Derek Brooks
12th August :

CW01431851

HARVARD HISTORICAL STUDIES, 158

Published under the auspices
of the Department of History
from the income of the
Paul Revere Frothingham Bequest
Robert Louis Stroock Fund
Henry Warren Torrey Fund

Margaret Meserve

Empires of Islam in Renaissance Historical Thought

HARVARD UNIVERSITY PRESS

Cambridge, Massachusetts, and London, England   2008

Library of Congress Cataloging-in-Publication Data

Meserve, Margaret.
    Empires of Islam in Renaissance historical thought / Margaret Meserve.
        p.   cm.—(Harvard historical studies ; 158)
    Includes bibliographical references and index.
    ISBN-13: 978-0-674-02656-8 (alk. paper)
    ISBN-10: 0-674-02656-X (alk. paper)
        1. Turkey—History—Ottoman Empire, 1288–1918—Historiography.   2. Islamic Empire—
Historiography.   3. Historiography—Europe—History—To 1500. I. Title.
    DR438.8.M43   2008
    956'.015072—dc22   2007015308

Contents

Note on Nomenclature

The Ottoman Empire comprised a cosmopolitan population of various national, religious, ethnic, and linguistic groups. The ruling elite called themselves "Ottomans" (in Turkish, Osmanlı), after Osman, the founder of the dynasty. In classical Ottoman usage, "Turk" was a pejorative term. The Italian humanists—indeed, all European historians of the early modern period—had no idea of this distinction, and called both the rulers of the Ottoman Empire and their subjects "Turks" (in Latin, *Turci*, occasionally *Turcae*). They also used the name *Turci* for earlier Turkic peoples. In fact, their inability to distinguish between the different Turkic polities which flourished in central Asia, the Caucasus, and Anatolia between the sixth and fourteenth centuries A.D. caused most of their historiographical confusion. In this book, I identify pre-Ottoman Turkic peoples (Western Türks, Khazars, Oğuz, Seljuks) where necessary to elucidate the content of the late antique and medieval source material which Renaissance historians used. When discussing Renaissance texts, however, I follow the practice of the authors themselves and use "Ottoman" and "Turk" interchangeably. In doing so, I purposefully replicate one of the central assumptions Renaissance historians made about Ottoman identity: that the "Turks" were members of a single genetic race whose history could be traced back across the centuries to a genesis in remote antiquity.

List of Figures

No question has exercised the writers of histories more than the origins of peoples.

—Jean Bodin, *Method for the Easy Comprehension of History* (1566)

All Nations have their fabulous Originals.

—John Stevens, *The Kings of Persia* (1715)

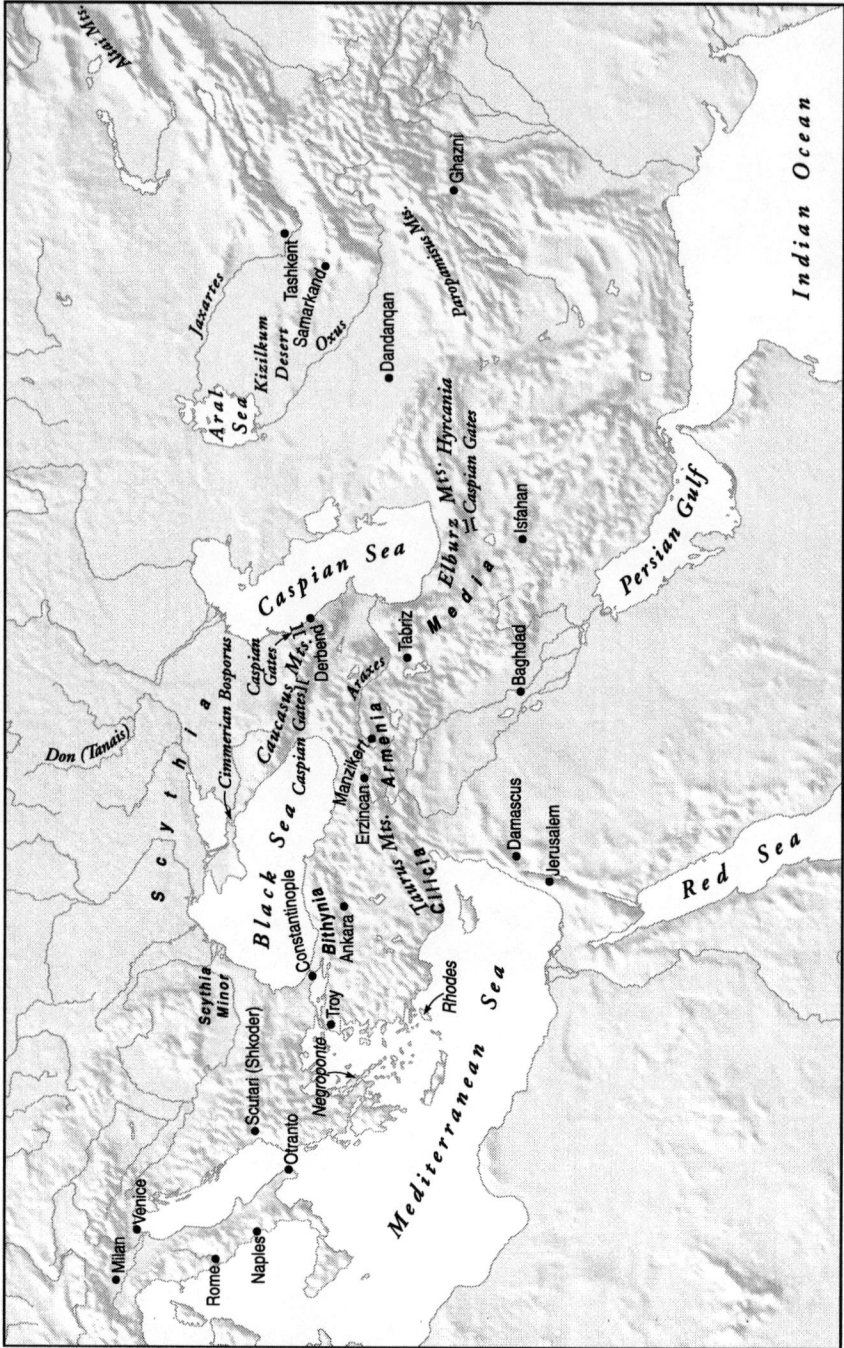

Figure 1. Western and Central Asia

Introduction

On July 21, 1453, the bishop of Siena, Aeneas Sylvius Piccolomini, wrote a letter to his friend Cardinal Nicholas of Cusa. The bishop's
mood was black, for some two weeks earlier news had reached him in
Austria, where he sat as papal envoy and counselor to the Hapsburg emperor Frederick III, that Constantinople had fallen to the Ottoman Turks.
To Aeneas, it seemed that the glory of Greece was destroyed, the empire
of "New Rome" overthrown. The Turks had raped and pillaged their way
through the city, he wrote, burning books and smashing statues, slaughtering all in their path till the streets ran thick with Christian blood. The carnage had been horrific. What was more, he lamented, Greek learning had
been dealt a fatal blow; its modern revival was over before it had really begun. Last, the Turkish triumph made depressingly clear to Aeneas the fragmented and impotent condition of the Christian states of Europe, which had
barely lifted a finger to help the beleaguered Greeks. It seemed that the
Turks had exposed a rent in the very fabric of civilization.

Aeneas's despair over the fall of Constantinople was shared by others
across Renaissance Europe. Laments for the city's loss and nervous appraisals of the Turkish foe were widespread, and they have been widely studied
in modern times. What interested me most about Aeneas's famous letter the
first time I read it was a point he took pains to emphasize concerning the
ethnic origins of the conquerors: who the Turks were, where they had come
from, and—apparently just as important—who they were not. "Those who
are now called Turks are *not* Persians," Aeneas noted to the cardinal, with
palpable disapproval, "nor are they Trojans, as certain others think. They are
a race of Scythians, come from the depths of a barbarous land."[1]

This book represents an attempt to understand Aeneas's remarks in their
widest possible context. Why, when confronted by epochal catastrophe, did
an Italian humanist look to history, and in particular to the question of ethnic origins, for explanation, clarity, assurance? And why was his next step to
criticize the historical research of his peers?

What did Aeneas mean when he identified the Turks as Scythian barbarians? What did those terms mean to him, and why was he so sure he was right? Indeed, who were those irresponsible "others" who traced the origins of the Turks back to Troy, or back to ancient Persia, for that matter? What was so objectionable about their ideas?

Aeneas's compulsion to look to the past in order to make sense of a messy and disturbing present was one his fellow Renaissance humanists felt intensely. It is a habit of mind which the humanists borrowed from their classical predecessors, which they passed on to later generations of European historians and political theorists, and which arguably has continued to inform our interest in history, and our sense of its value, down to the present day. The appropriation of historical narratives by politicians and pundits alike still has the power to shape perceptions of both our own past and that of the wider world.

Aeneas himself was a remarkably versatile Renaissance individual, and his many professional identities each contributed something to his theories on the historical antecedents of the "problem" posed to European Christendom by a militant, expansionist Islamic empire. As a humanist scholar and poet, he cared for the fate of Greece, its books, language, and culture, which he believed were under assault by new barbarian hordes. As a faithful believer, he was distressed by the idea that a new infidel scourge had been unleashed on Christian souls. As a high-ranking churchman, he also cared for the security of Christendom and the health of the European political economy, which the Turks seemed to threaten. And as a scholar and historian, he was determined that his own theories about the historical background of the present crisis be accepted as convincing, important, and true.

Tracing these various strands in Aeneas's historical thought led me to read the works of other Italian humanists writing on the same set of questions: who were the Turks, where had they come from, and what did their appearance signify—for Europe, for Christendom, for the course of world history, and for the project of its retelling? Most of the writers who treated the question shared the same concerns and convictions—cultural, political, pastoral, and scholarly—that inspired Aeneas. Their interests shaped the histories they wrote, often in ways that were difficult to parse.

The result of my reading is this book, a study of Renaissance humanist history writing on the origins of both the Ottoman Turks and other Islamic empires, both past and present. Starting in the early decades of the fifteenth century, Renaissance humanists (mostly but by no means exclusively Italians) engaged in a scholarly campaign aimed at illuminating the contemporary problem of Ottoman Turkish aggression and suggesting means of redress to it. To do this, they invoked one of their favorite heuristic devices, the narrative of origin.[2] In letters, historical treatises, political commentaries, biographies, geographical tracts, and even epic and elegiac verse, humanist authors devised various narratives of origin for the Ottoman Turks that tried both to account for their current success by making reference to the distant past and to make the case to contemporary Europe for a military campaign to reverse it.

Humanists like Aeneas Sylvius identified the ancestors of the Turks—and so, by extension, their contemporary descendants—as a barbarous race, ferocious, uncultured, and illegitimate, with no claim to rule over or even reside in any part of the civilized world. Moreover, they did not limit their researches to the question of Ottoman history alone. To emphasize the outlandish ferocity of the Turks, some authors also rewrote the traditional medieval history of the "Saracen" Arabs. By playing down or even denying altogether their impact on world history, humanist historians made the medieval Arabs seem relatively harmless. The Turks, by contrast, were a foe unlike any the world had seen before. Humanist historians also worked hard to endow certain other Islamic dynasties, especially those that challenged Ottoman hegemony in Asia, with as illustrious a pedigree as possible. By identifying states and dynasties of legitimate origin in the Islamic East, the humanists further highlighted the rogue status of the Ottoman Empire, as they saw it, while suggesting yet another means of reducing Turkish power: Christian Europe could join forces with the "good" empires of Islam to envelop the Ottomans in a war on two fronts.

Humanist research into the origins of Islamic empires thus both was prompted by and also purposefully contributed to contemporary political debates over the Ottoman Turkish threat. A close and often conflicted relationship bound historical scholarship on Islam to the dictates of policy, especially in the Italian states most directly affected by Ottoman expansionism: Venice, Naples, and above all papal Rome. But historians working in these courtly ambits were not just the paid mouthpieces of their patrons. Rather, Renaissance scholars working on the problem of Islamic history had to negotiate a series of competing imperatives: the pursuit of historical truth, the production of political propaganda, the strength of their personal convictions, and (very often) the promotion of their own careers. For in arguing for the relevance of history to contemporary political debate, the humanists were also arguing for their own relevance as participants in the conduct of modern politics. Yet another powerful limiting factor on their work was the influence of ancient and medieval tradition. Despite claiming for themselves revolutionary standards of critical inquiry, humanists investigating the origins and national character of the empires of Islam wrote as willing participants in a long tradition of "barbarian" ethnography, drawing from a diverse range of classical, early Christian, and high medieval sources. Their work reveals the often surprising extent to which humanist scholarship was shaped—and sometimes destabilized—by tensions between empirical experience, political expedience, and enduring cultural tradition.

Politics and Providence

Modern historians of the Ottoman Empire may well envy the clear picture of its origins which the humanists produced. In the past century, the character of the early Ottoman state has been the subject of intense scholarly debate: whether Osman and his followers were motivated by economic opportunism, tribal pride, or religious zeal (and whether this last was orthodox or heterodox in nature) remains a fiercely contested question. The secret of the Ottomans' early success has yet to be fully divined.[3] But Renaissance humanists had no inkling of these subtleties. The immediate origins of the Ottoman state were not "problematized" in the Renaissance as they have been in more recent years.[4]

But humanist speculation on Turkish history is itself problematic, as indeed is the humanist approach to Islamic history as a whole. What happened when classically educated humanists, cleaving to newly forged ideals of rational historical analysis, attempted to chart the history of an enemy of their faith? Many tried to explain the Ottomans' rise to power as a purely secular phenomenon—a clear departure from earlier, medieval accounts of the "infidel" foe. Crusade theorists of the High Middle Ages had generally treated the Saracens as a threat to the Christian religion and to the salvation of Christian souls. When twelfth- and thirteenth-century historians wanted to account for the origins of Saracen power, their inquiries almost always took them back to the life of Muhammad himself. Medieval polemical biographies of the Prophet emphasized his arrogance (he had dared to establish a new religion, with himself at its head) and his deviousness (his "law" was so attractive, allowed so many earthly pleasures and promised so many heav-

enly delights, that it had seduced whole nations).[5] The subsequent history of
his people was told as a story of continuing religious error, demanding cor-
rection by Christendom in holy war.

By contrast, the humanists' chief objection to the Ottoman Turks seems to
have been not theological but political. Osman, the founder of the dynasty,
was an upstart bandit prince, a local warlord who had seized territory and
power by illegal means. His followers had carved a rogue state out of the formerly Byzantine East. This was an act as illegitimate as it was destabilizing.
The language the humanists used was deliberate: the Turks were not just infidels, they were bastards, pretenders, usurpers, brigands, and thieves; they
broke promises, voided treaties, disrupted trade, and cruelly suppressed conquered peoples. The fact that they were Muslim, while reprehensible, was
not the crucial factor that determined their guilt, nor was it their unbelief
that demanded a military response from European states. Indeed, other Islamic nations were equally lacking in faith, but because they, by the humanists' lights, were engaged in the just exercise of legitimate power, European
states were free to cultivate them as allies and friends. From the humanist
perspective, there were good Muslims to be found in Asia as well as bad
ones; political considerations—and history—determined which was which.

On the face of it, then, it would seem that Renaissance historians tried to
account for the Turkish problem in the new vocabulary of Renaissance humanism—essentially, in mundane political terms. And yet the story they
told remained open to moral and even theological interpretation, for despite
the humanists' interest in locating the origins of Turkish power in the turn of
secular events, the sudden appearance of this fearsome nation could not
help but suggest the action of a larger providence, guiding the course of human history, raising up tyrants to punish the sinful, and calling the faithful
to both outward action and inner reform.

The Turks were an illegitimate nation, but they had grown powerful
thanks to Christian negligence or, put more bluntly, Christian sin. It was
possible, even likely, that God himself had sent them to scourge the negli-
gent Byzantine Greeks and the selfish, schismatic Christians of Europe. And
it seemed certain that God had also provided a possible remedy against the
Turkish threat in the form of other Islamic empires on the Ottomans' eastern
frontier. The Christian response to both kinds of Islamic state—to barbarian
usurpers and legitimate imperial heirs—would be a test of their faith in their
Lord and their willingness to reform themselves and seize the opportunities

he provided. These assumptions were only occasionally made explicit, but their influence can be discerned in almost all Renaissance humanist historical thinking about Islam.

In this book, I explore the tensions inherent in that historical thinking: between the political and providential heuristics the humanists brought to bear on the question of Islamic history and, more generally, between the Renaissance fascination with classical antiquity and its modes of expression and analysis, on the one hand, and the abiding power of medieval Christian traditions, assumptions, and mentalities, on the other. These tensions are not strictly diachronic; there is more at stake than just a bumpy transition from one era's way of thinking about faith, power, and global history to another's. The classicizing history that the humanists pioneered had from the outset inherent contradictions: between what Arnaldo Momigliano identified as the antiquarian impulse to use the critical tools of Renaissance philology to uncover objective, empirical facts about the past and a deep-seated conviction that history writing was above all a form of rhetoric, which its authors could and ought to use to argue passionate points of view.[6]

These competing visions of history and its uses coincide and frequently clash in the texts I examine—for the most part, fifteenth- and early sixteenth-century historical accounts of the Islamic empires, their origins, and their fortunes. I approach these texts from a variety of angles, from a close study of what sources their authors used and how they used them, to a broader consideration of what assumptions informed these scholars' researches, how they constructed their larger historical narratives, and what they constructed these narratives for. Along the way, I also investigate Renaissance perceptions of Muslim people and Islamic states and Renaissance debates over the relationship between Christianity and Islam; but this is primarily a book about history writing. It focuses on accounts of a crucial story in world history—the rise of Islam and its empires—in order to illustrate a key moment in the development of the European historical art.

A Renaissance in Historical Thought

The emergence of a new kind of history writing was one of the most important achievements of Renaissance culture, the foundation of an intellectual tradition that endures in the West to the present day. It is often said that the Renaissance saw the first appearance (in post-classical Europe, at least) of a critical approach to the historical past, part of that larger intellectual praxis which Burckhardt termed the "objective treatment and consideration of the state and of all the things of this world."[7] Though Burckhardt's vision of the Renaissance has been challenged in countless respects, the application of his thesis to Renaissance history writing long remained largely unquestioned, with humanist historiography understood to have been an essentially rational endeavor, secular, mundane, fact-based, pragmatic, interested in locating the sources of historical causation in the human realm rather than the divine.[8] Recently, however, some critics have begun to investigate just how Renaissance humanist historians went about their work and whether their methods and conclusions were as critically objective as they and their later readers liked to claim.[9] It is becoming clear that the development of humanist historiography was a slow and complicated process; "objectivity," if it has ever really obtained in European history writing, certainly did not take root all at once.

It is worth reiterating the point that there was no such thing as a professional historian in the quattrocento.[10] Many humanists wrote history, but they did so while performing other duties, primarily as civil servants. They were chancellors, notaries, secretaries, speechwriters, diplomats, librarians, and on rare occasions even heads of state. Inspired by the classical ideal of the *vita activa*, the humanist historian devoted his intellectual gifts to the service of his state and the pursuit of its policies. A humanist might, for instance, rewrite the history of his own city to support its claims for political legitimacy, or he might write a biography of his prince in order to justify the parvenu's right to rule.[11] Humanist polemicists also used history to assail the legitimacy and status of rival rulers and institutions, sometimes to devastating effect.[12] When humanists turned their attention to the question of the history of Islam and its empires, they carried on in this partisan tradition, now taking the whole of Christendom as the party whose interests were at stake.

I start, then, from the assumption that Renaissance humanist history writing was a political act. Investigating humanist histories of the empires of Islam reveals how this politicized historiography operated on a particularly challenging set of questions. The story these authors had to tell was at once longer than those treated by most humanist histories (encompassing a millennium or more of human history) and broader in scope (unfolding on a global scale). It was more remote (stretching in some cases far beyond the reach of the historical and geographical knowledge actually available to late medieval Europe) and more urgent (involving, as its writers saw it, the very survival of their way of life and the salvation of humankind).

This last point, however, poses a different challenge to our understanding of Renaissance history writing, and one I also address in this book. Renaissance history writing was never as objective or politically neutral as some of its early readers claimed, but there were characteristics other than objectivity that distinguished it from the history writing of earlier eras. In the first half of the fifteenth century, the well-known "heroes" of humanist historiography—scholars like Leonardo Bruni, Lorenzo Valla, and Flavio Biondo— turned a critical eye to the story of Italy's ancient and medieval past and sowed the seeds of a historiographical revolution. By the middle of the sixteenth century, their methods had become standard practice: the adoption of classical models, a skeptical approach to earlier authority, a renewed interest in rhetoric, secularized theories of causation. Over time, these were to have a profound effect on the kinds of history that were written in early modern Europe.

The question is whether this revolution happened all at once. It is unclear how quickly and how widely the movement spread at first, even among the intellectual elites of the quattrocento. How deeply did the new methods— and the new critical mindset these methods reflected—actually penetrate in the early years? I would argue that of all those who swore allegiance to the new history, few, if any—especially in the earliest phases—underwent what we might term a full "conversion." Many quattrocento humanist historians followed Bruni in attempting a methodical reconstruction of the rise and fall of political states. But did they in fact make the same conceptual leap that Bruni made in his *History of the Florentine People,* from a providential worldview to one in which human individuals and societies alone determine their fate? Many humanists likewise delighted in adopting Valla's provocative critical stance, exposing problems in the evidence, contradictions, gaps, and outright errors in their sources. But how completely did they accept the unflinching skepticism Valla brought to bear on the Donation of Constantine, his determination to question even the most firmly entrenched tradition if the evidence failed to support it? At issue here is a distinction between being and seeming, between how Renaissance humanists wanted readers to *think* they did their history and how they actually did it. Many humanists of the later quattrocento aspired to the critical standards their predecessors had forged; many paid lip service to them in their writings. But these were not the standards that the majority of them actually used. The larger implications of the new historiography could be risky, sometimes downright threatening, to deep-seated European views on the nature and order of the world, the direction and purposefulness of human history, and the role that Christian faith had to play in its unfolding.

This ambivalence—the sense that the new learning might be a mixed blessing—can be detected in almost every form of humanist writing, but it becomes especially clear in discussions in which Christian tradition stood in potential conflict with humanist convictions. One such problem was that of Islam. On the one hand, humanists believed they had special tools of historical and political analysis which could explain and perhaps even resolve the Islamic "problem" as no previous European theorists had been able to do. On the other, discussing the phenomenon of Ottoman Turkish aggression in purely secular terms stripped the crusade—still very much a live political issue, and one embraced by many humanists as well as their employers—of its entire rationale. In the end, thinking about Turks without thinking of and objecting to their religion was something that few humanists were willing or even able to attempt. Machiavelli was probably the first to do so in total seriousness.[13]

Humanist history writing claimed for itself several virtues: rhetorical elegance, sound moral instruction, and also a certain reliability, derived from the erudite and critical assessment of sources. When it came to writing the history of Islam, humanist historians found some of these values easier to embrace than others. A central concern of this book is to illuminate the tensions at play in their attempts.

Alterity, Expertise, Reform

Renaissance Europe's attention to Islam, to the Turkish "problem," and to the ideology of crusade has been the object of increasing critical attention in recent years, and the consensus on how humanists conceptualized all three has been significantly revised. Where earlier historians maintained that humanist interest in these issues was something of a retrograde phenomenon, a curious relic of medieval thinking in a Renaissance world,[14] more recent studies have argued that humanist attitudes toward Islam and its history were innovative, even revolutionary, involving a rejection of medieval, theological frames of reference in favor of classical cultural and ethnographical ones.[15] Some see this development as foreshadowing the emergence of the modern genres of anthropology, travel writing, and journalism. Approaching the humanist discourse on Islam through the lens of history writing opens up a sort of middle path between these competing views by distinguishing the traditional concepts that lie at the core of the humanists' thinking about Islam from the innovative idioms in which they articulated their thoughts. This is a crucial distinction. In the proliferating discussion of early modern perceptions and constructions of the Islamic "other," comparatively little work has been done to determine precisely how those perceptions were actually formed (from what materials?) and expressed (using what kinds of rhetoric?). History writing is particularly susceptible to just this sort of analysis; in most cases, I have been able not only to identify the sources of the humanists' information on Islamic history but also to show how they interpreted and at times purposefully manipulated that material to support their claims.

Tracing the rhetorical work the humanists performed on their sources can reveal a great deal. Because humanist historians were more likely to manipulate their sources when those sources proved incredible, uncomfortable, or fundamentally contradictory to their own convictions about Islam and its role in world history, retracing their steps can lead us to a better understanding of what those convictions actually were.

Focusing on *how* the humanists wrote their histories also allows a new consideration of the significance of their discussions for Renaissance intellectual and cultural history as a whole. Much recent Anglo-American scholarship has been concerned with locating premodern European writing on Islam within the Orientalist "discourse of alterity" which Edward Said first detected in European scholarly writing of the eighteenth and nineteenth centuries.[16] The operative questions in these investigations ask who the "other" is, how he is made to seem other, and what this process reveals about contemporary European prejudices, preoccupations, and concerns vis-à-vis the outside world. The establishment of alterity is the central point: individual studies tell us how Europeans from antiquity to the present—from individual authors to entire cultures—have gone about constructing and articulating difference, usually to negative effect.[17] The underlying assumption is that European writers have long engaged with the Orient as a way of establishing and reinforcing a position of cultural superiority over rival civilizations.

As fruitful as this exercise has proved for certain periods, detecting an Orientalist discourse in the early Renaissance is more problematic, for the very basic reason that there was no one Oriental "other" in the fifteenth and sixteenth centuries. Rather, the European states confronted a bewildering geopolitical chessboard of Islamic polities. Some (for instance, Ottoman Turks) were seen as mortal enemies, while others (Ilkhanids, Timurids, Karamanids, Aqqoyunlu, Crim Tatars, Safavids, and Mamluks) were potential allies. Sensitivity to the historical and political and even sectarian differences at play within the Islamic East was in fact crucial to the model of Islamic history the humanists devised. Hence, a central concern of mine is to identify just how the humanists discovered, understood, and articulated those differences, especially in the context of the universal or world histories they were trying to write.

Moreover, if the key point to be made about Orientalist writing is that it tells us more about the concerns and prejudices of European writers than it does about the Orient(s) they purport to describe, this observation still cannot account for what in particular any given group of Orientalist authors has chosen to say. At different times and in different places, European writers can be found saying radically different things about the Islamic East. Their statements may all be equally tendentious, defamatory, and untrue. But they are so in different ways. To consider them together under a single Orientalist rubric is to risk creating a monolithic Occident as undifferentiated and removed from reality as the Orient it is meant to have fashioned. Such a construct—of an uncomprehending, hostile, and imperialist Occident—may serve the purposes of certain apologetic strains of modern Western scholarship no less than a passive, servile, and irrational Orient served to support the imperialist aims of European scholarship in the past.

Renaissance humanists developed ways of writing about Islam that were peculiar to them and that, if parsed carefully, can reveal much about humanist ways of thinking as distinct from other scholarly and popular discourses. For example, even if the humanist version of Islamic history was tendentious, defamatory, and untrue, it was not *wildly* so. There were limits to the distortions allowed. Some ideas—that the Turks were avenging Trojans, for example, their history and their motivations rooted in a poetic, mythic past—were beyond the pale of respectable humanist history. Others—that the Ottomans were barbarian Scythians, newly arrived from the wilds of central Asia—enjoyed enthusiastic support among humanists even as the body of evidence to the contrary continued to grow. By discerning the self-imposed limits on the humanist discourse of alterity, we can learn more about what it was to be a humanist historian and what humanists thought

they were doing when they set out to write about remote peoples and
events long past.

So there are two aspects to the question: first, how and why humanists
used history writing to make sense of the problem of Islam; and second,
what the histories that they wrote can tell us about their ambitions for
themselves in Renaissance scholarly and political circles. The latter question
entails a consideration not just of what the humanists said about Islamic history, or even of how they said it, but of why they wanted to engage in this
discussion at all.

On the most idealistic level, the humanists wrote history as a way of ful-
filling the classical ideal of the *vita activa;* at a more prosaic level, they wanted
to be heard, valued, and (if possible) gainfully employed. For all these reasons, they were keen to interject themselves into contemporary debates
over political policy and the conduct of foreign affairs. To do this, however,
they had to frame the debates in terms favorable to their own expertise. Often this meant casting debates in historical terms, in particular in terms of a
history that *only they could recover.* Humanist pronouncements on Islamic history may well have been motivated by a desire to establish the cultural superiority of European Christendom (or perhaps Greco-Roman civilization) to
its Muslim "other." But the humanists' histories also had a great deal to do
with establishing their own authority in a European debate that had long
been the province of scholastic theologians.[18] The humanists wanted to join
the medieval conversation, as it were, on the problem of Islam; they did so
by framing the problem as a historical one and then advertising their unique
ability to provide historical answers to it. Their critical skills and knowledge
were indispensable—or so they claimed—to any ruler or state wanting to
engage with the problem of Islamic expansion in an effective way. Thus,
reading humanist writing on Islam as part of the Renaissance discourse of
expertise helps to explain some of the more peculiar aspects of these humanist texts: their concern to locate the origins of Islamic empires as far back
in the past as possible, preferably to a point in classical antiquity; their neglect of theological polemic in favor of political analysis; their insistence that
historical problems demanded philological solutions; and their almost total
disregard for the testimony of past or contemporary eyewitnesses to Islamic
history, from crusader chronicles to travel writing and the accounts of prisoners of war, in favor of more arcane and difficult textual authorities which
they alone could claim to control.

Finally, alongside the self-interest that led Renaissance humanists to offer the world their thoughts on the problem of Islam stands the larger question of why they imagined Islam to be a problem in the first place. For Europe at the close of the Middle Ages, the question was complicated. I have argued elsewhere that it is more accurate to say that what Renaissance Europeans confronted was not really the problem of Islam at all but rather the problem of the crusade.[19] Humanist crusade writers fretted over the decline of the crusade as an ideal and as a political reality. Why were the European states no longer able to launch one? Even the popes rarely concerned themselves with the project, and when they did, few outside the ranks of the Church could be bothered to respond. What did this failure say about the fragmented, self-interested state of Christendom, and what did it bode for its future?

Humanist histories of Islam, often composed to support arguments for a new crusade, both were shaped by and contributed to this larger European discourse of reform. At work in the humanists' thinking was more than a particular belief that Islam was bad or that Christianity was good and therefore deserved to triumph. These assumptions rested on more fundamental convictions: about the rightly ordered nature of the universe, the purposefulness of human history, and the centrality of certain political institutions and ideas (above all, the institutions and idea of Rome) to God's plan for humankind. History was useful as a tool for taking the measure of humanity's ability to stick to that plan at any given moment. On this view, the seventh-century rise of Islam was not the cause but rather the symptom of a far greater crisis in human history: the fall of Rome. The political and ecclesiastical fallout of that disaster had made Islam possible; now only a reunited Europe and a reformed Christendom could reverse the Islamic tide. So the Italian humanists investigated the story of Islam's rise—and its apparent triumph under the Ottoman aegis—as a way of better understanding how their own institutions had failed in the distant as well as the more recent past. The crusade they advocated would serve as an instrument of internal reform, one which would revive Christendom, restore the European political economy, and reinstate Rome at its proper place at the center of both.

In the chapters that follow, I offer a series of close readings of humanist accounts of Islamic history produced between about 1380 and 1510. Although many of these texts have been studied by previous scholars, only rarely have they been considered as examples of history writing. For over a century, crusade historians and Ottomanists alike have occasionally drawn on humanist texts on the Turks for their potential to illustrate the history of diplomatic and military relations between Western Christendom and the eastern Mediterranean world.[20] Of course, those diplomatic and military relations (to say nothing of the commercial economy of the late medieval Mediterranean) were in reality far less confrontational, far more often inclined to coexistence, than the humanists either wanted or were willing to admit.[21] Their comments must be taken as a window onto European imaginative spaces, not the halls of commerce or state. Other scholars, recognizing the fundamentally literary quality of humanist crusade propaganda, have included it in their investigations into the image of the Turk in the various national literatures of Renaissance Europe, together with poetry and drama, religious tracts, the tales of travelers and prisoners of war, even music and popular spectacle. From these varied sources modern critics have uncovered a wide range of attitudes to the Ottomans in the cultures of Renaissance England,[22] Germany,[23] Central Europe,[24] France, and Spain.[25] (There is no shortage of Turcica available for study. Göllner, in his bibliography of sixteenth-century literature on the Turks, arrived at a tally, since shown to be far from complete, of nearly 6000 printed editions.)[26] The persistence of crusading themes in Italian literature (especially romance) has been explored,[27] and more recently a growing circle of literary critics and historians has turned its attention to the vast corpus of Italian humanist rhetoric on the problem of the Turks.[28] This latter group has usually focused on how the humanists constructed rhetorical arguments for a crusade and—a closely related topic— how they perceived and represented the contemporary Turkish threat. Only a few consider how humanists researched and reconstructed earlier Turkish and Islamic history,[29] a topic which, rather inexplicably, has been treated only briefly in studies of Renaissance historiography.[30] None of these has thoroughly assessed humanist histories of Islam. As a result, some conclusions reached thus far need to be revisited.

One goal of my study is to clarify just who was writing these historical accounts, when, and with what materials. Scholars have tended to concentrate on the figure of Aeneas Sylvius, who thanks to his high profile (in 1458 he became Pope Pius II), as well as the sheer volume of his writings on the Turks, is usually hailed as the most important crusade propagandist of the fifteenth century and one of the first serious students of Islamic history. Aeneas Sylvius is a central figure in this book too, but I pay equal attention to other, less well known authors, some writing long before him. Andrea Biglia's extensive and unpublished *Commentaries* on Eastern history (1433), for example, have escaped the notice of most scholars of humanist literature on Islam, as has Theodore Gaza's treatise on the origins of the Turks (1472), an early (and unrecognized) example of the circulation of Byzantine chronicle material in Renaissance Italy. Finally, very few studies have examined Renaissance writing on Islamic dynasties other than the Ottomans, in particular, texts on Timur and the dynasties that succeeded his regime in Iran and western Anatolia. This is a literature whose significance is best understood in the context of contemporary writing on the Ottomans, with whom those dynasties contended.

I have also tried to clarify certain questions regarding the humanists' use of sources. Aeneas Sylvius and his fellow crusade advocate Francesco Filelfo were both given treatises on the origins of the Turks by Greek émigré scholars—Niccolò Sagundino and Theodore Gaza, respectively. Scholars have concluded from this that humanist information on the Turks—and indeed, interest in the question of their history—was a product of Byzantine influence.[31] Sagundino, however, wrote hardly anything about the Turks apart from the treatise commissioned by Aeneas Sylvius; he composed this *after* Aeneas had written several accounts of Turkish history himself, and his conclusions follow those of his patron quite closely. Likewise, Theodore Gaza did not write his treatise for Filelfo until 1472, long after Filelfo had developed his own ideas on the subject; Filelfo, moreover, did not commission Gaza to write the tract.[32] A third Greek author, Laonicus Chalcocondyles, has also been hailed as an important source for several Italian humanists, but recent scholarship has shown that he completed his Turkish history only in the late 1480s and so contributed nothing to the development of earlier humanist ideas on the subject.[33]

The Italian humanists did not, in fact, rely much on contemporary Greek scholars for information on Islam or its history. Still less did they turn to the eyewitness testimony of contemporary travelers, merchants, or escaped prisoners of war, even as an increasing number of such informants made accounts of their time in Islamic lands available to Western European readers. Instead, the humanists based their accounts instead on material from earlier Latin sources, especially medieval world chronicles.[34] I focus on the medieval elements in this body of humanistic literature because recent scholarship has tended to emphasize precisely the opposite, concentrating on what seems innovative in these texts rather than the continuities they share with earlier traditions. This preoccupation with singling out what seems new or modern about the humanist image of the Turk has sometimes produced a distorted picture of the opinions humanists actually held. Critics often high-light those theories that seem most characteristic of mainstream humanist scholarship, with its interest in classical antiquity, empirical observation, and secular political analysis, while neglecting the significance of ideas and con-cepts derived from medieval Christian traditions, which do not fit the ac-cepted view of humanist scholarly methods and modes of thinking quite as well.

A case in point is the theory that the Turks were descended from the an-cient Trojans and had entered on their campaigns against Byzantium as re-venge for the Greek sacking of Troy. This has long been considered one of the humanists' main contributions to the Renaissance debate on the origins of the Turks. The idea so resembles the sort of speculation humanists regu-larly ventured regarding the classical roots of other nations and institutions that many modern scholars have assumed it featured prominently in hu-manist historiography on the Turks as well. Chapter 1 surveys a wide array of texts in which this notion is expressed. The theory of the Turks' Trojan an-cestry, although frequently expressed in Renaissance poetry and popular lit-erature, appears only rarely in humanist historical writing. It may seem the sort of belief that humanists *should* have held, but very few authors actually did so.

The far more widely accepted theory that the Turks were barbarians from Scythia has also been interpreted as an example of the generally secular and classicizing tendency in humanist historiography. On this view, human-ist scholars like Aeneas Sylvius, Biondo, Filelfo, Sagundino, Gaza, Lauro Quirini, and Giorgio Merula identified the Turks as Scythians not only to give them an authoritative ancient pedigree, but also to portray them as age-old enemies of classical culture—and not, as medieval polemicists had done, as *infidels* opposed to the Christian religion. By representing the Turks as bar-barians, it has been argued, the humanists tried to revive some long-dor-mant traditions of classical ethnography and political science, in particular the idea, first suggested by Herodotus, that unresolvable cultural differences divided Europe from Asia, keeping the peoples of both continents locked in eternal hostility. But humanist notions about the Turks' Scythian origins derived almost entirely from medieval rather than ancient ethnographical sources, as I argue in Chapters 2 and 3. On a deeper level, they reflect medi-eval Christian ideas about monstrous races and their role in world history, as much as if not more than they do classical ethnographical categories.

Medieval notions of the providential purpose of world history also informed humanist attempts to account for the rise of Islam itself. Chapter 4 examines how three early Renaissance humanists—Biglia, Biondo, and Filelfo—conceptualized the origins and rise of Islam as a political morality play that reflected poorly on the seventh-century government of the East Roman Empire and presented important lessons for the empire's present-day heirs in Europe. The fall of Constantinople effectively cut off this line of reform-minded speculation, prompting a later generation of humanists to consider the rise of Islam in more confrontational, less self-critical ways.

Finally, in searching the distant past for a solution to the Turkish "problem," as they saw it, humanists turned their attention to other contemporary Islamic states, especially those lying on the eastern fringes of the Ottoman Empire, which might prove useful allies in a future war against the Turks. Medieval Europe had for centuries looked to distant Asian kingdoms for alliances against Islamic powers in the Levant; fifteenth-century diplomats and scholars continued this tradition of wishful political thinking, but humanist writers also transformed the ways in which it was articulated. Just as they deployed secular, historical narratives of origin to denigrate the Ottomans' political heritage and legitimacy, so they used history to aggrandize and justify the status of potential Muslim allies in the East, from Timur and Uzun Hasan in the fifteenth century to Shah Ismail, the founder of the Safavid dynasty, in the first decades of the sixteenth. Medieval authors had often tried to justify possible alliances with Asian rulers on the grounds that they were already crypto-Christians or might in future be induced to convert. Chapter 5 argues that the humanists too toyed with these notions but found it equally important to portray the objects of their interest as politically legitimate, often by inventing fantastic dynastic claims that linked these Muslim lords to the ruling houses of ancient Babylon, Persia, and Parthia. When discussing an Islamic empire which might prove a useful ally against the Turks, humanist authors cloaked the same acts of usurpation and violent conquest which they so decried in the Turks in a veil of heroic legitimacy. And as in their histories of the Turks, though humanist arguments in support of Persian kingship relied heavily on secular political reasoning and claims of ancient authority, they also derived a great deal of their force from both biblical and medieval Christian legends—in this case, legends about the wisdom and power of Oriental kings from Cyrus to the Magi, Prester John to the great Khan of Cathay.

Distortions of history in the service of policy are not so surprising to discover, in the Renaissance or any other age. What bears investigation is how the humanists engineered both the denigration of Europe's Islamic enemies and the rehabilitation of potential Islamic friends. Deftly intertwining their rhetorical tropes of alterity, expertise, and reform, Renaissance humanists wove the history of Islam into strikingly modern patterns; but the fabric was shot through with traditional strands.[35]

The Origin of the Turks

The story of the real origin of the Turks is neither simple nor short but needs to be told in order for us to understand the historiographical, geographical, and onomastic puzzles which beset Renaissance scholars.[36] The name

Figure 2. The origin of the Turks. Hartmann Schedel, *Liber cronicarum* (Nuremberg: Anton Koberger, 1493), fol. 165r. Photo Warburg Institute, London

"Turk" is recorded for the first time in A.D. 552, when, according to Chinese annals, a barbarian clan from Mongolia, the A-shih-na, revolted against their feudal overlords, declared independence, and began to call themselves Türks.[37] (Modern scholarship assigns the term "Turkic" to an even larger collection of Asian peoples related along ethnic or linguistic lines. Such "Turkic" peoples existed before the A-shih-na, of course, but it is a device of modern convenience to call these earlier peoples "Turks." Before 552, the name seems not to have been used.) The steppe empire the A-shih-na established did not last long, but its influence was felt from northern China to the Black Sea coast. The people made a considerable impression on the great empires whose borders they reached: China, Persia, and Byzantium. In all these places, various forms of the name "Turk" were used to describe them; the name was also applied to later Turkic tribal unions that succeeded them.

The western half of the A-shih-na confederation, known to modern scholars as the Western Türks, occupied territory north of the border with Persia and possibly as far west as the Volga.[38] In 563 they sent their first embassy to Constantinople. The historians who document the story of Byzantine-Türk relations—Menander Protector, Theophylactus Simocatta, and Theophanes Confessor—called these people "Tourkoi."[39]

Byzantine historians also used the name to describe the Western Türks' successors, the Khazars. Linguistically, and possibly ethnically, the Khazars were related to the Western Türks; they were also, at first, their vassals.[40] With the collapse of the Western Türk confederation in the 620s, the Khazars established an independent state in the west, centered on the north Caucasus and south Russian steppe. They struck an alliance with the Byzantine emperor Heraclius against Sassanian Persia in 626–627 and in later decades remained valuable friends of Byzantium. They engaged the Arabs, who by the 640s had replaced the Persians as the major threat to the empire's eastern frontier, in two extended wars (642–652 and 722–737) which kept Byzantine territories in eastern Anatolia and along the northern Black Sea coast safe from harm.

Theophanes Confessor is the major Byzantine source for the history of the Khazars and their relations with Byzantium. His *Chronographia* was translated into Latin at a very early date, around the end of the ninth century; as a result, several Western medieval chronicles preserve notices from Theophanes on the Khazar "Turks" of southern Russia ("Scythia," in classical parlance) and their activities around the mountain pass through the Caucasus known as the Caspian Gates. This tradition was one of the most important sources for Renaissance humanists investigating the origins of the Otto-man Turks. The Turkic Khazars also left their mark on Christian apocalyptic literature. Seventh-century Syriac authors in northern Mesopotamia, where Khazar incursions on behalf of Byzantium were greeted with little enthusi-asm, included these northern invaders in their visions of the impending end of the world. In Syriac prose romances, homilies, and laments, the Khazars were cast (alongside Ishmaelite Arabs, Red Jews, Gog and Magog, and other unclean races supposedly confined by Alexander the Great behind the Cas-pian Gates) as heralds of an imminent Antichrist. Translated first into Greek and then, around 700, into Latin, the best-known formulation of this leg-end, the *Revelations* of ps.-Methodius, inspired a tradition of historical and literary descriptions of apocalyptic barbarians which thrived well into the fifteenth century and also had a profound effect on humanist ideas about the historical origins of the Ottoman Turks.

In short, Renaissance humanists were bequeathed two traditions con-cerning the seventh-century Khazar "Turks" of the Caucasus—one positive (from Byzantine histories) and one negative (from the ps.-Methodian apoc-alyptic tradition). That they chose the fantastic but negative version over the factual but positive one already tells us something about their use of their sources. Equally important is the fact that the Khazar "Turks," despite the name Byzantine and Syriac authors gave them, had only the most distant connection to the Ottoman Turks. The secret of Ottoman origins lay in the history of a second group of Turkic people, whose trajectory west toward Christian Europe lay along a path very far removed from northern Scythia.

After the A-shih-na empire divided in two, and after the collapse of the Western Türks, a confederation of "Eastern Türks" continued to rule terri-tory around the Altai Mountains of Mongolia and southern Siberia until the late eighth century. After their state collapsed, a new Turkic confederation emerged, the Oğuz, who migrated south and west to form a central Asian state northeast of the Aral Sea.[41] A lesser chieftain of the Oğuz, the epony-mous and probably legendary Seljuk, is said to have led his followers into Persia from lands beyond the Oxus.

In the mid-eleventh century, the first historical figure to emerge from this migration, the Seljuk sultan Toghril Beg, led a rapid campaign of con-quest across the medieval Middle East. Toghril Beg destroyed the powerful Ghaznavids in Khorasan, captured Isfahan, the main city of central Per-sia, and in 1055 toppled the Shiite Buyid dynasty in Baghdad, protectors of the faltering Abbasid caliphate. The Great Seljuks then ruled over much of the Middle East for the next two centuries. In 1071, a cadet branch of the family defeated the Byzantines at Manzikert and went on to occupy much of Anatolia. The Seljuk sultanate of "Rum" (Rome) endured for nearly two centuries, until the Mongol invasions of the 1240s.[42] In the political vacuum left by the Seljuks' collapse, control of Anatolia devolved into the hands of a collection of independent Turkish warlords. One of these was Osman; his campaigns of conquest began shortly before A.D. 1300 and were continued by his *Osmanlı* (Ottoman) sons and followers.

In short, the ancestors of the Ottomans arrived in Anatolia in the wake of the Byzantine defeat at Manzikert; they came to Manzikert from Iraq, to Iraq from Khorasan, to Khorasan from Transoxania, and to Transoxania, ultimately, from the Altai Mountains of eastern Siberia. They never passed through Scythia or the Caucasus, where Renaissance scholars routinely placed them, for they came not from the north but from the east. The Anatolian Turks had four centuries of political and military distinction behind them, four centuries of contact and assimilation with Islamic civilization; four centuries as well of encounters with Latin Christians in various degrees, from crusade to coexistence. The humanists had their reasons for ignoring the legacy the Seljuk Turks bequeathed the Ottomans, but ignorance of these facts was not one of them.

CHAPTER 1

The Rise and Fall of the Trojan Turks

The Renaissance belief that the Turks were descended from Trojans is far better known from the contemporary criticism it attracted than from any statement written in its support. The most important—certainly the most frequent—critic of the idea was Aeneas Sylvius Piccolomini, who expressed his doubts and distaste for the idea on numerous occasions. In his *Europa,* a treatise on the history and geography of Europe written about 1458, Aeneas denied there was any truth in the notion: "I see that in recent years numerous authors, not only writers and poets but even historians, are so mistaken that they call the Turks *Teucri*—inspired, I believe, by the fact that the Turks now possess Troy, where the Teucrians once lived."[1] It was well known, Aeneas wrote, that the real Teucrians had come to Troy from Crete and Italy, they had been a literate nation, and latterly they had given rise to the Romans. All this proved they could have nothing to do with the Turks, who were in fact a barbarous nation of Scythia.

Aeneas voiced his objection to the notion of the Turks' Trojan origins in a variety of works—historical studies, crusade exhortations, and letters to European leaders—which circulated widely through fifteenth-century Europe. He almost always outlined his case against the idea as a prelude to presenting his own theory, which was that the Turks had emerged from the northern regions of Scythia. In the second half of the fifteenth century, his version of Turkish origins came to be accepted as the standard account of the subject. One unexpected consequence of its success—which Aeneas would surely have regretted—was that later humanist historians who copied his information on the Turks' Scythian origins also repeated his arguments against the possibility of their Trojan ancestry, giving rise to the misleading impression that the idea remained current among Renaissance historians.

Such are the risks of invoking *anasceua,* the rhetorical figure defined by Frank Borchardt as "the critical rejection of one myth in order to support and give greater credibility to another."[2] This straw-man device is ubiquitous in Renaissance historiography, especially among historians hoping to establish the superiority of their own erudition and methods over the misapprehensions of the crowd. But how much weight should be given to the claim that the earlier myth is truly widespread and in need of explosion?

Modern critics have noticed the frequency of Renaissance objections to the Trojan theory and arrived at just such a risky conclusion: that the conventional wisdom among fifteenth-century historians was that the Turks were Trojans; that Aeneas Sylvius was the first to argue against the idea; and that despite his best efforts, the notion lingered on in Renaissance historiography for decades.[3] Scholars have devoted more attention to this particular theory than to any other of the various strands of Renaissance historical scholarship on the empires of Islam, identifying both medieval sources for the notion and fifteenth-century texts where the idea is expressed.[4] And they have speculated on what the popularity of the idea may indicate about the nature of Renaissance history writing as a whole. Yet while this particular belief about the origins of the Turks was clearly current in fifteenth-century literature, it does not appear to have featured prominently in history writing per se. Why, then, has the idea come to seem almost emblematic of Renaissance historical thinking on the Turks, indeed on the whole "problem" of Islam?

It may help to clarify precisely what the Trojan theory entails. The idea has three distinct aspects. First is the simple practice of calling the Turks *Teucri*, to which Aeneas Sylvius draws attention, and which can be found in a great many contemporary texts. Second is the notion that the bitter enmity between the Turks and their most immediate neighbors, the Byzantine Greeks, could be explained as a continuation of the epic quarrel between the ancient Greeks and the inhabitants of Troy. Third, and finally, is the invocation of medieval authority. Two earlier traditions—that of the seventh-century *Chronicle* of "Fredegar" and a brief notice in the anonymous twelfth-century *Gesta Francorum*—serve as the original sources for the Renaissance idea that the Turks traced their origins back to Troy.

Taking these aspects together, it would seem that the Trojan theory was a highly determined, perhaps even overdetermined, historical idea, rooted in the medieval chronicle tradition but finding fullest expression in the century when antiquarian interest in classical languages, history, and the primordial roots of modern nations and nomenclature first began to dominate European intellectual culture. What might the popularity of such an idea tell us about the character of Renaissance historiography?

One interpretation holds that the popularity of the "Trojan" Turks exemplifies much of what was new (and at times irresponsible) in humanist thinking: an interest in achieving a pure, classical Latin style purged of barbaric neologisms, sometimes at the expense of historical accuracy; and, on a deeper level, a conviction that the realities of the modern-day world could be explained only by a proper grasp of their classical antecedents. An understanding of the state of the world in antiquity—the disposition of ancient peoples and the nature of their ancient quarrels—could illuminate the course of current events better than either direct observation or pragmatic political theory. Thus Edward Gibbon, more than two centuries ago, condemned the humanist historians of the quattrocento for "most absurdly" believing that the Turks were the avengers of Troy, and mocked "the grammarians" for classicizing the Turks into *Teucri*.[5] More recently, Robert Schwoebel also interpreted the Renaissance belief in the "Trojan" Turks as a particularly frivolous example of humanist pedantry: classically trained scholars, eager to explore the historical ironies of a quarrel between Greeks and Trojans carried forward to the present day, were satisfied to conclude that the Turks had taken Constantinople as revenge for the Greek sack of Troy. No further questions needed to be asked.[6] Nor was the problem merely academic. James Hankins has explored the political implications of the theory's widespread acceptance, arguing that some "philoturk" humanists took the notion of the Turks' Trojan ancestry to dangerous lengths, flirting with the possibility that the contemporary *Teucri* were actually justified in attacking the Greeks. They might have a rightful hereditary claim to Asia Minor or even, by virtue of their descent from Priam's house, to a place in the large family of European nations who claimed a Trojan pedigree.[7] On this interpretation, humanists who asserted that the Turks were Trojans made light of the crucial problem facing Christian Europe in the fifteenth century. More intrigued by historical ironies than by contemporary calamities, they fiddled with spellings, so to speak, while Constantinople burned.

A second and almost completely contradictory interpretation takes a far less negative view of humanistic scholarship by stressing the medieval roots of the notion of the Turks' Trojan past. Eckhardt, Runciman, and Spencer, for example, all point out that belief in the idea was already well established in the Middle Ages, thanks to the passages in Fredegar and the *Gesta Francorum* mentioned above. They argue that its survival in the fifteenth century was due primarily to writers of traditional chronicles unthinkingly repeating information found in older authorities, and to poets, forgers, and fantasists hoping to invoke the traditions of chivalric romance. As the Renaissance dawned, the idea of a Trojan origin for the Turks was—like similar claims made by the French, British, Germans, and various Italian city-states to ancestors of classical epic fame—simply waiting to be disproved. Pursuing this line one step further, Michael Heath maintains that it was the humanists themselves who finished it off. Over the course of the fifteenth century, they applied their constantly improving critical skills to the project of demolishing the theory. By patient compilation of information from earlier geographies and histories, the humanists were able to establish a more accurate identification: the Turks were Asiatic Scythians.[8] On this interpretation, the phenomenon of the "Trojan Turks" presents a story of historiographical progress, from medieval credulity to rigorous, almost modern critical discrimination.

Neither interpretation works entirely well. Scholars on both sides of the question have tended to interpret as a consistent whole the various fifteenth-century orthographical, literary, and historical traditions which equate the Turks with the Trojans. They assume that these traditions contributed equally to the formation of a single, uniform theory about the Turks' Trojan origins to which any author making a comment linking Turks and *Teucri* or Turks and Troy would have subscribed. But if we look closely at the Renaissance sources that discuss, or appear to discuss, the Trojan origins of the Turks, a different picture emerges. The three elements considered integral to this supposedly monolithic belief—orthographical equation of *Teucri* with *Turci,* belief in the modern Turks' innate desire for revenge against the Greeks, and the invocation of medieval sources that identify the Turks as scions of Troy—are rarely, if ever, cited in combination. Each tends to appear on its own, in a particular sort of context that does not necessarily admit the others.

This is not to say that no one in the Renaissance believed in the Trojan origins of the Turks. Rather, the idea was not nearly as widespread, as uniformly expressed, or as naively embraced as has often been assumed. Nor is there much point in trying to label the idea as a whole as either medieval or modern. The distinction that should be made is instead a generic one: on one side, poetic or imaginative works (both those following traditional medieval models and those influenced by the new learning), where references to the Trojan origins of the Turks are more frequent; on the other, more straightforward historical texts, again including works both medieval and humanistic in outlook, where the notion of "Trojan Turks" finds far less approval.

To begin with, there is no doubt that Renaissance authors often referred to the Turks as *Teucri.* But it is less clear exactly what, if anything, they meant to imply by doing so. Was the name *Teucri* always used to conjure up a Trojan past for the Turks, or was it sometimes just a name? Very few Renaissance authors who employ the term connect the Turks to the Trojans explicitly, or interpret their contemporary history as an extension of their supposed Trojan past.

Second, there is the rather smaller group of authors who maintain that contemporary Turkish policy actually reflects a desire for vengeance for ancient injuries done by the Greeks at Troy. The idea appears very rarely in formal history writing, tending to crop up instead in more imaginative contexts: epic poems, satires, prophecies, rhetorical exercises, and the like. Moreover—and this seems to be the crucial point—in these texts the idea is almost always presented as a quite ludicrous one, a notion that the credulous Turks may entertain about themselves but that no sensible European author or reader ought to accept. In these texts, the point is not that the Turks are actually Trojans but that they arrogantly *claim* to be Trojans. It is an accusation, not an explanation, used to underscore the outrageousness of Ottoman imperial pretensions, not to provide a plausible account of their motives or justification of their actions.

Nevertheless, even if these authors engaged in their own forms of *anasceua,* raising the possibility of a Trojan identity for the Turks only to mock and deride the notion, the idea still had to come from somewhere. The origins of the claim in the medieval chronicle tradition are beyond doubt. But it was not widespread. The modern notion that "Trojan Turks" appear everywhere in the medieval chronicle tradition and that the theory was demolished only by the work of careful humanist critics does not stand up to scrutiny. In fact, a survey of the medieval sources which appear to establish a direct genealogical connection between the Turks and the Trojans—all of them deriving from either Fredegar or the *Gesta Francorum*—shows that the "Trojan Turks" had their fair share of critics throughout the Middle Ages. Belief in their descent from Priam was by no means universal. By the start of the fifteenth century the idea had all but disappeared from serious historical writing. Nor was it humanism that led to its demise, but rather a shift, starting in the earliest decades of the high Middle Ages, in the notion of what universal histories, and the legends of national origin they propagated, were for.

The Turks as *Teucri*

Exactly when Latin authors began to refer to the Ottoman Turks as *Teucri* is not clear. The word itself was not common in ancient Greek (it was Virgil who popularized it as an alternate name for the Trojans). Byzantine authors

before the fifteenth century seem not to have used the term for any of the
Turkic states—Western Türk, Khazar, Seljuk, Ottoman—with whom they
came into contact.[9] Nor was it used in Latin literature on the crusades to describe the Seljuk or Mamluk opponents of the Franks in the Holy Land. The
earliest example of the practice I know is in a letter composed by the Florentine chancellor Coluccio Salutati in the late fourteenth century. Calling the
Turks *Teucri* may well have been his innovation.

In 1389, Salutati wrote to King Tvrtko I of Bosnia on behalf of the Signoria
of Florence, congratulating him on a recent military victory over the Ottomans; he referred to the Turks as both *Phryges* and *Troiani*.[10] Eight years later,
while discussing the Turks in a letter to the margrave of Moravia, Salutati
explained why: "You see these 'Teucrians' (for it is more pleasing to call
them this than 'Turks,' since they now rule in Teucria—though legend has it
they came down from Mt. Caucasus). You see, I say, these Teucrians, a most
fearsome race of men."[11]

Note Salutati's qualification of the usage: now that the Turks are in the
Troas, we may as well call them *Teucri*. He certainly does not say that the
Turks are the descendants of the Trojans. He is well aware that they have
come to "Teucria" from elsewhere, and even speculates about where exactly
their original homeland might have been. We will come back to his suggestion of a Caucasian origin for the Turks in a later chapter. What is important
here is that for Salutati, using the name *Teucri* did not amount to endorsing a
particular view about the origins or national character of the Turks. It was
simply a familiar classical name which, thanks to a coincidence of history
and geography, was convenient and pleasing to adopt for a newly emergent
nation. The real origins of that nation, however, lay far outside the boundaries of the classical world.

Salutati's later successor as Florentine chancellor, Poggio Bracciolini, expressed similar ambivalence about the practice of calling the Turks *Teucri*. He
often did so himself, in letters, orations, and dialogues written throughout
his long career.[12] In none of these works did he claim that the Turks were actually Trojans, or that they were descended from Trojans, or that memories
of Trojan defeat in any way determined their present policy. At one point
Poggio even admitted that it was probably inaccurate to call them *Teucri*,
though he saw the value of the term for the humanist intent on achieving
an authentic antique style. Writing to his friend Alberto Parisi in 1454,
Poggio acknowledged that there were really no grounds at all for believing
that the ancient Trojans had survived in Asia to become the modern-day
Turks: "Regarding your question whether the enemies of our faith should be

called *Teucri* or *Turci*, the rationale for these names is unclear to me. You know, of course, that the name *Teucri* is an ancient one, derived from *Teucer*, and that the Trojans were called *Teucri* after him. But after the fall of Troy we do not read of any nation of Asia using this name; it seems to have been revived only recently, in our own age."[13]

It would be better, Poggio says, to call the enemies of Christendom by their present-day name, *Turci*. Many other contemporary nations are known by modern names that have no classical antecedent; conversely, all sorts of ancient names for countries and peoples have fallen out of use without anyone calling for their revival. At this point, Poggio's argument becomes a bit unclear. He mentions some apparently analogous cases: the ancient Scythians are now known as Tartars, and the Sarmatians are now called Hungarians. From these examples, it may seem that Poggio thought the Turks really were descended from the ancient Trojans, but that out of respect for current usage, they ought to be known by the modern form of their name. But Poggio goes on to clarify that, unlike the history of the other nations mentioned, that of the Turks is not at all certain. No historical relationship between them and any people of antiquity can be determined: "The origins of the ancestors of our present enemy, and the name by which they were known before the past century, when they were contained within the borders of Asia Minor, remain unknown."[14]

Turkish history could be traced with certainty only from the fatal moment in the mid-fourteenth century when the Turks entered Europe as mercenaries in the pay of the Byzantine pretender John Cantacuzenus. Poggio recounts this episode in detail but then drops the question altogether, concluding that the truth of the matter remains obscure: "Let those who are more interested in such things determine what the proper name for them is."[15]

Salutati's letters to the rulers of Bosnia and Moravia and Poggio's missives to Alfonso and Frederick III were written while each was performing the duties of Florentine chancellor. The practice of calling the Turks *Teucri* was also followed in other European chanceries in the fifteenth century, but here too we should not assume that any historical or genealogical significance was attached to the use of the name. In papal bulls and briefs,[16] and in the official correspondence of the Venetian Senate,[17] King Alfonso of Aragon,[18] Emperor Sigismund,[19] and the Knights of St. John on Rhodes,[20] the Turks are called *Teucri* and the sultan of the day *Magnus Teucer;* but in none of these documents is it suggested that the Turks are *actually* Trojans, or even de-

scended from Trojans. Nor is there any speculation about the significance of
their name—no hint that the fact that the Turks are "Teucri" explains their
present animosity toward the Greeks, or gives them a right to occupy Asia
Minor, or makes it acceptable for Christian powers to enter into treaties or
truces with them.[21] The letters are either diplomatic reports detailing the latest Ottoman activities and movements or slightly more formal communica-
tions addressed from one state to another and appealing for joint action
against them; but in either case, although the Turks are called *Teucri,* their
character as Trojans is simply not an issue that is discussed. The only moralizing points made in these letters are religious in character: in letters issued
by the Venetian Senate, for instance, Mehmed II is called *Magnus Teucer* but
also *crucis persecutor* and *inimicissimus nominis Christiani;* he and his "Teucrian"
mob (*Teucrorum rabies*) are devoted *ad damna et exterminium Christianorum.*[22]

The Franciscan Bartolomeo da Giano expanded on the theme of the Turkish menace in a letter sent from Constantinople to a fellow friar at Venice in
1438. Here Fra Bartolomeo laments the ferocious attacks of the Turks on
Byzantine territory, the hopelessness of the Greek situation, and the dangers
of the current Latin policy of waiting and watching. He uses both *Teucri* and
Turci as names for the Turks, but in describing the Greeks' present humiliating predicament, in which obscure barbarians threaten to overthrow the
very heart of their empire, Bartolomeo makes no effort to assert a Trojan
identity for the Turks: "Alas, alas, it was only a few years ago that the *Teucri*
were unknown anywhere in the world, save for a few shepherds, living on
some hills or other on the outskirts of Damascus: rude, uneducated, wild, il-
literate, without any learning—as they remain even to this day."[23] *Teucri*
they may be, but these coarse Bedouin hail from the Syrian outback. They
are hardly dispossessed princes of Troy.

Western observers of the capture of Constantinople, fifteen years later,
took a similarly harsh view of the Turks, their character, history, and motivations. The Turkish sack struck those who witnessed it, and those in Europe
who heard of it soon afterward, as a calamity almost unprecedented in the
history of civilization. This is not the place to survey the dozens of eyewitness reports and even more numerous secondhand accounts of the city's fall
which circulated in subsequent years.[24] It is enough to note that even the
most hard-headed diplomats and canniest merchants were moved by the
city's tribulations. Many ventured to speculate on the significance of the disaster for the course of world history and, in doing so, to search for an explanation for the tragedy in the record of past events.

Cardinal Isidore of Kiev, often cited as a believer in the Turks' Trojan origins,[25] witnessed the fall of Constantinople at first hand, having been sent by Pope Nicholas V as papal legate to the Byzantine court. In his letters to Christian leaders describing the capture of the city, Isidore does on occasion refer to the Turks as *Teucri*, but without the slightest intimation that they actually are Trojans or that their actions represent any kind of revenge against the Greeks for ancient wrongs. Instead, he stresses the Turks' hatred of Christians and their barbarous cruelty.[26] Isidore sees the Turkish threat in theological rather than classical terms, despite the classical name he gives to the enemy. Sultan Mehmed, while called *Magnus Teucer,* appears in his works as the herald of Antichrist, not the avenger of Hector. In name and in title he is heir to the Prophet of the Hagarenes (that is, Muhammad) and a son of Satan.[27] Isidore clearly saw no real significance in the name *Teucri:* in letters written within days of those cited above he also used the forms *Turci* and *Thurci* and called Constantinople *Turcopolis.*[28]

Leonardo Giustiniani of Chios, archbishop of Mytilene, was with Isidore at the fall of Constantinople and, like his older colleague, wrote an account of it for Pope Nicholas V. He too uses the term *Teucri* for the Turks but, like Isidore, never suggests that the conquerors are actually of Trojan stock.[29] Leonardo interprets the loss of the Byzantine capital as a punishment visited by God on the Greeks for their failure to observe the union of Orthodox and Latin churches agreed to in Florence in 1439 and proclaimed in Constantinople in December 1452. He likens the city's captivity to that which, according to the prophets, Israel endured as punishment for its sins: where Isaiah lamented the fall of Zion, "tossed with tempest," Leonardo decries the fury of the *Theucri tempestas* that has enveloped Constantinople.[30] If any explicit historical comparison is intended for the Turks in this passage, it is to the Assyrians who persecuted Israel, not the defeated defenders of Troy.

More classical in tone is the Brescian humanist Ubertino Puscolo's epic poem *Constantinopolis,* which describes the fall of the city that he too witnessed at first hand.[31] Puscolo had traveled to Constantinople to learn Greek but was captured by the Turks during the sack of the city and forced to pay his own ransom in order to return to Italy. Arriving home in about 1455, he composed an account of his experiences in 3007 epic hexameters. Throughout the work, Puscolo calls the Turks *Teucri* and the sultan *Magnus Teucer,* while the Greeks appear as Homeric *Danai.* But despite the poem's heroic tone and many debts to Homer and Virgil, Puscolo makes only one rather indirect connection between the defeat of the original *Teucri* and the victory of their modern namesakes.[32] Puscolo, openly contemptuous of his Greek hosts, blamed the fall of the city on Byzantine inaction and cowardice.[33] According to his Virgilian model, then, we might expect him to side with the *Teucri* and present them in a positive light, but Puscolo does no such thing. In his view the Greeks were bad, and so it was their just reward to fall into the hands of an even worse nation, the Turkish *Teucri*, a mob of violent savages thirsting for Christian blood. Given Puscolo's perilous and frustrating experiences in the East, one suspects that he took a certain satisfaction in seeing the two nations now thrown together. The only heroes in his work are the few stalwart Latins ("fidi Latini")[34] like himself who selflessly come to the city's defense. Avenging Trojans have no place in his story.

The Florentine Platonist Marsilio Ficino has also been cited as a believer in the Turks' Trojan origins.[35] In two ironical letters addressed to Sixtus IV in the aftermath of the Pazzi conspiracy of 1478, Ficino calls on the pope to stop interfering in the affairs of Christian nations and turn his attention to the more serious threat posed by the *Teucri*. Despite using the classical name, however, Ficino expresses no opinion on the Trojan ethnicity of the Turks. He is more concerned with portraying them as savage barbarians and enemies of the faith, threatening Sixtus's Christian flock with apocalyptic ruin.[36] Moreover, in a letter of 1480 addressed to King Matthias Corvinus of Hungary, Ficino calls the Turks *Turci*. Here too his emphasis is on their barbarity and hatred of Christian culture. He compares them to the Egyptians under Pharaoh who so savagely persecuted the Hebrews (and calls Matthias a new Moses who must liberate his subjugated people); he also brands the Turks monsters whom Matthias, as a new Hercules, must slay.[37] Among these various ancient exempla, Ficino does not mention Troy.

References to Turks as *Teucri* appear in numerous other fifteenth-century accounts of Turkish affairs; most express even less interest in their significance for world history or Christian teleology than those just surveyed. The Genoese officials Angelo Giovanni Lomellino and Franco Giustiniani, for instance, each wrote eyewitness accounts describing how the *Teucri* stormed Constantinople, but neither makes any comment about their historical origins or motivations; they certainly do not claim they were ethnically Trojan.[38] Giustiniani, in fact, seems to consider the name *Teucri* no more than an alternate spelling of *Turci:* he uses both forms in his letter and calls the Asian side of the Bosporus *Turchia*.[39] Both names also appear, interchangeably, in the works of Fra Bartolomeo da Giano, Isidore of Kiev, and Marsilio Ficino, as they do in a slightly earlier account by Egidio Calerio of the death of Car-

dinal Giuliano Cesarini at the battle of Varna, written in 1447.[40] Letters from
the imperial chancery and the Knights of Rhodes also use both, or call the
sultan *Magnus Teucer* but the Turks as a nation *Turci*.[41] Likewise Henricus de
Soemmern, a papal official who drew up a summary of various accounts of
Constantinople's fall in the late 1450s, switches from *Turci* to *Teucri* without comment, depending on which source he is quoting.[42] Even the Greek
humanist Niccolò Sagundino, author of one of the most detailed accounts
of the Scythian origins of the Turks, did not scruple to use *Teucri*, alongside *Turci*, in his earliest work describing them.[43] The flexibility with which
both names can appear in the same text and sometimes even in the same
sentence suggests that most authors—and, perhaps just as important, most
copyists—saw no meaningful distinction between the two.[44] In the majority
of cases it seems that *Teucri* was no more than an alternate, more classical-
sounding, and thus aesthetically pleasing form of *Turci*. Use of it should not,
on its own, be taken as proof of an author's beliefs about the ethnic origins
or national character of the Turks.

What is more, many of the more emotional or imaginative fifteenth-
century texts on the Ottoman threat describe the "Teucrian" Turks in terms
that either implicitly contradict or explicitly reject the possibility of their Trojan ancestry. Authors who compare or even identify the Turks with biblical
villains like the Assyrians, the Egyptians, Gog and Magog, Antichrist, or Satan, for example, effectively exclude them from any connection to the classical world.[45] Even those authors who prefer to analyze Turkish aggression
in the context of secular history show little regard, in their choice of examples, for the supposedly widespread belief in the Turks' Trojan origins.

It was in fact quite common for writers to compare the fall of Constantinople (and other Greek cities) to the fall of Troy, likening the tribulations of
the Byzantine capital to those of Priam's city (and thus the modern-day
Greeks to the unfortunate Trojans), without, apparently, stumbling over the
fact that it was the Turks who were supposed to be of Trojan stock. "There
was never such impiety committed in the sack of Troy as that which the
Teucri, those savage henchmen of demons, inflicted on the Greeks,"[46] writes
Adam of Montaldo. The Genoese humanist Giorgio Fieschi makes the comparison even more explicit in his epic poem *Eubois*, which casts the fall of
Negroponte to the Turks in 1470 as a reprise of the fall of Troy. In his account, Mehmed II is cast as a formidable Greek warrior, a "new Achilles,"
while the Venetian colonial governor plays the role of white-haired Priam,
noble and doomed.[47] That such comparisons were made is not surprising:

the sack of Troy was the most famous urban catastrophe of all time and, along with the razing of Carthage and the capture of Jerusalem, offered an obvious parallel for any Renaissance writer wanting to ornament his description of the tragedy at Constantinople. Lauro Quirini, in fact, claimed Constantinople's capture was a far worse disaster than the fall of Troy or of any other ancient city: "When I consider the ancient fall of Troy, the unhappy sack of Carthage, the wretched capture of Jerusalem, the slaughter at Saguntum, and the destruction of many other very noble cities, it seems that none was ever more shameful, more cruel, or more pitiful."[48] But there is no suggestion in either Fieschi's or Quirini's text that the fall of Constantinople was *historically* connected to the capture of earlier cities, nor that the Turks themselves had acted to avenge any previous wrong.

Some Greek observers come closer to asserting a direct correlation between their ancestors' sack of Troy and their current predicament. The Greek eyewitness to the city's fall known as Nestor-Iskander, writing in medieval Russian, maintained that in capturing Constantinople, the Turks had "conquered the conquerors of proud Artaxerxes . . . and destroyed the destroyers of wondrous Troy."[49] Even this does not amount to the declaration of a direct historical or genealogical link between the Trojans and the Turks (or, for that matter, between the Turks and the Persians under Artaxerxes). Nestor simply notes the irony of the fact that the Greeks, conquerors of so many ancient nations, have now been laid low.

Another frequently cited proponent of the Trojan theory, the Greek historian Laonicus Chalcocondyles, describes how the "Romans" (that is, the Byzantine Greeks) viewed the fall of Constantinople to the Turks in 1453. Writing several decades after the fact, Chalcocondyles says that the loss was a punishment the Greeks deserved, as a result of their brutal sacking of ancient Troy: "It seems that this very great catastrophe surpasses in pathos all those which have ever occurred in the world, and almost approaches the catastrophe of Troy, and that justice was done for Troy by the barbarians, as the Greeks perished in all their strength. And this is how the Romans knew it had come to pass that the price had been paid by the Hellenes for the catastrophe which happened at Troy long ago."[50] Like Nestor-Iskender, Chalcocondyles identifies the Turks not as ethnically Trojan but rather as instruments of fate, sent to punish the Greeks for injustices done at Troy. In both texts, the emphasis is on Greek hubris, not the resurgence of some atavistic Trojan force on the geopolitical stage.

Observations like these were employed primarily as rhetorical devices, intended to illustrate by way of analogy the horror of Constantinople's fall while also—no minor consideration—demonstrating the author's own ingenuity, erudition, and command of the classical tropes of lamentation. In other texts, humanist authors compare the fall of the city to that of Jerusalem, or of Carthage, or of Rome to the barbarian hordes.[51] Even more common are comparisons between the Turks and various enemies of ancient Rome—Etruscans, Carthaginians, Armenians, Germans, Goths—or between Mehmed II and renowned world conquerors of the past like Alexander, Caesar, and Augustus, or less admirable tyrants like Ramses, Xerxes, Hannibal, Nero, and Caligula.[52] These ancient exemplars were used to illuminate the course of current history, but they were not meant to be understood as actual historical antecedents to contemporary political events. Most authors saw no more connection between the Turks and the Trojans than they did between the Turks and the Babylonians who captured Jerusalem, the Persians who threatened Athens, the Etruscans, Goths, or Carthaginians who besieged Rome, or indeed between the Turks and the *Greeks* who sacked ancient Troy.

One Florentine humanist, Niccolò Tignosi, even argued directly against the practice of calling the Turks *Teucri* in order to reinforce just such a rhetorical point. The Turks, he said, had behaved far more cruelly than the Goths who sacked Rome: "If you search through history, I believe you will find that no crime was ever committed more cruelly and detestably than what was done at Constantinople. Indeed, the enemy ought not to be called *Teucri*, as many people who notice the similarity of their names suppose, but rather *Truces* [savages], who, it seems clear enough, are allowed to defy the gods themselves, steeped as they are in human blood."[53]

Morbisanus: Trojan Avenger?

There were, of course, some authors who not only called the Turks *Teucri* but also commented on how a belief in their Trojan past contributed to their present actions. Aeneas Sylvius would hardly have objected to the notion as strenuously as he did had it not had some currency in his day.

In a few cases, authors identified the Turks as Trojans simply because they believed they were an indigenous people of Asia Minor. One historian who expressed ideas along these lines was the Augustinian friar Andrea Biglia. Biglia had taught Aeneas Sylvius in Siena in the late 1420s and is very likely one of the authors Aeneas had in mind when he complained that "not only writers and poets, but even historians" were using the term *Teucri* in their works. In 1432–1433, Biglia composed a survey of Eastern history from the time of Muhammad to his own day, in which he strove for a consciously classical prose style. He calls the Turks not only *Teucri* but also *Phryges, Dardani,* and *Mysi,* stating explicitly that they are the direct descendants of these ancient peoples of Asia Minor. Biglia used this nomenclature because he believed that the Turks had originated in Asia Minor and had not migrated there from anywhere else. But he never suggests that their Trojan ancestry somehow propelled them to attack the Greeks—indeed, the whole point of his work (written at a time when the Ottomans seemed less of a threat than they would at midcentury) is to portray the "Teucrian" Turks as a sympathetic nation, allied in spirit with the nations of the West but long subjected to a brutal enemy occupation. In Biglia's scheme, it is the Mongol "Tartars," who *do* hail from beyond the Mediterranean world, and not the indigenous Anatolian Turks who threaten to destroy civilization. (Biglia's historical ideas and reasoning are quite complicated, and receive a fuller treatment in Chapter 4.)

Poggio Bracciolini, in his letter to Alberto Parisi of 1454, hints at a similar belief in the autochthony of the Teucrian Turks, suggesting that up until the previous century they had been "confined" within Asia Minor. But Poggio may have meant only to contrast their present expansionist policy with the much more modest state in which they had lived in the fourteenth century. Indeed, he concludes by admitting that the question of the Turks' earliest origins is insoluble.

Biglia and Poggio are the only humanist historians I have found to even flirt with the idea that the contemporary Ottoman Turks were truly, historically descended from Trojan stock.[54] Did their speculations really warrant such a full-on attack from Aeneas Silvius? Or did the source of his irritation lie elsewhere? A much more influential text claiming Trojan origins for the Turks—and a far likelier candidate to be the target of Aeneas's ire—comes from a very different context altogether. A spurious letter addressed to the pope from a Muslim ruler variously called Morbisanus, Morbasanus, Amorbisanus, Marbassian, Morbosiano, and so on enjoyed widespread circulation across fifteenth-century Europe.[55] In the text, "Sultan Morbisanus" argues that the pontiff should call off the crusade he is organizing against him on the grounds that, as Italian and Turk, they are both descended from the Trojans and so bound by ties of Teucrian blood:

I am compelled to wonder and grieve at the fact that the Italians rebel against me, since a secret love inspires me to cherish them, for they and

their great works and their forefathers have sprung from the blood of Trojans. I know that their ancestors were Antenor and Aeneas, born of the
blood of Priam; and in their place I shall carry my empire into Europe, ful-
filling the promises which are known to have been made by my gods to my
forefathers. And I intend to restore great Troy, and to avenge the blood of
Hector and the ruin of Ilium by subjugating the empire of the Greeks to my
rule, and to punish the heirs of the original culprits for the injuries done to
my goddess Pallas.[56]

Here is the likely source of Aeneas's irritation: not widespread historical
error but a particularly mischievous piece of antipapal propaganda.

Aeneas's hostility to the idea of the Turks' Trojan origins was renowned;
furthermore, once elected pope, he not only organized a crusade against the
Turks but also composed a letter to Mehmed II (which circulated widely in
Europe after his death) exhorting him to convert to Christianity. Given all
this, it is not surprising that the spurious letter of "Morbisanus" was considered by some contemporaries to be a genuine text, written by Mehmed in
reply to Pope Pius's famous attempt at evangelization. The Morbisanus letter
was printed after the papal letter to the sultan in all but one of its several
incunable editions.[57] Some modern scholars have maintained that the text is
either the Latin translation of a genuine Turkish document or a European
forgery composed after the publication of Pius's epistle.[58] Although other
critics have simply rejected the letter as spurious without speculating on its
date or place of origin,[59] few seem to have realized that the text is in fact a
much older concoction, originally composed in Italian more than a century
before Aeneas Sylvius's elevation to the papacy.[60]

The earliest dated version of the text has the Turk addressing Pope Clement VI (r. 1342–1352) and is dated 1345.[61] In 1344, Clement directed
French, Genoese, and Venetian forces on a crusade against the Turkish emirate of Aydin and its capital, Smyrna (modern Izmir), on the Aegean coast
of Asia Minor. The emirate's aggressive new ruler, Umur Pasha, had been
threatening Italian trading interests in the eastern Aegean.[62] In the letter,
"Morbisanus" (that is, "Umur" plus "Bassanus," a common Latin transliteration of "Pasha") chides the pope for giving help to the Venetians, since, unlike the Turks and the Romans, they are not of Trojan blood. Whoever
forged the letter did so soon after Clement allied with Venice against Umur
Pasha; the Italian author may have been an opponent of Venetian interests
in the Levant—possibly Genoese or Florentine.

The letter remained in circulation long after Clement's Smyrniote crusade. Later scribes kept the text (now circulating in a Latin version as well as in Italian) current by changing either the date or the name of the pope addressed, or both.[63] A French translation, now addressed to Pope Nicholas V, was appended to an eyewitness account of the fall of Constantinople by the Florentine merchant Jacobo Tedaldi.[64] Latin and German versions of the letter addressed to Nicholas V are also known, though whether these derive from an earlier Latin text or from the French is unclear;[65] another German translation may also have been made.[66] Several versions of the French text of the letter, varying slightly in wording or dialect, are known; certain of them were incorporated, along with Tedaldi's account, into some popular French chronicles of the 1460s and early '70s, thereby ensuring the text's widespread circulation in French literature well into the sixteenth century.[67] The letter was equally well known in Italy, thanks to its publication alongside Pius's letter to Mehmed; an older version of the text, in Latin and addressed to Clement VI, also appeared on its own in a Roman broadside.[68]

The letter of "Morbisanus" probably inspired many, if not all, of those fifteenth-century authors who both comment on the Trojan ancestry of the Turks and attribute to them a thirst for revenge against the Greeks. It is to their works that I now turn. Filippo da Rimini, the Venetian chancellor of Corfu, wrote an account of Constantinople's fall in which he called the Turks *Teucri* and Mehmed II *Tros* (the Phrygian king after whom Troy was named). He also inserted into his report a (false) story that after entering the city, the sultan raped a Greek woman sheltering inside the church of Hagia Sophia in revenge for the rape of Cassandra by the Locrian Ajax.[69] Ajax had dragged Cassandra from the base of the statue of Pallas Athena to which she had clung, claiming sanctuary; Filippo may well have substituted this crime for the more general "injuries done to our goddess Pallas" which "Morbisanus" says he intends to avenge.[70]

Adam of Montaldo, the Augustinian friar, compiled an account of the fall of Constantinople derived almost entirely from earlier sources, sometime after 1476. Adam attributes *all* the atrocities committed by the Turks in the sack to their desire to avenge their Trojan ancestors. After describing at length the slaughter, pillage, and rape inflicted by the Turks on the inhabitants of the city, he comments: "I do not see any reason for surprise that this Asiatic race has vanquished its mortal enemy—mortal because of both [the difference in] religion and the ancient wrong done to the Dardanians." The great surprise, for Adam, is that Western Christian powers allowed the catastrophe to happen—and even colluded in the Turks' success—without offering the slightest resistance.[71]

The intention of "Morbisanus" to carry his revived Trojan empire into Europe finds an echo in another text, written shortly after the fall of Constantinople by Timoteo Maffei, a humanist cleric who later served as archbishop of Ragusa, professor of rhetoric at the Florentine *studio*, and architectural adviser to Cosimo de' Medici. In late 1453, Maffei wrote a letter to the princes of Christendom appealing for a new crusade. He too reported that Mehmed II had captured and sacked Constantinople in order to avenge his Trojan ancestors. And his next step, Maffei claimed, would be to attack Italy: because it had been settled in antiquity by Trojan refugees, the sultan believed—*falsely*, Maffei stressed—that the entire peninsula formed part of his birthright; now he was keen to reclaim it.[72] Note where the emphasis falls in Maffei's account: the Ottomans are dangerous because (like Morbisanus) they *think* they have a right to Italy, not because they actually do.

The Turks' outrageous presumption in claiming Trojan ancestry became something of a topos in crusade literature of the later quattrocento. In a 1471 poem exhorting the princes of Christian Europe to a new crusade, the Roman jurist Giovanni Luigi Toscani excoriates the sultan for shamelessly presuming to claim a Trojan pedigree. Likewise, in a vernacular lament for the fall of Negroponte addressed to the Venetian Senate in the following year, Antonio Cornazzano ridicules the sultan, who has "mentito al mundo el gran sangue di Troia."[73]

Another poetic text, related even more closely to the Morbisanus tradition, is the *Responsio Magni Turci*, one half of a spurious versified exchange purporting to take place between Pius II and the Turk. This fictional conversation is clearly based on Pius's (genuine) letter to Mehmed II and the letter of "Morbisanus" that sometimes masqueraded as Mehmed's reply.[74] In the *Responsio*, the Turk remonstrates with Pius for denying his Trojan heritage:

> Tu nos Dardanei generis posse esse negasti
> > Me Turchum tandem dicere non puduit
> Sum Theucer, Theucro natus de sanguine. Turcum
> > Quid, Pie, meque tuo carmine sepe vocas?
> Dic mihi, quis Theucer fuerit, quis denique Turcus?
> > Troiani fuimus, quicquid, pater, putas.
> Reliquie fuimus Priami quas perdere Graii,
> > Crudeli bello non potuere duces.

> Dardanide quanto fuerint cum Marte potentes
> Historie referunt: hystoriasque lege.[75]

You have said it is impossible for me to be a Dardanian by birth, nor have you blushed to call me a Turk. I am a Teucrian, born of Teucrian blood. Why, Pius, do you call me a Turk throughout your poem? Tell me, who was Teucer, and then, who was Turcus? Father, we were Trojans, whatever you may think. We were the remnants of [the nation of] Priam whom the Greek generals could not destroy in their cruel war. History tells how powerful in war the Dardanians were: you should read your history.

Later, Mehmed says he is coming to Italy to claim the lands of Ausonia for himself.[76] In fact, the project of establishing a Trojan world empire is more important to Mehmed than even the destruction of the Christian faith—the objective usually imputed to the Turks:

> Perdere non cupio Christum, sed regna priorum
> Dardanidum repetam que tua sceptra tenent.
> Aeneas mediis fuerat qui elapsus Achivis
> Tros urbem Romam condidit in Lacio
> Romoleasque arces repetam; instantibus ense
> Donabo mortem gentibus atque face.[77]

I do not wish to overthrow Christ, but I shall seek the kingdoms of the earlier Dardanians, which are part of your dominions. Trojan Aeneas, who escaped from the middle of the Greeks, founded in Latium the city of Rome; I shall seek the citadels of Romulus and I shall kill the people there with fire and sword.

A rhetorical exercise like this functions on several levels. It presents the Great Turk and his policies in a way meant to seem particularly threatening to Italians, to be sure. At the same time, however, it mocks the Turk for his Trojan pretensions: he appears simultaneously dangerous and deluded. Last, the poet works in a clever dig at the pope's own intellectual postures; how better to subvert the crusade propaganda of the humanist pope than by countering the force of his trademark *anascuea:* "you should read your history." Spurious letters from Oriental potentates had long been used as a tool of satire or social criticism in the medieval West; the Morbisanus letter seems to function primarily on this level, pointing out the inertia and ineffectiveness of Europe's political (and intellectual) defenses.

The most extensive poetic elaboration of the themes expressed in

Morbisanus's letter has, to my knowledge, escaped the notice of all commentators on the Renaissance belief in the Turks' Trojan origins, despite a helpfully descriptive title: the epic *De destructione Constantinopolitana sive de ultione Troianorum contra Graecos,* written in November 1458 by a little-known French jurist, Florentinus Liquenaius of Tours. A transparent reworking of the first two books of the *Aeneid,* the poem opens with a suitably Virgilian statement of purpose, in which the interpretation of Constantinople's fall as an act of Trojan revenge is clearly established:

> Impia barbarici (Danaas invasit ut urbes)
> Scribimus acta ducis, Troum qui maximus ultor
> Marte lacessitos intravit vindice mortis
> Hectoree cinctus armato milite muros.[78]

I write of the impious deeds of the barbarian leader, how he stormed the city of the Danai, the great avenger of Troy who, surrounded by a host of armed companions, penetrated the walls assailed by Mars, in revenge for the death of Hector.

But despite being branded impious and barbaric, the Turks are also, in Liquenaius's view, heroic and tragically wronged. The sultan, "Morbezanus," is haunted by thoughts of Greek treachery and the loss of his ancient city. A downcast Venus beseeches her father, Jupiter, to help him, and in a night vision Mars encourages him to fight for his patrimony:

> Morbezane, Phrigum in Danaos validissimus ultor
> Quid piger hic, et nulla facis? Memorare tuorum
> Fata patrum, immerito, qui Troie marte perempti
> Argolico, parte vindicta posse potiri
> Exoptant. Graium te profer menibus ipsos
> Cinge armis, et ego quocumque vocaveris, illic
> Mars adero, solamen ubique tibique parabo.[79]

Morbezanus, bravest avenger of the Phrygians against the Danai, why are you idle, why do you do nothing? Remember the fate of your ancestors who, slain unjustly in the Greek war at Troy, long for you to win back and take possession of that which is your due. Take yourself to the very walls of the Greeks, and surround them with arms, and from wherever you summon me, there I, Mars, shall be, and everywhere I shall bring you comfort.

The pathos of these opening scenes notwithstanding, Liquenaius is no "philoturk." Once the siege is under way, the true heroes of the work appear: the pious Greeks, led by the snowy-haired and dignified Emperor Constantine, cast in the unmistakable role of King Priam.[80] Supported by their own heavenly patrons (the Virgin and Child, who repeatedly appear in visions, as well as a lion speaking on behalf of a jealous and protective Hercules), the Greeks mount a fierce defense of Constantinople's walls. Defeat comes at last, but only after numerous examples of heroic martyrdom and pious sacrifice. Ultimately the battle for Constantinople is lost, and a great deal of rape and slaughter ensues. But the war is still to be won: Liquenaius concludes the poem looking forward in hope to the time when the injustice of the Turkish victory will be righted, the Turks expelled from the lands of the Greeks, and the sultan made to pay for his sins.[81]

Liquenaius seems at first to cast the Turks as heroic Trojans and to portray their capture of Constantinople in a positive light, but in the end his work offers a thoroughly conventional assessment of the city's fall and its significance. The same cannot be said of Giovanni Mario Filelfo, author of a much better known epic poem on the same subject, the *Amyris*, written about 1476. In the first draft of the poem, at least, the interpretation of the Turkish capture of Constantinople as the justified and thoroughly honorable act of a pious son of Troy is expressed without reservation.

As in Liquenaius's epic, Filelfo's *Amyris* opens with the young Mehmed pondering what course to take in life. The goddess Bellona approaches, reminding him of the ancient wrongs done to his people by the Greeks and urging him to avenge his vanquished forebears.[82] She pauses to underscore exactly how Mehmed is related to the Trojans, for the relationship is not one of direct descent. Rather, the Turks are a race far older than Troy: the founder of the race, Othman, was the ancestor of Erichthon, from whom in turn were born Tros, Ilus, Laodemon, and finally King Priam himself. Thus the Turks are not so much Trojans as the Trojans were originally Turks! Mehmed must remember his Turco-Trojan heritage and strive to avenge the injuries his race has sustained.[83] Filelfo then recounts Mehmed's succession to the Ottoman throne, his early campaigns, and finally the siege and capture of Constantinople. In accomplishing this, Mehmed at last realizes his destiny. The losses of the Trojans are redeemed and the Greeks suitably punished. Filelfo taunts the conquered Byzantines:

> Namque Phryges nisi vos, Graeci, tot funera passos
> oppressissetis, regnumque a culmine totum
> corporaque ampla virum vinclis et carcere duro
> vestra manus traheret, nisi tanta incendia belli

> ex Helenes moechae vitio commissa fuissent,
> rex Mahomettus ea nunc vos non mente tulisset
> in praeceps, nec vellet eis committere bellum
> cum quibus ulla foret non causa, nec ullus habendi
> adiectus stimulus. Sed fatis denique vestris
> principium veteres vestri struxere parentes.
> Vos luistis poenam.[84]

For if you Greeks had not crushed the Phrygians, who have suffered so many losses, and if your troops had not brought down the whole kingdom from the top, and dragged countless bodies of men away in chains and in harsh imprisonment, and if the crime of the adulteress Helen had not sparked such great conflagrations of war—then King Mahomet would not now be plunging you headlong into peril in this way, nor would he desire to wage war against a people with whom he had no quarrel, nor any incentive to create one. But your ancient forebears laid the foundation for your fate: you are paying the penalty.

Does Filelfo, then, exploit the Trojan origins of the Turks for "philoturk" ends? Yes and no: his unconventional approach to his subject is explained in large part by the fact that he was commissioned to write the work by an Anconitan merchant, Othman Lillo Ferducci, who had family and business connections to the Ottoman court. It is not known whether Filelfo, or Ferducci, ever sent the work to Mehmed II, although a dedicatory letter by Ferducci to the sultan precedes the work.[85] But the depth of Filelfo's attachment to the idea can be gauged by the fact that after Ferducci died, Filelfo abandoned his initial concept for the poem and added a fourth book, now calling for a new crusade to defeat the "Trojan" infidel and adroitly rededicating the whole work to Duke Galeazzo Maria Sforza of Milan.[86] Filelfo is the only author I know of, humanist or otherwise, to claim in all seriousness that the Turks deserved to reclaim their (genuine) Trojan patrimony, and he was paid to say so. Patrons willing to underwrite such sentiments were rare in Renaissance Europe. There is but one more: a wedding oration discovered by Anthony D'Elia, composed by Lodovico Carbone in the 1460s, in which the orator identifies the Ferrarese groom, one Zarabinus Turchus, as a descendant of the Trojan Turks. Zarabinus, Carbone explains, can trace his family tree back to a distinguished ancestor ("Amorbassanus," no less), a Turkish ambassador who defected to the Christian West with papal encouragement. Amorbassanus in turn was one of the Turkish *Teucri*, and "what is more noble than their origins, which go back to those from which the Latin race, the Alban fathers, and the walls of Rome [arise]? . . . The same place where the Turks are is where Troy was and the glory of the Trojans."[87] Marriage to a man of such distinguished pedigree, Carbone concludes, would be an honorable state.[88] The festive context, as D'Elia argues, rather blunts the political impact of Carbone's startling claim.

The Byzantine Greek Critoboulos of Imbros was connected even more closely to Mehmed II than either Filelfo or the Ferducci of Ancona (to say nothing of the Turchi of Ferrara). Critoboulos, born a subject of the Byzantine Empire, remained in the East after the Turkish conquest and was appointed governor of his native island of Imbros by the sultan in 1456. His *History of Mehmed the Conqueror*, written in Greek sometime after 1467 and modeled on Thucydides, is one of the more important sources for this period of Ottoman history. It is thanks to a particular passage in the *History* that Mehmed himself has at times been credited with a belief in the Trojan ancestry of his people. While on campaign in Asia Minor, Critobolous reports, the sultan diverted his army in order to visit the site of Troy:

> He himself with his army crossed the Hellespont, marched through Phrygia Minor, and reached Ilium. He observed its ruins and the traces of the ancient city of Troy . . . He also inquired about the tombs of the heroes—Achilles, Ajax and the rest. And he praised and congratulated them, their memory and their deeds, and on having a person like the poet Homer to extol them. He is reported to have said, shaking his head a little, "God has reserved for me, through so long a period of years, the right to avenge this city and its inhabitants. For I have subdued their enemies and have plundered their cities and made them the spoils of the Mysians. It was the Greeks and Macedonians and Thessalians and Peloponnesians who ravaged this place in the past, and whose descendants have now through my efforts paid the just penalty, after a long period of years, for their injustice to us Asiatics at that time and so often in subsequent years."[89]

And yet even here Mehmed does not claim the Trojans as his direct ancestors. Although he marvels at Trojan accomplishments and mourns the sack of their city, the only connection he draws between the Trojans and his own people is to describe them all as "Asiatics," locked in an eternal struggle with Greece. Critoboulos's point in relating the story is to present Mehmed not as a victorious Trojan returning home but as a cultured and sensitive ruler, versed in classical culture, aware of the poignancy of his own conquests, and nostalgic for the glory of heroic ages past. Given the eloquent rhetoric of the speech as reported and Critoboulos's many other debts to Thucydides, we must question whether the text is largely the author's invention. Mehmed appears here not as a ranting Morbisanus but instead as a world conqueror in the mold of Xerxes, Alexander, and Caesar—all rulers known to have visited Troy in the course of their conquests. On arrival, each of these ancient commanders is also said to have mused on the passing of heroes and the fall of great empires.[90] Critoboulos's portrait is certainly intended to flatter the sultan, but the emphasis is on Mehmed's eloquent and poetic sensibility, not his actual pedigree.

In contrast to the authors examined so far, some other commentators accepted the Turks' Trojan ancestry as genuine, only to interpret it as a reason for hope, not despair, for Christian Europe. Annius of Viterbo, for example, claimed the Turks were doomed because of their Trojan pedigree. His *De futuris Christianorum triumphis in Turchos et Saracenos* purports to be the text of a sermon delivered in Genoa in 1471 in which he predicted, on the basis of complex astrological calculations, that the Turkish empire would collapse in nine years' time. (It is rather more likely that Annius composed and backdated the work shortly after the Turkish occupation of Otranto in the summer of 1480; the first edition was printed on 8 December of that year.) Come the year 1480, Annius "prophesies," "The good fortune of the Turks will begin to fade . . . nor will anyone be surprised at [Mehmed's] invasion of Apulia, because the road to salvation will come from where you least expect: from a Greek city. Indeed, I think that just as the sack of Troy was begun by Apulians, so the fall of the Turks will be begun by the prince of Apulia."[91]

Trojan origins are seen as a disadvantage for the Turks in another imaginative text, the idiosyncratic *Opus Davidicum* of the Franciscan friar Johannes Angelus of Leonessa, written about 1497. Dedicated to Charles VIII, the text celebrates the French invasion of Italy in 1494 and exhorts the king to return to complete his project, defined not only as the conquest of Naples but also as a crusade for the reclamation of the Holy Land.[92] Johannes Angelus outlines the descent of the French royal house from David and the kings of Israel. This, according to the friar, entitles the "most Christian" kings of France to rule not only France but also the rest of Christian Europe, as well as Jerusalem, original seat of the Davidic kings. Almost every other contemporary work of historical and imaginative literature that touches on the origins of France traces the ancestry of the French kings back to the royal house of Troy (see below). But Johannes Angelus rejects this notion outright, claiming instead that a pure line of descent could be traced from the kings of Israel to the house of Valois. The Trojans, in his wholly original view, took on the allegorical role of an unholy and inglorious counterpart to righteous Israel; at one point he conflates them with the Ishmaelites of the Old Testament. They were an idolatrous and immoral nation, driven by sensuality and impulse (witness Paris's foolish dalliance with Helen) rather than reason and the will of God. For Johannes Angelus, the work of the chosen people of Israel had been continued in modern times by their descendants the French, while the role of the pagan Trojans had now been taken by their offspring, the nefarious Muslim Turks.[93] It was thus Charles VIII's destiny to defeat his historical enemies, the Trojan/Ishmaelite Turks, and reclaim his heritage in the Holy Land. His foray into Italy was to be celebrated as the first step in fulfillment of this ancient project.

Johannes Angelus's theory of a Hebrew origin for the French monarchy seems not to have been adopted by any later author, nor was his opinion that Trojan ancestry was a mark of a nation's infamy or pagan disregard for God. It was more common, in fact, for authors of crusade exhortations to stress the Trojan ancestry of *European* nations and to decry the Turks' presumptuous appropriation of both Trojan territory and identity, rightly the property of Christian Europe.[94] Early on, Coluccio Salutati took up this theme in a letter to the Angevin duke Charles of Durazzo, exhorting him to strike against the Saracens.[95] Likewise, in 1451, Francesco Filelfo exhorted Charles VII of France to move against the newly elevated sultan Mehmed II by urging him to reclaim his Trojan birthright: "What is your ancient country? Surely it is Troy, which once was called Teucria. But now we see it is called *Turcia* instead of Teucria or Troy; for all those who used to be called Teucrians and Trojans have now been overwhelmed by the shameful and savage inhumanity of the Turks."[96]

Such comments were not limited to exhortations to French princes. Two years later, after the disaster of Constantinople, Publio Gregorio Tifernate composed a poem warning of the danger the Turks posed to Italy. The entire peninsula, and Rome in particular, he said, seemed powerless to stop the rising tide of Turkish aggression: "My country, my once invincible land, now you lie open for all to plunder. Unspeakable crime! Woe to you, who enclose your seven hills with a rampart and trace the origins of your nation back to Troy."[97]

The humiliation inflicted by the Turks on "Trojan" Europe was a favorite theme of the poet Jean Lemaire de Belges. In his *Illustrations de Gaule et Antiquitez de Troye*, a highly imaginative survey of French history begun about 1500 and published 1511–1513, as well as in a poem purporting to be a letter from the French king to the supplicant ghost of Hector, Lemaire repeatedly appeals to the French nobility ("noz princes Troyens") to take up arms against the Turks and recover their hereditary patrimony in Asia Minor.[98] At the start of the *Illustrations*, Lemaire explains that he will recount the Trojan origins of France in order to demonstrate the presumption of the Turks in laying claim to both Trojan territory and Trojan ancestry.[99] They may boast that they are Trojans avenging the wrongs done to their ancestors by the Greeks, he says, but in reality the Troas has been occupied by impostors:

> Tout cela tient gent estrange et Turquoise
> Gent dissolue, infidele, bastard
> Gent toute infame. . .[100]

The real injury is that which has been done to the honor of the true Trojans—the nobility of France—and it is they who should now be demanding satisfaction.

There can be no doubt that the claim that the Turks were descended from the Trojans was often aired in the fifteenth century. But it should be clear by now that the idea was not nearly as widely essayed, nor as naively accepted, as has sometimes been claimed. We cannot assume that any author employing the name *Teucri* for the Turks automatically believed in their Trojan origins. As Salutati's letter of 1397 shows, use of the name was probably first inspired by the fact that the Turks had recently come to occupy "Teucria." It does not follow that Salutati—or later authors who also called the Turks *Teucri*—thought they were the direct descendants of the Teucrians. In fact, the name *Teucri* was applied to the Turks in some highly emotive accounts of Constantinople's fall where an assertion of their Trojan origins would be completely out of place, contradicting and undermining the points the authors wished to make about their barbarous, infidel, or even apocalyptic character. If the authors themselves do not state that the Turks were Trojans, we cannot assume they believed so solely because they use a word which often functioned as no more than a classicizing alternative to *Turci*.

We are left, then, with a smaller set of texts which state that the Turks either were descended or—more frequently—*thought* they were descended from the Trojans and so interpreted their deeds as acts of revenge for ancient wrongs done at Troy. It is worth asking what the purpose of these texts was. On the whole, their authors' intent was not to explain but to inflame, using the Turkish claim to Trojan ancestry in order to reinforce some other rhetorical point. Whatever the intended effect—to underline the ferocity of Turkish attacks on Greece; to stress the danger in which Italy itself lay; to encourage European princes, the true heirs of Troy, to take an interest in the Turkish threat; or (perhaps most common) to mock the Turks for their imperial pretensions—invoking the Trojan ancestry of the Turks was for all these authors essentially a rhetorical device. And as we have seen, other writers were just as able, in similar circumstances, to invoke other historical exempla which ignored, contradicted, or even indignantly denied the possibility of a Trojan heritage for the Turks.

Modern readers have either criticized the humanists for falling victim to "absurd" antiquarian preoccupations that skewed their perception of the Ottoman threat or regarded Renaissance "praise" of the Trojan Turks seriously, taking their claims at face value as proof of sincere and enlightened "philoturk" tendencies. In fact, Renaissance authors who invoked the Trojan origins of the Turks almost always did so in an ironic, mocking, sometimes even blackly humorous way. Their remarks were not meant to be read as statements of historical fact.

What of the alternative and almost entirely contradictory modern interpretation, that the theory of the Trojan Turks was in fact a medieval phenomenon exploded by humanist critical scrutiny? The Trojan Turks certainly do appear in numerous medieval chronicles. Even if few in the Renaissance found them believable, there must have been a time when the Trojan Turks did hold historical value, both for the authors who told their story and for the readers who embraced it. Nevertheless, the phenomenon in the medieval chronicles—and in the historiographical tradition derived from them, which continued well into the sixteenth century—has its own rhetorical intricacies and critical complications.

Chronicles of the Trojan Turks

The first known reference to the Trojan origins of the Franks appears in a Latin chronicle compiled by a series of unknown authors sometime in the late seventh century and attributed to a fictitious author, "Fredegar."[101] The parts of the chronicle covering the years from Creation to A.D. 584 derive largely from earlier histories; into these excerpts Fredegar interpolates much apparently original material, including a legendary account of the flight from Troy of both the Franks and a people called "Turks."[102] According to Fredegar, the Franks were the direct descendants of a group of refugees from the city. Their first king was Priam, who was succeeded by Friga, after whose reign the group split in two. One half went to Macedon, where they intermingled with the native population and in due course gave rise to the nation of Philip and Alexander. The second group wandered through Asia Minor for many years before finally choosing a king for themselves, called Francio; it was from him that the nation derived its name. These Franks migrated to Europe and at last settled down "between the Rhine or the Danube and Ocean," a vague enough address but one which does coincide with either of the two territories the historical Franks inhabited before their migration into Gaul: Pannonia and the Rhineland. It was around this time, according to Fredegar, that another group of people detached itself from the main body of Franks:

> It is said that the third nation born of this same stock is that of the *Torci:* for, after the Franks had wandered across Asia, encountering numerous battles along the way, upon entering Europe one part of them settled along the banks of the Danube between the Ocean and Thrace. They chose for themselves a king by the name of Torquotus, from whom the nation of *Turqui* derive their name.[103]

The *Torci* or *Turqui,* then, dwelled somewhere to the east of the Franks, in the area known in antiquity as Scythia Minor or Scythia Inferior.[104] The Franks remained along the Rhine, resisting a famous attempt by Pompey the Great to conquer them. Fredegar ends the story with another reference to Torquotus's departure.[105] After this, the *Torci* disappear from the *Chronicle.*

Much ink has been spilled over the legend of the Trojan origins of the Franks.[106] Whether the story is Fredegar's invention or whether it derives from some earlier, now lost tradition remains unclear. But the function the story was meant to perform is clear enough: the seventh-century chronicler hoped to provide the parvenu Franks with an ancient pedigree that would justify their conquest of the old provinces of Gaul and put them on an equal footing with the "Romans" (whether in Italy or Byzantium) whom they now faced as political rivals. Fredegar's attribution of Trojan origins to the mysterious *Torci,* on the other hand, is less easy to explain. Various attempts have been made to identify this people, none completely satisfactory. Still,

it is worth considering whether Fredegar meant to indicate any historical Turkic people, as the question has some bearing on the reception of
Fredegar's *Torci* in later medieval and Renaissance historiography.

One nineteenth-century scholar, Wilhelm Wilmanns, argued that
Fredegar's *Torci* were meant to represent Hunnish tribes who migrated into
eastern Europe in the fifth and sixth centuries A.D.[107] The Franks were in
frequent conflict with peoples claiming descent from Attila (most notably
the Avars), and a patriotic historian could well have wanted to trace the
source of their enmity back to a falling-out of legendary Trojan heroes. But
there are no historical or ethnographical grounds for identifying either Huns
or Avars as "Turks": neither was an ethnically Turkic nation, nor did they
speak a Turkic language, nor did any of the civilizations with whom they
came into contact ever call them "Turks." Moreover, elsewhere in the *Chronicle* Fredegar mentions both Avars and Huns by name.[108] If the author really
meant to invoke their presence at the very dawn of Frankish history, we
should expect him to have used their proper names.

To get around this problem, Wilmanns argued that Fredegar must have
derived their name from a different source. The name may reflect that of the
first Turkic people to be known as "Turks," the Western Türks, who had
made contact with Byzantium in the late sixth century and were regularly
called *Tourkoi* in Byzantine sources (see Chapter 2). News of these "Turks,"
Wilmanns suggested, would have reached the Frankish kingdom from Byzantium by way of Italy, and it was probably in Italy that authors hostile to
both the Türks and the Franks composed the legend of origin relating the
two to each other. But Fredegar's *Torci* are even less likely to be Western
Türks than Huns or Avars. The Franks themselves knew nothing of this central Asian people and certainly had no longstanding quarrel with them that
would have inspired a Frankish author to either adopt or fabricate a story of
prehistoric kinship. It is hardly more probable that an Italian author would
have concocted a legend linking the two nations in this way. Last, there
were no grounds for anyone to locate the Western Türks in the Danube region, where they had no political presence or influence (much less to identify them with the Huns or Avars who did occupy these lands).[109]

Later critics have tried to connect Fredegar's *Torci* with other central Asian
migrants into early medieval Europe. Claude Cahen argues that Fredegar
meant to indicate the Torcilingui, a tribe listed by Jordanes among the allies
of Odoacer and who (according to Cahen) were Turkic-speaking Huns.[110]
The Torcilingui were probably a Germanic people, however, and they did

not have much connection with the Franks.[111] Norbert Wagner suggests that Fredegar refers to the Turkic-speaking Proto-Bulgars, a nomadic people who settled along the middle Danube in the seventh century and did come into contact with the Franks. According to Wagner, not only do Fredegar's *Torci* reflect the Turkic ethnicity of the Proto-Bulgars, but both *Torquotus* and *Torcoth* are approximations of the name Turxanthos, a contemporary Turkic prince.[112] Eugen Ewig combines the theories of Wilmanns and Wagner, arguing that Frankish diplomatic links with Byzantium (in particular, a Frankish embassy of 578–581) brought information on the central Asian Türks back to Western Europe, and this knowledge inspired Fredegar both to use the name of the Türks when describing the Turkic-speaking Proto-Bulgars on the Danube and to transform the historical Turxanthos into Torcoth, the companion of Francio.[113] But just as the *Torci* are unlikely to represent the Western Türks, they almost certainly cannot be Proto-Bulgars. Although these migrants into eastern Europe spoke a language identified by modern linguists as Turkic, they never called themselves or were known by others as "Turks." Moreover, Turxanthos (a name known only from Byzantine sources) was not a Proto-Bulgar prince but khagan of the Western Türks; his domains lay in central Asia, his capital near Tashkent, and he had not the slightest political or ethnic connection with the Proto-Bulgars on the Danube.

In short, Fredegar's *Torci* probably do not represent any people of central Asian origin. Most migrants from central Asia to eastern Europe in the centuries up to and including Fredegar's (including the Huns and later tribes claiming descent from them) were not ethnically Turkic; neither they nor any of the true Turkic or Turkic-speaking peoples (such as the Proto-Bulgars) whom Fredegar might have known ever called themselves, or were called by others, "Turks."[114] It remains unclear which historical people, if any, are really intended by Fredegar to be the Trojan cousins of the Franks, but we can dismiss the possibility that this seventh-century Frankish chronicler knew anything of actual, Asiatic Turks.[115]

Few authors of the early Middle Ages took much interest in Fredegar's *Torci*. None imagined they were related to the true Turks of Asia, knowledge of whom did not become widespread in Western Europe until reports of the First Crusade began to circulate in the early twelfth century. For one thing, Fredegar's version of the story of the Franks' Trojan origins had been challenged—and at times almost entirely superseded—by that of a later chronicle, the eighth-century *Historia Francorum regum*. According to this text, the

Franks had escaped from Troy alone, unaccompanied by either Macedonians or "Turks."[116] The eighth-century chronicler Freculph, for example,
repeats only this version of the story, omitting all mention of Torcoth and his
Torci.[117] The tenth-century monastic chronicler Aimoin, too, begins his history of the Franks with the later version of the story; he then rehearses
Fredegar's account, but only as a clearly inferior "altera opinio." In repeating the story, Aimoin uses the names *Torchotus* and *Torchi;* among the variety
of forms of the name given by Fredegar (*Torci, Turqui, Turchi*), these are
the least similar to those for actual Turks which were then in use in contemporary Byzantine and (on rare occasions) Latin literature (for example,
Tourkoi, Turci). Fredegar himself almost certainly did not mean to refer to
any historical Turkic people; it seems equally unlikely that Aimoin, three
centuries later, saw the name as indicating any real Turks either.[118]

Only after the start of the crusades does the form *Turci* appear in the
text of any chronicler repeating the Fredegar story, or even in any of the
manuscripts of Fredegar's *Chronicle* itself.[119] When Hugh of St. Victor, whose
Chronicon dates to around 1130, retells the story, the leader of the tribe is not
Torquatus or *Torquotus* or *Torcoth* but simply *Turcus*. Some people believe,
Hugh says, that it is from him that both the cousins of the primeval Franks
and the modern-day Turks derive their name.[120]

The connection between Fredegar's *Turci* and contemporary Turks was developed further by the crusade historian William of Tyre, writing in Palestine
in the early 1180s. William's history of the Latin Kingdom of Jerusalem contains some of the most detailed and accurate information on the peoples of
the East produced in the entire medieval period.[121] He writes a great deal
about the Seljuk Turks, whom he identified as the chief opponents of the
first crusaders, describing their early movements in Transoxania and their
invasion of Persia in the eleventh century. William prefaces his information
on the Seljuks' central Asian origins with a brief retelling of the Fredegar
tale, possibly derived from Hugh of St. Victor:

> From earliest times, the nation of the Turks, or Turcomans (they both come
> from the same stock), was a northern one. But they are named after a cer-
> tain leader of theirs called Turcus, as they themselves assert, and as is found
> in our chronicles, who after the fall of Troy led them to the Hyperborean re-
> gions, where they abandoned the use of arms and wandered about tending
> their flocks and herds. They were an uncivilized race, without any fixed
> abode.[122]

William then explains how the Turks emerged from their nomadic existence in the wilds of Asia to establish the Seljuk sultanate in Persia.[123] There is a tension in his account which is difficult to resolve: he starts by asserting that the Turks from earliest times ("ab initio") lived in the north, then concedes that their name, at least, is said to derive from that of a Trojan exile. Whatever William may have really thought of this story, he integrates it neatly into his information on the Turks' more recent activities by recasting it slightly, so that Turcus now takes his followers not to eastern Europe ("between the Danube and Ocean," as Fredegar says) but rather to the far north of Asia, from where they emerge in historical times. Why the shift? William's European source may have specified the land settled by Trojan Turcus as "Scythia" (specifically, the territory of Scythia Inferior, which Isidore of Seville locates between the Danube and Ocean), which William may have misread as classical Scythia, the territory stretching east from the Black Sea to the central Asian steppes. Or he may have been trying, on his own, to reconcile the Fredegar legend with his own knowledge of the Seljuks' Transoxanian past.

Despite the enormous popularity of William of Tyre's work in Latin Europe, his particular version of the Fredegar story was not taken up in any subsequent retellings of the origins of the Franks.[124] (In fact, the passage describing how Turcus led the Turks north into Asia from Troy is preserved in only one manuscript of William's work, identified by his editor as the one closest to the archetype. An early copyist seems to have excised the story, an omission which persists in all subsequent copies.)[125] In later chronicles, emphasis falls on the origins of the Franks alone and their connection to Troy; if the *Turci* appear at all, it is almost incidentally. In the early thirteenth century, for example, Hugh of St. Victor's version of the story was modified by another French monastic historian, Rigord, who identifies Francio (in some editions of his text he is even "Francus") as a son of Hector and his cousin "Turcus" as a son of Troilus, making both characters grandsons of Priam.[126] This is the version of the story adopted by the two most popular and influential chroniclers of the later Middle Ages, Vincent of Beauvais and Martin of Troppau.[127]

The transformation of Torquotus into Turcus effected by Hugh of St. Victor and Rigord probably testifies to nothing more than a natural desire to substitute a familiar (although notorious) name for an unfamiliar one. It is not clear how many of these authors followed William of Tyre in imagining a historical or ethnic connection between Fredegar's Turks and the contemporary Seljuk rulers of the Middle East. Hugh of St. Victor, Rigord, Vincent of Beauvais, and Martin of Troppau (and most authors who followed them) are careful to say that "some people" believe that the legendary "Turcus" and his followers are the direct forebears of the modern-day Turks; they do not endorse the view themselves.[128]

Rigord, in fact, proposes a different destiny altogether for the Trojan Turks: after arriving at the Danube, he says, Turcus's descendants migrated north and east to become the ancestors of various Nordic peoples who would later challenge the Franks for control of Gaul—Goths, "Vandals" (that is, Wends), and Normans.[129] Rigord says nothing that would link these northern peoples to the modern-day Turks. He may simply have regarded the name Turcus as a familiar and pleasing form to use when recasting an old legend; or he may have wanted to emphasize the pagan origins of the Franks' northern neighbors, using the term "Turk" in the more general sense of "infidel."[130] Whatever the case, Rigord does not suggest any historical or ethnic connection between the legendary, Nordic Turcus and his contemporary namesakes in the Muslim East. He may have borrowed the name of the Turks for his account of Frankish prehistory, but he saw no significance in this for the history of the Turks themselves.

Later in the thirteenth century, the monks of St. Denis who compiled the *Grandes chroniques de France* introduced Rigord's version of the story, including his proposal that Turcus was the ancestor of the Goths and the Normans, to the French vernacular historiographical tradition, where it was to enjoy widespread popularity.[131] It was also repeated by the Latin chronicler Guillelmus Armoricus (c. 1223–1225).[132] But while these historians tried to excuse the presence of "Turks" in early French history by transforming them into proto-Scandinavians, other contemporary authors found it easier simply to dispense with the Trojan Turks altogether—as a brief survey of the *fortuna* of Fredegar's story up to the end of the fourteenth century shows.

The well-known and influential chronicles of Frutolf of Michelsberg and Ekkehard of Aura (1101), Sigebert of Gembloux (1111), and Otto of Freising (1158) all preserve the story of Francio and his Franks without mentioning Torquatus or Torcoth or Turcus at all.[133] Hugh of Flavigny (1102) keeps "Turchot" in the story, but only as a later ruler of the Franks, without any mention of a separate people descended from him. The thirteenth-century Latin version of the *Chronicles of St. Denis* makes Francio and "Torgot" the joint successors of Antenor, and thus cofounders of the Frankish race.[134]

The figure of Antenor came to occupy a prominent place in the story of Frankish origins as told by certain German and Italian historians, a development which usually saw Turcus and his Turks expelled from the story altogether. In the eighth-century redaction of the legend preserved in the *Historia Francorum regum*, it was recorded that the Trojan leader under whom the Franks founded their Danubian city of Sicambria was Antenor.[135] This was an unusual claim: Antenor was more commonly reputed to have led a group of Trojans to Italy, where he founded the city of Padua. Godfrey of Viterbo (in his *Pantheon,* written c. 1185–1187) solved the problem by claiming that the Franks were led to Sicambria not by Antenor but by a companion of his, the younger Priam; the entire group had set out from Padua. This was a significant change. The legend of the Trojan Franks was valuable to French historiography because it conferred antiquity and nobility on the French monarchy: the Franks were a separate people, directly descended from a Trojan leader and therefore just as ancient and noble as the Romans, who claimed descent from Aeneas. For Godfrey, however, the value of the legend lay in the suggestion that Trojan kinship might actually unite and identify the Germans (that is, the Franks) and the Italians.

For Godfrey, there was only one exodus from Troy, one group of noble refugees who later divided into two branches, Italian and Teutonic.[136] The former was established by Aeneas, while the latter traced its roots back to Antenor, founder of Padua, and his companion the younger Priam (who was Aeneas's brother and thus a nephew of the Trojan king whose name he shared). It was not Antenor but this younger Priam who left northern Italy for the Danube, where he founded the city of Sicambria; from him the entire German (Frankish) nation descended.[137] Godfrey's substitution of Priam, companion of Paduan Antenor, for the Frankish Duke Antenor of Sicambria, who according to the *Historia Francorum regum* arrived at the site of his city directly from Troy, proved that the Germans were descended from the Trojans of Italy. The *translatio* of imperial power to Charlemagne was thus really an act of reinstatement: Charlemagne had done no more than unite the two long-separated branches of Trojan exiles; he and his successors were fully entitled to call themselves Roman emperors.[138]

Godfrey's innovation proved popular among later Italian authors, either because it fit well with their own ideas about the legitimacy of the empire or simply because it appealed to patriotic convictions that Rome—and by extension Italy—should be considered first among European nations. Brunetto Latini (writing c. 1262–1266)[139] and Giovanni Villani (d. 1348)[140] both follow Godfrey in tracing the origins of the Franks back to Antenor and the younger Priam of Padua or Venice. The Milanese historian Galvano Fiamma (d. 1344) takes the idea even further, maintaining that almost all the nations of Europe can trace their origins back to the Trojans of Italy. According to Fiamma, the younger Priam left Antenor at Padua in order to found Sicambria in Hungary, but he was not the ancestor of the Franks. Rather, the Trojan Paris (who on first fleeing Troy had settled in Sicily) crossed the Alps to found his namesake city, as well as the kingdoms of France and Germany. Francus was a companion of his, whose achievements were limited to the foundation of Troia (that is, Xanthen) on the Rhine.[141] Latini, Villani, and Fiamma, having reduced the Franks to junior members of the Italian branch of Trojan exiles, saw no need to confuse the line of Trojan succession between Rome and northern Europe with tales of other exiles. Turcus and his Turks simply dropped from the story.[142]

Patriotic sentiments prompted other authors outside France and Germany to doubt even the story of the Trojan origins of the Franks. Boccaccio chauvinistically questioned whether any nation other than Rome descended, even indirectly, from the Trojans; he cast doubt on the claims of the Franks in particular.[143] In England, Matthew Paris (d. 1259) enthusiastically accepted the Trojan origins of the Romans and Britons (via Brutus, according to a legend first told by Geoffrey of Monmouth) but maintained that the Franks only emerged into history when the emperor Valentinian engaged their services in a local campaign against the Alans in the fourth century A.D.[144] The fourteenth-century chronicler Ranulph Higden dated the emergence of the Franks even later, to around A.D.425.[145] Paris's contemporary, the encyclopedist Bartholomaeus Anglicus, recorded an even less illustrious account of their origins: the Franks took their name from "a certain executioner" called Francus, who inherited the crown of the king of Paris and in whose memory executioners remain held in high esteem by the kings of France to this day.[146] This claim is repeated in the anonymous encyclopedia *Rudimentum novitiorum*, printed at Lübeck in 1475.[147]

It hardly needs saying that in works such as these, where the aim is to demolish the entire tradition of the ancient origins of the French, Turcus and his Turks were not considered necessary to the discussion. They simply do not appear. This is not an exhaustive catalogue of medieval chroniclers who reproduce, as a whole or in part, Fredegar's material on the Franks and the "Turks." But even a limited survey indicates that the legend of the Trojan Turks, while no doubt current, was far from universally accepted by medieval chroniclers. Renaissance historians were not the first to doubt the story.

The other medieval document frequently cited as a source for the Renaissance belief in the Trojan origin of the Turks is a brief notice in the *Gesta Francorum*, an anonymous crusade history written shortly after 1099, which reports that the Seljuk Turks themselves believed that they were related to the Franks: "[The Turks] say that they are of the same stock as the Franks and that no man is by nature a soldier apart from themselves and the Franks."[148] Note that there is no mention of any shared *Trojan* ancestry. The author attributes the Turks' belief in a relationship between the two nations to the fact that they are equally accomplished as soldiers.[149] The notice appears in the *Gesta* immediately after a description of the battle between the Franks and the Turks at Dorylaeum in July 1097, the earliest major conflict of the First Crusade, from which the Franks emerged the clear victors. Rather than simply celebrating the Turks' defeat, the author pauses at this point to praise their accomplishments in war.[150] He does so primarily to establish that God must have been on the side of the Franks: in the face of such a formidable enemy, they would have lost the battle had it not been for divine intervention.[151] Moreover, by praising the Turks, the author also praises the Franks, noting that the Seljuks had easily subdued every other nation in the region (including Arabs, Armenians, Syrians, and Greeks) but were no match for Frankish might.[152] And the Turks themselves knew it: so impressed were they by the Europeans' performance at Dorylaeum that they even tried to fabricate a blood tie with them.

This is the context in which the report of the Turks' belief in their kinship with the Franks should be seen. Far from invoking the rather obscure Merovingian tradition of a common Trojan ancestry for the Franks and the *Torci*, the author of the *Gesta* simply reports that it was a belief *of the Turks* that the two nations were related, with no reference at all to who their common ancestor may have been. The author does not seem to have much faith in the idea himself—perhaps an early instance of the charge of presumption that so many Renaissance writers would level against the Ottoman Turks. His aim throughout the passage is to establish the Franks and the Turks as the only two truly warlike nations in the Holy Land, equally matched in strength and courage and regarding each other with respect. With the two sides presented as such worthy opponents, the Franks' ultimate victory over the Turks appears all the more glorious, the will of God more clearly on their side.

The *Gesta Francorum* was an important source for later historians of the crusades, most of whom follow it in reporting that the Turks believed they were related to the Franks.[153] But none suggests that this relationship was based on a common Trojan ancestry. The story is always recounted simply to enhance the reputation of the two nations, setting them apart from the rest of the local population and elevating the importance of their conflict. Guibert of Nogent (c. 1109), for example, elaborates on the *Gesta* text:

> But perhaps someone may object [to the claim that Dorylaeum was a great victory], arguing that the enemy forces were merely peasants, scum herded together from everywhere. Certainly the Franks themselves, who had undergone such great danger, testified that they could have known of no race comparable to the Turks, either in the liveliness of spirit, or energy in battle . . . It was the Turks' opinion, however, that they shared an ancestry with the Franks, and that the highest military prowess belonged particularly to the Turks and Franks, above all other people.[154]

Baudri of Dol, author of another crusade history (c. 1110) based largely on the *Gesta Francorum*, also repeats the story, adding that the Turks further supported their claim by maintaining that their ancestors had been Christians.[155] Baudri's version of the story was repeated by Vincent of Beauvais in his account of the First Crusade.[156] None of these chroniclers specifies a connection to Troy.

By contrast, the fourteenth-century chronicler Jean de Paris includes the anecdote (quoting Baudri) but puts the story at the start of his history, citing it as support for Fredegar's Trojan legend as told by Rigord and Vincent of Beauvais:

> Francio the son of Hector and Turcus the son of Troilus . . . escaped after the fall of Troy together with a great multitude of people . . . and divided themselves into two nations. Some followed Francio and made him their prince; but others attached themselves to Turcus and went with him into Scythia, where they lived subject to his rule and are called after him *Turci* . . . just as the Franks are called, to this day, after Francio himself. This is supported by what Baudri says in his *Historia Hierosolymitana:* "The Turks," he says, "boast that they are born from the same stock as the Franks, and that their ancestors descended from the Franks. And therefore, they say, no one else apart from themselves and the Franks ought to fight in war.[157]

The two traditions are thus at last combined. But Jean de Paris turns out to be an exceptional case. Apart from one very late French history (that of Nicole Gilles, d. 1503, discussed below), I know of no other history treating either the origins of the Franks or the First Crusade which combines the two stories in this way. Fifteenth-century Italian historians who discuss the crusades—for example, Andrea Biglia, Flavio Biondo, Antoninus Florentinus, and Benedetto Accolti—do not mention the *Gesta* story at all.

Early Italian humanists seem to have accepted the Trojan origins of the *Franks,* by contrast, without reservation. Salutati and Filelfo both refer to the story in letters to French princes,[158] as does Aeneas Sylvius in his chorographical account of European history, but without mentioning Turcus.[159] Filelfo retells the whole legend in verse, in an ode accompanying his letter to Charles VII of 1451, though he removes the embarrassing Turcus from the story by changing him into an unobjectionable "Teucro."[160] Indeed, only a very few fifteenth-century authors chose to preserve the Trojan Turks in the story.

By the end of the thirteenth century, as we have seen, most historians had excised the Turks from the ancient legend of Francus and his Trojan Franks. One exception was Vincent of Beauvais, who did report (although as an opinion held by others, not by himself) that the Turks were descended from Turcus, the cousin of Francus. Several of the most popular and widely circulated chronicles of the fifteenth century draw heavily on Vincent's work, but even in these, Vincent's qualified statement is barely preserved. The Carthusian monk Werner Rolewinck of Cologne (d. 1502), author of perhaps the most popular work of history written in the fifteenth century— certainly the most frequently printed—preserves the story of Francus and Turcus in a single entry on his graphical timeline of world history: "Francio et Turcus, Troiani fugientes, duo regna constituunt, longe tamen post."[161] Rolewinck's brief entry was repeated by Hartmann Schedel in his *Liber Cronicarum* (1493), with a woodcut genealogical tree showing the descent of Francus and Turcus from the royal house of Troy. Unlike Rolewinck, however, Schedel adds a qualification to the story echoing that made by William of Tyre four centuries earlier: "These two, fleeing from Troy, established two kingdoms, although a long time later: Franco the son of Hector . . . ; and Turcus the son of Troilus the son of King Priam. Some say that the people descending from him are called Turks. *But others say the Turks are Scythian in origin.*"[162]

Turcus survived a little longer in France. At least three (and likely many more) French history rolls from the late fifteenth century record the separate escapes of Aeneas, the younger Priam, Helenus, and Turcus from Troy,

Troyanum bellū decēnale primo Esebon siue Abesson iudicis anno(teste eusebio)surrerit. quo tpe sequētes claruerūt. Troya eñi quā Jlion tros regis troyanox filius amplissimā instaurauit mille τ quingentis passibus a mari remota erat: vbi oim rerum vbertas erat: Jpsa quippe que decēnalem grecozum obsidionem passa fuit: et ab eis tandē deleta.

Hercules

Hercules ille cū Jasone troyā vastauit que statim a pamo fuit reedificata. Jdez hercules agone olimpiacuz cōstituit et bella multa cōfecit quē dicūt duodecim insignes et inhumanos pfecisse labozes.

Hector

Jste bector fuit pmogenitus pami ex becuba vxoze incōpabilis fortitudinis et strēnuitatis. Jo ob maximū et° militie fulgorem apud troyanos maxio i precio habitus est. Jlla ob incredibilē et° prudētiā atz fortitudinē nō solū parētes: sed et patriā nobilitate atcz glia splēdidā fecit. hic ex Andromacha ꝗinꝗe plures genuit filios. Ed ꝗb°frāc°vn°fuit Aꝗ (vt aityuincēt° hystorial°burgūd°)frāci originē habuere.

Menelaus   Helena

Paris

Hercules ille cū Jasone... zauris abstulit et Troyam pdurit. Ex qua rapina bellum decēnale grecoz aduersus troyanos susceptū est. Hic cū troyanis vrbem obsidentib° multa strēnue gessisset: A pirrho achillis filio occisus fuit.

Helena

Helena fuit vxoz menclai regis: a pari de filio priami rapitur. τ ad troyā pducitur. ppter ꝗd troyanū bellū exortuz. Jpsam tñ post troye excidium Greci menelao red dixerūt.ꝗ gaudēs nauim cū illa cōscendit patriam petitur° : sed tēpestatib° acti in egiptū ad polibuz reges deuenere. Jndecz discedentes octo āis errates (vt testis est eusebi°)tandes in patriam redierunt.

Paris qui et Alexāder dict° est eiusde hectoris frater: ex pamo τ becuba nat°: sꝛ specie legatiōis cū.xx.nauib°in greciā mittitur Et a menelao hospicō suscipi�: Cuꝰ cū asperisset vxozes illas.absente marito tandē cū oibus regiis the

Agamenon

Agamenon fuit frater regis Menelai dux totiꝰ exercitus grecoz. cōtra troyā bellauit.ꝗ tandem traditorie et turpissime capiꝦ.fuitcz Atrei regis filiꝰ. ab omni exercitu imperatoz designatus.ad bellū pergens Clitemestram conuiges ex qua multos susceperat filios reliquit. Et apud troyam multos passus labozes.τ simultates principum pro quibus ab imperio depositus τ illi palamedes suffectꝰ est. Que cum vlixes occidisset ipse maioz gloria imperium reassumpsit. Tandes Troya capta et diruta cum ingenti pzeda et cassandra priami filia in patriam redi turus naues conscendit Uerum τ ipse tempestate actus.p annū ferme errauit.

Turcus

Jsti duo de Troya fugientes duo regna constituūt: longe tamē post.

Franco quidē ex bectoze filꝰ pami nepos a quo francoz nome tractū est.a troya fugat° postea tota Asia puagata in danubiꝺ ripis tandē puenit. Jbi cū aliꝗdiu cōsedisset.deinde locum querēs a cōmuni hominū societate seiunctū; ad thanai fluentia τ paludes meotidas secessit. vbi Sicambriā condidit vrbem.

Franco

Turcus filiꝰ Troili filij regis Priami.A ꝗ pplm ab eo descendentē. quidem turcos denoiari dicūt. Alij eozū origine ex Scythia referunt.

as a prelude to the establishment of European nations, although, curiously enough, Francus himself is not included in these lists.[163] Turcus and Francio do appear together in the French historical compendium of Nicole Gilles (d. 1503).[164] Gilles starts his *Annales* with an account of the legendary origins of all the nations of Europe. Jupiter had two sons: Danus, the founder of the Greek nation, and Dardanus, who gave rise to the Trojans, from whom the French, Venetians, Romans, English, Normans, Turks, and Austrians are all descended.[165] After the fall of Troy, the various founders of these nations (among them Aeneas, Antenor, Helenus, Brutus, Francio, and Turcus) made their way into Europe. After separating from Francio, Turcus went north into Scythia, where the inhabitants are still known as Turks and claim they are related to the French.[166]

The history rolls and Gilles's work together represent a late revival of a deeply conservative trend in French historiography which had perpetuated the Trojan legend over the centuries with little or no alteration, usually preserving even the awkward figure of Turcus.[167] Given the centrality of the Trojan legend to their country's history, it is understandable that many French historians hesitated to discard even the smallest detail concerning the crucial moment of national foundation. But even in France, around the turn of the sixteenth century a new generation of historians began to question the validity of the Trojan Franks and so, by association, the Trojan Turks.[168]

Robert Gaguin, in his *Compendium de originibus et gestis Francorum* (1495), was among the first to cast doubt on the Trojan origins of the Franks. The idea that they had come from Troy was quite widespread, he said, and other nations claimed the same about themselves;[169] but this did not necessarily make the story true. Gaguin expressed doubt about the story of Sicambria, supposedly built by the Franks in the time of Valentinian, since Caesar mentioned *Sycambri* already living in Germany several centuries earlier. As for the "Turks" of the story, Gaguin removed them altogether, claiming instead that the companion of Francus was one "Thorgorus" and that it was he and his followers who went to Macedon (not, as in Fredegar, the second group of Trojans under Friga), where they served Philip and Alexander and were known as the Thorgori.[170]

Later scholars of early French history tried to disprove the Trojan legend altogether.[171] In his *De regibus Francorum* (1505), Michele Riccio argued that the true origins of the French lay among the Gauls, who were descended from the ancient Galatians and ultimately from Polyxenus and Galatea. They could not be descended from Hector, for Homer says the Trojan hero had only one son, Scamander, also called Astyanax. Later dramatists tell of Hector's fathering numerous sons by women of easy virtue, but even among this bastard progeny the name of Francus is never found. The story of the Franks' Trojan origins is false, but probably of ancient origin, for throughout history people have always claimed heroic and notable ancestors for themselves.[172] A year later, the Volterran humanist Raffaele Maffei repeated that the original Frenchmen had been the Gauls; barbarian invasions (including that of the Franks) added to the mix of peoples, but there was no ancient authority for the claim that the Franks had come from Troy. The earliest evidence Maffei could find for their whereabouts was a reference by the Byzantine historian Agathias, writing in the sixth century A.D., who referred to them as Germanic barbarians dwelling on the northern fringes of Italy.[173] After these skillful displays of humanistic criticism, it is hardly surprising that neither Riccio nor Maffei bothered to mention the legend of the Trojan origins of the Turks. Scholarship on the origins of France had moved on to different questions altogether.[174]

Even the notorious historical forgers Annius of Viterbo and Johannes Trithemius found no place for the Trojan Turks in their spurious compendia on the origins of nations.[175] Annius traced the genealogy of all European nations back to Japhet; anticipating the more sober researches of Maffei and Riccio, he claimed that the original French had been Celts, not Franks. Moreover (and here he departed from authentic historical sources), the founder of their race had been Samotus, the fourth son of Japheth. In Annius's scheme, Francus was a very late arrival on the scene, who gained power over the primordial Celts only by marrying into the ruling family. Annius makes no mention of his companion, Turcus.[176] Trithemius, too, was eager to show the antiquity of the Frankish nation, and although he stands by the Franks as the oldest inhabitants of Germany, he plays down their Trojan origins in favor of an even older pedigree. The people now known as "Germans" are so ancient that their true origins are not known. When they lived in Troy, they were called Trojans; after migrating to Scythia, they were known as Scythians; when they lived on the Danube, they were known as Sicambrians; and after Francus led them, they were called Franks. It is only recently that they have come to be called Germans.[177] In casting the escape of the "Germans" from Troy as just one event in a history reaching back much further into the mists of prehistory, Trithemius, like Annius, had no need to clutter up the story with another set of Trojans; Francus's "Turkish" companions simply do not appear.

By the late Middle Ages, references to Turcus and his Trojan "Turks" had all but disappeared from historical accounts of the fall of Troy and the origins of European nations. The middle of the fourteenth century, however, saw a revival of the tradition in another context: in discussions of the origins and history of the Turks themselves.

The Venetian doge and historian Andrea Dandolo (d. 1354) takes much of the early material in his chronicle from Vincent of Beauvais (via an intermediate chronicle), including his remarks on the Trojan origins of the Turks.[178] But in an interesting echo of William of Tyre, Dandolo maintains that the Turks also came from the Caucasus. After escaping from Troy, he says, the Turks headed east into Scythia; it was from Scythia that they were to emerge in modern times: "The country of the Turks lies on the other side of the Caspian Mountain [that is, the Caucasus]. They are descended from Turchus, the son of Troilus, who was the son of the Trojan King Priam and who took flight into those parts with a huge retinue after the fall of the city."[179]

Whether Dandolo knew of William's twelfth-century account of the Trojan Turks' flight into the "Hyperborean regions" or arrived at his quite similar conclusion independently is unclear. As Coluccio Salutati's letter of 1397 demonstrates, by the fourteenth century, theories of a Caucasian or Scythian origin for the Turks were beginning to multiply in Western Europe.

A century later, Bishop Antoninus of Florence (Antonio Pierozzi, 1389–1459), like Vincent of Beauvais a member of the Dominican order, followed the thirteenth-century chronicler in composing a vast scholastic encyclopedia of which his universal history, the *Chronicon*, was only a small part. In his description of the fall of Troy, Antoninus repeats Vincent's information on Francus and Turcus, including the claim that "some people" say the modern Turks are descended from Thurcus, son of Troilus.[180] Then, later in his chronicle, he discusses the origins of the Turks again, in an entry on the Seljuks for the year 1048 taken directly from William of Tyre. Antoninus follows his source almost verbatim, including his reconciliation of the two apparently contradictory theories about the Turks' primordial origins, Trojan and Scythian.[181]

Yet another Dominican, Friar Felix Fabri of Basel, preserves a similar two-stage account of the origins of the Turks in his report of his two pilgrimages to the Holy Land, undertaken between 1480 and 1484.[182] In his description of the Troas, Fabri repeats (and cites) both the text of Vincent of Beauvais on the Trojan exiles Francus and Turcus and Antoninus's extracts from William of Tyre on the wanderings of the Trojan *Turci* in Scythia, before producing a long, barely digested collection of texts—culled from the Church fathers, medieval chronicles, and more recent historians—on the barbarians of Scythia in general and the Turks in particular, as well as their more recent activities in the Islamic world.[183]

Fredegar's *Torci* enjoyed a long run through the traditions of medieval historiography. But if we return to the question set out at the beginning—whether fifteenth-century references to the Trojan origins of the Turks represent an essentially medieval or an essentially humanist strain of thinking—it should be clear by now that the Trojan Turks cannot be classified along such simplistic lines. The term *Teucri* was used by all sorts of writers, some humanist, some not. Few explored the implications of the nomenclature. Those authors who do elaborate further on the Trojan character of the Turks turn out to regard the notion with a certain degree of ironic distance, echoing the satiric character of their most likely source, the fourteenth-century forgery of "Morbisanus." Once again, some of these authors were committed humanists; others were more traditional in outlook. When considering the significance of the theory of the Turks' Trojan origins, then, we should make the distinction not between medieval and modern ideas about historical truth but between types of literature where such fables either were or were not considered acceptable. In poetry, prophecy, satire—not to mention wedding orations—an author could toy with the idea and its ironic possibilities. But this was less acceptable when writing history, no matter the style.

The medieval historiographical tradition which gave rise to the notion of the Trojan Turks began to reject it long before the Renaissance began. The *Torci*, while almost certainly not real Turks, presumably meant something to Fredegar and his audience, though we will likely never know who this collateral branch of the Trojan Franks was meant to represent. But if the *Torci* played an integral part in the seventh-century myth of Frankish origins, they quickly lost their value to later authors in France and even more so elsewhere in Europe. A different story—that of the Franks' foundation of Sicambria—was preferred to the tale of their split from the obscure and (by now wholly irrelevant?) *Torci*. Even after the First Crusade, when the *Torci* changed into the more familiar *Turci*, their survival in the historiographical tradition was hardly assured. Other questions came to hold greater importance. In France, the focus fell on establishing the ancient origins of the Franks alone. Where *Torcoth* or *Turcus* survived, he was often transformed into a later member of the Frankish dynasty, without a separate nation to his name. In Germany and Italy, the material from Fredegar and the later *Historia Francorum* was recast to serve an entirely different political end, that of establishing the antiquity and legitimacy of the Holy Roman Empire by defining it as an inheritance from the *Italian* Trojans: Aeneas, Antenor, and the younger Priam. Fredegar's Turks had no part to play here. Elsewhere—for example, in England—patriotic pride rejected even the Trojan Franks, and there was no question of admitting their Turkish cousins.

The medieval chronicle tradition, while based on the repetition of authorities, was far from static. Even the foundation myths with which the chronicles often begin were extremely flexible: names, peoples, entire stories could change or even disappear as political and cultural orientations shifted. Authors exercised critical judgment—or perhaps creative license—in recasting their material to suit new purposes. The Trojan Turks did not often survive the process. By the fifteenth century, virtually the only historical works to preserve the story of the Turks' origins in Troy were those written by conservative, monastic compilers (Antoninus, Rolewinck, Fabri) relying on the notices of Vincent of Beauvais and William of Tyre. And even these authors usually qualified their presentation of the Turks as refugee Trojans with a second account of their origins. In Andrea Dandolo's work, written in the middle of the fourteenth century, as well as in Coluccio Salutati's comments on the question fifty years later, the alternate theory of the Turks' origins in Scythia was already established. It later found approval in the era's monumental *summa* of historical erudition, the *Nuremberg Chronicle*. This Scythian theory, too, originated in various medieval chronicle traditions; it would find fullest expression in the writings of quattrocento humanist historians.

CHAPTER **2**

Barbarians at the Gates

One reason the notion of the Trojan Turks may have seemed implausible to most fifteenth-century authors is the fact that it completely contradicted the most widespread contemporary assumption about the Ottoman foe: that of their extreme barbarity. Western observers certainly recognized other qualities in the Turks that were cause for amazement and concern: their military skill and strategic cunning; the ease with which they exploited and frequently flouted diplomatic conventions; the sultan's brilliant leadership and the remarkable obedience of his subjects; and, not least, the seductive dangers of their faith. But even as they expressed interest in and alarm at the formidable efficiency of Turkish military, political, and religious culture, European authors voiced their strongest concern over a much more basic element of the Turkish character as they saw it: an inborn ferocity which seemed to propel the Turks to acts of barbarous cruelty and violence unprecedented in human memory. Such savagery also placed them firmly outside the family of historically civilized nations, Trojan or otherwise.

The Turks' reputation for brutality grew together with their conquests in the Balkans and Mediterranean in the first half of the fifteenth century. After the fall of Constantinople, references to their savagery became a commonplace in European literature. The siege and sack of Constantinople were undoubtedly traumatic events. Eyewitness reports nonetheless exaggerated the extent of the atrocities the Turks committed, describing the Ottoman capture as a relentless melée of rape, pillage, and murder.[1] Over time the prurient details lost none of their appeal; later accounts, some written decades after the city's fall, still brim with tales of children, virgins, matrons, monks, and nuns defiled, slaughtered, or led into slavery, churches and holy relics profaned, and streets flowing with Christian blood.[2] Later Ottoman conquests gave rise to similarly lurid tales: in eastern Europe and the Mediterranean alike, it was said, the Turks tortured and murdered innocent Christians and compelled survivors to repudiate their faith. Western observers concluded that the ferocity with which the Turks pursued their conquests was more than just brutal strategic expedience: an irrational and immutable hatred of all things Christian and civilized seemed to lie at the heart of their character and direct their every move.[3]

This method of characterizing the enemy was by no means new. A long tradition of Christian rhetoric, dating back at least to the First Crusade, had aimed at dehumanizing the Muslim foe; for centuries the "Saracens" were portrayed as both monstrously cruel and driven by all-consuming hatred of Christians and their faith.[4] A fifteenth-century innovation was the portrayal of the Turks as enemies of Western secular culture as well as the Christian religion. As Nancy Bisaha has shown, some Italian humanists dwelled with particular gloom on the fact that the Turks threatened to destroy not only the Greek empire and people but also the last surviving traces of ancient Greek learning.[5] Even before the capture of Constantinople, Leonardo Bruni had lamented that Greeks under Turkish rule were forgetting their ancient language.[6] After the city's fall, some European observers mourned the loss of Greek books in the catastrophe just as keenly as the loss of Greek lives. Lauro Quirini claimed that the Turks had destroyed 120,000 volumes during the sack; now, he said, they threatened to destroy the Greek language itself.[7] Aeneas Sylvius worried less about the living language and more about potential losses to scholarship: by destroying the Greek books of Constantinople—many perhaps as yet unknown to Western scholars—the Turks were bringing about a new dark age, a second death for Homer and Plato.[8] Marsilio Ficino too condemned the Turks for trampling not only the Christian faith but also the rule of law and the liberal arts.[9]

Humanists were horrified by Turkish violence against Greek books, learning, and culture, largely because these were things they themselves held dear. But they never lost sight of—or their taste for—the older, more traditional charges that could be leveled against a Muslim foe. In exhortatory letters to princes or harangues to the general public, even in their private correspondence and learned dialogues and treatises, humanists described the Turks not only as enemies of culture and learning but also as a potent threat to European political and military security and, even more traditionally, as idolatrous infidels thirsting for Christian blood. Taken as a whole, these multifarious charges produced a terrible picture: every aspect of the Turks' character and culture was irredeemably base. Not only heretical, violent, and cruel, they were also lustful, proud, crude, unlettered, and ignorant—despicable in every respect.

Such a universal condemnation of the enemy may well reflect, as Robert Schwoebel once argued, a wider sense of pessimism in fifteenth-century Europe, a morbid interest in the monstrous and sensational.[10] In the case of the humanists, however, it seems just as likely that the motivation for attacking the Turks on so many fronts was rhetorical. By exploring every avenue of defamation and so amplifying their verbal assaults on the Turkish enemy, the humanists hoped to reinforce arguments for the advantageousness (*utilitas*) of a new crusade. The Turks, they argued, posed a threat to European security in all its aspects: political, religious, moral, and cultural. At the same time, it was an affront to the honor of European princes that so vile an enemy should have conquered so much Christian territory.[11]

Humanists invariably turned to this last point in their crusade appeals, emphasizing the contrast between the lofty splendors of Christian civilization and the baseness of the enemy who attacked it. Bessarion mourned the loss of Constantinople for precisely these reasons: "A city which only recently was blessed with such an emperor, so many distinguished men, so many famous and ancient families, and such an abundance of resources—the capital of all Greece, the splendor and glory of the East, the nursery of the most noble learning, the repository of all that is good—has been captured, stripped, plundered, and pillaged by the most inhuman barbarians, the most savage enemies of the Christian faith, the most ferocious wild beasts."[12]

Lauro Quirini expressed similar thoughts: the fall of such an ancient, noble, and wealthy imperial city was certainly to be lamented.[13] What made it intolerable was the fact that the city had fallen into the hands of such unworthy attackers: "a barbarous race, an uncivilized race, living without set customs or laws, careless, wandering, arbitrary, full of treachery and tricks."[14] Francesco Filelfo phrased the antithesis in even starker terms: "The more humble the men who inflict it, the more humiliating is the indignity—if, indeed, the Turks should be called men and not some sort of completely unrestrained and savage beasts, since they have nothing of humanity in themselves beyond a human form, and that deformed and depraved on account of the disgusting filthiness of their shameful habits."[15]

A further layer of criticism which the humanists added to this line of attack—and another involving an issue close to their own intellectual interests—drew on arguments from history. In crusade letters and appeals, humanists claimed that the Turks were as bad as, sometimes far worse than, any previous enemies civilization had ever known. The ancient Assyrians had at least taken some pity on captive Israel, allowing the nation to survive in Babylonian exile, but the Turks had scattered the Byzantine Greeks and destroyed their nation forever.[16] The Persians under Xerxes and Darius, despite their epic designs on world domination, had hoped to annex the city-states of ancient Greece, not obliterate them. The Romans, too, had invaded Greece, but they had shown respect for Greek learning and letters—indeed, had eagerly embraced Greek culture for themselves.[17] In more recent times, the Goths, even as they subjected Rome to fearful trials, did not desecrate churches or shrines, as the Turks seemed ready to do.[18]

Some humanists went beyond historical comparisons like these and tried to reconstruct the ancient and medieval history of the Turks themselves, aiming to prove both that the Turks were more savage than any previous enemies of civilization and that they had always been so—from their genesis in a barbarous part of the world through a long history of uncivilized activity. Humanist historians maintained that the Turks were originally Scythians, inhabitants of the vast territory which, according to ancient geographers, stretched north and east of the Black Sea to the very limits of the known world and which had been known in antiquity, as well as in more recent times, as home to an array of wild and unsavory peoples—nomadic raiders, bandits, even cannibals. Humanists also asserted that the Turks had made their way south into Asia Minor in a violent invasion through the Caucasus Mountains, another area notorious throughout history for producing barbarian invaders hostile to civilization.

The barbarism which classical geographical and ethnographical literature associated with Scythia and the Caucasus—and, more generally, with the colder regions of northern Europe and Asia—was invoked by humanists not only to describe the condition of the original Turks but also to make a polemical point about their contemporary descendants: the harshness of their native land was forever ingrained in their character. In the oration Aeneas Sylvius delivered at the Diet of Frankfurt, convened in September 1454 by Frederick III to discuss a German response to the fall of Constantinople, Aeneas roundly condemned the Turks as barbarians from a barbarous land: "They are a nation of Scythians, originating in the heart of Barbary, having their home beyond the Black Sea towards the northern ocean . . . an unclean and disgusting race, fornicators indulging in every kind of depravity . . . They set out from the Caspian Mountains [that is, the Caucasus] and took themselves by a long path into Asia; and there they have remained ever since."[19]

No matter how many centuries had elapsed since they invaded Asia and, later, Greece, their occupation of these milder climes had done nothing to soften their essential savagery. Their diet was still monstrously unclean (including the meat of horses, bison, and vultures), they were slaves to lust, and—worst of all—they despised literature and the arts. "Despite the fact that they have lived so long under sunnier skies and in gentler territory, and seem a little more civilized, nevertheless they still retain about them some flavor of their primitive crudity; they have not washed the barbarian completely away."[20]

Francesco Filelfo, too, maintained that the Turks had carried their uncivilized habits with them from Scythia into the civilized world. As early as 1444, he condemned the Turks as "a race of people who, having abandoned their homeland and ancestral hovels among the vast and frightful crags of the Caucasus, where day and night they polluted themselves with every kind of shameful filthiness, have raged long and hard, using every kind of mockery and insult, in almost every part of the world, against the name of Christ."[21]

Humanists even introduced this kind of geographical denigration into their poetry. In a prophetic poem composed just after the fall of Constantinople, Publio Gregorio Tifernate imagined that the Turks who would soon overrun Italy were a barbarian race, a "great evil" spreading down from the frozen North.[22] Nicola Loschi, in a poem addressed to Aeneas Sylvius, lamented that a "Caspian race" should threaten the West and in particular that Christian authority should be challenged by Mehmed II, a lowly "Scythian boy."[23] In 1472, the poet Antonio Cornazzano decried the Turks as descendants of "Caucasian tigers" who had emerged from their mountain lairs to ravage the lands of the Greeks.[24] In describing the fall of Negroponte to the Turks in 1470, Paolo Marsi pictured a monstrous horde descending across the frozen plains of Scythia and down through the Caucasus, driven by ravenous greed for fertile southern soil. Marsi praised those Venetian husbands who killed their womenfolk rather than consigning them to slavery under a "Caucasian" mistress.[25]

Many of the negative comments Renaissance humanists made about the Scythian or Caucasian character of the Turks can be identified as commonplaces deriving from either classical ethnographical writing about Scythia and its inhabitants, or—as the verse by Tifernate suggests—a parallel Judeo-Christian tradition that associated northern, nomadic races with apocalyptic disaster.[26] But some historians relied on more than the general and longstanding reputation of Scythia as a breeding ground for barbarians when they proposed it as the homeland of the Ottoman Turks. They invoked the authority of classical and medieval texts which explicitly referred—or appeared to refer—to Turkic peoples living or campaigning in the region. This made it possible for them to construct a chronological account of the movements and activities of Turks through the centuries. The information these scholars collected was frequently wrong—either derived from corrupt texts or, more usually, simply irrelevant to the history of the Ottoman dynasty. On the other hand, despite the difficulty of some of the texts they used (and the obscurity of almost all of the historical events they investigated), the humanists were not entirely the victims of their sources. They were not above manipulating the material they found in order to make negative polemical points about the contemporary Ottoman Turks. In several cases it can be shown that they knowingly did so. Still, an examination of their researches can provide some basic and perhaps unexpected insights into their historiographical methods, including their knowledge of medieval history, their attitudes to medieval source material, and their ability to interpret it.

This chapter and the next one examine how humanist historians developed and amplified their theory of a Scythian ancestry for the Turks as well as the larger questions their researches raised. At first glance we seem to confront a group of scholars who typify the central values and concerns of Renaissance humanism—interested in recovering facts from ancient texts, in searching for classical antecedents to contemporary issues, in reviving an ancient literary genre (in this case, ethnography) and its attendant vocabulary, and in applying the fruits of their labors to modern policy debates. In all this they seem to depart from the medieval preoccupation with the divine as the motivating force behind human history, with religion as the key criterion for determining whether a foreign people were friends or foes.

And yet, despite the fact that the humanists uncovered much new historical and ethnographical source material in their researches, I still question whether their approach was in fact all that new. What exactly did the humanists mean by calling the Turks "Scythians" and constructing a barbarian past for them? How faithfully did they revive classical concepts of barbarism? Just as their theories about Turkish origins derived from a mixture of ancient literary commonplaces and medieval historical sources, those theories were shaped, in a larger sense, by an equally complicated combination of classical and Christian notions of barbarity itself, and of the role barbarians had to play in world history.

Scythian Commonplaces

The reputation of Scythia as a harsh country, home to tough and sometimes savage peoples, was established early on in both the classical and the biblical tradition. The fifth-century B.C. Hippocratic treatise *Airs, Waters, Places* describes the cold, damp climate of the regions north of the Black Sea and its ill effects on the people who dwelled there.[27] Herodotus, in a famous ethnographic essay, also remarks on Scythia's difficult climate and the habits of the people who endured it.[28] The winters, he wrote, lasted eight months, gripping the country in intolerable cold. The ground froze solid and snow fell constantly, while the short, cold summers were racked by violent storms. The treeless plains were drained by enormous rivers, a terrain which allowed the Scythians to breed horses but little else; as a result, most of them were nomadic, wandering from place to place in their wagons, and knew nothing of agriculture. There were no towns. North and east of the plains stretched empty deserts, thick forests, and impassable mountains. Here dwelled strange nations like the Hyperboreans, the Amazons, the Issedones, who worshipped their ancestors' skulls and ate parts of their bodies, and the Androphagi, "the most savage of men, [who] have no notion of either law or justice. They are herdsmen without fixed dwellings; their dress is Scythian, their language peculiar to themselves, and they . . . eat human flesh."[29]

All the Scythian tribes were notoriously fierce in war: they fought on horseback, using bows and arrows, drank the blood of their slain enemies, wore their scalps on their belts, used their skulls as drinking cups, and were known to take captives for use in human sacrifice.[30] They had invaded Asia once, descending through the Caucasus in pursuit of the Cimmerians (the previous rulers of Scythia, whom they had conquered and expelled), after which they subjected Media to a harsh occupation. Herodotus recounts: "During the twenty-eight years of Scythian supremacy in Asia, violence and neglect of law led to absolute chaos. Apart from tribute arbitrarily imposed and forcibly exacted, they behaved like mere robbers, riding up and down the country and seizing people's property."[31]

Herodotus reports much of this information—sensational as it may seem—in a fairly neutral tone. The historian did not consider the Scythians, despite their rough habits, morally outrageous or a threat to civilization; he found them interesting, and in some respects admirably virtuous. In fact, from Herodotus on, there developed a long tradition of eulogizing the primitive simplicity of the Scythians. Many classical authors portrayed them as noble savages, morally pure (even if violent) when compared to the soft and corrupt civilizations of the Mediterranean world.[32]

The Scythians and their neighbors nevertheless earned their fair share of calumny in antiquity. The traumatic impression made by the Cimmerian and Scythian invasions of Media in the eighth and seventh centuries B.C., for instance, left powerful echoes in the prophetic books of the Old Testament. Jeremiah describes the future enemies of Israel as horse-riding warriors from the north. In Ezekiel, they are personified in the figure of Gog from the land of Magog, leader of a terrifying horde which will descend on Israel in the last days, "from the uttermost parts of the north."[33]

Some Greek and Roman authors also expressed alarm at the ferocity of the Scythians, and especially at those uncivilized habits which Herodotus described with such detachment. The Scythians' penchant for cannibalism and human sacrifice and their taste for raw or half-cooked meat held a special fascination, but it was their nomadic life that most disconcerted ancient authors. Because they would not settle in any one place and showed no interest in agriculture, urban life, or organized government, the Scythian nomads seemed to threaten the very foundations of classical civilization.[34] In the *Politics*, Aristotle classified the various ways a nation could earn its living. He put pastoral nomadism firmly at the bottom end of the scale, below agriculture, hunting and gathering, and even piratical raiding, though this last practice was also frequently attributed to the Scythians.[35]

Roman authors transferred many of these stereotypes to the European barbarians they encountered in the course of their conquests in Gaul, Germany, and Britain. Cicero established the *immanitas* of the unstable and violent northern barbarian as a commonplace in Roman oratory.[36] Nor was the Roman stereotype limited to northern Europeans. Distant Scythia was still regarded as the quintessential land of harshness and barbarity.[37] Imperial campaigns brought news of enemies beyond the Danube and in the Caucasus, such as the Alans and Getes, who were described in traditional terms. The Romans also assigned their archrivals the Parthians a Scythian ancestry.[38] The peoples of the Caucasus, the mountainous barrier separating the Scythian north from the civilized south, were considered particularly savage: in the first century A.D., a legend developed that Alexander the Great himself had tried to contain them in the course of his conquests in Asia. The wild tribes behind Alexander's "Caspian Gates" featured in Roman poetry, geography, and historical writing and enjoyed a long afterlife in medieval Christian apocalypse and romance. The legend also had a profound, if mostly indirect, impact on Renaissance ideas about the origins of the Turks.

Some Roman authors still found qualities to admire in the northern barbarians, often inverting familiar ideas regarding their rugged poverty and simplicity for moralizing or ironic effect. The self-deprecating respect Tacitus expressed for the hardy Germans, in whose virtuous society he saw the mirror image of corrupt imperial Rome, can also be detected in some descriptions of Scythia.[39] In the *Georgics,* Virgil painted a cozy picture of Scythian life, the hardy shepherds spending wintry nights wrapped in furs, drinking beer, and tossing logs on the fire.[40] Cicero and Horace, as well as the Greek geographer Strabo, composed similar eulogies of Scythian simplicity.[41] Trogus (author of a *Philippic History* which survives only in the third-century A.D. abbreviation of Justin) found the Scythians a magnificent race, whose valor in war had produced an impressive record of conquest and whose simple, nomadic lifestyle left them blissfully ignorant of the vices associated with property and wealth.[42] To illustrate his point, Trogus lists familiar Scythian characteristics, now offered as tokens of their abstemious virtue: for instance, their ignorance of agriculture, codified law, architecture, coinage, even woven clothing—for the Scythians wear only furs.[43] In all, he concludes, the Scythian way of life constitutes a model of moderation and restraint which the rest of the world would do well to observe: "It seems amazing that nature should bestow on the Scythians what the Greeks have been unable to achieve with all the protracted teachings of their sages . . . and that a refined morality should suffer by comparison with that of uncultured barbarians. So much more has ignorance of vice benefited the Scythians than knowledge of virtue has the Greeks."[44]

The philosophical and literary tradition of praising barbarians gave way once and for all—understandably enough—at the start of the barbarian invasions. In the fourth century, Ammianus Marcellinus demonstrated the unsavory character of the Huns by reciting a list of topics taken directly from Trogus but without his charitable interpretation. For Ammianus, the harsh climate, primitive diet, precarious nomadic existence, and political anarchy which characterized Hunnish life were causes for scorn and fear, not admiration:

The nation of the Huns . . . live by the frozen ocean beyond the Maeotic marshes, and exceed every standard of savagery . . . Their diet is so crude they have no need of fire or savory food, but eat the roots of wild plants and

the half-cooked flesh of any sort of animal . . . They do not live in houses . . .
but wander over mountains and through frozen forests . . . They obey no
kingly authority but are content to follow the disorderly leadership of various powerful men . . . No one among them plows or ever even touches a
plow handle; for they all live without fixed abodes and wander about without homes or laws or any stable source of nourishment . . . a wild race of
men, tied to no particular place, burning with savage greed for plunder.[45]

Fifteenth-century humanists revived many of these ethnographical commonplaces to describe the Ottoman Turks—usually, it should be stressed,
adopting the negative interpretation of Ammianus and only rarely taking
Trogus's more positive view. One example of the latter approach is Coluccio
Salutati's letter on the Ottoman Turks, written in 1397, in which he praises
the Turks for their simplicity of life and strict military discipline. Trained
from boyhood in the arts of war, Salutati says, the Turks spend their days
hunting and exercising in the field. They live happily on dry bread or game
or, when necessary, the roots of plants; they endure extreme cold or heat or
foul weather without complaint and sleep on the bare earth. In short, what
other men find intolerable, they not only endure but enjoy.[46] Did Salutati
sincerely admire the Turks? In this case, as with the ancient sources, context
is everything. Salutati recites this list of Turkish virtues to the margrave of
Moravia in order to encourage him and other northern European princes to
resolve the present schism in the Church and thereby restore their Christian
subjects to their own inherent virtue. Doing so will have the useful side effect of preparing them to withstand a possible Turkish attack. "We Christians," he says by way of contrast, "are mired in debauchery and sloth; we
aim at only indulgence and gluttony."[47] Standards are slipping, morals are
weak, and, worst of all, without a legitimate pope, the health of Christendom itself is in danger. "Shall we wait until this dispute escalates (alas!) into
war? Or until the Turks in their boldness . . . attack Christians and throw
them into turmoil? It will be too late to seek reconciliation then."[48] Salutati
presents the harsh discipline and endurance of the barbarian Turks as a provocative moral example to the people of Europe: if *they* can achieve such a
virtuous life, surely we can too.

   As the Turkish threat grew more serious, however, especially after the fall
of Constantinople, few humanists followed Salutati in praising the habits of
the Turks for rhetorical purposes, no matter how worthy the cause.[49] Emphasis shifted to the danger they posed. As a result, ancient truisms regarding the negative aspects of barbarian behavior were revived. Aeneas Sylvius

was clearly following the tradition established by Ammianus when he recounted the hideous diet and uncouth practices of the Turks through the
ages. Other Renaissance writers attributed typically Scythian habits specifically to the Ottomans of their own day. Lauro Quirini lamented that Constantinople had fallen to "a barbarous, uncivilized race, living without set
customs or laws, careless, wandering, arbitrary, full of treachery and
tricks."[50] Filelfo too condemned the contemporary Ottomans as "a restless
and wandering people."[51] Niccolò Sagundino composed perhaps the most
elaborate pastiche of ancient ethnographical commonplaces in the account
of Turkish origins he wrote for Aeneas Sylvius in 1456. Sagundino presents
the Turks as the direct descendants of the original Scythians, in a passage
that may well owe a debt to Ammianus: "The Turkish nation traces its origins back more than six hundred years, to the Scythians who lived across
Don, on the Asian side, with no settled home, no cities, no fixed or permanent abodes; they wandered here and there over the broad plains and seem
to have flowed out from there like a stream from a fountain." Moreover, the
habits of the contemporary Ottomans are still obviously Scythian: "To this
we can add the similarity of their customs, the appearance of their bodies and their costume, their method of riding and shooting arrows, a certain military discipline that is common to their nation, and that which can
prove the matter beyond doubt to anyone, the similarity of their very language and manner of speaking." Last, their political institutions (such as
they were) retained the anarchic flavor of their Scythian forebears: "At first,
these Turks followed no single prince; but different groups of them, as if in
factions, obeyed different leaders and various authorities. It was from this
nation, about a hundred and fifty years ago, that a man called Ottoman . . .
began to maraud about and plunder where he could."[52]

Sagundino had spent a year in Turkish captivity after the fall of Thessalonica in 1430, so he had more reason than most to describe the Turks as
harsh and barbaric. On the other hand, he had recently accompanied a Venetian legation to Mehmed II, intended to secure Venetian trading privileges
in the wake of the fall of Constantinople. It is curious that Sagundino's 1456
description of Turkish culture—or rather the lack of it—gives no hint of the
cosmopolitan court and urban society he would have encountered on his
mission just two years before. Rather, his account reveals his debts to the
topoi of classical ethnographic description.

Scythian history was a topic which ancient writers discussed less frequently.
The subject tended to be raised in the context of positive appraisals of the

country rather than negative ones. Although Herodotus described the Scythian occupation of Media as chaotic, he admired the way the nation later resisted the invading Persians.[53] Trogus, too, thought the Scythian record in war was impressive: not only did they repel Darius, Cyrus, and Alexander; earlier in their history they also invaded Media three times, made war on Egypt, and exacted tribute from all of Asia for some 1500 years until the establishment of the Assyrian Empire. Later they gave rise to the formidable kingdoms of the Bactrians, Parthians, and Amazons.[54]

As with the stock collection of Scythian habits and traits, the course of Scythian history came to be interpreted in wholly negative terms once the Hun invasions began in the fourth century A.D. Some later historians reviewed the same events Herodotus and Trogus described, but now as evidence of the Scythians' ferocious rapacity, not their empire-building skills. Many more identified new and far more sinister aspects to the Scythian past, drawing on traditions from both Christian apocalyptic literature and the romantic legends then beginning to circulate regarding Alexander the Great's adventures at the edges of the earth. All influenced the way Renaissance humanists described the "Scythian" origins of the Turks—far more than the original classical sources did.

When the Huns swept through the Holy Land in 395, coming south from the Pontic steppe through the Caucasus, Jerome identified them as the descendants of those ancient Scythian raiders Herodotus had described, who invaded Media by the same route and demanded tribute from Egypt and Ethiopia. They were also, he added, completely inhuman. They slaughtered children and the aged and spared no one in their path: "Pray Jesus keep such beasts outside the Roman world."[55] Other Christian authors of Jerome's time also identified the barbarian invaders as offspring of the ancient Scythians, but most concentrated on more notorious and fantastic aspects of their lineage, as they saw it, above all by identifying them as the descendants of Gog and Magog, the fearsome northerners of Ezekiel and Revelations. Josephus, writing in the late first century A.D., had first drawn a direct connection between Magog and the ancient Scythians, but the idea lay fallow until fourth- and fifth-century theologians began to promulgate it widely. In doing so, they often attached an eschatological significance to the Huns' appearance: the barbarians threatened to usher in the apocalypse, if they had not already done so.

The story that Alexander the Great built gates in the Caucasus to restrain the Scythian tribes, another idea first mentioned by Josephus, likewise took

re qð vocať regio folis. vbi cõfpexit gẽtes inmũdas et afpe-
ctu hoꝛribiles. fũt aũt ex filijs Japhet nepotes. quoꝛũ imun-
diciẽ videns exhoꝛruit. Comedebãt enim bÿ omnẽ cãticoꝛũ
fpeciẽ ofñe coinqnabile. i. canes: mures ferpẽtes: moꝛticinoꝛ
carnes: aboꝛtiua infirmabilia coꝛpa. et ea que in aluo nõdum
p lineamẽta coagulata funt. vel ex aliq parte mẽbꝛoꝛum pro
ducta. vnde compago figmenti poffit perficere foꝛmã vel fi-
gurã expꝛimere iumẽtoꝛ: necñ etiã ⁊ omnẽ fpẽm feraꝝ imũ-
darũ. moꝛtuos aũt neqꝗ̃ fepeliũt fed fepe comedũt illos.

Quõ alexãder magnꝰ. Gog ⁊ Magog ꝓ̃t eoꝛ turpitudinẽ in cafpijs mõtibꝰ incluferit

ⱳbool ex q̃
natꝰ eft Alex-
ander. Jfte te-
xtꝰ ipugñt õcm
Oꝛofij q̃ dicit
philippũ regẽ
macedonũ fu-
iffe patrẽ puta
tiuũ Alexãdꝛi
magni Alexã
der magnꝰ oc
cidit Darium
regẽ medoꝛũ
q̃ et pfaꝝ vlti-
mꝰ fuit qm̃ in
ipo ceffauit re
gnum Perfa-
rum et fuit fi-
lius Arfamiõ
ifto Dario ha
betur Danielᷞ
rj. capitulo.

Figure 4. Alexander seals up the Caspian Gates. ps.-Methodius, *Revelationes*
(Basel, 1498), sig. b4r. By permission of Houghton Library, Harvard University,
INC 7738

on new life at the time of the Hun invasions, as a vivid illustration of how longstanding and serious a threat the northern barbarians had posed to the Western world.[56] In his letter describing the invasion of the Holy Land, Jerome explicitly identified the Huns as the Caucasian tribes whom Alexander had excluded: "Behold, suddenly . . . great swarms of Huns, flying this way and that on their swift horses, filling the whole world with terror and death, have erupted from among the monstrous tribes of Massagetes around the frozen Don, where the gates of Alexander confine wild peoples within the crags of the Caucasus."[57]

From the fourth to the seventh century, Latin and Greek historians and geographers identified a whole series of contemporary barbarians with the monstrous tribes behind Alexander's Caucasian gates. In the seventh century, the apocalyptic strains in the legend came to the fore as a group of Syriac Christian authors (among them the author of the hugely influential *Revelationes*, known to us as ps.-Methodius) began to suggest that the barbarians still swarming behind the gates included in their number Gog and Magog themselves, who might yet break through the barrier and precipitate the end of the world. And just as other attributes of the Huns—and ultimately of the Scythians—were applied to later barbarians in the Middle Ages, so too the notion that these later invaders could actually be Gog and Magog and could trace their origins back to an eruption from Alexander's gates in the Caucasus became a commonplace of medieval historiography: Alans, Goths, Khazars, Magyars, and Mongols were all identified in turn with both Gog and Magog and the tribes Alexander had excluded.

The regularity with which medieval authors assigned each new wave of barbarian invaders the same identity, place of origin, and early history was to a certain extent justified by historical events: these migrants *were* for the most part nomadic peoples, and they did launch their incursions into Europe from north of the Black Sea, the ancient Scythian heartland. But the phenomenon also reflects a more basic assumption on the part of medieval historians; to them, Scythia seemed a region almost immune to historical change or progress. Over the course of the centuries the steppes had poured out ("like a stream from a fountain," as Sagundino puts it) an inexhaustible torrent of the *same* barbarians, a single nation untouched by the passage of time. Even as the new barbarian kingdoms of Europe developed elaborate histories for their own forebears, it was assumed that the Scythians, or their later incarnations, had little real history of their own. The most that might be mentioned was their descent from or identity with Gog and Magog and the record of later destruction they caused.

In the twelfth century, for instance, the universal chronicler Sigebert of Gembloux set out to recount the history of the world. In all of recorded time, he writes, there have been only nine principal nations: first of all the Romans and Persians, and then the newer arrivals: Franks, Vandals, English, Lombards, Visigoths, Ostrogoths, and Huns. All other nations can be included in one of the nine major groups. Sigebert includes the peoples of Scythia—including the Turks—under the rubric "Huns." They are a people so barbarous they would scarcely be worth mentioning were it not for the fact that they had dared to attack Roman territory.[58] This is the only aspect of Hunnish history worthy of notice, and the only thing that justifies mentioning their later descendants. All of them, Sigebert concludes, should be identified with Jeremiah's northern scourge: "In addition to these [Huns] there were other nations who attacked the Roman Empire, such as the Gepids, Alans, Turks, and Bulgars, and many others who all came out of the northern zone. The prophet was, perhaps, speaking of them when he said, *Out of the north an evil shall break forth upon all the inhabitants of the land.*"[59]

These various medieval images of Scythians—as perennial invaders, as enemies of Alexander and the imperial civilization he embodied, as inhuman monsters outside the realm of Christian history—were also invoked by fifteenth-century humanists when describing the origins of the Ottoman Turks. In his *Decades* of Roman history, completed in the early 1440s, Flavio Biondo referred directly to Jerome's letter in order to identify the Turks as the tribes behind Alexander's gates: "The Turks themselves were Scythians, from among those whom Alexander of Macedon shut up in the Hyperborean Mountains by means of iron gates, as other authors relate, and which the blessed Jerome confirms."[60]

Biondo's account was immediately and widely influential, repeated by, among others, the papal historian Platina and the universal chroniclers Jacopo Filippo Foresti of Bergamo and Hartmann Schedel of Nuremberg.[61]

Aeneas Sylvius revived a different topic, the historical progression of Scythian empires, which he derived from the histories of Diodorus Siculus and Trogus. In his geographical treatise the *Asia* (c. 1460–1462), Aeneas includes an expanded, updated genealogy of the Scythian peoples, drawing on classical historians like Diodorus and Trogus and extending to later nations like the Huns and Turks. He starts with a survey of the nations who inhabited Scythia in antiquity. Here, at least, he is willing to reproduce descriptions of peoples both mild and barbarous.[62] When he turns to the question of what the Scythians have achieved in recent history, however, he abandons the ancient topos of Scythian virtue, offering an interpretation far

closer to the dark pessimism Jerome and Sigebert expressed when considering the record of the northern barbarians.

Aeneas begins this Scythian excursus by quoting from Diodorus Siculus;
significantly, he reproduces only those details that present the Scythians in a
poor light.[63] They were an insignificant race to begin with, possibly descended from a certain Scythes, son of a monster who was half woman, half
viper. They conquered much of Asia and gave rise to formidable nations like
the Sacae, Massagetes, Arimaspians, and Sarmatians, as well as (here he begins to follow Trogus) the Parthians and Bactrians. They defeated Darius,
Cyrus, and Alexander, made war on Egypt, and extracted tribute from Asia
for 1500 years.[64] At this point Aeneas takes exception to his source. In enu-
merating the Scythians' many successes in war, Trogus asserts—as evidence
of their rugged independence—that "they heard of Roman arms but did not
experience them."[65] Aeneas cannot agree: this is no more than a pretty
phrase. Trogus must have got it from a Greek source, and Greeks are known
to exaggerate. In fact, Aeneas says, both the Greeks and the Romans often encountered and defeated Scythians in battle. Alexander, Pompey, and
Claudius won victories against them, and both Rome and Constantinople
saw innumerable Scythian triumphs celebrated in their streets.[66] If Rome
never conquered Scythia itself, this was only because it was an unpleasant
land where there was nothing worth capturing. "Who would take up arms
and risk death, knowing the victory will be empty?"[67] The Scythians were
no more invincible than brute elephants or bulls, who can be tamed by a superior intellect.

The subtext here is obvious: as Aeneas laid preparations for his crusade
against the Ottomans, he refused to accept that the "Scythian" enemy could
have an illustrious record in war. Rather, his whole account of their history
aims to prove how easy it will be to overcome their modern descendants.
Aeneas concludes his appraisal of ancient Scythian history with some faint
praise: "Nonetheless, I admit that many Scythians have done great deeds;
for those who live in a barren country do find it easy to migrate, and many
are drawn by the prospect of better land."[68] He then proceeds to the history
of the Huns and, finally, the Turks themselves.

Francesco Filelfo also used—but at the same time reacted against—information on the Scythians from Trogus. In his crusade letters, he sometimes claimed that the Turks were not actually Scythians themselves but
the fugitive slaves of that barbarian race—in other words, the lowest of
the low.[69] This seems to be a veiled borrowing from Trogus, who, in his

account of the origins of the Parthians, asserts that the etymology of their name shows they were originally exiles or fugitives from Scythia.[70] It is not clear whether Filelfo, in transferring this story of origin to the Turks, meant to identify them as Parthians. He certainly did not reproduce the *spirit* of Trogus's remark—namely, that it was a cause for wonder and admiration that such an obscure nation could have grown so powerful.[71] Filelfo stresses exactly the opposite: it is shameful and embarrassing that such a lowly power should now threaten the civilized world: "What a disaster, what miserable fortune, that things should have sunk to so low a level that the ignoble and uncouth horde of Turks, descended from the lowliest, starving shepherds and the fugitive slaves of the Scythians, should now lord it far and wide over Christian peoples and kings, and with every day increase their power to such an extent that they now lie scarcely sixty miles from Italy!"[72]

Filelfo's identification of the Turks as fugitive slaves was not repeated by later historians of the Turks, as far as I know. Aeneas's borrowings from Trogus, on the other hand, like Biondo's citation of Jerome, enjoyed widespread acceptance. The chronicler Foresti repeated Aeneas's résumé of Scythian history more or less completely at the start of his *Supplementum chronicorum,* first printed in 1483.[73] Foresti also set it within a biblical framework. His work begins with a geographical survey of the countries of the world, followed by an account of Creation and early Old Testament history. After the destruction of the Tower of Babel, he proceeds directly to the history of the Scythians, whose kingdom, he says, sprang into life at this very early moment in human history.[74] The progenitor of the nation was Magog; their numbers included the Amazons, the Scythians who repelled Darius, the Bactrians, the Parthians, and Attila and his Huns. To this list of Scythian nations, taken from Aeneas Sylvius, Foresti adds the Lombards, Hungarians, Goths, Catalans (whom Foresti says are descended from Alans) and finally the Turks.[75] Despite this long pedigree, Foresti says, the Scythians are still a breed apart from civilized nations. Their country, though ancient, has always been barbarous, "and for this reason is not counted among the four principal kingdoms."[76] The reference is to the scheme of world empires set out in the Book of Daniel (2:31–45 and 7:1–27), which Foresti probably derived from one of his regular sources, the slightly earlier chronicle of Werner Rolewinck.[77] In four thousand years of history, Foresti concludes, the habits of the Scythians—including the Turks—have remained the same: "All the Scythian nations carry bows while riding and feed upon, not the fruits of the

Quomodo Gog et Magog exeūtes de caspys montibus obtinēt terrā Israhel

In nouissimis vero temporibus secundum Ezechielis propheticam que dicit. In nouissimo die consumatiōis mūdi exiet Gog et Magog in terram Israhel: que sunt gentes et reges quos reclusit Alexander magnus in finibus aquilonis et in finibus septentrionis Gog et Magog Mosach et Tubal et Anog et Ageg et Athenal et Cephar: et

Hec ppheria habet Ezech. xxxviij. ca. et xxxix.ca. eiusdem. Apoca. xx.ca. Johannes pdixit de illis gentibus q faciunt seuā psecutionem sup eccl'iam in hec Vba. Cū consumati fuerint.2C.

Figure 5. Gog and Magog break through the Caspian Gates. ps.-Methodius, *Revelationes* (Basel, 1498), sig. b5r. By permission of Houghton Library, Harvard University, INC 7738

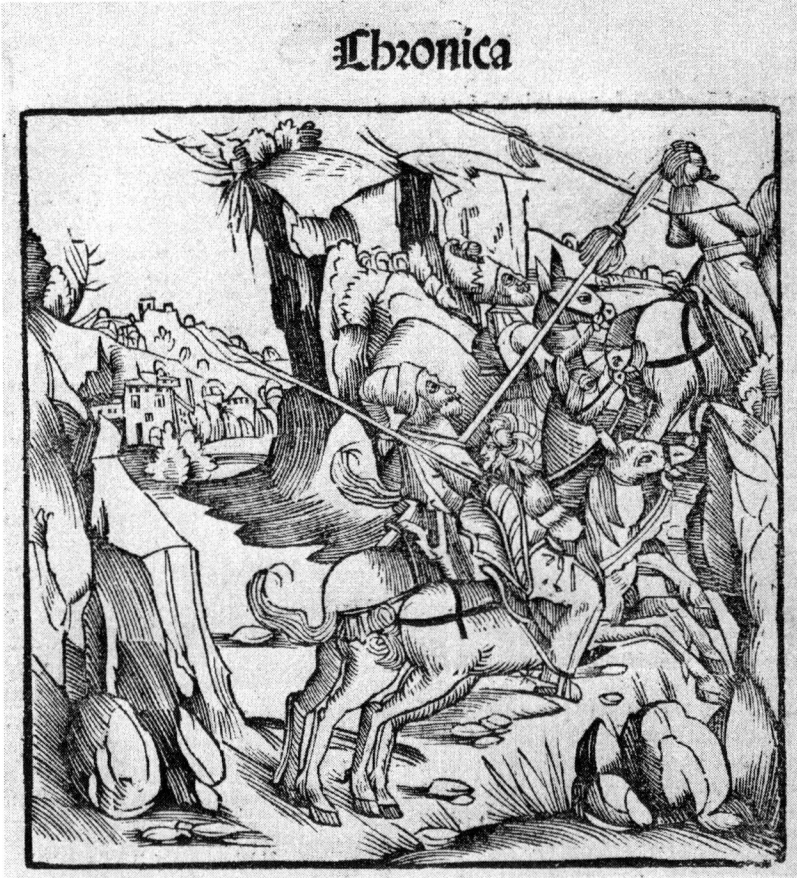

Figure 6. The Turks break through the Caspian Gates. Johannes Adelphus, *Turkisch Chronica* (Strassburg, 1512), sig. A6r. By permission of Houghton Library, Harvard University, OTT 150.10*F

plough, but the meat of beasts which they hunt . . . They are a barbarous race, and respect no rule of law or justice."[78]

   Later in his chronicle, Foresti also repeats Biondo's identification of the Turks as the wild tribes behind Alexander's gates. And so we see gathered in a single fifteenth-century historical work the entire range of medieval topoi regarding the barbarous Scythians—primitive habits, formidable military record, conflict with Alexander, exclusion from Christian history—now invoked to explain the origins and early history of the Ottoman Turks.

Foresti's chronicle cannot, perhaps, be considered an example of strictly humanist historiography; nevertheless, he derived most of his information on the Turks from Aeneas Sylvius and Biondo. The debt of these two indisputably humanist authors to the medieval tradition is more surprising. This is especially so since, on the surface at least, their comparisons between the Turks and the peoples of ancient Scythia seem to indicate a departure from the polemical attacks on the infidel characteristic of medieval chronicles and crusade rhetoric, toward a more classically inspired form of ethnographical description. Indeed, much of the information reported by Sagundino and Aeneas Sylvius—both their historical accounts of the kingdoms of Scythia and the more general commonplaces regarding Scythian behavior—can be traced back to classical sources. Yet the interpretation these humanists applied to that information and the spirit in which they presented it were largely shaped by later medieval traditions of confronting apparently apocalyptic forces of destruction, from the legendary Gog and Magog to the Huns and Mongols of more recent and bloody experience.

Bastards and Pretenders

It may seem from the preceding examples that humanist historians identified the Turks with the ancient Scythians, as well as with later northern barbarians, purely on the basis of analogy. In other words, they equated, and thus identified, these latest foes of Christendom with previous generations of nomadic invaders the world had known, particularly those whom the pious Alexander was meant to have restrained behind the Caspian Gates of the Caucasus. The reputation of Scythia and the Caucasus as nurseries of barbarian invaders certainly rendered them likely places for a troublesome new nation like the Turks to have originated. But there was more to it than that. The identification was especially attractive to the humanists because they had at hand a number of Byzantine and Latin historical sources that actually mention Turkic peoples (as *Tourkoi* or *Turci*) inhabiting Scythia and the Caucasus in the sixth, seventh, and eighth centuries A.D. On occasion, some of these texts even relate that these "Turks" emerged through the Caspian Gates—referring here to a real mountain pass in the Caucasus—to invade or plunder territory to the south.

   The humanists did not discover these references to Turks in the Caucasus in ancient texts. The information had been preserved and transmitted in medieval Latin universal chronicles and was accessible to earlier historians.

William of Tyre, for example, writing in the twelfth century, located the ancestors of the Seljuk Turks in the "Hyperborean" regions of northern Asia, while two centuries later, Andrea Dandolo claimed that the original Seljuks dwelled on the farther slopes of the "Caspian Mountain." Coluccio Salutati suggested much the same of the Ottomans—that they had "come down from Mount Caucasus." These authors may simply have wanted to associate the Turks with the wild tribes Alexander met during his legendary exploits in the Caucasus and the lands of Asia beyond it; but it seems just as likely that they knew of the historical references to Turks preserved in earlier chronicles and other texts.

Fifteenth-century humanist scholars also knew and relied on these earlier texts when they argued for a Scythian origin for the Ottoman Turks. They tended to cite their sources more explicitly and extensively than medieval chroniclers did. For a scholarly community of book-hunters, citation served as an advertisement of knowledge and expertise, of course, though the practice also hints at a certain deference to medieval authority that is perhaps less expected. For us, the humanists' editorial practices make it far easier to identify not only which sources they used but also how they manipulated them to their own ends.

Francesco Filelfo was probably the fifteenth century's most prolific advocate of a new crusade against the Turks.[79] In the course of a long and eventful career, he wrote dozens of letters to both friends and European princes urging a campaign to turn back the Ottoman tide; he also composed several crusade orations. He had personal reasons for taking an interest in the Turkish threat: in his youth, he served for seven years as secretary to the Venetian *bailo* at Constantinople. There he studied Greek with John Chrysoloras and married his daughter, Theodora; it was from her, he later declared, that he acquired true fluency in the Greek language. He also learned a great deal about the political crisis gripping the Byzantine East; on one memorable occasion he encountered the Ottoman enemy at first hand, when he accompanied a Venetian legation to the court of Murad II. When Filelfo returned home to Italy in 1427, he was not only one of the few Italian humanists who could read, write, and speak Greek like a native but also one of very few who had traveled in Turkish lands and seen the Ottoman threat for himself.

Filelfo's interest in the Turkish problem and his desire for Western action to defend the Greek East were unquestionably sincere. He did not shrink, however, from exploiting his personal knowledge of the problem and expressing concern for its resolution in a manner calculated to reflect well on himself and advance his own career. His precarious personal circumstances frequently compelled him to do so.[80] His crusade letters were crafted as pieces of advice and encouragement, but also as advertisements of his readiness to serve a new patron as a scholar, ambassador, or adviser on Turkish affairs.[81] He used them as opportunities to display his own eloquence, erudition, and expertise.

Filelfo's self-serving approach to the problem of the Turkish threat has so disconcerted modern scholars that few, if any, have recognized how well informed on the subject of Turkish history he really was.[82] In addition to his own experience of the Eastern political situation, he had access to and was able to read a variety of Greek historical sources. He also drew on a surprisingly wide range of Western medieval chronicles and histories.

In November 1444, Filelfo addressed a letter to King Wladyslaw III of Poland and Hungary just days before the king was to lead his forces into doomed battle against the Ottomans at the Black Sea port of Varna. The letter, an exhortation to victory over the Turks, offers a good example of Filelfo's rhetorical technique: a combination of overblown flattery of the warrior king and denigration of the Turkish enemy as lowly in origin, with a long history of shameful behavior.

Filelfo starts by congratulating the king on the great victory he is about to achieve over the Turks, a barbarous and inhuman race.[83] He laments that the irresponsible Western powers have allowed such savages to rise so far above their station. All will be well now, however, because Wladyslaw has come forward to take up the banner of Christ: "The Lord has chosen you alone of all Christian princes, to raise up, support and safeguard his prostrate people, to turn back, put to flight, cast down, overcome and destroy his most foul enemies—a restless and wandering people—and in doing so, to earn for yourself an immortal, splendid reputation, to be admired by all the world for generations to come."[84] Wladyslaw is like a new star in the sky, rising triumphant over the East. He will defeat the Turks, cross the Hellespont, and march not only to the Holy Land but all the way to India. He will be a new Alexander, but even greater than Alexander, for he will lead Christian armies in triumph and spread the Christian faith through Asia. His victory is certain, Filelfo concludes, because the enemy he goes out to face is nothing more than an unruly rabble: "Who is that you must fight? Surely it is not the French or the English or the mighty and unconquered Italians? Indeed, it is the Turks, shepherds and fugitives, who undertake everything, not by the rules of war, but instead by treachery and brigandage."[85]

Such a base people must be treated carefully, nevertheless, for they are capable of great mischief, as their early history shows. At the start of the letter, Filelfo traces the original Turks back to the Caucasus, where, he says, they had long dwelled in "hovels among the vast and frightful crags."[86] Here he goes on to explain that for a long time (presumably, he means throughout classical antiquity) the Turks remained a nation of little consequence, to whom no one paid much attention. But suddenly, in the time of Justinian, they swooped out of the Caucasus and captured the city of Bosporos in the Crimea in a surprise attack, under the leadership of one Bochamos, their bandit chief.[87]

Filelfo here refers to a very early event in the history of Western Türk relations with the Byzantine Empire: in A.D. 576, only a decade after they sent their first embassy to Constantinople, the Western Türks sent a raiding party, led by a captain known by the name or title of "Bokhan," to sack the Byzantine outpost of Bosporos on the northern Black Sea coast. This did not occur in the reign of Justinian (the date Filelfo gives) but slightly later, in the reign of Justin II.[88] The mistake is not Filelfo's but derives from his source, the late tenth-century Byzantine lexicon known as the *Suda*, a copy of which he had purchased during his stay in Constantinople.[89]

The *Suda* contains two entries which mention "Bochanos" the Turk, both of them extremely terse:

Bosporos: a city on the Hellespont, which Bochanos the Turk sacked in the time of Justinian.

Bochanos: a royal title, being the leader of the Turks, who sacked Bosporos in the time of Justinian.[90]

It is in fact only in another source, the sixth-century Byzantine historian Menander Protector, that any really informative details of the event are preserved.[91] Filelfo almost certainly did not know the text of Menander, so it is intriguing to see how far he develops the rather sparse information he had. The *Suda* entries say nothing about sudden surprise raids (Filelfo's *clandestinis latrociniis*), nor do they portray Bokhan as a leader of bandits (*duce latronum*); both are Filelfo's embellishments, intended to present these early Turks in as poor a light as possible.

In the oration he delivered on behalf of his patron Francesco Sforza at the Congress of Mantua in 1459, Filelfo returned to the subject of the Scythian origins of the Turks, emphasizing again their baseness and the dishonor their present success had brought to Christendom. He repeated the story of their capture of Bosporos, this time in order to demonstrate the Turks' innate and bloodthirsty greed for Christian territory, and again he added extra details to emphasize their treachery and cunning. The Turks took the Crimean city with sudden violence (*repentina vi*), while Bokhan—a figure about whom modern Turkologists know practically nothing—was a "most wicked warlord and brigand" whom the delegates at Mantua were apparently meant to recognize as a familiar villain.[92]

As a historical anecdote with which to blacken the name of the modern-day Turks, Filelfo's Bokhan story was fairly lame. No other fifteenth-century humanist seems to have repeated the tale. Despite Filelfo's best efforts to embroider the story, it was probably simply too obscure to mean much of anything either to readers of his letter to Wladyslaw or to his audience at Mantua. Filelfo's next claim, however—that the Turks soon embarked on a second expedition out of their lair in the Caucasus, this time south into Persia and into permanent contact with the civilized world—was to enjoy much wider acceptance among fifteenth-century historians.

Soon after their early display of force in the Crimea, Filelfo told Wladyslaw, the Turks went on the offensive again: "And scarcely had they withdrawn within their craggy Caucasian redoubt, when they emerged again during the reign of Heraclius, this time into Persia."[93] In his oration at Mantua in 1459, he further embellished the story, asking his audience: "Who on earth is unaware that the Turks are the fugitive slaves of the Scythians, the same shepherds who burst out of the confines of that vast and forbidding Mount Caucasus . . . and descended into Persia and Media for the purpose of pillaging; settling in no particular place except wastelands and bristling lairs in the forests?"[94]

Here, too, Filelfo refers to actual historical events, although in terms so vague it is impossible to tell precisely where he derives his information from. Nevertheless, there can be no doubt as to what, in general terms, he is talking about: during the reign of the Byzantine emperor Heraclius (r. 610–641), the Turkic Khazars, sometime vassals of the Western Türks, emerged as a political and military power in the area north of the Caucasus; in 626 they entered into an alliance with Byzantium which led them into direct conflict with the armies of Sassanian Persia.

The ninth-century Byzantine historian Theophanes Confessor (c. 755–818) provides by far the most extensive account in a Western language of the Khazars and their activities in the southern Caucasus in the seventh century.[95] It is unclear whether Filelfo read the text of Theophanes'

Chronographia in Greek. He may have relied on the ninth-century Latin translation of the text prepared by the papal librarian and sometime anti-pope Anastasius, or else used one of several later Latin chronicles which took information from Anastasius. (Anastasius's translation was a direct or indirect source for Sigebert of Gembloux, Otto of Freising, Vincent of Beauvais, and Martin of Troppau, among numerous other medieval authorities.)[96] But Theophanes is certainly the ultimate source for the anecdote he reports. The Byzantine chronicler preserves a good deal of information on these events: seven references in total to the Khazar "Turks" and their services to Byzantium in the Caucasus. Almost every Renaissance historian who maintained that the Ottoman Turks were Scythians from the Caucasus based his claims to some extent on one or more of these references—although they were almost always taken out of context and presented in a way that obscured the fact that these early "Turks" were actually accorded a very positive role in Byzantine historiography.

A brief survey of Theophanes' information on the Khazar Turks, together with an account of the historical events to which they refer, can illuminate how Filelfo and later historians made use of it.[97] In his chronicle, Theophanes usually refers to the Khazars as *Tourkoi* because the Khazars had originally been vassals of the Western Türks.[98] The first two of his seven entries on the Khazar "Turks" describe the formation of their initial alliance with Heraclius in 626–627; the remaining five cover various events of the second Arab-Khazar war in the eighth century.

Heraclius concluded his alliance with the Khazars at a moment of crisis for the Byzantine Empire. After a series of losses to Persia under the rule of Chosroes II, culminating in the capture of large parts of eastern Anatolia in 613, Jerusalem in 614, and Egypt in 619, Heraclius reorganized the Byzantine army, ejected the Persians from Anatolia, and in 623 invaded Persia itself.[99] In 626 he was campaigning in Lazica in the south Caucasus. Seeking support for a new campaign to the east, he contacted and concluded an alliance with the Khazars, who had just raided Persia themselves in 625–626.[100] The Khazars joined the emperor on a successful campaign against Chosroes in late 626; the next year, however, they declined to accompany him on his final push into Persia, where he destroyed the Sassanian army at Nineveh in December 627.[101] In 628, Chosroes was deposed and Persia ceased to present any serious threat. Byzantium regained territories in Armenia, Mesopotamia, Syria, Palestine, and Egypt.[102] By the 640s, Persia had fallen to the Arabs, who soon emerged as the major threat to Byzantium's eastern frontier. Their ascent to power ensured that the Byzantines continued to rely on the Khazars, who engaged the Arabs in two extended wars (642–652 and 722–737) which effectively prevented the latter from crossing north through the Caucasus and attacking Byzantine territory on the Black Sea coast.

In the *Chronographia*, Theophanes recounts the circumstances surrounding the Byzantine-Khazar alliance of 626 as part of the general buildup to Heraclius's final triumph over Persia. At first the Khazar "Turks" appear a fairly unruly and violent people:

> 1. [A.D. 624/625][103] The third part [of the army], [Heraclius] took himself and advanced to Lazica. During his stay there he invited the eastern Turks, who are called Khazars, to become his allies . . . Now the Khazars broke through the Caspian Gates and invaded Persia, that is the land of Adraigan, under their commander Ziebel who was second in rank after the Khagan. And in all the lands they traversed they made the Persians captive and burned their towns and villages.[104]

It is very likely that this passage was the source for Filelfo's statement in his letter to King Wladyslaw that the Turks invaded Persia during the reign of Heraclius—and furthermore, that they did so "for the purpose of pillaging," a detail added in his oration at the Congress of Mantua. But if Filelfo took his information on the early Turks directly from Theophanes or Anastasius's translation, then he must have purposefully ignored the rest of the story, which the *Chronographia* preserves. Immediately after the passage quoted above, Theophanes goes on to stress both the value of the Khazars' support for Byzantium and the sincerity with which it was offered:

> The emperor, too, set out from Lazica and joined them. When Ziebel saw him, he rushed to meet him, kissed his neck, and did obeisance to him . . . And the entire army of the Turks fell flat on the ground and, stretched out on their faces, reverenced the emperor with an honor that is unknown among alien nations. Likewise, their commanders climbed on rocks and fell flat in the same manner . . . After picking 40,000 brave men, Ziebel gave them to the emperor as allies, while he himself returned to his own land. Taking these men along, the emperor advanced on Chosroes.[105]

The characterization of the Turkic Khazars is here entirely favorable: they are honorable, devoted to Heraclius, and generous in their support of him. This contrasts nicely with Theophanes' account of the desperate but comical tyrant Chosroes, who relied on an army of slaves and foreigners and kept the corpse of a disgraced general preserved in salt so he could abuse it when the impulse struck. Chosroes is the chief villain throughout this particular period of Byzantine history, and Theophanes is so pleased to report Heraclius's final victory over him in the following year that the sudden desertion of his Khazar allies is reported with hardly a note of disapproval:

2. [625/626]: In this year the emperor Heraclius, by invading Persia together with the Turks starting in the month of September—an unexpected move, since it was winter—threw Chosroes into a state of distraction when the news had reached him. But the Turks, in view of the winter and the constant attacks of the Persians, could not bear to toil together with the emperor and started, little by little, to slip away until all of them had left and returned home.[106]

Despite this setback, Heraclius rallied his troops and destroyed the Persian army. There is no suggestion that the Khazars were at all perfidious; instead, they appear merely weak-willed and rather easily discouraged.

Theophanes has little to say about Khazar activities in the Caucasus for about a hundred years after this incident. Then, under the years 728–732, he notes three further occasions when the Khazars stormed out of their mountain strongholds to attack their southern neighbors:

3. [727/728] In this year the son of the Chagan, that is the ruler of Khazaria, invaded Media and Armenia. In Armenia he encountered the Arab general Garachos, whom he slew together with his army. After devastating the lands of the Armenians and the Medes and causing great fear to the Arabs, he returned home.[107]

4. [728/729] In this year [the Arab general] Masalmas invaded the land of the Turks. He joined battle with them, and there were many casualties on both sides. Seized by cowardice, Masalmas took to flight and returned through the mountains of Khazaria.[108]

5. [730/731] In this year Masalmas invaded Turkey. He reached the Caspian Gates and withdrew in fear.[109]

All three notices refer to historical events which can be confirmed from other sources.[110] So favorable is Theophanes' appraisal of the Turks, however, that he omits to mention how, before, between, and after these three Khazar successes, the Arabs inflicted a series of heavy blows, destroying armies, capturing towns, and finally, in 737, defeating the Khazars so conclusively that their khagan was forced to convert (although only temporarily) to Islam.[111] Theophanes prefers to report good news, and it is Khazar victories and Arab defeats which fall under this rubric. The two final notices on the Khazars in Theophanes' *Chronographia* report similarly good results:

> 6. [762/763] In the same year the Turks went out of the Caspian Gates, killed many people in Armenia [then an Arab province], took many captives, and returned home.[112]
>
> 7. [763/764] In this year the Turks went forth again to the Caspian Gates and to Iberia. They fought the Arabs and there were many casualties on both sides.[113]

Throughout this part of the *Chronographia*, Theophanes presents the Khazar Turks in an almost heroic light. He emphasizes their ferocity in battle and the fear they struck in Persian and Arab hearts, but even so, there is little in the original text to support Filelfo's contention that the early Turks were scarcely human, a barbarian rabble. Theophanes also makes it clear that the Turks who emerged from the Caucasus to fight first Persians and then Arabs represented a state with whom Byzantium maintained formal relations, a fact which Filelfo ignores in his repeated claims that they were fugitive slaves, driven to invade Persia by their desire for plunder and slaughter. Of course, there is no way to be sure that Filelfo knew the text of Theophanes in its entirety. His source for the Khazar invasion of Persia in 627 could well have been a later Latin chronicle which excerpted only the few details which Filelfo himself repeats.[114]

Flavio Biondo, on the other hand, was undoubtedly familiar with the whole text of Theophanes, in the translation of Anastasius Bibliothecarius. It is one of the main sources he used in compiling his enormous survey of late antique and medieval Italian history, the *Decades*.[115] Biondo began work on the *Decades* in the late 1430s; a draft may have been complete by 1442, but the work was not published until about 1444.[116] In his account of the emergence of the Turks, Biondo, like Filelfo, reproduces information from Theophanes-Anastasius regarding the Khazars, and he too presents this material in such a way that these ancient Turks appear as violent and lawless barbarians. He omits any mention of the helpful role they played in Byzantine foreign policy and instead associates their appearance with a period of difficult times for both the empire and Italy.

Unlike Filelfo, Biondo does not draw an explicit connection between the ancient Turks he discusses in the *Decades* and the contemporary Ottoman

Turks. There is nevertheless political significance to his remarks. They come close to the start of Biondo's second *Decade*, in the midst of a discussion of the papal crisis of 755, when the Lombard Aistulf besieged Rome, sending Pope Stephen II in flight to Pepin, king of the Franks.[117] Biondo clearly considered this papal crisis an important turning point in Italian history, with significant implications for the peninsula's future.[118] The pope's flight should have been a matter of grave concern to the Byzantine emperor Constantine V, Biondo argues, an opportunity for him to reassert imperial authority in Italy. Instead, the hapless Constantine neglected his responsibilities to the Italians and allowed both Lombards and Franks to exercise power unchecked. At the same moment, Constantine saw new troubles erupt on his eastern frontier:

> While Rome and Italy were agitated and distressed by such great losses and dangers, Emperor Constantine took no steps to alleviate the problem, although this was a change in fortunes which was hardly of advantage to himself. And afterwards this emperor had a second such change of luck, because it was at this time that the Turks first invaded Asia, molesting the Alans, then the Colchians and Armenians, and thereafter the peoples of Asia Minor and finally the Persians and Saracens, seizing land and slaughtering great numbers of people whom they found there or who dared to gather [in opposition].[119]

Once again we see Theophanes' tale of Khazar heroism recast as an example of Turkish violence and greed.

We should not, perhaps, read too much into the fact that Biondo here associates the growing divide between papal and imperial authority in Italy with the first appearance of the Turks in the East. He himself makes no further comment on the significance of these two events taking place one after the other, beyond presenting them as examples of Constantine's (and, by extension, the empire's) ill fortune in these years. But Biondo did firmly believe that the rift that developed in the eighth century between imperial Constantinople and papal Rome marked the final collapse of the ancient empire.[120] Elsewhere in his writings, he expressly asserts a connection between the decline of ancient Rome and the inability of modern Italians to beat back the Turkish threat. In both the preface and the conclusion to his antiquarian treatise, *Roma triumphans*, which he completed while attending the Congress of Mantua in 1459 as a papal secretary,[121] Biondo called on Aeneas Sylvius, as Pius II, to lead a revival of ancient Roman institutions, mores, and values. In doing so, he argued, Italy would regain the strength it had enjoyed under Roman rule and thus be in a position at last to triumph over the Turks.[122] Furthermore, later in the *Decades,* in his account of Urban II's sermon launching the First Crusade, the words he puts in the pope's mouth describe the new expedition against the Saracens and Turks as a campaign not so much for the recovery of Jerusalem as for the restoration of the territories and prestige of the ancient Roman Empire.[123]

Whether or not Biondo intended to treat the emergence of the Turks in eighth-century Asia as an event of direct historical significance for the political fortunes of contemporary Italy remains unclear. Still, there can be no question that his reference to the Khazar invasion as an example of the empire's increasing woes directly contradicts his source, Theophanes-Anastasius, who interpreted Khazar interventions in the Caucasus and Persia as positive contributions to Byzantine policy in the East. This is the only point in the *Decades* where Biondo repeats information from the *Chronographia* on the Khazars, although he had access to the complete text of Anastasius's translation and repeated much else from it in this part of his history.[124] It seems it was not only the violence that Theophanes attributes to the Turks here but also repeated references to the Turks coming through the Caspian Gates that caught Biondo's eye, for immediately after recounting their eighth-century invasion of Asia Minor, he concludes with the statement (examined above) that these Turks were in fact identical to the wild Scythian tribes Alexander the Great had enclosed behind the Caspian Gates in antiquity.[125] Biondo seems to have been the first Renaissance historian expressly to identify the Ottoman Turks with Alexander's tribes.

The Renaissance idea that the Ottoman Turks originated in Scythia and the Caucasus was both inspired by a widespread romantic tradition—that unclean races were enclosed behind Alexander's legendary Caspian Gates—and firmly based on Byzantine historical sources recording real "Turks" breaking through the real Caspian Gates on raids undertaken on behalf of the eastern empire. Filelfo, while citing historical information about the Turks from the *Suda* and (at whatever degree of remove) from Theophanes, seems also to invoke the legendary tradition implicitly in his crusade exhortations. He lays particular stress on the moment of the Turks' emergence from the Caucasus, dwells on their unclean and inhuman behavior, and on one occasion describes their initial invasion as a release from mountainous imprisonment.[126] Biondo simply makes explicit the identification with Alexander's enclosed tribes.

Later historians were often reluctant to follow Biondo in repeating such a fantastic claim. No matter how closely the story fit their own prejudices regarding the character and intentions of the Ottomans, it may have seemed inappropriate to include it in historical works meant at least to appear sober and factual. Platina, for instance, used most of Biondo's entry on the travails of Constantine and Pope Stephen in his *Lives of the Popes* but tried to historicize the deed Alexander was supposed to have performed: "Some writers say that the Turks were Scythians, in particular those whom Alexander, king of Macedon, shut up in the Hyperborean [mountains] by means of iron bolts—by which they mean, metaphorically, that he had isolated this unconquerable race in that corner of the world as if in a prison."[127]

Aeneas Sylvius Piccolomini also constructed a Scythian history for the Turks, using many of the same devices Filelfo and Biondo employed. Aeneas, too, refers to the emergence of the Khazar "Turks" from the Caucasus, quoting information from the Theophanes tradition out of context and to negative effect. He also portrays these Turks as primitive and disgusting savages, hinting at their association with Alexander's unclean tribes while carefully disguising the legendary and apocalyptic nature of the source he cites to support his claim.

Aeneas was by far the most prominent and vocal advocate for a crusade against the Turks in the fifteenth century.[128] His writings in support of a campaign against the Ottomans were enormously influential, enjoying widespread circulation for decades after his death. While Filelfo probably composed more words on the subject in his dozens of crusade letters, more of Aeneas's letters were copied and distributed independently in manuscript; he also delivered more orations at important public events, where they were heard by prominent leaders and—just as significantly—soon found their way into print.[129] As a result, Aeneas's ideas about the origins of the Turks, which he introduced into almost every one of his crusade appeals, were quickly accepted as historiographical orthodoxy, repeated by historians and orators well into the sixteenth century.

Given the central role Aeneas was to play in the campaign for a new crusade in the decade after Constantinople's fall, it is surprising that his interest in the Turkish threat developed only late in life. The disaster at Varna, in 1444, may have stimulated his concern. Coming only a year after he quit the Council of Basel for Frederick III's imperial service, the destruction of the Hungarian and Burgundian army and the death of its prominent leaders, including Wladyslaw of Poland and Cardinal Giuliano Cesarini, may have confirmed him in his recently adopted conviction that only the emperor could free Europe from internal dissensions and overcome the enemies who threatened it from without.[130]

It was not until the 1450s, however, when the Ottoman threat grew far graver (and Aeneas began his rapid advance through the clerical hierarchy),[131] that he started to pronounce regularly and at length on Turkish affairs. He made the topic a central theme of an oration delivered after Frederick's imperial coronation in Rome in March 1452: here he outlined the need for a new crusade, presented Frederick as the best candidate to lead it, and called on Pope Nicholas V to lend his support. After the fall of Constantinople, his impassioned letters to Pope Nicholas and Cardinal Nicholas of Cusa, written days after news of the catastrophe reached him in Austria, convey his real and personal distress over the crisis. The same sense of urgency also pervades his speeches on behalf of the emperor at the Diets of Frankfurt and Regensburg in 1454 and Wiener Neustadt in 1455, and before Pope Calixtus III in Rome later that same year—compounded, perhaps, by his growing realization that Frederick had no real interest in resolving the Turkish problem after all.

Above all, after his election to the papacy in 1458, when he declared that a new crusade was to be his most important priority, the Turkish question dominates his writings: these include open letters to various Christian leaders as well as private diplomatic correspondence; his orations at the Congress of Mantua in 1459; extended passages in the geographical treatises, *Europa* and *Asia,* which he wrote in 1458 and 1460–1462, respectively (and which were intended at least in part to support the crusade project); scattered comments in his autobiographical *Commentaries;* and the bull "Ezechielis prophetae," with which he formally launched the crusade in 1463.

In these compositions, Aeneas took the commonplaces of humanist crusade rhetoric to new heights, drawing on political arguments, historical examples, and emotive rhetorical appeals. He lamented the extent and frequency of Turkish victories, the atrocities they visited on the innocent and weak, the territories and treasure that had been lost. He called for concord between the Church and the princes of Europe, reproached them for neglecting their Christian neighbors in the East and betraying the crusading traditions of their ancestors, and urged prompt action to reverse the Turkish tide. To these principal arguments he added figures from a seemingly limitless stock of persuasive ornamentation: examples of classical and biblical heroes for contemporary princes to emulate; references to barbarian wars fought by ancient emperors and crusader kings; disquisitions on the spiritual benefits of crusading; examples of the Turkish contempt for European literature and arts; breathless accounts of their insults against the Eastern Church and the Holy Land and the threat they posed to European security; exhortations regarding the glory to be won by fighting and dying for Christ.

While this mixture of pragmatic and idealistic arguments may seem incongruous or inconsistent to a modern reader, it came perfectly naturally to Aeneas, as did his protean attempts to make the crusade seem a compelling endeavor to the wide variety of audiences he addressed, whether chivalry-minded Burgundian knights, humanist cardinals nostalgic for the glories of Greece, or German and Italian princes jealous of their dignity and keen to promote their own interests. He strove to excite concern and secure commitment wherever he could find it; embracing the rhetorical principle of *amplificatio*, he could leave no argument untried. To this end, his rhetoric could shift even on the question of the actual goal of the crusade—and consequently on the very identity of the enemy. Aeneas usually argued for a crusade directed against the Ottomans, with the aim of liberating Constantinople, relieving Hungary, and reclaiming the Aegean, but he could redirect attention when it suited his purposes to the "Saracens" (that is, the Mamluks of Egypt) then ruling the Holy Land and to the old crusading ideal of recapturing Jerusalem. At times he inveighed, even more vaguely, against infidels in general—an undifferentiated mass of enemies including Turks in eastern Europe and Asia Minor, Mamluks in the Holy Land and Egypt, Moors in North Africa and Spain, even pagan Tartars in southern Russia and remote, primitive tribes along the furthest reaches of the Baltic Sea and in northern Scandinavia. These godless hordes surrounded Europe on all sides. Christians everywhere must strike out from the tiny corner to which they had been confined or else be overwhelmed.

In his earliest crusade oration, delivered after Frederick's coronation in Rome in 1452, Aeneas made little effort to distinguish the Ottomans, their history and character, from other Muslim nations. He described Turkish aggression as part of a universal assault on Christendom by somewhat disingenuously conflating recent Ottoman victories in Greece with the longstanding Muslim occupation of Jerusalem and the Holy Land. Frederick had three reasons for wanting to lead a crusade, Aeneas began: pity for the oppressed, his own advantage, and the honor of the cause.[132] He felt pity for the Holy Land, where the holy places lay in the hands of "filthy, unclean, horrible Saracens."[133] But the plight of Greece, "mother of letters, inventor of laws, cultivator of ethics, and teacher of all the good arts," and her people was equally moving.[134] Indeed, wherever Frederick looked, he could see infidels pressing against Christendom: Hungary, Poland, Spain, and the Mediterranean islands all suffered. This was the result of negligence on the part of generations of selfish Christian princes, Aeneas concluded, in somewhat portentous terms.[135] But Frederick was a different sort of prince. He knew that both advantage and glory would come to him by undertaking a new crusade, and he longed to strike out as soon as he could. The aims of this crusade would be as universal as the host of enemies who Aeneas imagined had provoked it: Frederick would first liberate Hungary and Greece, then free the Holy Land from Muslim domination, and finally wipe Islam itself from the face of the earth.[136]

In defining the Ottoman threat as part of a larger Muslim attack on Christendom in this early oration, Aeneas also presents the Turks as a nation very like, if not identical with, the other Islamic empires of the East. In the lament with which he begins the speech, he deplores the fact that the Turks have conquered the Greeks, descendants of the hardy citizens of ancient Athens, Sparta, and Thebes, later led by the great Alexander. This mighty race was now subject to the Turks, by contrast a shamefully "effeminate" people.[137] But Frederick knew that they, like the other Eastern peoples, would put up no real resistance to a new crusade. For the Turks, "Assyrians," and Egyptians were all weak and unmanly nations, with no talent or taste for war. Who could fear the stocky little Turks in their turbans, or the Egyptians in their flowing trousers?[138] Certainly not the brave warriors of Europe, who had never been defeated by an Asiatic army—except in those rare cases when they had been completely outnumbered.[139] The forces of Christendom were far superior; for one thing, they were constantly proving themselves in battle against one another (here, another passing swipe at Europe's lamentable lack of unity). They stood ready to fight, and win, worthier battles abroad.[140]

The Turkish capture of Constantinople in the next year proved Aeneas lamentably wrong on this point. After the events of May 1453, the idea of the Ottomans as a soft, easily conquered Asiatic race from whom Europe had nothing to fear was a conceit he no longer tried to sustain. In the letters he wrote that year and in his later orations, he abandoned this particular line of attack, replacing it with a new account of the Turks' character which stressed their primitive origins, their violent early history, and the great danger they posed to contemporary Europe.

On 12 July 1453, apparently just after hearing news of Constantinople's fall, Aeneas composed a consolatory letter to Pope Nicholas V.[141] At first, echoing the themes of his oration of the previous year, he lamented that the city had fallen into the hands of effeminate Turks and blamed the Western powers for allowing such a catastrophe to occur.[142] But he changed his tone very quickly, now emphasizing the brutal, perhaps irresistible force of the Turkish attack on the city, cataloguing the atrocities they had committed during the siege, mourning their destruction of Greek books, and comparing them unfavorably to the Goths.[143] Within a fortnight, in a letter to Cardinal Nicholas of Cusa, Aeneas had converted completely to this new, harsher view of the Turkish character, asserting without reservation that they were ferocious northern barbarians. In this letter he imagined the Turkish rampage through the city in the most grisly detail. The Turks he described here were not soft, effeminate, or marked by any other stereotypically Asiatic characteristics. Indeed, Aeneas argued, they were not to be identified with any nation of Asia at all: "For those who are now called Turks are not Persians, nor are they Trojans, as certain others think. They are a race of Scythians, come from the depths of a barbarous land, who are said to have made their original home beyond the Black Sea and Pirrichean Mountains, towards the northern Ocean, as Aethicus the philosopher says."[144]

This was the first time Aeneas referred to the Scythian origins of the Turks. He would repeat the claim, usually citing the authority of the mysterious "Aethicus" alongside later, additional authorities, at least nine times in subsequent works: in a letter to Johannes Troster written in July 1454; in orations at the Diets of Frankfurt in September 1454 and Wiener Neustadt in January 1455 and before Calixtus III at Rome in March 1455; in his autobiographical *Commentaries;* in his geographical treatise *Europa,* written about 1458; in his oration at the Congress of Mantua in 1459; and in two separate passages in his *Asia.*[145] The letter to Nicholas of Cusa also marks the first time Aeneas argued against the idea that the Turks had come from Troy, raising the possibility of their Trojan origins only to reject it. He would repeat the *anasceua* in most of his later compositions, always as a prelude to his own account of their Scythian past. The connection is significant. Although the identification of the Turks as *Teucri* or avenging Trojans was well established in European imaginative literature well before the fall of Constantinople, Aeneas never expressed any doubts about it before his remarks in his letter to Nicholas of Cusa. In fact, in an oration delivered early in his career, at the Council of Basel in 1436, he came very close to suggesting that Turkish aggression against Europe was indeed intended as a campaign of revenge for the loss of Troy.[146] And in his private correspondence in the 1440s as well as the official letters he drafted for Frederick III at the time, he used the form *Teucri* to refer to the Turks—perhaps following a stylistic practice of the imperial chancery dating back to at least 1412.[147]

Now, in 1453, he began to argue against the idea that the ancestors of the Turks had anything to do with the Trojans. His objection to it seems closely linked to his newly acquired conviction that the contemporary Turks were dangerous barbarians: any theory associating them with a nation of classical antiquity now became unacceptable. It is interesting to note, in this context, that Aeneas never tried to argue against the idea of the Trojan Turks on the grounds that it was *historically* improbable. He rejected the notion because it contradicted what he believed to be true of their character: the Trojans had been a literate and cultured nation.[148] What could they—or, for that matter, the ancient and illustrious Persians—have to do with the Turks? In short, Aeneas assumed what he was ostensibly trying to prove: the Turks were innately barbarous.[149]

The account of the Scythian origins of the ancient Turks which Aeneas developed to support his campaign against their modern descendants was very similar to the versions Biondo and Filelfo had put forward only a few years earlier.[150] His sources were different from theirs but derived from the same literary and historiographical traditions, which placed earlier generations of *Turci* in Scythia and the Caucasus. Furthermore, like Filelfo and Biondo, Aeneas often manipulated the information he found in his sources in order both to enhance the credibility of his account and to make his portrayal of the original Turks—and so, by extension, their Ottoman descendants—especially damning.

In his letter to Nicholas of Cusa, Aeneas explains that the Turks could not possibly be either Trojans or Persians, since according to "Aethicus the philosopher" their original homeland lay "beyond the Black Sea and Pirrichean Mountains, towards the northern Ocean." He then quotes a passage from Aethicus describing the habits and character of the original Turks, who were "a shameful and unknown nation, promiscuous in every sort of lewdness, lovers of debauchery, who ate anything disgusting and had no knowledge of wine, grain, or salt. They kept no religious holiday except in the month of August, when they sent a tribute of alluvial gold to Augustus Caesar; they were not compelled to do this but did so of their own accord when they saw that other territories were offering tribute." Nor had the Turks come very far from such ignoble beginnings: "And there is still a little flavor of their origins about them, even though, having lived in Asia a long time, they have shed some of their original baseness and made themselves a little civilized; for they still shun wine and eat the meat of horses and bison. They are steeped in lust, care little for the study of letters and are incredibly haughty and proud."[151]

Aeneas prized Aethicus as an authority on the Turks. He must have owned a copy of his geographical treatise, entitled *Cosmographia,* or else copied out the full text of the description of the Turks it contains, for when he repeated information from the work in later years, he sometimes added or substituted various details from the text. At the Diet of Frankfurt, for instance, he said the Turks lived on the meat not only of horses and bison but also of vultures.[152] In his treatises *Asia* and *Europa,* he added further information on the exotic geography of their homeland: they lived near the "Taracuntan islands"—apparently lying in a distant bay of the Black Sea or Northern Ocean—and the mountains known as the *ubera aquilonis* or "breasts of the north." In the geographical works he also changed the list of unclean foods they ate, now including the flesh of beasts of burden, wolves, vultures, and (*quod magis horreas*) the corpses of stillborn human infants.[153] One can see why Aethicus's account appealed to Aeneas. It traced the Turks to a distant part of Scythia far removed from the lands of classical civilization, attributed to them primitive and disgusting habits, and, perhaps most valuable of all, fixed them in such conditions at a relatively early moment in history, during the reign of Augustus.[154]

This last point is especially important. Although Aeneas was most concerned with establishing the primitive character and habits of the original Turks—and demonstrating the survival of these traits among their descendants—it was important, too, that his description be historically credible. In the geographical works, he repeated Aethicus's curious story about the alluvial gold offered by the Turks as tribute to Augustus—not only, one presumes, because it portrayed them as childishly awed by Roman civilization. In the later works he glossed the story with a sentence borrowed from Trogus's account of the ancient Scythians ("They heard of the power of Rome rather than had direct experience of it") in order to highlight the antiquity of the information he had discovered regarding the primeval Turks.[155] Filelfo had traced the history of the Turks back as far as Justinian, and Biondo to the age of Jerome. Aeneas would go one better, developing a history for the Turks as ancient as the empire itself.

On what authority did Aeneas base this claim? The *Cosmographia* purports
to be a translation of and commentary on an ancient geographical work by
a Greek philosopher, "Aethicus."[156] It is even written in the third person,
as if the Latin translator were merely reporting on the contents of the earlier Greek text. Some manuscripts name this supposed commentator as
"Hieronymus Presbyter," a figure sometimes identified by later medieval authors as St. Jerome, so adding another layer of apparent authenticity.

In fact there never was a Greek geographer called Aethicus, nor did Jerome
play any part in the text's composition. The *Cosmographia* was composed in
Latin; modern scholars have proposed dates for the work ranging between
the fourth and eighth centuries A.D. and various places of composition—
all in northern Europe—ranging from Ireland to Dalmatia. It now seems
most likely that it was composed in the mid-eighth century, probably at a
Carolingian court school or monastery.[157] Aeneas could not have known
just how complex and uncertain the text's pedigree was, but even so, he can
hardly have believed that this was a genuine work of classical geography.
The *Cosmographia* consists of a haphazard collection of legends, geographical
curiosities, reports on monstrous races, and details of the impending terrors
of the apocalypse, derived primarily from the Bible, the *Etymologies* of Isidore
of Seville, and the recently translated *Revelations* of ps.-Methodius, all re-
hashed in a syntax and vocabulary so bizarre as to render the text almost
unintelligible.[158]

Aeneas cleaned up the section of Aethicus's text that he cited in his letter
to Nicholas of Cusa, not only classicizing the grammar, syntax, and orthog-
raphy but also editing out some of the more outrageous aspects of early
Turkish culture detailed in the medieval work. The original passage in the
Cosmographia offers a rather less credible portrait of the Turks than the one
Aeneas offers. Here is the original:

> Other texts pass over the Turks in silence. For the poets and philosophers
> never make any mention of them, but Aethicus, in addition to the affairs of
> other peoples, says much. He says they inhabit islands, or the mainland, of a
> gulf of the Black Sea, enclosed by the Birrichean mountains and the islands
> of Taraconta, facing the "breasts of the north"—a nation shameful and un-
> civilized, monstrous, idolatrous, promiscuous in every kind of lewdness and
> debauchery, truculent (from which epithet they derive their name [that is,
> *Turci*]), born of the seed of Gog and Magog. Everything they eat is abomina-
> ble, even stillborn human infants, as well as the flesh of children, horses

and bears, vultures, ravens and kites, owls and bison, dogs and apes. They are hideous in appearance, never wash in water, have no knowledge of wine, use no salt, and have never eaten grain . . . Locked up with their wicked offspring behind the Caspian Gates, this nation will make great devastation in the time of the Antichrist. In appearance they are black as soot, with hair like a raven's and very strong teeth. They possess a multitude of camels, the kind bred in Bactria, a number of extremely swift mules . . . and massive dogs so much stronger than any other breed that they can kill lions, leopards, and bears.[159]

It is easy to see why Aeneas excluded so much of this account. Aethicus's use of dubious etymology (equating *Turci* with *truculenti*) and references to the Turks' descent from Gog and Magog and their imprisonment behind the Caspian Gates (as well as their black skin and peculiarly strong teeth) could hardly support Aeneas's claim to have discovered plausible historical grounds for identifying the modern Turks as Scythians—and to have established at the same time a credible, ancient alternative to the legend of their Trojan origins. In this regard, the most significant aspect of Aethicus's description of the Turks omitted by Aeneas occurs immediately after the passage just quoted:

Alexander the Great of Macedon could neither capture nor defeat this nation; he sent his army against them on numerous occasions but could not overcome them. Mindful of this . . . he is said to have declared: ". . . Alas, may these demons of hell, this phalanx of enemies, never hear or catch sight of the wider world, fertile and flowing with honey as it is, or of its wealth and famous kingdoms, all its goods and treasures and the glory and beauty of its people! Else they will swarm over the whole face of the earth and snatch it all up like a piece of bread and gorge themselves on it. O North, mother of dragons and nurse of scorpions, snake pit and pool of demons, it would be better for there to be an impenetrable barrier against you, like the gates of hell, than for you to spawn such a race."[160]

Aethicus here preserves one of the earliest Latin accounts of the legend of Alexander's gates in the Caucasus in its apocalyptic form.[161] Since Aeneas's whole point in citing Aethicus was to demonstrate the inherent barbarity of the Turks by invoking the authority of an ancient and reliable-sounding historical account of their Scythian origins, it is not surprising that he edited his source so that its fantastic character was disguised.

Although Aethicus's information on the Turks amounts to little more than a retelling of the ps.-Methodian legend of Alexander's gates, the text does nonetheless explicitly mention "Turks" as a race Alexander encountered in his journey beyond the Caucasus.[162] This is almost certainly a reference to the Turkic Khazars.[163] In the eighth century, when Aethicus most likely wrote, the Khazars were the dominant ethnic group in the Caucasus and the steppes north of the Black Sea; they were routinely called "Turks" in Byzantine literature; most important, they very likely provided the inspiration for the Syriac ps.-Methodius's apocalyptic description of the unclean nations behind Alexander's gates, which was clearly Aethicus's source for the story told here. The only problem with this putative debt is that, to the best of my knowledge, no extant version of the ps.-Methodian legend, either in the original Syriac or in any Greek or Latin translation, actually identifies the unclean races as "Turks," even though the Khazar Turks clearly provided the inspiration for the story. But Aethicus's work is a very early Latin witness to the ps.-Methodian tradition and may preserve a version, otherwise lost, in which the identity of the unclean races as "Turks" was made clear.[164]

In the oration Aeneas delivered at the Diet of Frankfurt in 1454, he offered another piece of evidence to support his claim that the Turks were Scythian in origin. The chronicler Otto of Freising, Aeneas said, preserved a report that the Turks had emerged from their home in Scythia during the reign of Pepin, king of the Franks. They came south out of the "Caspian Mountains" (the Caucasus) and took themselves into Asia, "and there they have remained ever since."[165] As he did with the information from Aethicus, Aeneas repeated this story in later compositions, changing details, sometimes crediting Otto and sometimes not. In his geographical treatises, for instance, he reported that the Turks had come out of the Caspian *Gates*, not the Caspian Mountains, and added that afterward they engaged in a battle with the Avars in which many lives on both sides were lost.[166]

The passage Aeneas cites from Otto's *Chronica* derives, via several intervening Latin chronicles, from Theophanes' final entry on the Khazar raids through the Caspian Gates in the eighth century (entry 7 from the *Chronographia* as numbered above).[167] This is one of the entries that Biondo, working directly from Anastasius's translation, also used for his account of the emergence of the Turks from the Caucasus. Like Biondo, Aeneas gives no hint of the original, positive interpretation of the incident as told by Theophanes. In Aeneas's case, however, this was not an editorial decision of his own making: Otto himself preserves only this entry in his *Chronicle*, where it appears in isolation from any other information on contemporary events in the Byzantine East.

Otto copied his note on the Khazar "Turci" from an earlier Bavarian chronicler, Frutolf of Michelsberg, who in turn took it from an Italian, Landulphus Sagax, a chronicler who relied directly on Anastasius's translation of Theophanes.[168] In his *Historia Romana* (written in the 1020s), Landulphus divided up the text of Anastasius, distributing excerpts among information from other sources, but he still preserved all seven of Theophanes' reports on the Khazars.[169] About eighty years later, Frutolf incorporated parts of the *Historia Romana* into his own historical compendium but included only the last of Theophanes' references to the Khazars.[170] Writing for a German audience, Frutolf probably imagined that events in the distant Caucasus would be of little interest to his readers—unlike the Italians Anastasius and Landulphus Sagax, who wrote for an audience more interested in news of the Greeks and their foreign relations. More important, perhaps, is the fact that the original entry in Theophanes described (correctly) the Khazars encountering *Arabs* in battle, while the reference in Frutolf is to a conflict between Khazars and *Avars*. This slip goes back as far as Anastasius, who either misread Theophanes' *Arabōn* ("Arabs") as *Abarōn* ("Avars") or emended it to the latter reading.[171] Landulphus reproduced the incorrect reading,[172] as did Frutolf after him.

It is strange that Anastasius should have changed the Turks' enemies from Arabs into Avars—to an Italian author of the ninth century, the Arabs were a familiar enough nation. Moreover, Anastasius translates Theophanes' narrative word for word, and at this point in the story the Arabs are seldom far from center stage. It is easier to understand why the wrong reading made sense to the German Frutolf. The Avars, who occupied lands around the Middle Danube in the sixth century and in the eighth century had engaged in bitter struggles with Charlemagne's Franks, were still remembered in eleventh-century Germany. It seems likely that Frutolf selected only this passage from Theophanes on the Khazar "Turks" precisely because it seemed to associate them with a people who were once close neighbors of, and so might be of interest to, his Bavarian readers.

While this incorrect detail assured the anecdote's inclusion in the chronicles of Frutolf and Otto, still, important information was lost. The Turks appeared no longer as Byzantium's allies against the Arabs, Christendom's greatest foes, but instead as the opponents of a tribe more usually associated with eastern Europe—participants, as it were, in a local Scythian dispute.[173] This was precisely how Aeneas interpreted the story when he repeated it in his *Europa;* here, he explained that the Avars whom Otto described in conflict with the Turks were none other than the Hungarians—thus suggesting that Hungary, universally regarded as the *antemurale Christianitatis* by fifteenth-century crusade propagandists, had been defending Europe from the Turks for over six centuries![174] After this battle with the Avar-Hungarians in the eighth century, Aeneas concluded, the Turks retreated back into the Caucasus and then moved south to invade Asia. To describe how these events unfolded, he turned to a third and final source, the treatise on the origins of the Turks written for him in 1456 by the humanist scholar and diplomat Niccolò Sagundino.

Sagundino, a Greek émigré who spent most of his life working in the Venetian civil service, first in colonial administrations in the Aegean and later as an ambassador to the Italian courts, was personally familiar with the Turkish situation.[175] Born in 1402 in the Venetian colony of Negroponte, he was working in Thessalonica, another Venetian possession, when the city was captured by the Turks in 1430. He and his family were held prisoner for a year. Once freed, he returned to Negroponte and continued to serve Venetian interests; he worked as an interpreter at the Council of Florence-Ferrara in 1438–1439 and was then appointed apostolic secretary by the Venetian Pope Eugenius IV. After Eugenius's death in 1447 he again returned to Negroponte and Venetian service. In 1453 he joined the Venetian legation sent to negotiate trading privileges with Mehmed II after the capture of Constantinople. He then returned to Italy and continued to travel on missions between Venice, Rome, Naples, and the East until his death in 1464.

In the spring of 1456, Sagundino was in Naples at the same time as Aeneas Sylvius, who as bishop of Siena had traveled to the Aragonese court to try to resolve a dispute between the citizens of his episcopal see and King Alfonso.[176] Aeneas stayed in the city for four months. It was during this time, and apparently at his request, that Sagundino composed his treatise on the origins and early history of the Turks.[177] The text enjoyed considerable popularity in the fifteenth and sixteenth centuries, being printed once in the 1470s (in Poland) and copied in numerous manuscripts.[178] In 1503 the owner of one such copy, Marino Sanudo, tried to interest Aldus Manutius in printing the text, although no Aldine edition ever appeared.[179] The text eventually found its way into several sixteenth-century compilation volumes on Turkish history, where later historians praised Sagundino for his erudition and elegant style.[180] The information which Aeneas Sylvius quoted in his own works, to which the discussion here is limited, became even more widely known.

The character and quality of Sagundino's treatise have never really been properly assessed. Babinger expressed high regard for the text, identifying it as the first European attempt at a survey of Ottoman history—a judgment that most later students of Renaissance literature on the Turks have accepted.[181] Although it probably is the first self-contained work on Ottoman history produced in the Latin West, Sagundino's treatise offers very little information on the Ottomans' origins and the careers of the early emirs that Filelfo, for instance, had not already presented in his letters to Wladyslaw III (1444) and King Charles VII of France (1451). On certain points Sagundino's account is actually less accurate than Filelfo's. Babinger's prejudice against Filelfo ran deep, however, and he seems to have resisted crediting him with any original or accurate research into Turkish history.

Pertusi, too, saw great value in the treatise, detecting in it evidence of both Sagundino's firsthand knowledge of Turkish affairs and important borrowings from the Byzantine historian Laonicus Chalcocondyles.[182] Chalcocondyles's history of the Ottoman Empire, written in Greek, certainly did contain more information on early Turkish history than was yet known in the Latin West, but recent scholarship has shown that he completed his work at least thirty years after Sagundino, who cannot be credited with introducing his findings to Europe.[183] Moreover, there is very little in Sagundino's short, somewhat vague, and entirely polemical account to compare with Chalcocondyles's more thorough researches. Schwoebel, finally, recognized the tendentious nature of Sagundino's work, but he still saw it (or rather, Aeneas's commissioning of it) as evidence of a new and healthy interest among the humanists after 1453 in obtaining reliable information about the Turks—an approach reminiscent, Schwoebel argued, of the investigations into barbarian ethnography made by classical historians like Herodotus.[184]

In fact, Sagundino's treatise reproduces an entirely conventional humanist view of the barbarian origins of the Turks, which owes more to well-worn clichés about the habits of earlier Scythian peoples than to his own direct observation or historical research. Furthermore, Sagundino did not compose his history completely independently. His account of Turkish origins closely resembles Aeneas's own earlier comments on the subject. We know Sagundino wrote his treatise at Aeneas's request. It seems he also wrote precisely what the bishop of Siena wanted to read.

Sagundino starts with an account of the Turks' primitive origins. He describes the rootless, lawless existence they led in the Scythian plains around the River Don, their primitive habits, and their resemblance to the modern-day inhabitants of the area, the Tartars. He cites no source for these descriptions, which probably derive from the ethnographic accounts of Herodotus or Ammianus Marcellinus (who specifically located the homeland of the Huns "around the Don" and described their nomadic life, exceptional horsemanship, and ignorance of law) rather than from direct observation of the modern Turks.

For his account of the earliest events in Turkish history, Sagundino probably relied on the accounts in Theophanes (or one of his later Byzantine or Latin followers) describing the Khazar Turks' emergence from Scythia through the Caucasus in the seventh and eighth centuries. Once again he cites no specific source. According to Sagundino, the Turks were still living in Scythia "more than six hundred years ago"—a vague figure which, if we take it at all literally (*ab sexcentis annis* could also simply mean a very long time ago), produces a date sometime before A.D. 856—within a century or two of Theophanes' notices on the Khazars. At this time, he says, the Turks left Scythia: "They migrated first through Pontus and Cappadocia, and then slipped gradually into the other neighboring regions [of Asia Minor]."[185] Sagundino does not mention the Caspian Gates or the Caucasus specifically, but the route he maps out for the Turks' expansion, from the Don to the Black Sea coastal region of Pontus and Cappadocia to its south, assumes a passage through just this territory. It was a common assumption among Byzantine historians (as it was, increasingly, among Western authors) that all Turkish peoples descended from the Khazars whom Theophanes described. (In Chapter 3, we will see how the eleventh-century chronicler Skylitzes, writing relatively accurately about the very recent arrival of the Seljuks from central Asia, was still convinced that their original homeland lay on the northern slopes of the Caucasus.) The influence of Theophanes' account was simply too strong to allow a Greek author to imagine that there could have been any other, later Turks who originated elsewhere.[186]

Sagundino's account of how the Turks spent the next five centuries after they "slipped gradually" out of Pontus and Cappadocia is remarkably vague, punctuated by few details regarding dates or places but emphasizing instead their treachery and avarice. The Turks achieved their conquests by stealth, Sagundino says, raiding and robbing their neighbors of vast amounts of territory:

> At first, these Turks tried to increase their strength in small groups in the manner of thieves, by undertaking some secret raids. And thereafter, as happens, a multitude of men of this same sort came together and, having taken possession of certain mountains and mountain passes which were conveniently located for launching raids, they so grew in strength and confidence that now they did not fear to compete openly and with equivalent force of arms with their neighbors over the possession of land. Finally, in the ensuing time, whether by the negligence of the Greeks with whom they were in contention, or by a certain destined inevitability and the variety of human fortunes, or by the authorization of the gods who had decided to bestow dominion on another people, their power grew so quickly (as all agree) that they conquered and brought under their sway not only Pontus and Cappadocia, but also Galatia, Bithynia, Pamphylia, Pisidia, both Phrygias, Cilicia, Caria, and all the territory known as Asia Minor, up to the shores of the Ionian Sea and the coast of the Greek [Aegean] Sea. Nor did they follow any one prince, but different groups of them, as if in factions, obeyed different leaders and various authorities. It was from this nation, about a hundred and fifty years ago, that a certain Ottoman . . . began to maraud about and plunder where he could.[187]

Sagundino goes on to recount the careers of Osman and his successors, still emphasizing their humble origins and treacherous methods of conquest. The lack of detail in his account of pre-Ottoman Turkey can be attributed partly to his misinterpretation of the real chronology of events. The ninth-century "Turks" of Scythia whom he mentions first are almost certainly the Khazars. But the Khazars never did intrude into Asia Minor itself, much less conquer Pontus and Cappadocia. Since Sagundino maintains that they did, however, he then has to account for what happened in the centuries between their arrival and the eventual occupation of all of Asia Minor by Turkish tribes—a process which, historically, began only after the Seljuk invasions in the eleventh century, and which was quite unrelated to the much earlier activities of the Khazars.

In Sagundino's mistaken view, the Turks had maintained a continuous presence in Asia Minor for over six hundred years. Because no historical source or tradition exists which might shed light on their activities in the area (no Turks were actually there), Sagundino must invent a history for them. Little wonder that he describes their conquest as slow and gradual, achieved by means so subtle and devious as to be almost imperceptible. Starting as bandits, occupying desolate places which no one else wanted, they managed to gather men and resources to support ever more ambitious campaigns of acquisition. Sagundino is at a loss to explain exactly how they achieved control of the entire region: divine will must have decreed it, or else that favorite humanist device, the "variety of fortune," made it so, or else the Greeks by their negligence allowed it. The Turks themselves certainly did not deserve such a prize.

The final state of events Sagundino describes—and which he implies was the culmination of these centuries of territorial conquest—saw various Turkish tribes, including the Ottomans, in control of various parts of Anatolia ("as if in factions"). But far from marking the high point of Turkish political achievement, the rather disordered patchwork of beyliks and emirates to which Sagundino refers was, historically, a step backward from a much more impressive political structure which Sagundino does not mention at all. The partitioning of Anatolia among a collection of Turkish "factions" came about only after the defeat of the Rum Seljuks by the Mongols in the 1240s. And this brings us to the real puzzle in Sagundino's account: his failure to mention the Seljuk Turkish Empire.

Sagundino skips over a long and important period of Turkish history—information which would have been familiar to any educated Greek. He neglects to mention the initial movement of the Seljuks out of central Asia and through Persia, their conquest of Baghdad and absorption of the Abbasid caliphate, or the catastrophic defeat they inflicted on the Byzantine army at Manzikert in 1071; nor does he acknowledge the subsequent century and a half when the sultanate of Rum encompassed almost all of formerly Byzantine Anatolia. These events were widely discussed in Byzantine histories of the period, recounted as essential background information to explain the disaster at Manzikert and the subsequent arrival of the Frankish crusaders.[188] But Sagundino passes over these events in order to dwell instead on the state of political anarchy in Asia Minor after the collapse of the sultanate of Rum and immediately before the rise of the Ottomans. His silence on these matters seems a deliberate misrepresentation of the facts: by passing over the Seljuks in silence, he can portray the Turks as a people who had remained until quite recent times in the deepest political obscurity. From their nomadic origins in the wilds of Scythia to their stealthy annexation of the whole of Anatolia, they had continued as an illegitimate, lawless, leaderless mob, who in their habits, appearance, and language had hardly progressed from their barbarian origins. At the conclusion of the treatise, he drives the point home with the familiar rhetorical truism that the rise of such lowly barbarians was an affront to the dignity of civilized nations:

> And so, reverend father, I have written this little work, which I confess is inelegant and slight and hardly worthy of you . . . From it one may easily grasp how swiftly, and in how quick a sequence of events that despicable and barbarous race, led by Osman, grew up from obscure and nomadic origins; to what end they have finally arrived; how many and how great their achievements; what lands they now hold and occupy; what peoples they rule over (unworthily and shamefully), whom they now threaten, and where they boldly plan to go next.[189]

Sagundino composed his treatise at Aeneas's request. Aeneas had already written several letters and orations making similar points about the barbarous origins of the Turks, their rapacious excursions out of the Caucasus, and their eighth-century occupation of Asia Minor. In his 1454 oration at Frankfurt, for instance, Aeneas claimed that after the Turks invaded Asia through the Caspian Gates in the time of Pepin (as he learned from Otto of Freising), "they have remained there ever since."[190] In his 1455 oration to Calixtus III, he even made a passing reference to the manner in which they had achieved their occupation ("In the time of King Pepin they migrated into Asia and *little by little* made that province subject to their rule"), which seems to anticipate Sagundino's more extensive account of their gradual (*sensim*) annexation.[191]

One wonders whether Sagundino knew much at all about the origins of the Turks before Aeneas asked him to produce an essay on the topic. He may have been prompted (or perhaps shrewdly decided) to produce a historical brief that perfectly agreed with Aeneas's own views on the subject. In his other works, Sagundino expresses little concern for the question of Turkish origins or history. The rest of his oeuvre—translations of ancient and patristic Greek texts, dialogues and essays on philosophical, theological, and rhetorical topics, and urbane *epistolae familiares* addressed to his wide circle of friends—reflects his interest in literary and philosophical issues rather than politics or history.[192] Some of these compositions do touch on Turkish affairs, but in a very different way from the approach he took in his treatise for Aeneas. In January 1454, for instance, shortly after returning from his mission to Mehmed II, Sagundino delivered a report on the current state of the Turkish empire to Alfonso of Aragon, in which he made no reference whatever to the Turks' barbarian origins.[193] Instead he presented a dramatic account of the fall of Constantinople (probably derived from one or more earlier eyewitness reports, since it repeats most of the standard catalogue of atrocities) and a fascinating sketch of the sultan's mercurial character, his emulation of Alexander the Great and interest in Roman and Greek history, his ill will toward Christendom, his sadism and sexual perversions, and his elaborate schemes for the conquest of Italy.[194] This portrait is executed with a great deal of imagination and rhetorical flair, and there are several stirring set speeches. The overall impression is of a classic Oriental despot, cruel but cultivated. Sagundino makes no attempt to establish the historical antecedents to Ottoman expansion or the national character of the conquerors; there is no mention of a Scythian pedigree. The Mehmed he portrays here is a barbarian, to be sure, but a very different sort of barbarian: Asiatic, decadent, despotic, and cruel, not northern, primitive, or unclean.

Other works of Sagundino's which may indicate an interest in Turkish affairs include two translations: one of Demosthenes' First Olynthiac oration, in which the orator warns the citizens of Athens to beware Philip of Macedon's aggression from the East,[195] and the other of a spurious ancient Greek oracle on the destruction of the Hexamilion wall guarding the isthmus of Corinth. Sagundino prefaces this with an essay on the history of the wall, from its construction as a defense against the Persians in the fifth century B.C. to its renewal by Justinian against the Goths and its recent destruction by the Ottomans, remarking on the similarities between these various waves of "barbarian" invasion.[196]

These little-known works by Sagundino reflect a common humanist view of the Ottoman threat, in which the Turks are likened, by analogy alone, to earlier "barbarian" invaders (Persians, Macedonians, Goths). Sagundino's approach in these texts suggests that his modern reputation as an expert on Turkish history and culture has been somewhat exaggerated. The treatise he wrote for Aeneas was his only attempt to survey the Ottoman past, and it was based more on classical literary models and contemporary rhetorical clichés than historical fact and corresponds closely to his patron's own ideas on the subject.

Other humanist scholars in the late 1450s and early 1460s produced accounts of early Turkish history based on, or at least heavily influenced by, Aeneas's writings on the subject. As mentioned above, Nicola Loschi dedicated a poem to the pope in which he called the Turks a "Caspian" race and

Mehmed II a "Scythian boy."[197] In another poem, also composed to celebrate Aeneas's crusade, Bartolomeo Pagello neatly summarized the whole humanist narrative of Ottoman origins, from Scythian beginnings to marauding through Asia, crossing the Hellespont, and capturing Constantinople. Remarkably, he squeezed all this into just eight economical lines.[198] Several poems in the collection of *Epaenetica* written for Aeneas during his papacy also repeat these motifs.[199] Yet another set of verses, describing his efforts to launch a crusade and sometimes paired with the poetic version of the spurious letter addressed to him by "Morbisanus," has been ascribed to Aeneas himself, a questionable attribution.[200] The author of the poem, in an apostrophe directed to God, describes the pope's efforts against the Turks; he also recasts Aeneas's familiar historical arguments against their Trojan ancestry in verse.[201] Another poem, written in the same vein and also attributed to Aeneas—but likewise more apt to have been composed by someone seeking to celebrate his dedication to the crusading cause—rehearses his account of the Turks' emergence from Scythia into Asia.[202] Humanist scholars writing to Aeneas about the Turks may have decided it was simply prudent to echo his own ideas about their historical origins. Ludovico Carbone, for example, in his wedding oration for Zarabinus Turchus, showered the groom with praise and remarked in particular on the Trojan origins of his supposedly Turkish ancestors. Significantly, Carbone acknowledged that on a previous occasion, in an oration before the pope, he had rejected the idea that the Turks could be Trojan; but, he explained, he had done so only to please the pontiff (*utque pontifici blandiri voluerim*) and had since changed his mind.[203]

After his election to the papacy, Aeneas compiled little new information on the origins and early history of the Turks. In his crusade appeals and geographical works, even in a description of his own papal coronation, he essentially reproduced his earlier account, still relying on the information he had found in Aethicus, Otto of Freising, and Sagundino.[204]

In the oration with which he opened the Congress of Mantua in 1459, for example, Aeneas rehearsed the origins of the Turks in order to show how their violent force had accelerated the spread of Islam: "A great many Christians remained in Asia up to the time of Pepin, king of the Franks . . . At that time the Turks came out of Scythia and occupied Cappadocia, Pontus, Bithynia, the Troas, Cilicia and all of Asia Minor, and having grown powerful thanks to our negligence, not only drove true Christians out of Asia, but crossed the Hellespont in boats and invaded Macedonia, Thrace, Attica."[205]

The date, "in the time of Pepin," comes from Otto, while the list of prov-

inces conquered is derived from Sagundino. Aeneas also seems to have
accepted the larger ideas implicit in Sagundino's vague and misleading account of how the Turks conquered Asia. He, too, makes the Turks seem a far
older enemy than they actually were, suggesting that they began their assaults on Christendom in the eighth century and continued them, without
interruption, for six hundred years, culminating in their occupation of European territory in the mid-fourteenth century. He likewise follows Sagundino
in refusing to give the Turks ("who thanks to our negligence amassed their
power") real credit for these achievements.

In his geographical treatises, *Europa* and *Asia*, Aeneas repeats his account
of Turkish origins a further three times. As befits the more discursive and descriptive style of these works, he quotes all three of his authorities on early
Turkish history—Aethicus, Otto, and Sagundino—at greater length than he
had done in any previous composition, giving particular emphasis (in emulation of his main classical model for the works, Strabo's *Geographia*) to the
information from Aethicus and Sagundino on Turkish habits, mores, and
culture. In *Europa*, he mentions the Turks in an early chapter devoted to the
countries of eastern Europe. After describing the topography and peoples of
Hungary, Transylvania, and Thrace, he rehearses the Turks' eighth-century
emergence from Scythia and conquest of Asia, then describes their more recent activities in the countries under consideration, especially their capture
of Constantinople (included here as the capital of Thrace) and their unsuccessful attack on Belgrade in 1456.[206]

In *Asia*, Aeneas repeats his account of Turkish history twice more. He does
so first in an early chapter on the peoples of Asiatic Scythia, ancient and
modern, where he sets Aethicus's description of the primitive Turks' unclean diet and Sagundino's account of their lawless brigandage alongside descriptions of ancient barbarians like the Massagetes and Amazons as well as
more recent invaders, including Huns, Goths, and Lombards.[207] At the conclusion of the treatise he repeats the story again, this time in an account of
the geography and history of Asia Minor. The description of Asia Minor actually takes up more than two thirds of the whole treatise as it survives—
Aeneas clearly considered it the most important of the areas of the continent
he had yet surveyed.[208] It is significant, then, that he concludes both the description of the province and this section of the work itself with yet another
rehearsal of the origins and early history of the Turks. Once again he stresses
their barbarous origins, arguing particularly vehemently against the possibility of their Trojan ancestry, and the lawlessness with which they had pur-

sued their conquests since the time of Pepin. He then carries the story of the
Ottoman emirs forward to the reign of Mehmed II, before ending with a
long lament for the Christian relics and classical monuments of Asia which
have been lost to the terrible onslaught of the Turks.[209]

To construct a Scythian past for the Turks, Aeneas Sylvius, Filelfo, Biondo,
and Sagundino relied on a common set of texts and methods. All four differ
from most of their humanist contemporaries in that when they set out to
represent the Turks as barbarous enemies of civilization, they did so by presenting what seemed a true, historical account of the Turks' origins, identifying their genetic forebears rather than simply likening them by analogy
to notorious barbarian invaders of ages past. In order to substantiate their
historical accounts, they quoted references to *Turci* from various medieval
sources: the *Suda;* Theophanes' *Chronographia,* whether in the original Greek
or in Anastasius's translation; Otto of Freising's world chronicle; and the
apocalyptic *Cosmographia* of Aethicus. They pieced these together to form a
coherent (or at least coherent-seeming) sequence of events in Turkish history, from primitive origins in Scythia, to invasion by way of the Caucasus
in the seventh, eighth, or ninth century, to the subtle and treacherous occupation of Asia Minor and the emergence of Osman (himself a subtle and
treacherous figure) in the early fourteenth century.

That these scholars knew of and were willing to refer to these medieval sources at all may seem remarkable, given the prejudice that fifteenth-
century humanists are often assumed to have held against "barbaric" post-
classical texts. The assumption is not without merit: Aeneas himself once
famously denounced medieval chroniclers as "ignorant," their work "a clob-
ber of nonsense and lies, without attraction in form, in style, or in serious
reflection," and advised the young student to steer clear of their worthless
tales.[210] The prudent scholar should stick to the more reliable authorities of
antiquity. Indeed, the way Aeneas and his fellow humanists manipulated
the material they found in their unlikely sources suggests that even though
they were happy to extract and repeat their references to early *Turci,* they
were not entirely comfortable with the way medieval authors presented this
information.

For the humanists, good history writing had to be authoritative, elegant,
and plausible all at the same time. For political reasons, humanists writing
after 1453 also wanted to show the Turks in as poor a light as possible.
The operations they performed on their source material reveal that they

pursued all four objectives simultaneously. Aeneas edited the fantastic text of Aethicus so that it read like an ancient geographical authority, toning down—but not completely—the outlandish details of the original text. Likewise, he and Filelfo described the Turks' emergence through the Caspian Gates in the eighth century in a way that hinted at an association with the legendary unclean tribes enclosed behind Alexander's prophylactic gates, but did not make the fabulous identification explicit (although Biondo, an exceptional case, did precisely that). Filelfo and Sagundino revived ancient commonplaces regarding the primitive diet and nomadic customs of Scythian barbarians and applied them to the medieval Turks as though they wrote on the strength of direct evidence concerning the Turks, when they almost certainly possessed no such thing. Biondo and Filelfo extracted information from Theophanes on military maneuvers by the Khazar Turks in the Caucasus while obscuring the positive context in which that information appeared in Byzantine historiography. Filelfo, Sagundino, and Aeneas all made it clear that the Turks, after their eighth-century emergence into Asia, could claim no subsequent political or cultural achievements of note; all pointedly ignored the existence of either the Great Seljuks or the Seljuks of Rum. The four authors focused most of their attention on the earliest appearances of Turks in the historical records they found—in keeping with prevailing preferences for ancient over more recent history, but also in order to attribute to the Turks the longest possible history of violent, anti-Christian behavior. But they passed over in silence the question of the Turks' more recent and impressive political history, and thus were able to argue that even the contemporary Turks were a backward, uncivilized, and illegitimate race.

CHAPTER **3**

In Search of the Classical Turks

The Italian humanists imagined themselves, indeed declared themselves, to be classical scholars—readers, writers, and critics of the texts of classical antiquity. Thus it is somewhat surprising to see how extensively they relied on medieval sources (both Byzantine and Western European) when investigating the prehistory of the Ottoman Turks. The willingness of scholars like Aeneas Sylvius, Filelfo, Biondo, and Sagundino to accept the testimony of monastic chroniclers, apocalyptic visionaries, and somewhat muddled encyclopedists and geographers suggests a broader and perhaps more open-minded approach to their medieval heritage than we have come to expect.

But this point carries two important provisos. First, the humanists were willing to accept information on the Turks from medieval texts—but only if it could be used to present them in a negative light. No matter how loudly the humanists may have trumpeted each new and obscure discovery, their concern was never to uncover all the information available, for they undertook their research for political and polemical reasons, not scholarly ones. Their selective and subjective approach can be illustrated by two brief examples, which we will examine next: one of the earliest references to Turks in Byzantine history, which was positive and which the humanists suppressed; and a contemporary tale celebrating a similar instance of Persian piety, which they eagerly accepted.

Second, the lure of antiquity was powerful. The humanists were willing to accept information on the Turks from medieval texts, but they still preferred earlier sources (provided, of course, that those sources were disparaging to the Turks) to later ones, no matter how unlikely their provenance. In the historical excurses examined in Chapter 2, we saw the humanists straining to push the barbarian Turks ever further back into ancient history—to the era of Justinian, of Jerome, of Augustus —often on the flimsiest historical grounds. This impulse grew yet more powerful among humanists in the generation after Aeneas Sylvius. By the 1470s, philological researches into the texts of ancient geographers began to yield important clues—or so their humanist readers imagined—to the whereabouts of the Turks in antiquity. As in previous cases examined thus far, powerful contemporary impulses (not just a political belief in Turkish barbarity but also, increasingly, a typically humanist concern for scholarly reputation) determined how the next generation of historians uncovered, read, and interpreted their sources.

Two Conversion Tales: Tattooed Turks and a Christian Queen

Humanist historians had access to one very early notice on the Western Türks (it was well represented in medieval chronicles) but chose to ignore it. They seem to have disregarded this account because, despite its antiquity, it directly contradicted their polemical model of the early Turks as barbarous infidels.

The story concerns a group of Western Türks presented to the emperor Maurice in A.D. 591 because they had Christian crosses tattooed on their foreheads. First recorded in the seventh-century *Histories* of Theophylactus Simocatta,[1] a slightly shorter version of the tale is reported by Theophanes. According to both authors, these Turks were prisoners of war sent to Maurice by the Persian Chosroes II during a brief alliance which the two had formed in order to oust the usurper Bahram from Persia.[2] Theophanes reports: "[588/589] . . . The Turks were sent to the emperor in Byzantium. The Turks had on their foreheads the symbol of the cross tattooed in black, and when asked by the emperor how they came to have that sign, they said that many years earlier there had been a plague in Turkey,[3] and some Christians among them had suggested doing this and from that time their country had been safe."[4]

Like Theophanes' several references to the later Khazar "Turks," his notice on the tattooed Turks was translated into Latin in the ninth century by Anastasius Bibliothecarius and copied verbatim by Landulphus Sagax in the early 1020s.[5] It was also repeated by the Benedictine chronicler Sigebert of Gembloux,[6] although in a slightly different context. Landulphus followed Theophanes in dating the incident to the late sixth century, but Sigebert moved it to a later date, appending it to one of Theophanes' later entries on the Khazar Turks under the year 762.[7]

This transposition somewhat obscures the importance of the story as one of the very earliest extant reports on "Turks" in Greek and Latin literature. Nevertheless, the tale did not disappear from view. Sigebert's *Chronica* was one of the most influential historical works of the entire medieval period.[8] His most celebrated reader, Vincent of Beauvais, repeats Sigebert's account of the tattooed Turks almost word for word in his *Speculum historiale,* placing the entry under the year 762 and citing Sigebert as his source.[9] The Venetian Andrea Dandolo, writing in the middle of the fourteenth century, also seems to have liked the story. He repeated it twice in his *Chronica extensa,* probably under the influence of two separate sources. First, under the year 591, he tells the story much as Theophylactus and Theophanes do, adding comments on the Turks' Caucasian homeland and descent from the Trojan Turcus,[10] though his precise source is unclear. By contrast, there can be no question that when he repeats the story, under the year 761, he is following Sigebert and Vincent of Beauvais.[11]

Nevertheless, despite the relatively wide diffusion it enjoyed in medieval historiography, Theophanes' notice on the tattooed Turks found little favor among Italian humanist historians. I have discovered no humanist text that repeats the story.[12] It did, however, continue to circulate in histories written in the scholastic tradition: for instance, the *Chronica* of Antoninus of Florence—the very antithesis of a humanist historical text.[13] Like his fellow Dominican Vincent of Beauvais, Antoninus wrote his chronicle as part of a much larger scholastic encyclopedia, treating the history of the world as one of many areas in which divine wisdom may be discerned.[14] It is a conservative work, relying almost exclusively on the compilations of earlier ecclesiastical chroniclers and showing little critical intervention beyond a rigorous organization of information into sacred and secular categories.[15]

Antoninus almost certainly took the story of the tattooed Turks directly from Vincent of Beauvais.[16] The story's appearance here may imply that Antoninus saw in it some special manifestation of divine will, or it may simply illustrate his method of compilation, rejecting nothing his authorities had thought fit to preserve.

Antoninus copied the story into his *Chronica* sometime in the 1450s—a decade when concern over the Turkish threat dominated Italian political discourse, oratory, preaching, and literature. He himself, as archbishop of Florence, led legations to Rome to pledge his city's support to Calixtus III and Pius II for their respective crusade projects. He was deeply engaged in the contemporary political debate over the Turkish threat.[17] But this involvement seems not to have influenced his scholarly activities: in his *Chronica,* he included without comment a story that portrayed the early Turks as a people marked by naive but powerful respect for the central symbol of the Christian faith. He was followed in this by the Carthusian world-chronicler, Werner Rolewinck.[18]

The positive light which the story could cast on the primordial Turks is almost certainly what led humanist historians of the period to exclude it from their discussions of Turkish origins and early history. Arguments from silence are impossible to prove, but given the widespread diffusion of the story in medieval historiography and its repetition by a respected and prominent Florentine author in the 1450s, it seems likely that contemporary historians like Filelfo, Biondo, Aeneas Sylvius, and Sagundino would have encountered it at some point. In the version reported by Theophanes, it provided evidence for the Turks' activities in the late sixth century, fixing them at a date earlier than almost any other extant historical source. Even in the later chronicles, which moved the story forward to around 762, the entry is still roughly contemporaneous with the notices on the Khazars that Biondo and Aeneas Sylvius cited explicitly as proof of the Turks' barbarian origins and that seem to have led Filelfo and Sagundino to reach similar conclusions.

By way of contrast, we can track the fortunes of another Asiatic conversion story, also rooted in the early Byzantine chronicle tradition, which Italian humanists *were* inclined to repeat. In this tale, significantly, it is not primitive Turks but a Persian queen who embraces the Christian faith.

Platina, in his *Lives of the Popes*, reports that in the year 683, during the reign of Pope Vitalian (r. 657–692), a certain "Caesarea," queen of the Persians, made a secret visit to Constantinople. Her husband, the king of Persia, knew nothing of her trip:

> The queen was welcomed with honor by the emperor, and not long after she received the sacrament of baptism, for this was why she had come. When the king of Persia heard of this, he straightaway sent ambassadors to Constantinople to request that the emperor return his wife. But the emperor declared it was up to the queen whether she stayed or left; the question should be put to her. The queen replied that she would never return to her country unless her husband the king became a Christian. On hearing this, the king set out at once for Constantinople at the head of a peaceful throng of some 40,000 men. He was received warmly by the emperor and was baptised along with his men. Then he returned with his wife to his realm.[19]

Like the story of the tattooed Turks, this anecdote has its origins in the *Histories* of Theophylactus Simocatta. The Byzantine historian relates that Chosroes II, after Maurice helped him to oust Bahram from the Persian throne, exhibited first tolerance (*Histories* 5.1.7–8) and then genuine devotion (5.2.4) to Christianity: "Confessing that the Christ who is reverenced and honored among the Romans is the greatest God of all, [Chosroes] repudiated his former religion." Theophylactus makes no mention of his queen or her conversion, though other traditions identify Chosroes's wife Shirin or Sira (whose name may find a distant echo in the curious "Caesarea") as a Christian.[20]

It was Latin chroniclers who recast the story in the courtly terms that Platina repeats. Fredegar offers a lengthy account of Queen "Caesara's" clandestine visit to Constantinople, her baptism (with the Greek empress herself standing as godmother), the efforts of the king to retrieve her, and the subsequent conversion of the entire Persian nation. Fredegar dates this

Figure 7. Cesarea, queen of Persia. Hartmann Schedel, *Liber cronicarum* (Nuremberg: Anton Koberger, 1493), fol. 155r. Photo Warburg Institute, London

event around A.D. 587.[21] Paul the Deacon, in his *History of the Lombards*, tells much the same story, but, crucially, he transposes it forward to the reign of Constantine IV, Heraclius's son (r. 668–685).[22] Here the story takes on more urgent significance: the Persian monarchs accepted Christianity *after* Islam had spread to their domains.

This pleasing tale enjoyed some diffusion among medieval historians: authors from Bede and Gregory of Tours to Landulphus Sagax, Ekkehard of Aura, and Sicard of Cremona repeated the story of Caesara's pious journey to Constantinople, stressing that by her bravery and noble constancy the queen had ensured the conversion of the entire Persian nation.[23] It seems that Platina, writing in the late 1470s, took his version of the story directly from Paul the Deacon. Its polemical utility was clear. In a 1490 crusade oration delivered before Pope Innocent VIII, for example, the bishop of Cesena argued for a new crusade to Asia on the grounds that it was historically Christian territory: early Christians had sown the seeds of the faith in the East, and in 680, during the reign of Vitalian, the king of Persia had been baptized along with 40,000 of his subjects.[24] How could the popes have allowed that early flowering of the faith to wither? Now was the time to reclaim Persia for Christ. From Platina's *Lives,* the story was also picked up by the chronicler Foresti da Bergamo and through him made its way into Hartmann Schedel's *Nuremberg Chronicle.* There, the exploits of "Cesarea, Queen of Persia" were retold beside a woodcut portrait of the noble lady, resplendent with crown and scepter.

It was not until 1504 that an Italian humanist, Marcantonio Sabellico, expressed doubt about the story (though he, too, includes it in his world history). Perhaps the tale had migrated to the wrong century, Sabellico suggests, for after the Arab conquest there were no independent kings or queens of Persia, and even if there were, they would not have dared to convert, given the predominance of Islam in the region by that time. Or perhaps the exploit was attributed to the wrong queen. A queen of the distant Parthians (Huns? Mongols?) might have been able to embrace Christianity in the seventh century, Sabellico grants, but in Arab-dominated Persia such a move would have been impossible.[25] In adopting this skeptical stance, however, Sabellico (as in other cases) is the humanist exception and not the rule.

So we have two conversion tales: the tattooed Turks and the queen of Persia. Both concern Asiatic peoples who come to recognize the power of the Christian religion and who declare their devotion to the Greek emperor at Constantinople. In their medieval retellings, both tales migrated in time from the late sixth century to the late seventh, and thus came to seem to describe the continuing vitality of Christianity in Asia after the rise of Islam. As a result, both tales acquired a tinge of romantic fantasy, a whiff of wishful thinking. But only one found its way into humanist favor.

If humanist historians knew of the early notice on the tattooed Christian Turks—so early that in most circumstances it should have been highly valuable to them—then their rejection of it suggests that they carefully selected the kind of information they did choose to repeat to support a polemical contention. Humanists described the Turks as a primitive and unclean race, emphasized their origins behind the Caspian Gates made famous by association with Alexander, and documented (or, when necessary, invented) evidence of their later eruptions into and depredations in Persia, Media, Armenia, and Asia Minor. This enabled them to argue that the Turks had always been a frightening, ruthless, and untrustworthy race driven by greed for conquest.

But this narrative of origins did not apply to all Asian or even all Islamic nations. As the decision of Platina and his followers to accept the parallel tale of Caesarea suggests, it was entirely possible for humanists to imagine that other Eastern peoples were sympathetic to Christianity. Indeed, by the 1470s, when Platina wrote, a new dynasty had emerged in eastern Anatolia and western Iran (the Aqqoyunlu chieftains, hailed by European observers as resurgent "kings of Persia"), one that seemed poised to strike a blow against the Ottoman East and bring much-needed relief to beleaguered European interests in the Mediterranean. The Aqqoyunlu were devoutly Muslim, just like the Ottomans, but Italian humanist observers chose to play up their "Persian" identity instead (see Chapter 5). Here it is enough to note that the humanists embraced a historical anecdote that seemed to support their model of imperial Persia as a courtly and sympathetic ally in the struggle against unbelief while rejecting a closely similar tale that cast positive light on the ancestors of the Turks.

Theodore Gaza on the Caucasian Seljuks

By the 1470s, the theory of the Scythian origin of the Turks had achieved the status of orthodoxy among humanist historians. Scholars continued to investigate the question, following their predecessors in creatively interpreting and sometimes willfully misconstruing their sources. But this second phase of research was marked by a few differences as well. The next set of texts to be examined rely on different sources and were written for very different purposes from those produced in the decade or two after Constantinople's fall. Their authors—Theodore Gaza, the aged Francesco Filelfo, and Giorgio Merula—shifted their attention from medieval to classical sources in a series of (often improbable) attempts to locate Turks in the texts of ancient geographers. Interestingly, their aim was not to establish that the Turks were innately barbarous (each took it for granted that the Turks were originally primitive inhabitants of either Scythia or the Caucasus), nor did they aim to illuminate contemporary political events. In each case, the question of Turkish origins first arose in a discussion of Ottoman policy, but the argument quickly veered off in a more personal direction, toward demonstrating the author's command of ancient philology, geography, and history and thereby demolishing the scholarly reputation of a rival.

Over the course of the fifteenth century, as humanist scholars increasingly shored up their political advice with reference to hard-won bits of historical information, debates over the control of that information became fiercely contested. The origin of the Turks had become a topic worth having an opinion about—and worth defending. It was not just the future of Christendom that hung in the balance; academic reputations were also at stake.

Theodore Gaza wrote his treatise on the origins of the Turks (1472) as a polemical attack against an old intellectual adversary, the Platonist philosopher George Gemistos Plethon.[26] In order to rebut a passing remark Plethon had made some seven decades earlier about the whereabouts of the Turks in antiquity, Gaza introduced his Italian readers to an important Byzantine source for the history of the Seljuk Turks. In doing so, he acknowledged the historical relationship between the Seljuks and the Ottomans and the Persian milieu from which both had emerged—issues that earlier scholars like Sagundino, intent on portraying the Turks as Scythians without history, had either avoided or denied outright. But far from challenging conventional wisdom concerning the Turks' very earliest origins, Gaza interpreted his source in such a way that it ended up supporting the traditional belief that all Turks were barbarian plunderers from the Caucasus. He also introduced evidence from a classical source, arguing that a passage in Strabo's *Geographia* describing the peoples of the Caucasus, if interpreted in a creative (but not entirely convincing) way, included Turks among them.

Gaza's treatise takes the form of a letter to Francesco Filelfo, an old friend.[27] Gaza composed the work in Rome and addressed it to Filelfo in Milan, signing it with an ancient Greek date formula, which (in light of Gaza's own interpretation of the Greek calendar) should probably be resolved as 25 July.[28] There is no indication of the year, but it was almost certainly 1472: in a letter dated 1 July of that year, Filelfo asked Gaza why he referred to the Turks with the Greek form *Turkoi* when the Byzantine sources Filelfo knew used the spelling *Tourkoi:* "Besides these things, I would like some information from you concerning this: you always write *Turkos* and not *Tourkos*. What rule are you using when you write this? For I find your [Byzantine] writers always spell it not *Turkos* but *Tourkos*. You could look, if you wanted, at the *Suda*, which uses this form when it says *Bokamos, Tourkos*. So reply giving the reason for your spelling, and in doing so, do something pleasing to me. For it is a pleasant thing to be freed from ignorance."[29]

Gaza almost certainly sent his treatise on the origin of the Turks in reply. Although, as we shall see, he never addresses Filelfo's question directly in the work, toward the end he does explain why he thinks the spelling *Turkioi* (not *Turkoi*)[30] is closer to the original form of their name than *Tourkoi*. It is hard to imagine Filelfo asking his question had he already received this information.

Still, Filelfo's query is puzzling. Aside from the treatise examined here, Gaza hardly mentions the Turks in his extant writings. Most of these treat philosophical or philological matters; in those which do touch on contemporary events, such as the letter to the Byzantine emperor Constantine XI which he composed in Greek for Nicholas V in 1451, he refers to the Turks as *barbaroi*.[31] Gaza's two other extant letters to Filelfo contain no reference whatever to Turks.[32]

In his letter, Filelfo gives a hint of where Gaza used the form *Turkoi*. Filelfo thanks Gaza for a previous letter, dated 3 June 1472 (and now lost), in which he described the recent ceremonies in Rome celebrating the betrothal by proxy of Grand Duke Ivan III of Russia to Zoe Palaeologina, daughter of the late and last despot of Mistra, Thomas Palaeologus. Sixtus IV had officiated at the ceremony, which took place in St. Peter's and was attended by an array of distinguished guests.[33] In other extant accounts of the event, the betrothal is linked with the almost simultaneous departure from Ostia of the papal fleet, which Sixtus had assembled with the support of several Italian states in order to renew the war against the Ottomans in the eastern Mediterranean.[34] The two events, considered together, were regarded as promising signs of a renewal of Christian unity against the Turks. There was even talk that the grand duke might send his own army against them, approaching Constantinople overland from Moscow, through the country of the Golden Horde.[35] Perhaps it was in his lost letter describing the wedding that Gaza also referred to the Turks with the form *Turkoi*, which Filelfo found so curious.

Although Gaza sent his treatise in reply to Filelfo's query, he probably did not compose it for the occasion. The work is mostly concerned with the question of the origin of the Turks as a nation rather than the correct spelling of their name. Gaza's real purpose in pursuing the issue was to mount an attack on the conflicting statement about the origins of the Turks put forward by Plethon.

Gaza's enmity for Plethon had its roots in the long-running controversy over the relative merits of Plato and Aristotle which occupied so many Greek émigré scholars in Italy in the middle years of the fifteenth century.[36] Early on in the quarrel, Gaza aligned himself with his friend and patron Cardinal Bessarion, the defender of Plato, even though his own philosophical sympathies lay more with the Aristotelian view. But Gaza's loyalty did not extend to the more passionate Platonism of Bessarion's teacher, Plethon, who had made several virulent attacks on Aristotle, which prompted Gaza to compose, in 1459–1460, three polemical tracts defending Aristotle against Plethon.[37] Nor did Gaza confine his quarrels with Plethon to debates over philosophical matters. He also criticized him in his 1470 treatise on the Greek months, pointing out flaws in the plan Plethon had proposed in his *Nomoi* to reintroduce the ancient Greek calendar and its religious festivals. In short, Gaza's attack on Plethon's Turkish history was part of a general campaign of polemic which he pursued in a variety of scholarly arenas.

Despite the unconventional philosophical and theological views which Plethon expressed in the *Nomoi*—he wanted, it seems, to revive the paganism of the ancient Greek Neoplatonists—his ideas about the origins of the Turks were not particularly sensational. Sometime between 1407 and 1418, while resident in the Peloponnese, Plethon composed an oration "On Peloponnesian Affairs," addressed to Theodore Palaeologus, despot of Mistra.[38] The oration treats the topic of good government, with Plethon suggesting how Theodore should reorganize the administration of his territory and strengthen its defenses against enemies both domestic and foreign. Among these, the Turks pose a particularly urgent threat: "But most of all we are beset by these particular barbarians, our new neighbours, who have taken the greatest and best part of our dominions, these Paropamisidae of ancient origin, who were tricked and defeated by Alexander the son of

Philip and his Greek soldiers when he was on his way to India. Now, even so long afterwards, they still seek satisfaction from us Greeks, and having achieved power many times greater than our own, they plot against us on every occasion and threaten us with the ultimate penalty."[39]

The Paropamisidae whom Plethon calls the ancestors of the Turks inhabited the Paropamisus Mountains, the classical name for the Hindu Kush range, around Kabul and Nuristan in modern Afghanistan. Alexander the Great met the Paropamisidae in the course of his eastern campaign, while crossing the Hindu Kush from Arachosia to Bactria in the winter or spring of 329 B.C. Almost all the ancient historians of Alexander attest to this.[40] None of these sources, however, tell us much more about the Paropamisidae than that they were a primitive mountain people whom the Greeks barely saw as they passed through the mountains, since their low huts lay covered in deep drifts of snow.

Why did Plethon call these remote mountain people the ancestors of the Turks? Modern commentators have suggested that Plethon knew of and was making a classicizing reference to the Turks' true origins in the Altai Mountains of Mongolia. These are distant, but from a Westerner's perspective not all that distinguishable from the Hindu Kush.[41] But Plethon adds the detail that the Greeks "tricked and defeated" (*epibouleuthentes te kai kratēthentes*) these people, while the ancient sources indicate that the Paropamisidae were one of the few Eastern peoples whom Alexander left relatively untouched. It is more likely that when Plethon equated the Turks with the Paropamisidae, he intended to identify them with the wild tribes supposedly enclosed by Alexander behind the Caspian Gates.

Plethon would certainly have known the legend, which was as popular in Byzantine literature as it was in the West, and the tradition identifying contemporary threats to civilization like the Mongols and Turks as descendants of the ancient nations Alexander was supposed to have enclosed. But he probably also knew that the legend was historically impossible: Alexander never visited the true Caucasus between the Black and Caspian Seas and so could not have battled against any barbarian tribes who lived there. But he may have thought there was some kernel of historical truth to the story. Both Strabo and Arrian record that during the same campaign on which Alexander met the Paropamisidae, he or his followers began to call the Hindu Kush by the name "Caucasus." This was a deliberate attempt, these ancient authorities say, to associate Alexander with those gods and heroes of Greek myth who had also had adventures in the East, among them Prometheus,

Hercules, and Jason. Their exploits had taken place in the true Caucasus, and Alexander, despite having traveled much further afield, wanted to be known as an explorer of the same region.

By calling the Turks "Paropamisidae," Plethon was trying both to equate them with Alexander's legendary enclosed nations and to relocate those enclosed nations to a part of the world where Alexander was known to have campaigned. The story was that they had been locked up in the Caucasus, where Alexander had in fact never been; but since he *had* traveled through the Paropamisus (Hindu Kush) and had tried to rename it "Caucasus," Plethon concluded that the primitive people whom Alexander met in this false Caucasus—the Paropamisidae—were the historical inspiration for the legend of the enclosed nations. Thus, they could also stand for the ancestors of the Ottoman Turks.

The two main classical sources of information on the Paropamisidae and the false appellation of their country as the "Caucasus" were Arrian and Strabo. Plethon knew the relevant passages from both these authors. A manuscript in Vienna preserves a number of extracts Plethon made from classical authors early in his career.[42] The extracts include the passage in the *Anabasis* where Arrian gives his most comprehensive summary of the problem of the true and false Caucasuses and explains why the Macedonians began to call the Paropamisus by this incorrect name.[43] Plethon also took a special interest in the text of Strabo. In 1439 he wrote a short treatise on a section of Strabo's *Geographia* for the benefit of the Latins at the Council of Florence, as the work was almost unknown in the West at the time. The section Plethon chose to examine (2.5.12–32) includes a description of the eastern lands visited by Alexander and refers to the country of the Paropamisidae (2.5.32), although Plethon does not mention these people specifically in his commentary. He continued extracting, annotating, and commenting on the text of Strabo throughout his life, and so certainly knew the various passages of the *Geographia* in which Strabo, like Arrian, comments on the Greek practice of calling the Paropamisus by the name "Caucasus."[44]

Plethon's remark in his oration to Theodore was an attempt to historicize the legend of Alexander's enclosed nations. It was a neat rhetorical device to show the despot how longstanding the enmity which the Turks felt for the Greeks was. In addition, unlike some other invocations of the legend of Alexander's gates we have seen (in which the "enclosed nations" might be identified as Gog and Magog, or Hyperboreans, or simply "barbarian" or "unclean" races), Plethon's equation of the Turks with Paropamisidae had an air of classical authority about it.

Taking on this brief (one might even say throwaway) remark of Plethon's, Gaza composed a treatise in three sections. In the first part, he summarizes an excursus on the early history of the Seljuk Turks by the eleventh-century Byzantine chronicler Johannes Skylitzes.[45] In the second, he uses information gleaned from Skylitzes to launch his main attack on Plethon. In the third, he marshals further evidence from Skylitzes—and introduces an argument based on a creative reading of a passage in Strabo—to construct his own account of the origins and early history of the Turks. It is only at this point that he reveals the reason for his peculiar spelling of their name, which derives from his interpretation of these earlier authorities. Thus his idiosyncratic spelling also constitutes part of his attack on Plethon.

Gaza does not declare his polemical intent at the start of the treatise, nor does he mention Plethon's ideas about the Turks outright. He begins by noting that there is generally little agreement on the subject he is about to discuss, adding what may be a subtle dig at Plethon: "It is not at all easy to say who the Turks originally were, and from where they first emerged to occupy the lands they now inhabit; for those authors who have treated the subject before me do not describe the same events in the same way. And, because there is so little that is agreed upon, it happens quite frequently that even those things which are clear, even things about which there is no confusion whatsoever, are called into doubt."[46]

He then launches into a summary of Skylitzes's historical excursus on the Seljuks. Skylitzes (c. 1045–1110) wrote his *Synopsis historiarum* as a continuation of Theophanes' *Chronographia*, covering the period 811–1057.[47] His comments on the Turks appear in the book devoted to the reign of Constantine Monomachus (r. 1042–1055), but the events he describes cover a much wider range of dates, from the first appearance of the Seljuks south of the Oxus in 1026 up to their final conquest of Baghdad in 1059. Skylitzes wrote in the 1070s, shortly after the Seljuks' rout of the Byzantine army at Manzikert in 1071; it was to explain how this disaster had come about that he inserted into his text his brief survey of their origins and early history.[48]

The information Gaza found in Skylitzes gave a very different picture of early Turkish history—based on the Seljuks' rise to imperial power in eleventh-century Persia—from the vague account of anarchic brigandage which Sagundino and Aeneas Sylvius had proposed a few years before. Here at last was a historical source that shed light on the true forebears of the Ottoman

Turks and their political heritage in the medieval Middle East. But Gaza's knowledge of this material did not lead him to question the traditional account of the very earliest origins of the Turks. This was, of course, what Plethon had tried to do when he moved the Turks, as Alexander's "enclosed nations," from the Caucasus to a more historically probable location in central Asia. While Gaza ridicules the notion that the Turks had anything to do with Alexander the Great or the barbarian tribes he supposedly enclosed, one of his main objections to Plethon's theory is that it contradicts the evidence of ancient and medieval authorities, who place the earliest ancestors of the Turks in the Caucasus. He puts great trust in these sources (which, it must be said, contain confusing and sometimes corrupt information that could support such a reading. But his very conservative approach to these texts, as well as his determination to prove Plethon wrong, must also be factors in his interpretation.

For example, Gaza interpreted several passages from Skylitzes recording the historical movement of the Seljuk Turks from Transoxania into Persia as proof that they came from the Caucasus. He starts by quoting directly from Skylitzes (whom he calls "Skylax")[49]: "Skylax (a man whose opinion is by no means contemptible, despite his amateurish prose style) compiled a history of the emperors from Nicephorus of the Genicon to Isaac Comnenus, in whose reign he himself lived. He relates that the Turks were a Hunnish nation, who inhabited the northern slopes of the Caucasus mountains."[50]

Skylitzes probably based this claim on information from Theophanes' *Chronographia*—the text which he was continuing and which makes several references to the Khazar "Turks" in territory north of the Caucasus in the seventh and eighth centuries A.D., as we have seen. Next Gaza explains how the Turks descended from the Caucasus into Persia. At this point his source, Skylitzes, actually describes the arrival of the Seljuk Turks, not the Khazars, but he does not make the distinction clear. As a result, Khazar and Seljuk history appear seamlessly connected in the original chronicle, a conflation which Gaza reproduces.

The account of Seljuk history which Gaza borrowed from Skylitzes can be summarized briefly. During the reign of the Byzantine emperor Basil II (r. 976–1025), Gaza says, the ruler of Persia, a certain "Moamet, the son of Imbrael," was at war with both Babylon and India. To help him on these campaigns, Moamet sent an embassy laden with gifts to the "Lord of Turchia," who replied by sending three thousand Turkish archers under the command of a general called "Tancrolopix Mukalet, the son of Mikeel."

With the Turks' help, Moamet was able to defeat "Pissasirus, Lord of the Arabs" (the ruler of Babylon), but failed to convince his mercenaries to accompany him to India. The Turks then withdrew into the "Carbonitan Desert" and pillaged the Persian border country. Moamet pursued them with an army of twenty thousand men but could not persuade his soldiers to enter the desert. Then, in a surprise nighttime raid, the Turks seized the entire Persian supply train and set off in pursuit of Moamet himself, who was killed in flight. Immediately, Tancrolopix was acclaimed king of Persia. The remainder of the Turks (still in Turchia) then entered Persia, hailed Tancrolopix as their sultan, and went on to conquer "Babylon," "Arabia," and finally the Byzantine province of Media Atropatene.

It is possible to identify the historical events which this somewhat garbled account describes; in most cases, the confusion lies in the text of Skylitzes rather than Gaza's reading of it. Gaza's "Moamet," whom Skylitzes calls "Muchumet," is undoubtedly Sultan Mahmud of Ghazna (r. 998–1030), whose regime in Afghanistan and Khorasan was at this time reaching the apex of its power.[51] Historically, Mahmud led campaigns against both the Shiite Buyids of Baghdad ("Babylon") and the Hindu kingdoms of the Punjab ("India").[52] And it is a historical fact that during Mahmud's sultanate, the Seljuks first began to filter south from Transoxania into Ghaznavid territory in Khorasan, although the main thrust of their invasion occurred a few years after Mahmud's death. This happened in 1035, under the leadership of Toghril Beg Muhammad b. Mika'il b. Seljuq—Gaza's "Tancrolopix Mukalet, son of Mikeel," whom Skylitzes calls Tangrolipax.

The account Gaza found in Skylitzes of the Seljuks' arrival in and subsequent conquest of Persia contains much that is either incorrect or told out of sequence. The story that Mahmud received the Seljuks as a gift or loan from the "Lord of Turchia," for instance, is without foundation. The Seljuks' position in the lands beyond the Oxus had always been precarious: while members of the clan served a number of local Turkish princes in Transoxania as mercenaries and guardsmen, including Karakhanid emirs and the western Khwarazmshahs, most of these Turkish lords were hostile to Mahmud of Ghazna and could hardly have been persuaded to send him military aid. In fact, the Seljuks entered Persia as refugees rather than auxiliary troops, after various of their Turkish patrons were defeated by the Ghaznavids. They never served Mahmud in the way Skylitzes describes.

Moreover, Skylitzes says that the first thing "Muchumet" had his Turkish soldiers do was attack and overthrow "Pissasirius, Lord of Arabia." This is the Turkish general Arslan al-Basasiri, Shiite commander of the Buyid armies in Baghdad, a figure whom Mahmud, however, never fought. The conflict Skylitzes describes actually took place twenty years later, after Toghril had driven Mahmud and the Ghaznavids from Persia altogether and made his triumphant entry into Baghdad, where he was received by the Abbasid caliph in 1055.[53] Al-Basasiri, ousted by Toghril, eventually gathered an army and attempted to reclaim his position. In 1059, Toghril had him killed and thereby established his rule over the eastern caliphate for good.[54]

Skylitzes assigns the victory over Pissasirius to the period when the Seljuks were still serving Muchumet as auxiliary troops. Next, Muchumet decides to take his Turkish soldiers on campaign to India. The Turks grow fearful, refuse to follow him, and eventually withdraw into the "Carbonitan Desert"—probably the Karakum, south of the Aral Sea, territory where the Seljuks were in fact granted grazing lands after they crossed the Oxus.[55] Muchumet is furious; he sends some twenty thousand men against them under the command of ten "very noble" Saracen generals. After the Turks make a surprise attack, put the Persians to flight, and take possession of their baggage train, Muchumet's soldiers desert him and go over to the Seljuks' side.[56]

With his army growing ever larger, Tangrolipax decides on an open fight against Muchumet, who meets him with five hundred thousand troops and a hundred armed elephants, in a place called "Aspachan." There, in a terrible battle, Muchumet is killed and the Turkish leader is declared king of Persia. The decisive battle which Skylitzes describes actually took place a few years later, in 1040, at Dandanqan on the fringes of the Karakum Desert, with Mahmud's son Masud in command. Masud was not killed in battle, but he did flee to his lands in Afghanistan, leaving Toghril and his Seljuks in control of all Ghaznavid territory in eastern Persia; he was murdered by his generals in the following year. Skylitzes finishes his account with Toghril's acclamation as sultan—an event which actually occurred fifteen years later, in Baghdad.[57]

It is possible, then, to get to the real story that lies behind Skylitzes's account. But in telling his tale, he garbles so much of it, rearranging the chronology of disparate events and often conflating them with one another—perhaps out of sheer confusion, perhaps for the sake of a concise and dramatically interesting narrative—that very few useful details remain.[58] Especially problematic is his neglect of the sort of topographical details that might help to locate the story geographically. Skylitzes says, for example, that the "Lord of Turchia" was happy to send his archers to Muchumet, "because he was hoping that if his men could defeat the enemies of the Saracens, they would easily render passable the bridge across the Araxes—which was defended by high towers on both sides and guards everywhere and which therefore made access to Persia impossible for the Turks—by overwhelming the guards and so making the land of the Persians subject to him."[59]

There is certainly some truth to this story. A river did form a natural boundary between the Ghaznavid territories of Khorasan and the Seljuks and their Turkish patrons to the north, and the Seljuks did not enjoy free access to its southern bank. But this river was not the Araxes, which flows into the western side of the Caspian Sea south of the Caucasus, but the Oxus. It is not clear why Skylitzes refers to the wrong river. He may have genuinely believed the action took place on the Araxes, or he may have understood that the Seljuks crossed the Oxus but decided, since the events he next discusses happened in Persia, to shift the scene to a river in the Caucasus in order to fit better with his previous statement that the Turks originally came from north of those mountains. (The ambiguity arises from the fact that Skylitzes never specifies where the original land of "Turchia" is.) Finally, Skylitzes may actually have *meant* to locate the action at the Oxus River but simply called it "Araxes"—a misappellation with classical precedents. Aristotle mentions an Araxes River to the east of the Caspian Sea, by which he means either the Oxus or the Jaxartes.[60]

Perhaps more to the point, Herodotus also mentions an Araxes east of the Caspian Sea in his account of the Persian king Cyrus's campaign against the barbarian Massagetes. In order to reach them, Cyrus builds a pontoon bridge—interestingly, also fortified with towers—across a river which Herodotus calls "Araxes" but which is clearly the Oxus.[61] Rather than referring to any real bridge which the Seljuks wanted to cross, Skylitzes may have been trying to recall this classical story, casting "Muchumet" as another king of Persia with barbarian problems on the other side of the fortified "Araxes" bridge.[62] Whatever the source of Skylitzes's confusion, this one detail certainly made it possible for Gaza, centuries later, to locate the point of the Seljuks' invasion not in Khorasan, where it historically happened, but in the southern foothills of the Caucasus.

Other details in Skylitzes's account further obscure the location of the events he describes. He says the climactic battle between the Seljuks and the Ghaznavids, which actually took place at Dandanqan in eastern Khorasan, occurred in a place called "Aspachan"—most likely the Persian city of Isfahan.[63] The Seljuk prince Toghril Beg besieged Isfahan twice in the 1040s, captured it in 1050, and made it his capital for the last twelve years of his reign. In transferring the battle to Isfahan, Skylitzes compresses an important series of events, merging Toghril's early defeat of the Ghaznavids at Dandanqan with one of the final moves in his conquest of Persia, the capture of Isfahan, much farther to the west. In doing so, he makes it seem that this western city was actually the site of the Seljuks' first major victory.

Skylitzes gives a similarly ambiguous account of the final triumph of Toghril's career—his entry into Baghdad in 1055, when the city opened its gates to receive him and the Abbasid caliph acclaimed him as sultan and protector of the orthodox Sunni faith. Skylitzes describes this victory of Toghril's without mentioning Baghdad at all. Instead, he simply reports that Tangrolipax defeated Pissasirius, "Lord of the Arabs."[64] This title probably reflects the army of Iraqi Arab soldiers which al-Basasiri assembled while in exile from Baghdad and so is not entirely inaccurate. To a reader unfamiliar with these events, however, the scene of the early Seljuk triumphs would seem to have shifted once again westward, away from Iraq and toward the broader (if vaguely defined) land of "Arabia"—at the time, a term used by Latin Christians for the whole of the Muslim Middle East and Levant. Skylitzes concludes the excursus with an account of how the remainder of the Turks, whom Tangrolipax left behind in "Turchia" (the north Caucasus?), descended south across the "Araxes" to join him in Persia: "After proclaiming a triumph, and destroying the guard on the bridge over the Araxes, he [Tangrolipax] immediately opened the crossing into Persia for the Turks, and they all joined him . . . and having overcome the Persians and the Saracens, they made Persia their own."[65]

The text of Skylitzes, whether accidentally or intentionally, made it possible to interpret the whole story of the Seljuks' rise to power as taking place much farther to the west than it actually did. They seem to have started out as subjects of a "Lord of the Turks" in the northern Caucasus, not in Transoxania; they entered the Middle East by crossing the Araxes, not the Oxus; they defeated Muchumet not at Dandanqan near the Karakum Desert but at Isfahan in the heart of Persia; their defeat of al-Basasiri did not win them Baghdad but was a victory over all of Araby. In reading Skylitzes, Gaza seems to have made precisely these inferences. To conclude this part of his treatise, he summarizes the history covered so far: "Therefore, the Turks, as Skylax says, came out from the Caucasus Mountains, defeated the Arabs and then ruled over the Romans [that is, Byzantines]."[66]

In the second part of his treatise, Gaza launches his attack on Plethon's theory, namely, that the Turks were Paropamisidae from the Hindu Kush. He begins by quoting Plethon's own words from the oration to Theodore: "But Gemistus Plethon, who in our own times has claimed for himself a knowledge of history exceeding that of all others, says that the Turks are the same as the Paropamisidae who were tricked and defeated by Alexander the son of Philip and the Greeks who were accompanying him on their way to India; and who have now come back, after so many years, to exact their revenge on the Greeks."[67]

Gaza wonders how the two authors he has examined—Skylitzes and Plethon—can disagree so completely. He understands the confusion that arose in antiquity concerning these two mountain ranges and suggests (correctly, I think) that the ancient practice of calling the Paropamisus "Caucasus" inspired Plethon's statement. Gaza still prefers the text of Skylitzes, however, so no matter what the explanation for Plethon's statement is, there is no question in Gaza's mind that he is wrong:

> For it is clear that by "Caucasus," Skylax did not mean the mountain in India which the Macedonians absurdly called by that name—which is in fact part of the Taurus range—but rather that mountain which rises between the Pontic [that is, Black] and Caspian Seas . . . which is more than thirty thousand stades distant from India. This is what he means when he uses the name "Caucasus." The Paropamisus, by contrast, is part of the Taurus range, close to the Imaus range and India, and it was from this mountain that the Macedonians, as Aristobulus says, invaded India.[68]

Plethon's claim seems completely improbable to Gaza. The true Caucasus, as everyone knows, rises east of the Black Sea, while the association of the Paropamisus with the name "Caucasus" was a novelty introduced by the Macedonians. Since Gaza trusts Skylitzes completely, he cannot imagine that he would have used the name "Caucasus" in such a late and corrupt sense. Authority counts for a great deal with Gaza, as he goes on to show. He marvels that Plethon should be so sure that the Turks are Paropamisidae, when no one else has ever called them such, or equated them with any other race from that part of the world, or even suggested that they passed through the Paropamisus from an original homeland located somewhere else. From what secret source did Plethon find this information? How can he be so sure that Skylitzes, writing four hundred years before him, was wrong, and how did he, so many years later, happen to light upon the truth? "This idea of Plethon's seems wholly unbelievable, a statement aimed more at impressing his audience than describing the truth."[69]

Indeed, Gaza continues, Plethon's theory hardly makes sense. Again he takes the facts in Skylitzes's story as given and criticizes Plethon's account for failing to square with them. If, he says, Skylitzes really did mean to say that the Turks came from the Hindu Kush, how can this be reconciled with his later statement that "Moamet" sent ambassadors to a ruler there (of all places!) to seek help for a campaign against India? Clearly, Skylitzes's story can make sense only if the true Caucasus is meant.[70] And Plethon's association of the Turks with Alexander the Great seems equally far-fetched: it would be amazing, Gaza comments, if a tribe defeated by Alexander should retain the memory of it and still burn with a desire for revenge more than eighteen hundred years after the event. If this were the case, should not the Persians and Bactrians and Sogdians—all of whom Alexander was known to have conquered—also now seek revenge from the modern-day Greeks? There is no evidence in the ancient sources that Alexander ever fought against, tricked, or defeated any people in the Paropamisus. Had he done so, Gaza concludes, such a feat would surely be mentioned somewhere. This last remark is a potent criticism of the legend of Alexander's enclosed nations, although we may wonder whether Gaza is perhaps being deliberately disingenuous in claiming he has never heard of this particular exploit of Alexander.[71]

After dismissing Plethon's remark equating the Turks with the Paropamisidae, Gaza concludes his tract with his own reconstruction of the origins and early history of the Turks. Though he wholeheartedly agreed with Skylitzes, who said that the Turks had their origins in the northern Caucasus, he apparently felt it necessary to produce an older authority than this Byzantine historian in order to clinch the matter. In the last part of his treatise, he advances a new theory, based on evidence from Strabo as well as further details in Skylitzes, which identifies the Turks as the descendants of the *Kurtioi,* a people known to have inhabited the mountainous parts of northern Media (that is, northern Iran, some way southeast of the Caucasus) in antiquity.

Earlier in the text, at the conclusion of his summary of Skylitzes, Gaza noted two passages in the Byzantine chronicle which could support this identification. Both describe attacks made by Abbasid caliphs against the Byzantine frontier in the ninth century; both mention in passing a people called *Kourtoi.* In both cases, the reading *Kourtoi* is probably no more than a scribal error for *Tourkoi*. But Gaza believed the name was a valid variant form, as he explains: "Skylax also calls these people *Kourtoi*. For he relates that the Amermoumnes [Amir al-Mu'minin, "Commander of the Faithful"—the Abbasid caliph al-Mu'tasim] sent at least ten thousand *Kourtoi* to his son, together with the entire army of Armenians, when Theophilus was still emperor; and again, [he says] that messengers returned to Basil from Mesopotamia, leading with them many captive *Kourtoi* and Saracens."[72]

The first passage cited from Skylitzes describes an expedition by al-Mu'tasim against the Byzantine frontier during the reign of Theophilus (r. 829–842); his army included ten thousand soldiers whom Skylitzes calls *Kourtoi*.[73] In his description of the subsequent battle with Theophilus, however, Skylitzes describes the deadly showers of arrows fired by the "Turks" (*Tourkoi*) of this same contingent; this juxtaposition is probably what led Gaza to assume that the two names were synonymous. But the reading *Kourtous,* is actually quite doubtful. There is no record of such a people outside of Skylitzes. Thurn, the most recent editor of the text, notes that even most Skylitzes manuscripts have *Tourkous* instead, and this is the reading he adopts. The choice makes sense in light of Skylitzes's subsequent references to *Tourkoi*. The reading *Kourtous,* on the other hand, introduces a hitherto unknown people, who then have to be considered the same as the *Tourkoi* mentioned immediately afterward.[74] The other reference to *Kourtoi* in Skylitzes may be more reliable. During an eastern campaign led by Basil I in 878–879, the Byzantine armies take large numbers of captives, including Saracens and *Kourtōn,* most of whom Basil puts to death.[75] Thurn accepts the reading *Kourtōn* at this point, although he notes two manuscripts which read *Tourkōn* here as well.[76]

Gaza maintains that the name *Kourtoi* is genuine and that they are the same people as the *Tourkoi*. He then draws a further connection between these *Kourtoi* and the ancient *Kurtioi*. Strabo mentions these people twice in his *Geographia* as nomadic raiders dwelling in the mountainous regions of Media.[77] Thus, Gaza argues, if the *Tourkoi* are really *Kourtoi*, and the *Kourtoi* are actually Median *Kurtioi*, then the Turks have been resident in Media since antiquity and cannot have migrated from the Paropamisus, as Plethon claimed. In arguing all this, Gaza uses a variety of historical, geographical, and philological arguments—and not a little textual obfuscation:

It seems to me, therefore, that the information from Skylax is more believable [than that given by Plethon] and also agrees better with the text of the geographer Strabo. For Strabo says that the northern parts of Media Atropatene, which are mountainous, rugged and hard, are home to the Kadusioi, a mountain people, as well as the Amardoi, Tapuroi, Kurtioi, and other similar peoples who he says are nomads and plunderers; and that the Zagros and the Niphates mountains keep these peoples scattered far and wide, so that the Kurtioi and Amardoi, who live in Persis, are of the same character as those who live in Armenia.[78]

Strabo, as Gaza's citation clearly shows, said that the *Kurtioi* of Media were *similar in character* to other mountainous peoples, such as the nomadic tribesmen of Armenia.[79] Gaza interprets this statement more broadly and asserts that the *Kurtioi* actually inhabited Armenia as well as Media. After moving the *Kurtioi* on these rather tenuous grounds northwest from Media to Armenia, he then argues that Armenia is really part of the Caucasus: "Therefore the *Kurtioi*, as Strabo says, inhabit not only the mountainous part of Media Atropatene, but also Armenia. Now, certain spurs of the Caucasus range, reaching down to the south, encompass central Iberia [Georgia], and extend down as far as the related ridges of the mountains of Armenia. It is not beyond reason, therefore, to suggest that the *Kurtioi* who once lived in Armenia are identical with those people whom Skylax says occupy the northern parts of the Caucasus and whom he calls *Kourtoi* and *Tourkoi*."[80]

It is for this reason, we discover at last, that Gaza spells the name of the Turks *Turkioi* instead of *Tourkoi*, the usual Greek spelling of the name. It is to emphasize his identification of the Turks with the *Kurtioi* of ancient Media (or, as he would have it, of Media, Armenia, and the Caucasus) and thereby to signal his rejection of Plethon's theory that they came from the Paropamisus.

Throughout his treatise, Gaza repeatedly invokes Strabo as an important authority; in several places he also relies on the geographer without mentioning him explicitly. He cites information from Aristobulus on Alexander's campaign in the Paropamisus—a topic treated in only one extant fragment of Aristobulus, preserved in Strabo.[81] And when casting doubt on Plethon's statement that the Paropamisidae were tricked and defeated by Alexander, Gaza copies several lines from Strabo's text on the Paropamisus verbatim, without citing Strabo as his source.[82] Finally, when discussing how the name of the ancient *Kurtioi* changed into the more familiar *Tourkoi*, Gaza turns to the text of Strabo once again. Here he draws an analogy between this onomastic corruption and that of another Asian tribe, the *Aineianoi*, who lived by the Hyrcanian Sea and were later known to the rest of the world, Gaza says, as the Huns.[83] Strabo is the only ancient source to describe the *Aineianoi*. But neither he nor any other geographer, as far as I know, links the historical *Aineianoi* with the Huns—the genealogy seems to be Gaza's invention. His theory is based on more than just the similarity of their names. Strabo locates the *Aineianoi* in the southern foothills of the Caucasus around the mountains of Armenia and notes that like their neighbors, they are warlike plunderers rather than farmers (*ethnē lēistrika kai makhima mallon ē geōrgika*).[84] Gaza construes the relationship between the *Aineianoi* and the Huns as parallel to that which he posits between the *Kurtioi* and the Turks— a wild tribe of antiquity, inhabiting the southern fringes of the Caucasus and renowned for its savage ways, whose original name became corrupted after later, far-flung campaigns of conquest.

Gaza had been studying Strabo's *Geographia* with some attention before writing his treatise. He owned a complete and rather famous copy of the Greek text, a manuscript bought by Ciriaco d'Ancona in Constantinople in 1447 and brought to Italy, where it was divided into two parts and given, by order of Pope Nicholas V, to Guarino of Verona and Gregorio Tifernate to translate into Latin.[85] Gaza acquired the two codices after the translations were completed, in the late 1450s.[86] A decade later he helped Giovanni Andrea Bussi, editor for the early Roman printers Sweynheym and Pannartz, prepare his edition of Guarino and Tifernate's translation, presumably using his knowledge of Greek to correct the versions made by the Italian scholars.[87] It may have been at this time that he extracted from the text the information on the *Aineianoi* and the *Kurtioi* which he used in his treatise on the origin of the Turks.[88]

By the early 1470s, Gaza enjoyed some renown in Italy as an authority on Strabo. But he had a rival. The first Greek scholar to explicate Strabo's text to the Latin West had been none other than Plethon. Manuscripts containing his extracts and commentaries on Strabo's text traveled to Italy after his death c. 1454, and some ended up in the possession of Gaza's friend and patron Cardinal Bessarion.[89] There is evidence that at the same time that Gaza was working on the text of Strabo for Bussi in the late 1460s, other Greek émigré scholars were taking a similar interest in the *Geographia* and in particular in the extracts in Plethon's manuscripts. In Rome in 1467, a friend and former student of Plethon made a series of extracts from one of Plethon's autographs of Strabo.[90] And Bessarion, in the act of donating his library to Venice in 1468, kept his three copies of Strabo—including the one which was originally Plethon's—back for his private use until his death; he had another Greek scholar make copies from these in 1470.

This minor flurry of activity around the text of Strabo in Rome in the late 1460s may allow us to see Gaza's treatise on the origins of the Turks in a slightly different context from that associated with most contemporary works on Turkish history. Rather than investigating the origins of the Turks in order to make a political point about their innate barbarity or evil intentions toward Christendom, Gaza sought out information on them from earlier sources in order to attack the theories of an intellectual rival. It is significant that Plethon was widely considered the best contemporary source of texts from and commentary on Strabo. Gaza may have thought it would be particularly wounding to attack Plethon using a classical text on which he was reputed to be the foremost modern authority. He may even have hoped to overthrow Plethon from his posthumous position of authority in the Roman scholarly community, using the treatise to present himself as the more reliable and expert interpreter of Strabo's text.

In the final section of the treatise, Gaza adds a few more arguments to show that the Caucasus was the original homeland of the Turks. He notes that Byzantine sources record other "Turks" inhabiting areas north of the Caucasus. They are more likely to have migrated to those territories from the Caucasus itself than from the Hindu Kush: "Thus, it would also be reasonable to assume that those Turks who live around the Danube migrated there, during the reign of Leo, across the so-called Cimmerian Bosporos from the Caucasus, and not from the Paropamisus. For Skylax also locates some Turks in Pannonia, near to the Danube. He clearly puts some Turks in Asia, and some in Europe; he says that Leo, the son of the emperor Basil, sought help against the Bulgars from the Turks and Hungarians who were living beyond the Danube."[91]

Skylitzes's Danubian "Turks" are actually Magyars, who occupied territory on the Danube in the ninth century and whom the Byzantines called on for help against the Bulgars. Because of their perceived kinship with the Khazar "Turks" (a relationship much debated in modern scholarship), they were often called *Tourkoi* in Greek sources.[92] By taking the Magyars to the Danube by way of the Cimmerian Bosporos, Gaza may be trying to associate them with those earlier *Tourkoi,* the Western Türks, who captured the Crimean city of the same name in 576, as recorded in the *Suda.* Gaza either does not know or chooses to ignore the distinctions between these peoples. He assumes that all the Turks mentioned in earlier Byzantine historiography are the same people, and he suggests that the history of this one people can be reconstructed by stringing together their various appearances in the historical record, whether these locate them in Europe or in Asia.

His argument can be summarized as follows. According to Gaza, Strabo put the ancestors of the Turks in the southern Caucasus (Strabo in fact meant the *Kurtioi,* who had nothing to do with the Turks—or the Caucasus, for that matter). Skylitzes, on the other hand, put the Turks in the northern Caucasus (Skylitzes, relying on Theophanes, was probably referring to the Khazars). Later on, some Turks went north out of the Caucasus by way of Cimmerian Bosporos (here Gaza may refer to the Western Türks, who actually came directly west from central Asia when they attacked the city). They then migrated to the Danube, where they helped Leo the Wise against the Bulgars (these "Turks" were Magyars, who followed the westward path of the Western Türks across southern Russia toward the Danube in the ninth century). Gaza acknowledges that Skylitzes mentions other Turks in Asia (here he means the Seljuks), but far from suggesting that they came from the Hindu Kush, Gaza argues that Skylitzes's text shows that they came from the northern Caucasus, entered Persia by crossing the River Araxes (the name he used for the Oxus of central Asia), and thereafter invaded Byzantine Anatolia. The original homeland of both the European and the Asian Turks, Gaza concludes, must lie somewhere between the western and eastern extremes of their conquests, and this territory can only be the Caucasus.

Gaza ends the treatise with a last (and fairly weak) attempt to show how this one Caucasian race could have been known by three different names (*Kurtioi, Kourtoi,* and *Tourkoi*), this time arguing on philological grounds. He suggests that the *Kurtioi* became *Kourtoi* as part of a general shift in Byzantine orthography which saw *u* replaced everywhere with *ou.*[93] Later, Greek-speakers inverted the consonants in the name, turning the *Kourtoi* into *Tourkoi*—either because the name sounded better that way or because they heard the name pronounced this way by the Turks themselves (a suggestion which, if true, would undermine his whole argument!). With this point, Gaza concludes his treatise: "So after they had lived a long time among one another, and grown used to one another, it happened that those whom the [ancient] Greeks called *Kurtioi,* they [the Byzantines] called *Turkioi* and not *Kurtioi.* And so for this reason we too write *Turkioi,* or, when we wish to contract it, *Tourkoi.* Let us conclude, therefore, that these are the same as the *Kurtioi* whom Strabo says lived as nomads and plunderers around Media and Armenia, and not the Paropamisidae as Plethon believes."[94]

It is only in these closing paragraphs that Gaza addresses directly the question of the spelling of their name, the subject of Filelfo's original question. The cursory treatment he gives to the problem suggests that Gaza wrote the bulk of his treatise before receiving Filelfo's letter. He probably added these last few sentences in order to make clear the connection between his theory about the Turks as Caucasian *Kurtioi*—the real subject of the treatise—and his use of the spelling *Turkoi,* which puzzled Filelfo. If the date I propose for the treatise, 25 July 1472, is correct, Gaza would have had around three weeks (or less, allowing time for Filelfo's letter of 1 July to travel from Milan to Rome) to prepare the work. It seems likely, then, that the major part of his treatise consists of research done over a longer period of time, undertaken for the purpose of rebutting Plethon's statement that the Turks were Paropamisidae from the Hindu Kush and thus scoring another point against the older scholar's reputation.

Name Games

What did Filelfo make of all this? The Italian scholar seems not to have acknowledged Gaza's treatise at all. Filelfo had made his own researches into the early history of the Turks, and so far as the authentic form of their name was concerned, he could claim the *Suda* as a fairly early authority for the spelling *Tourkoi.* He may have found Gaza's theory that the Turks were descended from the ancient *Kurtioi*—and so should be called *Turkioi*—unconvincing. Or he may have kept his thoughts to himself because Plethon had been a friend of his.[95] Whatever the reason, Filelfo never mentioned the treatise in any later letters to Gaza nor, with a single exception, in any other later works.[96]

The only evidence that Filelfo even knew Gaza's work dates from about eight years later, when he was caught up in a humanist quarrel with the Alessandrian humanist Giorgio Merula.[97] The issue was once again the correct way to spell the name of the Turks. Filelfo and Merula argued over a completely different set of texts from those Gaza drew on in his treatise. Perhaps the best evidence for Filelfo's opinion of Gaza's work is how little he relied on it, even in a contest where it could have provided valuable ammunition.

Compared with Gaza's treatise, the argument between Merula and Filelfo is even less concerned with any political or historiographical debate over the origins and innate character of the Turks. It was a purely philological quarrel, and a particularly nasty one at that. Merula, a former pupil of Filelfo, had kept up an amiable correspondence with his teacher throughout the 1470s.[98] But in the summer of 1480, Filelfo wrote a letter to the Venetian patricians Bernardo Giustiniani and Francesco Diedo in which he derided Merula for calling the Turks *Turcae* instead of *Turci*—in his opinion, the correct form of their name.[99]

Merula's use of the form *Turcae* for the Turks seems to have been a recent stylistic decision. In his *Bellum Scodrense,* an account of the Turkish siege of the Albanian city of Scutari, or Shköder, from May to August 1474, Merula mostly uses general terms such as *hostes* or *barbari* for the Ottomans; in the three places where he refers to them by name, he calls them *Turci.*[100] By 1480 he had changed to *Turcae:* in a later letter in the controversy (12 December 1480), Merula proudly mentions using the latter form in some recent letters about Turkish attacks on Rhodes and Calabria.[101]

Mehmed II's siege of Rhodes began on 23 May 1480 and was raised on 28 July. On this same day, a separate Ottoman force landed in southern Italy and besieged the city of Otranto; it fell on 11 August, and the Turks retained possession of it until the summer of 1481.[102] So Filelfo must have taken exception to an account of these doings of the "Turcae" written by Merula sometime in the summer of 1480. Filelfo, too, had written about the capture of Otranto—possibly in his crusade exhortation of 13 September 1480. His words were to supply Merula with a pretext for broadening the quarrel: Merula countered Filelfo's criticism by attacking him in turn, not only for misspelling the Latin name of the Turks but also for misconstruing the classical names and locations of the places they were attacking.

The first surviving document from the quarrel is Merula's letter to Bartolomeo Chalco of 7 October.[103] Here Merula rejects the charges Filelfo had made in his letter to Giustiniani and Diedo, producing the ancient geographer Pomponius Mela as his authority for the spelling *Turcae:*

Francesco Filelfo, whose tongue is as unrestrained as it is unlearned, has criticized me very bitterly in a certain letter to . . . Bernardo Giustiniani and Francesco Diedo, because in writing to you I called the Turks *Turcae* and not *Turci.* Filelfo is too petulant—or should I say reckless—unless in his old age he has gone senile. He condemns a word which the ancient geographers use . . . Let my censor read Pomponius Mela, who puts a race of *Turcae,* much given to hunting, near the Euxine Sea and Maeotic Lake.[104] Nor does any rule of declension stand in the way; for *Turca* will be inflected like *Scytha,*

Geta, Dalmata and many another word of that ending. I, relying on the authority of the ancients, call nations and peoples by their original names.[105]

Filelfo replied to this argument in a letter dated 12 November, which he addressed to another third party, the Venetian Benedetto Aliprando,[106] who had written to Filelfo with a warning about Merula's attack. Filelfo starts by reassuring his friend, airily dismissing his former student and his abilities as a scholar:

Have you perhaps forgotten the Greek proverb, "He who spits at the sky gets spit in his beard"? Surely the Indian elephant pays no heed to the gnat, nor the nightingale to the crow? In fact, I have always considered that Alessandrian George, or rather that *Chezergius*,[107] to be rather dim; but now I find him foolish and demented as well, as he shows himself ungrateful to the man under whose tutelage he has achieved some reputation for himself.[108]

Filelfo then proceeds to the main point of his argument: his spelling (*Turci*) is not only correct but also supported by none other than Pomponius Mela. Merula, he insists, either misread the ancient geographer's text or relied on a corrupt copy:

He says that I reproach those people who say *Turcae*, in the first declension, when they ought to be called *Turci*. The mangy schoolmaster lies and says he has found a race of *Turcae* in Pomponius Mela . . . But the text of Pomponius Mela, near the end of the first book, reads verbatim as follows: "The domains of the Amazons contain plains fertile with grass but in all other things barren and empty. The Budinoe live in Gedomon, a city built of wood, while nearby the Thyssagetoe and Turcoe inhabit vast forests and live by hunting." Surely the *Turcoe*, spelled with the diphthong *-oe*, are to be called by us *Turci*, just as the *Thuscoe* become *Thusci* and the *Italoe, Itali*, and other names of this sort. Now, why don't we find all [Greek] names written with the same diphthong?[109] I believe this is the fault of copyists; for we see that almost all singular Greek names obey the same rule observed by Pomponius, for example *Peloponesos, Rhodos, Chios.*[110]

The argument here is very weak. The tribal names recorded by Mela are in fact first-declension nouns (*Thyssagetae, Turcae*), nor are any variants noted in modern critical editions to support Filelfo's contention that they belong to the second declension. Mela, writing in Latin, does sometimes use *-oe* to represent the Greek ending -*oi* for certain ethnonyms, just as -*ae* was used, far more commonly, to represent Greek -*ai*.[111] But the particular names *Thyssagetae* and *Turcae* are never spelled this way. It is unclear what manuscript of Mela Filelfo consulted. It seems likely that he is offering his own conjectural emendation here, rather than an authentic reading from an otherwise unrecorded textual tradition.[112]

To support his claim further, Filelfo employs arguments of varying flimsiness: many singular Greek toponyms, he says, are second-declension nouns (and so, presumably, all plural ethnonyms should be). Those tribal names which do appear to be of the first declension are actually corrupt, the products of scribal error, when confused copyists substituted the more familiar ending -*ae* for -*oe*. Next Filelfo offers some analogies, but rather oddly, he does not cite any of the commonly accepted nouns ending in -*oe* which *are* to be found in Mela's text—some of them quite near the passage in which the Thyssagetae and Turcae appear. Instead he proposes the forms *Thuscoe* and *Italoe*, which are almost certainly impossible.[113] Finally, Filelfo plays what he believes is his trump card. Hinting at firsthand knowledge of the Greek books bequeathed by Cardinal Bessarion to Venice, he announces that the proof that his spelling is the correct one is to be found among them: "But why should I bother to argue any further? If anyone is in doubt about the matter, let him seek out the Library of St. Mark, where he will find not only Scylax, who thoroughly describes the lives and deeds of the emperors, from Nicephorus to Isaac, to the one called Comnenus, but all the books of Cardinal Bessarion; [in these] he will come across—not *Turcae* in the masculine gender—but everywhere *Turci*."[114]

Filelfo is of course right in saying that Byzantine authors uniformly refer to the Turks as *Tourkoi*, a second-declension noun. But his suggestion that he is personally familiar with Bessarion's library seems rather dishonest. It is most unlikely that Filelfo ever saw a copy of Skylitzes in the Biblioteca Marciana. (Bessarion's books, bequeathed to Venice in 1468, had all arrived in the city by 1474, but access to them was extremely difficult to obtain.)[115] Instead he simply copied out the description of Skylitzes's work which Gaza had included at the start of his treatise of 1472 ("a history of the emperors from Nicephorus of the Genicon to Isaac Comnenus"), assuming that the manuscript of the work Gaza had used in Rome was part of Bessarion's collection and so would now be in Venice. Though correct, the argument is built on devious premises. The passage at least provides proof that Filelfo had received—and read—Gaza's work.

Merula got sight of Filelfo's letter on 30 November.[116] He then wrote another letter in reply, this one addressed to his fellow Alessandrian Johannes Jacobus Chilinus, dated 12 December 1480.[117] Here Merula just about demolishes Filelfo's arguments for the spelling *Turci* instead of *Turcae:*

> He [Filelfo] has tried to corrupt sound manuscripts; for he says that the word *Turcae,* with an *-ae* diphthong, is not the correct reading in Pomponius Mela, but rather *-oe,* making it the nominative plural of the Greek word *Turcos* [that is, *Tourkos*], and that spellings of this sort were commonly used by our [Latin] writers. You blockhead Philepsius, how can you so boldly, and ignorantly, quibble over a true reading as if it were a false one? . . . You say: "The rules of Greek declension are on my side"; but they are, rather, on the side of Merula. For the names *Tissagetae* and *Turcae* were spelled by the Greeks with *-ai,* as in *Basternae, Massagetae, Piangitae, Tentyritae, Tyrragetae* and *Tanaitae.* Do you want more, you ignoramus Philepsius? *Exobigitae* and *Nigritae.* All these names of races and peoples were written with the diphthong *-ai* by the Greek authors whom you accuse, and we see them transcribed in our language with *-ae.* But anyone who argues that the nominative plural of those nouns which appear in Greek in *-os* are inflected with the diphthong *-oe* unwisely entangles himself in difficulties. This is a form which is not only never found, but which even uneducated boys would scarcely dare to say in jest . . . *Turcoe* and *Tissagetoe,* spelled with *-oe,* are plainly neither Greek nor Latin words.[118]

Although Merula is wrong to say that the ending *-oe* never appears in Latin, the gist of his argument is correct: Filelfo invented the reading *Turcoe* in Mela and used faulty logic to support it. To clinch the matter, Merula then reveals that a second classical authority also preserves his spelling: Pliny the Elder.[119]

Merula touches only briefly on Filelfo's appeal to Greek sources, offering no counterargument but a forceful attack *ad hominem* instead: "But if anyone is in doubt about these [the names as they appear in Mela and Pliny], let him go to the Greek exemplars, and let him examine them more carefully than did that gaping great white arse, who is by far the most stubborn of schoolmasters, more obstinate than combative in his opinions; for he does not know how to fight, nor can he defend himself. He was always a slave to sloth and licentiousness, a preceptor of frivolous learning, more often a groper of harlots than books."[120]

Merula's point is not entirely clear, but we can be quite sure that, like Filelfo, he never actually examined a manuscript of Skylitzes. He seems instead to assume that Greek sources will repeat the spelling he has found in Mela, and it is Mela whom he regards as the very best authority for the word: "He is amazed at me, or rather he berates me, for speaking of a race of *Turcae*. Why, I ask? Have I departed from the truth of history, or put forward a new and unfamiliar word? Or have I expressed, like a paraphraser, the sense of Pomponius in words other than his own?"[121]

The extent to which Filelfo and Merula rely on the testimony (real or imagined) of ancient authors to support their arguments—as opposed to, say, later medieval histories, prevailing current usage, or the testimony of travelers, traders, or diplomats in direct contact with the Turks—reveals something fundamental, and not very attractive, about their quarrel. It was not really about the Turks at all, nor were their appeals to ancient texts part of any attempt to define the historical or political character of the contemporary people.[122] Each was mostly concerned with asserting his command of ancient authorities. The other orthographical points the two raised in the course of their quarrel demonstrate how far they were diverted, while ostensibly trying to discuss important political events of the day, into philological quibbling.

Merula, for instance, accused Filelfo, "this master of inappropriate invention,"[123] of committing several other toponymic infelicities when discussing the Ottoman threat. He had used the medieval Latin form *Scutrium* for the Venetian colony of Scutari in Albania (besieged by the Turks in 1474) instead of the ancient form *Scodra*.[124] And he called Otranto (then under Turkish occupation) *Hydrotum*, not *Hydrus or Hydruntum* (as attested in Pliny) and, even more egregiously, referred to it as a city on the border between Apulia and Calabria, when in fact, as not only Pliny but any modern-day sailor knew, the city lay deep in southern Calabria.[125] Filelfo tried to retaliate: "Merdula," the "dung-dropping little turd," was an untrained grammarian, who was clearly unable to understand how Filelfo had interpreted Pliny and whose arguments were weak and unconvincing.[126] In his second letter, Merula crowed that he had corrected the ignorant and puffed-up pedant, who had dared to contradict "the opinion of the noble geographers":[127] "How drunk was the man when he wrote those things? What was he dreaming? How blind he is, not even aware of where in the world he once lived and is now living! You whores who share his bed, wake up your Philepsius! . . . Let me just add here, in order to instruct little boys and the old man alike, that the word is declined *Hydrus, -druntis*. Believe me, the man did not read his Pliny."[128]

Filelfo and Merula's quarrel over how to spell the name of the Turks illustrates a key aspect of the humanist debate about Turkish history. Historical events—the Ottoman attacks on Scutari in 1474 and Otranto in 1480—prompted all four points which the two disputed: the correct Latin spelling of the name of the Turks, of Scutari, of Otranto, and of the province to which it belonged. Both authors had written letters or tracts discussing these Turkish incursions and the serious threats they posed to Italy.[129] Yet ultimately each man was less interested in debating the best political or military course of action that Christian Europe should take than in demonstrating that his own command of ancient history, geography, and philology was beyond reproach. Filelfo had once touted his expertise in Turkish history while offering his services to crusading princes north of the Alps; now, in order to defend the value of his findings, he had to prove his expertise in Latin philology against that of a rival in a contest for the attention and approval of Italian bureaucrats.

This concern with identifying the very earliest and most authentic references to modern-day peoples and places highlights one last problem in the quarrel: the weakness of Filelfo's response. Filelfo, having challenged Merula's usage, had at his disposal a lifetime of reading into the history of the Turks which he could have drawn on to support his claim that they were *Turci* and not *Turcae*. He could have cited the entry on *Bōchanos Tourkos* which he had found in the *Suda* decades earlier, or the many references to *Turci* he had found in Byzantine and medieval Latin chronicles; he could at least have discussed in greater depth the references to *Tourkoi* which Gaza sent him from Skylitzes. It seems the only reason he did not is that he was completely confounded by Merula's discovery of a different spelling in such an *early* source, Pomponius Mela—the first classical testimony of the name to be identified in the Renaissance.[130]

In Italian humanist discourse, debating the particulars of Turkish prehistory started out as a rhetorical device—*anasceua*, the demolition of one theory in order to reinforce the statement of another. But in the early years, at least, it was a device pressed into the service of real policy debates. Aeneas Sylvius may have played fast and loose with his medieval sources, but he and his followers constructed their histories in an effort to persuade European leaders to launch a crusade against the Turks. Throughout the 1470s, Ottoman assaults on European territory continued, as did European attempts to repel them. The epoch-making alliance between Russia and the last of the Palaeologan dynasty and the Italian defense of Otranto against Turkish occupation were both events of enormous importance. The humanists who wrote about these events continued to follow in Aeneas Sylvius's footsteps, uncovering new (and ever earlier) sources that put the Turks either in the barbarous plains of Scythia or on the lawless slopes of the Caucasus. But as we have seen, they also tended to lose sight of the larger picture, getting lost in the details of their quarrels as they defended their reputations as classical scholars, to the neglect of other contemporary concerns.

What, in the end, should we make of the humanists' Scythian researches? Compared with the popular notion that the Turks were resurrected Trojans, humanist attempts to reconstruct a Scythian past for the Turks certainly sound more historically plausible, more like the results of proper historical inquiry. Rather than repeating a well-worn but improbable tale of Trojan exile, the humanists argued for the Turks' Scythian origins on the strength of earlier texts that referred (or seemed to refer) to Turks in Scythia and the Caucasus at various moments in ancient and medieval history. And they attempted, as those who toyed with the idea that the Turks were avenging Trojans did not, to account for the movements and activities of these Turks between their supposed origins in ancient Scythia and their most recent conquests in Anatolia, the Mediterranean, and eastern Europe. However tendentious, defamatory, and inaccurate their accounts of these events may have been, the humanists did at least try to retrace the course of Turkish history over the centuries. Moreover, when they identified the Turks as classical Scythians, they revived certain classical ethnographical categories to describe them, treating such topics as how the early Turks ate, lived, traveled, and waged war. All this suggests that the humanists were interested in and sensitive to the possibilities of reconstructing a full and accurate history of the Turkish people in a way that those who fancifully called them Trojans, or indeed, those who saw them only through the prism of religious difference, as "blasphemous infidels," did not.

Still, we should not credit the humanists with too much critical judgment or even curiosity in their discussions of the origins of the Turks. Their accounts of Turkish history relied largely on literary commonplaces derived from earlier descriptions of Scythian barbarians. The discovery of Caucasian or Scythian "Turks" (*Tourkoi, Turcae,* even *Kurtioi*) in classical and early medieval texts certainly provided compelling support for the idea, but the humanists could provide no evidence for the activities of these "Turks" between their early appearances in these regions and the eleventh-century conquest of Asia Minor by the Seljuks—because none existed. No text or tradition indicated a connection between the Khazar "Turks" and the Seljuks and therefore between them and the Seljuks' political heirs, the Ottomans. The humanists had to invent a history—usually a vague account of continuing barbarous obscurity—to account for the activities of the supposedly Scythian Turks in the later Middle Ages. At the same time, they passed over in silence the most notable aspect of all medieval Turkish history: the rise and rule of the Seljuks. Even Greek scholars like Niccolò Sagundino and Theodore Gaza, who had access to Byzantine accounts of Seljuk history, largely neglected the record of the Seljuks' political, military, and cultural presence in Asia Minor.

Moreover, Byzantine chronicles were not the only sources available to Renaissance historians for the history of the Turks in the Middle Ages. Latin chroniclers of the High Middle Ages, from William of Tyre to Vincent of Beauvais, preserved a great deal of information on the Seljuks, including the story of their migration west from Transoxania through Persia and into Asia Minor in the eleventh century and their political hegemony in the Middle East until the time of the Mongol invasions. This information could have helped the humanists construct a more accurate account of both the Turks' central Asian origins and their political history from the eleventh to the fourteenth century. Most notable is the account in William of Tyre's *Chronicon,* composed around 1184, a history based on the author's own experience in the Latin East as well as on several Greek and Arabic histories to which William had access in the royal library at Jerusalem, where he was chancellor of the Latin Kingdom. William's excursus on Seljuk history is comparable, in terms of accuracy and level of detail, to the account given by Skylitzes, and his history enjoyed enormous circulation in Western Europe in the thirteenth and fourteenth centuries.[131] In the next century, Vincent of Beauvais copied into his widely studied world chronicle a report by a missionary to Asia, Simon of St. Quentin, which includes extensive notes on the Seljuk Turks in Iraq and their Turkic cousins in the central Asian interior. Later still, Marco Polo (and his later emulator, "Sir John Mandeville") recorded the presence of Turks in eastern territories beyond Persia, either in "Turquie," north of the Oxus, or "Turquestan," west of Cathay.[132]

It is possible that the humanists simply did not know these medieval accounts that reveal the true, central Asian origins of the Turks and acknowledge the political achievements of the Seljuks in western Asia. It is impossible to prove that they read but rejected them. On the other hand, since they seem to have assumed from the start that the Turks were savage barbarians, we can say that they were well disposed to accept and repeat the characterization suggested by their earlier authorities: that the original Turks were primitive bandits from northern Scythia, the country beyond the Caspian Gates of the Caucasus which had unleashed so many other barbarian scourges on civilization in the past. The humanists seem to have regarded these early sources as more respectable and acceptable authorities than later texts like crusade histories and vernacular travel accounts.[133] Even those authors who had firsthand knowledge of Turkish affairs (Filelfo, Sagundino, Gaza) rarely touted this expertise, preferring to present themselves as well versed in ancient texts rather than in current events. These three considerations—scholarly interest in fixing the origins of the Turks at as early a date as possible, the rhetorical utility of locating them in a notorious barbarian landscape, and the professional advantages of confining the argument to a realm of texts that only they could interpret—kept the humanists from investigating other possible answers to the question.

There is, in the end, something paradoxical about the humanists' efforts to establish an authentically ancient pedigree for the Turks. They revived literary commonplaces from classical ethnographical writing about barbarians, and they tinkered with their medieval sources to make them sound more historically credible, more like classical historical texts, than they really were. But the *spirit* of their portrayal is hardly classical at all. Ancient writers from Herodotus to Tacitus observed the habits, history, and society of barbarians with a detached and neutral curiosity which ultimately derived from a sense of cultural confidence, bolstered by the political and military security that empire affords. This was a view which authors writing in the fractured polities of mid-fifteenth-century Europe could hardly understand, much less emulate. Rather, as they contemplated the origins and rise of the conquerors of Constantinople, their responses recall the fear and doubt expressed by fourth- and fifth-century Romans, both pagan and Christian, in the face of the encroaching "barbarian hordes" of their day.

Indeed, the Christian element in the humanists' theory of the Scythian origins of the Turks should not be underestimated. Although they claimed that the Ottomans were descended from an ancient race, the humanists actually took very little of their information from ancient sources. Filelfo, Merula, and Gaza cited references by classical geographers to Scythian or Caucasian peoples whom they believed to be the ancestors of the Turks. But they put these theories forward several decades after the main arguments for the Turks' Scythian origins had been developed by Aeneas Sylvius,

Sagundino, Biondo, and Filelfo himself. These earlier scholars based their accounts not on classical texts but on references to Scythians (sometimes explicitly identified as "Turks") in medieval Latin and Byzantine universal chronicles and apocalyptic literature. In these sources, biblical prophecies regarding Gog, Magog, and the hordes of Armageddon combined with contemporary horror at the depredations of Huns, Goths, and Khazars[134] to form an image of the barbarian that was more terrible than anything classical geographers or ethnographers contemplated.[135] Renaissance humanists, despite the classical veneer they gave their descriptions of the Scythian Turks, ultimately perpetuated a medieval Christian image of barbarity: the Turks were a monstrous, inhuman scourge, sent by a vengeful, interventionist God against a sinful civilization. The humanists' idea of what it meant to be "Scythian" owed very little to classical notions of the primitive.

It is important to stress the medieval Christian background to the humanists' ideas about Turkish ethnography because most modern critics have interpreted their idea of a Scythian origin for the Turks as evidence of exactly the opposite. It is often claimed that the fifteenth-century humanists faithfully revived a classical model of barbarism while rejecting, or at least playing down, the medieval model of the "infidel" Turks as enemies of Christ and the Church.[136] The Latin translation of Herodotus, the foremost ancient authority on the Scythian peoples, which Lorenzo Valla completed shortly after the fall of Constantinople, is thought to have contributed to this revival.[137] Some scholars have also suggested that the identification of the Turks as Scythians reflects an even broader change in Renaissance ideas about world history, as humanist observers began to consider the rise of the Ottoman Empire as the latest phase in an ancient and perpetual contest between civilized Europe and barbarous Asia. This, too, was an idea first developed in detail by Herodotus. Where medieval crusade propaganda saw Islam as a new, emergent phenomenon, inspired by irrational hatred of the Christian religion and quite possibly unleashed by a wrathful Christian God, the humanists, it is claimed, put forward an altogether more rational and secular assessment of the situation, as one of age-old tension between two world systems divided by political and cultural incompatibility.[138]

But the humanist portrayal of the Scythian Turks owed little in its particulars to classical precedents. As we have seen, the ancient geographies of Pliny, Pomponius Mela, and Strabo were introduced only late in the day, long after the basic outlines of the Scythian theory had been developed. What is more, I have found no evidence that any humanist writing on the

Turks in the fifteenth century used Herodotus, in particular, as a source, either for specific information on barbarian habits or for a more general interpretation of the patterns of interaction between barbarians and the civilized world. None of the humanist authors who read Greek—Filelfo, Sagundino, Gaza, Merula—based his history of the Scythian Turks on information from the *Histories*.[139] Those who could not read the language—Biondo and Aeneas Sylvius—first proposed accounts of the Turks' Scythian origins well before Valla completed his translation: Biondo in the 1440s, Aeneas in 1453. Aeneas, moreover, had a perfect opportunity to consult the translation once it was finished: when he visited Naples in the spring of 1456, less than a year had passed since Valla had presented Alfonso of Aragon with the work. Aeneas was pursuing new information on Turkish history at the time. It was then that he commissioned Sagundino to write his treatise on the Scythian origins of the Ottomans. He could have consulted the new translation of Herodotus in order to search out information on the habits and history of the ancient Scythians, but I find no evidence that he did so.[140] Although the *Histories* are today considered the most authoritative classical source of information on the ancient Scythians, they seem to have enjoyed no such reputation in the fifteenth century, even among scholars busily turning up every scrap of information about Scythians they could find.

In fact, Herodotus's reputation in the early Renaissance was relatively poor. Arnaldo Momigliano has proposed various reasons that this might have been so, concluding that it took decades for the translations of Herodotus and other Greek historians made by Italian humanists in the middle decades of the fifteenth century to affect the thinking of educated Europeans in any significant way. "Perhaps," he notes with respect to the quattrocento, "the revolution just did not happen."[141]

There is another, more basic problem with this putative Herodotean revival in humanist political thought: in Herodotus's view, the Asiatic barbarians who threatened civilized Greece were not the Scythians but the Persians. His ethnographic essay on the Scythians in Book IV of the *Histories* has little to do with his meditation at the start of Book I on the timeless rivalry between Europe and Asia, embodied in his day in the Persian Wars.[142] Indeed, throughout the classical period, from the defense of Athens against Xerxes to the Roman wars against Parthia, it was Persian, not Scythian, "barbarians" who were regarded as the perennial opponents of classical civilization.[143] If humanists of the fifteenth century revived the ancient concept of a struggle between East and West in any way, we should look for signs of such a revival in works that relate the history of the Turks to that of the imperial dynasties of ancient Asia—to the Persians, Parthians, Sassanians, or even the Arabs, not to the Scythians of the barbarous north.

There were such texts in the Italian Renaissance, but their genesis, development, and purposes were complex. Not all addressed the problem of crusade, nor were all written in the service of anti-Turkish polemic. What is more, these texts drew inspiration and information from medieval as well as ancient history writing. The idea that the Turks—and Islam as a whole—represented the latest phase in the ancient struggle of Asiatic imperial aggression against Western freedom, faith, civilization, and culture was not an invention of the fifteenth century but one first essayed in the twelfth. As with humanist ethnography, so with humanist political theory and historical analysis: we must weigh up the extent to which the humanists revived exclusively classical models and modes of thinking against their debts to more recent, medieval Christian traditions and heuristics.

CHAPTER **4**

Translations of Empire

The Ottomans were not the dusty shepherds the Renaissance humanists liked to imagine. The dynasty rose to power, in the early fourteenth century, on the ruins of the Seljuk sultanate of Rum, from which they consciously borrowed claims to both political identity and authority. The Seljuk Turks had been a political presence in Anatolia, Mesopotamia, and the Iranian plateau for two centuries. And long before the Seljuks made their entrance from central Asia, other Islamic dynasties—Ummayids, Fatimids, Abbasids, Ghaznavids—had had their hour on the medieval Middle Eastern stage. None of these latter dynasties could be claimed as direct political (much less ethnic) predecessors of the Ottomans, but all played a part in the story of how Islam came to rule over so many territories of the old Roman Empire and so many sites of importance to Christians, and these were questions with which the humanists were deeply concerned.

In their narratives of Ottoman origins, however, as they insisted on the Turks' total barbarity, the humanists generally played down the connections between the Ottomans and earlier Islamic empires. Humanist historians identified the Ottomans as Muslims and decried their allegiance to the heretical and blasphemous "Mohammedan" sect. But there were rhetorical risks in connecting the Ottomans too closely to earlier Islamic states with whom Christian Europe had clashed. A crusade advocate who emphasized the long presence of Islam in the eastern Mediterranean might find it hard then to present the Ottoman case as especially urgent. If Muslims had been in the Levant for centuries—if even Anatolia had long been subject to Turks—why mount a campaign now? Moreover, imagining Islamic history as the story of a series of dynasties rising and falling, one after the other, with the Ottoman Turks merely the latest in the line of succession, could lead to the dangerous conclusion that Muslims, like the Christians of Europe, were political animals after all, "civilized" in the Aristotelian sense. Such a conclusion could undercut the central premise of the Scythian theory which the humanists propagated with such care: that the Turks were a

155

people without history, who had come from nowhere and stood for nothing but anarchy and destruction.

Ironically, these considerations seem not to have bothered medieval historians investigating the origins of Islam. Not that there was a strong interest in Islamic history in the Latin Middle Ages. Most medieval writers on Islam focused their attention on the biography of Muhammad and the objectionable qualities of the "law" he imposed on his followers. But alongside these traditions of hostile biography and theological polemic, a minor strand of medieval history writing sought to locate the Arabs—and the emergence of Islam as a whole—within precisely the sort of political narrative which Renaissance humanists took pains to avoid.

Prevailing ideas about the integrity of universal history and the continuity of empires prompted some medieval historians to imagine the "Saracens" as the latest in a long line of Eastern imperial conquerors. From the Latin version of Theophanes' *Chronographia*, twelfth-century historians like Hugh of Fleury and Sigebert of Gembloux discovered how Muhammad's Arab followers established themselves as a new power in the East in the seventh century, filling the political vacuum left by Sassanian Persia and quickly capturing the same Byzantine cities—Jerusalem, Antioch, Damascus—which the Sassanians had taken during their final war with Heraclius. The Saracens, these historians claimed, continued without interruption the political role that Persia had played throughout ancient history, as the chief rival to Western power, whether Greek, Roman, or Byzantine.

With the advent of Turkic and Mongol invaders from the eleventh to the thirteenth century, some chroniclers began to entertain a less monolithic view of the peoples of the Islamic world, trying instead to distinguish among Arabs, Turks, and Tartars. Authors following this line of thought usually assigned a less favorable combination of ethnic identity and character traits to whoever was the most recent arrival. In their hands, the familiar "Saracen" Arabs took on the role of mild and essentially harmless indigenous locals who were being overwhelmed by newer and fiercer peoples, whether Mongols or Turks. The terms used to establish these distinctions were rarely applied with consistency. Some historians claimed that the newcomers represented a resurgence of ancient Persian or Parthian aggression and thus were a cause for alarm, while others identified the invaders as barbarians who had swept away an older, Arabic-Persian political order—in their view, a cause for regret.

In short, there was no one medieval paradigm of Islamic political history, nor one medieval model for the relationship between ancient Persia and Islam. But three things are certain. First, it was medieval historians, not Renaissance ones, who devised the analogy between Christian-Islamic conflicts of the present era and Greek-Persian or Roman-Persian rivalries of the past. In fact, it may have been an almost exclusively medieval idea, for although the analogy did persist in the works of a few Renaissance historians, on the whole the notion seems to have fallen out of favor by the mid-fifteenth century. The more viscerally compelling identification of the Turks with Scythian barbarians took its place. Second, in their efforts to fit the Islamic empires into various universal history schemes, medieval historians seem to have paid rather more attention to the recent political history of the Islamic world than their Renaissance successors did. The humanists were not the first to take an interest in the secular aspects of Islamic history. In fact, given the treatments of the subject which were available to them in the medieval Latin tradition, it seems that the relative *inattention* of the humanists to the subject can be the result only of deliberate neglect. Third, one thing Renaissance historians share with their medieval predecessors is the tendency to exploit their narratives of Islamic history to rhetorical ends, as a device for emphasizing the dangerous character of whatever Islamic empire sat in ascendance at the moment of writing.

Medieval Views of the Empires of Islam

Between the twelfth and fourteenth centuries, Latin writers on Islamic history—chief among them Hugh of Fleury, Guibert of Nogent, Sigebert of Gembloux, William of Tyre, William of Tripoli, and Hetoum of Korikos—developed a range of heuristic strategies to account for the origins of Islam and its empires.[1] At first their interest was more theological than political: in 1095, Pope Urban II launched the First Crusade because the holy city of Jerusalem lay captive in the hands of an "infidel" foe. At that point, few in Christian Europe cared to know more about the enemy than that he subscribed to an illegitimate and heretical faith. Early twelfth-century chroniclers rarely charted the political growth of the Arab Empire or the later Islamic powers that succeeded it, and often failed to recognize the ethnic and political distinctions among contemporary Muslim nations. These tended to be described as generic "Saracens," that is, as Muslims of unspecified ethnicity or, in an older sense of the word, as ethnic Arabs, direct descendants of the nation which Muhammad and the early caliphs had led to triumph five centuries before.

The development of this perspective among Latin Christian historians was closely bound up with the larger concerns of the crusading movement in the West. The Byzantine Greeks viewed the Seljuks as a political threat; accordingly, Byzantine historians like Skylitzes reported extensively on the central Asian origins of the Seljuk Turks and the military and political stratagems they had used to seize power first in Iran and Mesopotamia and then in Asia Minor. Latin crusade propagandists, however, shifted attention away from the localized political, military, and economic problems the Seljuks posed in Asia Minor to the greater goal of rescuing Jerusalem from the infidels who had held it (or so it seemed) without interruption since the original Arab conquest—and thereafter of eradicating the religion of Islam itself. The important thing about the enemy, in their view, was the fact that they were Muslims, not Arabs or Turks.[2] Accordingly, Latin authors who tried to provide a historical context for the infidel occupation of Jerusalem usually did so by recounting the life of Muhammad and the spread of his religion. A polemical biography of the Prophet, built up from scattered details in Byzantine chronicles, historical and theological works from Mozarabic Spain, and hearsay picked up on the ground in crusader Palestine, came to dominate twelfth- and thirteenth-century discussions of Islamic affairs, not only theological analyses of Muslim doctrine but also historical writing on the status and political goals of the contemporary Islamic powers.[3]

Three French Benedictine historians—Guibert of Nogent, Hugh of Fleury, and Sigebert of Gembloux—first assembled the various elements of this polemical portrait.[4] Their accounts, cobbled together from half-true details from the life of the Prophet and some outright fabrication, aimed not only to explain the historical origins of Islam but also to show that it was an erroneous, even ridiculous superstition. Muhammad, a poor orphan, had been corrupted by a renegade monk who planted in him the seeds of heresy; the doctrine he established was no more than a willful corruption of Christian beliefs. Starting life as a lowly desert trader, he gained wealth and status by seducing a wealthy widow; when he began to suffer epileptic fits, he claimed to be receiving messages from the angel Gabriel, which he then preached to those around him. His "law" was tempting and attractive: he promised his followers entrance to a paradise of carnal pleasures in the next life; while still on earth, sexual freedom would be their sacred right. He reinforced the appeal of his new faith through carefully stage-managed stunts (training a cow to follow him with the Koran tied to its horns, exhibiting a tame dove that whispered divine revelations in his ear), and when he died, possibly in a drunken debauch, his body was ripped apart by pigs, causing his followers ever after to despise their meat and shun the fruits of the vine.

The hostile biography of Muhammad (which in certain particulars—the emphasis on the founder's low birth and devious tactics—rather anticipates the humanist portrait of the warlord Osman) was practically the only information provided by many twelfth-century chroniclers to explain how Islam spread through the East. After describing the Prophet's lawless life and licentious creed, Guibert of Nogent, for instance, simply adds: "Then the shadow of this nefarious sect blotted out the name of Christ, and to this day it covers the furthest corners of almost the entire East, Africa, Egypt, Ethiopia, Libya, and even our neighbor Spain."[5] Guibert was not interested in how Muhammad's followers established and administered their empire, nor did he try to determine the identities of the other nations who later converted to Islam. The important point was that the "Saracens" had created a new religion which, as it spread around the world, made Saracens of all who embraced it.

Details of the historical context in which Islam developed were not entirely unknown, however, even at this early date. Hugh of Fleury begins his excursus on the origins of Islam with an account of the early Arab conquests, which he derives from Theophanes as translated by Anastasius, including the caliph Omar's campaigns against Damascus, Jerusalem, and Antioch and the establishment of Arab control over lands from Egypt to the Euphrates.[6] Hugh also reports briefly on the later Arab conquest of Persia.[7]

Sigebert of Gembloux pays more attention to the political implications of the Arab conquests, describing how the Saracens not only attacked the Sassanian rulers of Persia but overthrew and replaced them as the dominant power in the region. He explains this sudden change of political fortunes in a way that preserves (in fact, reinforces) his larger thesis that there were only nine principal nations in all of universal history: "The Saracens, who up until this point had been subjects of the Persian Empire, conquered them in battle and subjected them in turn to their own dominion. From this point on, instead of the Persian Empire we must call it the Saracen Empire."[8]

Sigebert thus integrates the sudden rise of the Arabs into a far older and more familiar political framework, that of a *translatio imperii* linking successive Eastern powers from antiquity to the modern day.

The historical elision between Persians and Arabs that Sigebert attempts was made possible in part by widespread European confusion over exactly who the "Saracens" were and where they had come from. Although some authors knew that Islam had its origins in the Arabian Peninsula, there was an ancient tradition of identifying the Arabs as tribal descendants of the biblical Ishmael (hence the alternate names *Ismaeliti* and *Hagareni*) rather than as inhabitants of any particular geographical area.[9] The uncertainty grew when the crusaders encountered the Scljuk Turks, the recent conquerors of Ghaznavid Khorasan, in the Holy Land.[10] Few historians understood the ethnic, linguistic, and cultural distinctions that separated Turks and Arabs. Hugh of Fleury thought it enough to say that Islam arose among "the Saracens, who are also called Turks."[11] A detail included in some of the polemical biographies of Muhammad can be interpreted as either a result of this confusion or perhaps a more conscious attempt to resolve it: according to both Hugh of Fleury and Sigebert of Gembloux, the Prophet's first wife was a noble lady who ruled over the province of "Corazania," or Khorasan. After marrying her, Muhammad won possession of the whole province, and it was from here that he launched his attacks on the Byzantine Greeks.[12] Neither the Prophet nor his wife had any connection to Khorasan, but this was the territory where the Seljuks, the predominant power with whom the eleventh- and twelfth-century crusaders had to contend, had first risen to power. If Muhammad was transformed into a lord of Persian Khorasan, the discrete origins of the Arabs and Turks could be reconciled.[13]

A few twelfth-century authors emphasized that the Turks had a separate history from that of the Arabs. Guibert of Nogent believed that the Seljuks were descended from the ancient Parthians.[14] He also stressed that they were a distinct nation from the Saracen Arabs. Muhammad's religion took root among the latter, he explains, in the general climate of heterodoxy that characterized the eastern empire in late antiquity. In other words, his Arab followers were merely weak and faithless Christians, apostates from Byzantine political and religious authority. But the Turks had an entirely different historical pedigree: "The kingdom of the Parthians, whom we, because of changes in the language, call the Turks, is pre-eminent in military matters, in horsemanship, and in courage."[15] In an account that seems to owe a distant debt to Byzantine reports on the Seljuk-Ghaznavid conflict, Guibert explains how, after rebelling against their overlord, the emperor of Babylon, and his army of "Assyrians,"[16] the bellicose Parthian Turks began to threaten Eastern Christians and thus prompted the launch of the First Crusade. He based his history on the anonymous *Gesta Francorum*, a text which asserts that the Turks thought they were related to the Franks because of their common talent for war. In his reworking of that passage from the *Gesta*, Guibert also remarks that the Turks were fundamentally different in character from all the other nations of the Middle East: Syrians, Arabs, Armenians, "Saracens" and the like.[17] His insistence that the Turks also had a different historical pedigree is original to him and not found in the

Gesta. But the statement should be understood in light of the broader theme Guibert borrowed from that earlier text: the Turks were a high-born and formidable enemy, divinely chosen to prove the even greater might of the Franks.

In his history (*Chronicon*) of the Latin Kingdom, William of Tyre (c. 1130–1185) also draws a distinction between the Arabs, with their history and culture rooted in the old Byzantine world, and the newly arrived—and in William's view, far less admirable—Seljuk Turks. Though he starts with a conventional description of Muhammad's nefarious career and how the "disease" of his heresy infected the Eastern world,[18] William goes on to review the political history of the early medieval Middle East in much greater detail than any previous Latin historian, distinguishing between the Byzantine-Persian wars of the early seventh century and the Arab invasions which began a few decades later. William held that the Arabs, rather than simply replacing Persia as the Eastern partner in a centuries-old stalemate with Rome, represented a new and totally different political presence in the region. He also believed that the seductive influence of their religion was not the only factor in their rise. It was also at least partly a political and military phenomenon: if Rome and Persia had not exhausted themselves fighting each other for so many decades, both could probably have withstood the Arab invasions.[19]

Still, in William's view, the triumph of Islam had not been an undifferentiated catastrophe. Under the Abbasids, especially during the reigns of Charlemagne and Harun ar-Rashid, Eastern Christians and Western pilgrims had been treated well in the Holy Land. It was only after Syria and Palestine fell to the Shiite Fatimids in the tenth century that conditions grew intolerable. And even their administration was to be preferred to that of their successors, the Seljuk Turks: "As long as the rule of the Egyptians [that is, the Fatimids] and Persians [Abbasids] continued, Christians enjoyed somewhat better conditions. But when, in turn, the power of the Turks began to flourish and they extended their sway over the lands of the Persians and the Egyptians, matters grew worse again."[20] It is not clear whether William means to draw genetic connections between the Abbasids and the ancient Persians, or the Fatimids and the ancient Egyptians, or whether the terms simply made geographical sense and good Latin. But, notably, William does not assign the interloping Turks a classical name.

Instead he offers an extensive excursus on the origins of the *Turci*, starting with their flight from Troy into northern Asia under the leadership

of Turcus. There, William says, they lost all knowledge of their Trojan ancestry and were transformed into a primitive northern race, lacking cities,
knowing nothing of agriculture, trade, or government, wandering with their
flocks wherever pasturage was good and paying tribute to local lords for
grazing rights and land to pitch their tents.[21] This is a fairly conventional description of nomadic Scythian habits, not unlike some Renaissance humanist accounts (though I have found no evidence that any fifteenth-century
proponents of the Turks' Scythian identity used this passage as a source).
William then recounts how the Turks conquered Ghaznavid Khorasan: after
they migrated into the territory of the lord of Persia (Mahmud of Ghazna),
they chose a ruler for themselves, a certain Selduc, a man of admirable qualities, who led them to attack and overthrow the Persians and then dominate
the whole of Asia.[22]

Selduc's leadership transforms the very identity of his people: those who
accept him as king and join his conquering army come to be known as *Turci*,
while the rest, who retain their anarchic nomadic ways, are afterward called
Turcomani, or Türkmens.[23] The *Turci* occupy Syria and Jerusalem, impose
harsh rule on the Christian population, and ultimately provoke the start of
the crusades: "And this happened only thirty or forty years before our Western princes started their journey of pilgrimage."[24]

As he recounts the story of the Seljuks' military and political achievements, William expresses some admiration for them. Nevertheless, by un-
derscoring the differences between their rule and that of the Arabs, he also
reveals a certain nostalgia for the old Arab regime. Life under their rule had
been quite acceptable; it was the Turkish newcomers who caused problems
for Christians in the East. In the following centuries, Western historians
would regularly draw distinctions between bad and good (or perhaps we
should say bad and less bad) Muslim powers. In doing so, they also followed
William in discussing the political or moral character of each state as well its
religious heterodoxy. Their conclusions were not always as negative as William's: it was also possible to imagine that the emergence of new Eastern dynasties heralded the dawn of a better age.

In the thirteenth century, in the wake of the Mongol invasions and the rise
of the Turkic Mamluks in Egypt, Latin models of Islamic history changed. As
attention focused on the new powers, the histories of earlier ruling powers,
whether Arab or Turkish, grew less distinct. William of Tripoli, author of the
tract *De statu Sarracenorum* (1273), makes no mention of the Seljuk con-

quests. He claims that the Arabs had ruled the Middle East continuously from the time of the Prophet until quite recently; forty-two successive caliphs, all of them directly descended from Muhammad, had held the reins of power. This ancient, homogeneous regime was finally swept away in the Mongol sack of Baghdad in 1258; leadership of the Islamic world then fell to the Mamluks.[25] Unlike the old caliphs in Baghdad, the Mamluks were Turkish, a difference William stressed since he hoped their rule would bring about an improvement in Christian fortunes.[26]

William of Tripoli's enthusiasm for Mamluk Turkish rule did not last long in the Latin West, but his perception that the Mongols had obliterated an ancient regime was widely shared. Confronted by the frightening prospect of a new wave of central Asian invasion, Latin attitudes toward the Seljuks soon changed. Some authors now saw them not as a menace but as objects of pity—helpless victims of barbarian hordes—or simply as harmless shepherds. Vincent of Beauvais, relying on reports by mendicant missions sent by the papacy to the Mongols in the 1240s, notes with dismay the Mongol devastation of Seljuk "Turquia" and its many rich cities.[27] Within a few decades, the Turks—indeed all the old Muslim powers—came to seem decadent and weak in comparison with the fearsome new invaders. Listing six basic types of political state in the world, Roger Bacon suggested that each could be distinguished by the thing its members considered best and most desirable: the soft "Saracens" cared only for pleasure, Bacon says, but the ultimate concern of the Tartars was raw power.[28]

The Armenian historian Hetoum of Korikos better recollected the Turks' imperial past, but he too described their history in order to highlight the achievements of the Mongols. In yet another realignment of political sympathies, Hetoum wrote his history to celebrate the conquests of the Mongols—a people whom he, as a prince of the Cilician Armenian royal family, had particular reason to praise. His work, *Flos historiarum terrae orientis*, enjoyed great popularity in the fourteenth and fifteenth centuries and was a major source for those few quattrocento humanists who did attempt to write the history of the medieval Arabs and Turks.[29]

In the seventy years since the Mongols had appeared on the scene in the Middle East, the Christian kingdom of Cilician Armenia, almost alone among the regional powers, had come to terms with the invaders. In return for acknowledging Mongol suzerainty, the Armenians were guaranteed safety and religious freedom within their borders. Cilician Armenians joined Mongol armies on campaign against the Mamluks; Armenian clerics were also quietly working on a plan to convert their Mongol overlords to Christianity. Hetoum's treatise was intended to draw Western Christians into the Mongol-Armenian alliance. He wrote it for Pope Clement V in 1306, while in residence at the papal court in Poitiers. Whether he was there as an official envoy of the Cilician Armenian court or as a private exile is unclear, but a political message certainly underlies his work: if the armies of Latin Europe were to join those of the Mongols, Hetoum believed, the Mamluks could be expelled for good from the Holy Land—and from the borders of Cilician Armenia.

Hetoum includes a great deal of information on the Turks in his work, even though at the time that he wrote the Seljuk sultanates had been obliterated by the Mongols and there was as yet little sign of resurgence among the Turkish splinter states that survived in Asia Minor. Nevertheless, in order to demonstrate just how ancient and powerful an empire the Mongols had swept away, Hetoum recounts the events of Turkish history at some length.[30]

His history seems at first to follow traditional Western models. He begins with the birth of Christ and introduces the Muslim conquerors as the "cursed spawn of the nation of perfidious Mahomet," sons of "iniquity" and "perdition."[31] But Hetoum goes on to pay as much attention, if not more, to the political consequences of Muhammad's career as to its religious implications. He traces the origins of the region's troubles as far back as antiquity, to the long conflict between the Roman and Persian Empires. It was in the reign of Augustus that the Persian Empire first began to "rebel" against Rome; the Saracen Arabs later usurped their position and continued their revolt. In other words, the contemporary problems of the East ultimately derived from an act of insurrection against the political authority of the ancient empire rather than from the religious apostasy of Muhammad.[32] The establishment of Islam added fuel to a much older conflict; it was certainly not the start of it.

Hetoum makes Persia the central locus of power in Islamic history. It was only after the Arabs conquered Persia, he maintains, that they were able to establish a proper kingdom of their own, with an "emperor" (the caliph) ruling from the capital at Baghdad.[33] Passing over in silence the rule of the Ummayad caliphs at Damascus (661–750), Hetoum conflates the Arabs' military conquest of Persia in the 630s and 640s with the establishment of the Abbasid caliphate at Baghdad in the middle of the eighth century.[34] Whether from ignorance or deliberate design, his conclusion is that the culmination of the first few decades of Arab history was their conquest of Persia. By simultaneously destroying the Sassanian Empire, appointing a new "emperor" for themselves, and establishing him in a Mesopotamian capital city, the Arabs effectively replaced Persia as the dominant power and chief irritant to Roman authority in the Eastern world. Like Sigebert of Gembloux and Guibert of Nogent two centuries before, Hetoum presents Persia as the territory of central importance throughout Middle Eastern history, the seat from which power over the region has always been exercised.

Later, Hetoum portrays the eleventh-century Seljuk conquest of the region as yet another transfer of Persian *imperium*. The Turks make their first entrance in Hetoum's text at a fairly early date. When the Arabs first invade Persia in the 630s, Hetoum explains how King "Asdaiorth" (that is, the last Sassanian ruler of Persia, Yazdgerd III, known in Greek sources as Isdigerdēs) appeals to the surrounding kingdoms to come to his aid. From "Turquestan," the closest neighboring country, some 60,000 "Turquemanni" cross the River Phison into Persia. But their progress is slow, and the Arabs are able to attack, force a battle, and kill the Persian king before his Turkish allies can arrive.[35] Despite his anachronistic use of the name "Turquemanni,"[36] there are historical grounds for Hetoum's claim that a Turkic people came to Yazdgerd's aid in the dying days of the Sassanian Empire. The Byzantine sources shed no light on the question, but the ninth-century Arab historian Tabari preserves several accounts of Yazdgerd's defeat. In each of his versions, the Persian king flees east after the Arab victory at Qadisiyah and takes refuge in a city of Khorasan, from where he sends desperate letters to the kings of Soghd, China, and the Turks asking for help.[37] The king of the Turks mentioned by Tabari is probably the khagan of the Eastern Türks, whose territory extended from Soghd on the Persian border to western China.[38] The Turks respond to Yazdgerd's plea, crossing the river "Djihoun" (the Oxus), which separates their lands from Khorasan, to come to his aid.[39]

After this almost incidental introduction to his story, the Turcomans assume a central role in Hetoum's Book II. The slow-moving mercenaries proceed as far as "Corascen" (Khorasan) before hearing of Yazdgerd's death. When the Arab army appears, the Turks propose a settlement: they swear obedience to the caliph, accept lands "beyond Khorasan" (from where, the Arabs hope, they will cause little trouble), and agree to pay annual tribute in the form of taxes and military service. Later the caliph convinces the elders of the nation to convert to Islam, and they persuade the rest to accept the new religion. Conversion was an easy enough step for the Turks to take, Hetoum explains, since they had little regard for any form of authority and even less tradition of deep religious belief.[40] The Saracens, however, fail to detect the cynicism of this act; they shower the Turks with privileges, which the latter ruthlessly exploit, becoming rich and numerous over time: "For the Turcomans wisely knew how to remain subject to the Saracens until such time as they could find a pretext for rebellion."[41]

This occurred, Hetoum says, after the Saracens had ruled Asia for 418 years (since he dates the start of Arab rule to A.D. 632, this brings us to the year 1050). With the Saracens quarreling among themselves and at the same time losing territory to the Byzantine emperor Diogenes,[42] the Turcomans seize their opportunity:

> In A.D. 1051 the Turcomans began to rule for the first time in Asia, [a cir-
> cumstance which occurred] in this way: when they had grown rich in trea-
> sure and great in numbers, seeing the discord among the Saracens, they
> thought they could easily usurp rule over Asia. Accordingly, they chose a
> king and master for themselves, although they had never before had an
> overlord or ruler . . . called Salioch [Seljuk]. Once this was done, they took
> up arms, continually assailing the Saracens everywhere and driving them
> out, so that in a short time they conquered all of Asia Major and held do-
> minion over the land. But they caused no trouble to the Caliph, but rather
> held him in great honour. And after the aforementioned Turcomans held
> dominion over the land of Asia without anyone protesting, the Caliph,
> more out of fear than love, for he wished to please the Turcomans in every
> way, ordained the aforesaid Salioch, their lord, as emperor over all the king-
> doms and lands of Asia.[43]

Hetoum then rehearses the history of the first Seljuk sultans and their conquests across the Middle East: "Dolcrilssa" (Toghril Shah, that is, Toghril Beg); his kinsman "Artot" (Artuq); son "Alp Asalem" (Alp Arslan); grand-son "Melecssa" (Malik Shah); and nephew "Solimanssa" (Süleyman b. Qutlumush), "the first infidel to offer resistance to the crusaders."[44] His ac-count of the role the Seljuks played in the crusades is in fact rather too par-tial to them. He oversimplifies the region's complex political relationships, identifying the Great Seljuk sultan, who in reality had little influence out-side Iraq and exercised minimal control over other Muslim states, as both "imperator Turquorum" and "imperator Persarum," who commands the feudal loyalty of the lesser sultans of "Turquia" (Anatolia) and "Mesopotamia" (Syria).[45]

This all-powerful figure orders his sultans to capture Antioch, but when the Frankish crusaders retake the city and then proceed south to Jerusalem, the Turks are thrown into confusion. Hetoum's account of subsequent events, from the crusader capture of Antioch in 1098 to the arrival of the Mongols in the 1240s, is telescoped almost beyond recognition. From Antioch, the Turks retreat "home" to Persia, where they become embroiled in civil war and are then ejected from Persia altogether. Here, as well as in Syria and Palestine, various petty princes retain what territory they can, but only the sultan of Turquia maintains truly effective rule over his domains. In the end, he too falls before the Mongol advance: "The sultan of Turquia ruled his kingdom in peace until the arrival of the Tartars, by whom he was afterwards defeated."[46] The stage is thus set for the Mongol invasions, subject of Hetoum's third book.

Hetoum's abbreviated Eastern history emphasizes the role of the Seljuk Turks to the exclusion of almost every other regional power. His undue emphasis on the Seljuks—especially the way he credits them with imposing a more formal dynastic and administrative structure across the region than they actually achieved—can be understood in light of the contemporary political message he wanted his history to convey. By suggesting that the Turks were the sole heirs to the Arab caliphate in Asia, headquartered in Persia but controlling a feudal hierarchy of sultanates in "Mesopotamia" and "Turquia," Hetoum implies that the Franks and Mongols together destroyed a single great empire, that of the Turks. The crusaders eject the Turks from Palestine and humiliate them at Antioch—an act which effectively topples the dynasty in the Turkish heartland of Persia. With the arrival of the Mongols (some 150 years later), the last Seljuk stronghold, Turquia, also falls. In other words, Christians and Mongols had already taken effective action against one hegemonic Muslim power; if they turned to face the Mamluks of Egypt, there was every chance they would meet with success again.

Hetoum's interpretation of the fall of the Seljuks is not entirely accurate, but the importance of his work as a source for the earlier history of the Turks is undeniable. He demonstrated that Turkic peoples had played a role in Islamic history almost from its very beginnings, and that the Seljuks, coming west from central Asia, had assumed a central position in Eastern politics for several centuries, protecting the caliph, exercising administrative control over much of the Middle East, and challenging Christian crusaders both in the Holy Land and in "Turquia," the Anatolian heartland they ruled for nearly three centuries.

Renaissance humanists who claimed that the "Scythian" Turks lacked a distinguished political history did so by choice: they certainly did not write in a vacuum of information. Medieval historians developed a variety of narratives to explain and contextualize the origins and rise of the empires of Islam. While some called all of them "Saracen" and focused on the objectionable qualities of Muhammad's "law," others identified the Arabs first and later the Seljuk Turks as political successors to the ancient empires of Assyria, Persia, and Parthia. Medieval authors like Sigebert of Gembloux and Guibert of Nogent claimed that these new Islamic dynasties continued a timeless struggle between East and West, reviving ancient antipathies between Assyrians and Israelites, Persians and Greeks, Parthians and Romans, and, most recently, the last Sassanians and the Byzantine Greeks. Later historians (mostly those with local experience of the Islamic East, like William of Tyre, William of Tripoli, and Hetoum of Korikos) were able to distinguish quite clearly between the Arabs and later Turkic and Mongol invaders, usually in order to support a particular interpretation of the contemporary political situation: the new arrivals heralded either a dramatic upswing or a dramatic downturn for Christian interests in the region. Despite the politicized nature of their speculations, these medieval authors were able to reconstruct the political history of the Islamic empires in remarkable detail.[47]

How did Renaissance humanist historians of Islam engage with these medieval traditions? Humanists arguing for a barbarous Scythian origin for the Turks pointedly ignored the stories their predecessors unearthed regarding the political fortunes of the Turks in the medieval Middle East. Humanists writing on the northern origins of the Turks also paid little attention to the connections previous historians had drawn between the medieval empires of Islam (Turkish or otherwise) and the ancient Assyrians, Persians, Parthians, and Sassanians. Rather than pursuing these various lines of inquiry into Islam's ancient and medieval past, the humanists engaged in what might be termed a sustained campaign of ignoring and forgetting.

It would be wrong to suppose, however, that these medieval traditions died out all at once, giving way overnight to a new humanist orthodoxy that stressed the Turks' lack of political history. The early fifteenth century marks a period of transition, during which innovative historians like Andrea Biglia and Flavio Biondo tried to make humanist sense of these medieval narratives.

Rome in the East: Decline and Fall

Writing in the 1430s and '40s, Andrea Biglia, in his *Commentaries* on the decline of Christianity in the East, and Flavio Biondo, in his *Decades* of medieval Italian history, adapted and updated the medieval model of Islamic history as a progression of empires in order to explain the current political situation in the eastern Mediterranean. Both authors identified the Ottomans as the direct successors of ancient Eastern empires. Both based their accounts on the medieval histories just examined: Biondo used Anastasius and Sigebert; Biglia relied extensively on William of Tyre and Hetoum. And both brought a fairly sophisticated political analysis to bear on these texts. In other words, they both took an approach to Islamic history which is far closer to what might be considered "typical" humanist historical thinking than that which developed later in the fifteenth century. That is, they rearticulated two well-worn medieval themes—interest in the local details of Islamic political history and a larger concern for the translation of empires across world historical time—in the new idioms of Renaissance humanism. Along the way, Biglia and Biondo also put their stories to work in the service of patriotic calls to Italian regeneration and reform.

The Milanese humanist Andrea Biglia (1394?–1435)[48] completed his *Commentarii de defectu fidei in oriente* shortly after May 1433.[49] His work stands out from the generally vague and tendentious treatments of Turkish history that humanists of the later fifteenth century produced. Unlike his successors, Biglia understood—or perhaps was more willing to acknowledge—the complicated political cycles of medieval Islamic history. He recognized that the Ottomans were the political successors of the Seljuk Turks and that the latter had achieved a remarkable empire in Asia; in fact, he believed that the Turks as a whole were the direct heirs of the ancient civilizations of the East. This gave them—though certainly not all Islamic nations—a claim to empire. Biglia developed his interpretation of Islamic history in order to illustrate a rather original theory of how and why Roman imperial and ecclesiastical authority had declined in the East. Unusually, possibly uniquely among Italian humanists, Biglia assigned the Turks a positive role in his scheme, manipulating his sources to present them as the sole surviving exponents of classical virtue, political integrity, and moral goodness in the Eastern lands once ruled by Rome. To support his model, he also modified the standard medieval portrayal of Persia as Greco-Roman civilization's perennial antagonist, leaving the Arabs out of the imperial succession altogether. In Biglia's scheme, ancient Persia (like ancient Rome) was a civilized and virtuous empire which had fallen after its own "barbarian invasions," in this case an assault by the Arabs. Later the (Seljuk) Turks restored imperial civilization in the East, but they in turn were overthrown by new forces of barbaric destruction—the Mongols and the Mamluks.

Biglia was one of the earliest humanist authors to treat the question of Islamic history, but he had few followers. This is partly because of the idiosyncratic perspective he brought to his work, made possible by the particular time in which he happened to write. His history shows the influence of recent developments in Florentine humanist historiography—in particular Leonardo Bruni's theories about the effects of imperial Roman rule on the indigenous Italian character. In style, structure, and approach to his material, Biglia's history of the decline of ancient virtues in the East seems to owe much to Bruni's account of how indigenous Tuscan values were eclipsed by ancient Rome, only to rise anew in recent times. Moreover, when Biglia wrote, in the early 1430s, the Ottomans had yet to reassert themselves as a major threat to Western interests, and his main sources for Ottoman history were written at times when they seemed even less of a menace—for instance, in the immediate aftermath of Timur's conquests. These circumstances made possible Biglia's positive view of the Turks and the Turkish character, which enabled him to reconstruct a relatively accurate account of their earlier history. His *Commentaries* offer a hint of the direction humanist studies on Islamic history might have taken had the Ottoman Turks not proved so successful so quickly in the following decades.

As a humanistically educated cleric and historian, an advocate of church reform, and a critic of popular religious movements, Biglia was mainly concerned not with the rise of Islam but rather, as his title suggests, the collective failure of Christendom to contain it. The success of Islam was for Biglia an aberration which the Christian Church had allowed to happen. Biglia also held the Byzantine Empire and the heirs of Roman power in the Latin West responsible for the loss of so much Christian territory to the Arabs and their Muslim successors. In the end, Islamic history was of interest to him because it highlighted how these once-great European institutions had declined.

In the course of a distinguished academic career, Biglia had already demonstrated his interest in both the problems of the Church and the writing of secular history. He entered the Augustinian order as a teenager in Milan before embarking on a course of humanistic study, reading philosophy at Padua and from 1418 lecturing on ethics, poetics, and rhetoric at the Florentine *studio*. In 1423 he transferred to Bologna, where three years later he was appointed professor of natural and moral philosophy. By the end of the decade he was teaching in the University of Siena, where he remained until his early death from plague in September 1435. Biglia was a prolific scholar, proficient in Greek and possibly Hebrew. His extant works include translations of Aristotle, a *Milanese History* in nine books, and several pamphlets on the contemporary religious and political crises afflicting Italy.[50] At Siena in the winter of 1431–1432, he taught the young Aeneas Sylvius Piccolomini.[51] He may also have known Francesco Filelfo; certainly their careers coincided at various points: at Padua in the second decade of the 1400s, at Bologna in the 1420s, and in 1434–1435 at Siena, where Filelfo arrived just a few months before Biglia's death. Filelfo undoubtedly read and used Biglia's *Commentaries* as a source for his own later work on Islamic history.[52]

Before composing his survey of Islamic history, Biglia had not shown much interest in Eastern affairs. The project was suggested to him, so he says, by Sigismund of Hungary during his progress through Italy in 1432–1433. Sigismund arrived in Siena in July 1432 and remained there until the end of April 1433. During this time, as Biglia explains in his preface, the emperor commissioned him to translate two letters written in Greek which had arrived from Christian princes in the East. When Biglia marveled that Christians still survived in such distant parts and wondered how they had managed to preserve their faith, Sigismund produced a book on Eastern history which had come from these same Christian regions—this was almost certainly Hetoum's *Flos*. He suggested that Biglia recast its contents in a modern idiom, "so that they might be better known to our compatriots."[53] Biglia completed his work after 31 May 1433, the date of Sigismund's coronation in Rome: it is with this event that he ends the twelfth and final book of his history.

Sigismund gave Biglia the material for his history, but Biglia did not dedicate his work to the emperor. Instead he inscribed different individual books to various churchmen and secular leaders: prominent cardinals at the Council of Basel, members of the imperial court, the pope, and a *condottiere* in the service of the duke of Milan.[54] These dedicatees seem hardly related, but as Diana Webb has shown, all were involved during the year Biglia wrote in a tense political stalemate occasioned by Sigismund's entry into Italy at the invitation of Filippo Maria Visconti of Milan.[55] In the spring of 1433, this crisis seemed close to resolution. Biglia's historical survey of the problems afflicting Christianity in the East, dedicated to leading figures on all sides of a dispute then disturbing Western Christendom, was probably intended as a work of both description and prescription. A strong critic of dissension in the Church, Biglia hoped to draw attention to the misfortunes which had befallen the East as a result of centuries of Christian discord. Moreover, now that political and ecclesiastical reconciliation seemed to be in the air, he may well have wanted to suggest a worthy cause—*recuperatio*—for the united powers of Western Christendom to adopt.[56]

Although the title of his work suggests that it is a history of Eastern Christianity, in fact Biglia devotes most of his attention to the secular political history of the Middle East from the rise of the Arab Empire in the seventh century to the most recent deeds of the Mamluks and Ilkhanids in his own day. For his first five books, he relies on Books II and III of Hetoum's *Flos*, covering events from the appearance of Muhammad to the death of Hetoum's contemporary the Mongol ruler Ghazan in 1304. For the sections on the early Arab conquests, he also draws on material from Theophanes, most likely in Anastasius's translation. Continuing the story where Hetoum leaves off, Biglia fills Books VI through IX with material adapted from two biographies of fourteenth-century Islamic rulers, the Mamluk sultan Barquq (d. 1399) and the Ilkhanid conqueror Timur (d. 1405), by Beltramo de' Mignanelli, a Sienese merchant who had traveled extensively in the East.[57] In Books X and XI, Biglia backtracks to the eleventh century, offering a summary history of the crusades from their inauguration in 1095 to the fall of Acre in 1291, which shows debts to William of Tyre as well as, possibly, the twelfth-century *Itinerarium Regis Ricardi*. Book XII, finally, recounts the events of Sigismund's career and ends with his coronation in May 1433. The scope of the work and the level of detail Biglia achieves are extraordinary: no previous Latin historian had attempted to isolate the question of the political history of the Islamic world in this way and to treat it at such length and in such detail.

The Ottoman Turks do not loom large in the *Commentarii*—primarily because Biglia's sources do not say much about them either. When his main source, Hetoum, was writing in 1306, Osman himself had just begun his illustrious career, and there was no way Hetoum could have known the heights to which the dynasty he founded would rise. Mongol dynasties still dominated in Asia, and the central section of Hetoum's work is devoted to them. Along the Mediterranean coast, meanwhile, the Mamluks were the preeminent power. Hetoum's last book consists of a crusade plan directed against them. Likewise, when Mignanelli composed his biographies in 1416, the Ottomans were just starting to recover from the chaos of Timur's conquests. The interregnum of 1402–1413 had been resolved with the accession of Mehmed I, but three years later the Ottoman emirs still did not seem to pose as great a threat as either the Mamluk sultans or Timur's successors in the East, the two powers to whom Mignanelli devoted his attention. Nowhere in his work does Biglia pause to review Ottoman history *ab origine*, as later humanists would do. This lack of concern is in itself intriguing, since it shows what a classically trained historian made of the political situation in the East just a few years before the Ottomans eclipsed—in the minds of Italian humanists, at least—every other power in the region.

Biglia's interest in the political history of the Islamic world and especially the political distinctions between various Muslim states echoes that of Hetoum. Biglia also identifies another factor distinguishing each successive Eastern power from its predecessors, which can perhaps best be described as cultural character. He judges Persians, Arabs, Turks, and Mongols in turn according to their level of political organization, their receptiveness to organized religion, the antiquity of their race and national traditions, and—proceeding from all of these—the more elusive qualities of innate dignity and *humanitas*. Biglia finds the rise and fall of these cultural values just as important an issue as the health of the Christian religion and the strength of Christian states. Overall, the picture is a gloomy one, for Biglia finds that the glories of the ancient East have for the most part faded away.

Biglia starts his history in the year 630, as an already troubled Christendom is thrown into crisis by the appearance of Muhammad. He moves quickly through the stock polemical phrases: Machomet, a "horrible beast of hell," deserved never to be born, rose to prominence by means of wicked tricks, copied elements of Christian and Jewish theology to make himself seem a prophet, and won converts far and wide.[58] But other factors, at least as important as the new religion, contributed to the Arabs' rise to power. Chief among these was the political weakness of the Byzantine Empire. From Constantinople, Heraclius laid titular claim to an empire in which his name was scarcely known or respected: "among the barbarians, he had no legitimate authority." He could neither keep hold of his eastern provinces nor protect his possessions in Italy and the rest of Europe; the barbarians were outraged that the empire should still be called Roman.[59]

The weakened empire thus laid itself open to both political and religious rebellion in every quarter. The Arabs posed the gravest threat, despite their lowly political and economic status: "The Arabs certainly possessed great expanses of territory, bounded by the Ocean on both sides (here the Persian Gulf, there the Red Sea) and extending all the way to Mount Lebanon; but as a nation they never enjoyed any renown nor took part in any of the glory of the East. They were neighbors of the Persians and Assyrians, who were always the preeminent rulers of the East. The Arabs themselves pursued brigandage rather than any sort of trade and always lived a disreputable sort of life."[60]

Their rise to power was the product of both religious and political upheaval; for Biglia, the decline of the faith in the East was the direct result of the decline and fall of ancient Rome.[61] When Constantine transferred the seat of the empire away from the seat of the Church, the move debased both institutions. The Christian faith grew susceptible to heresy from within and assaults from without; equally important, the empire itself was irreparably harmed.[62]

Just as Biglia interprets the establishment and growth of Islam as a process intimately connected to the Arabs' political and military achievements, so too he claims that Rome's religious and political authority faltered *pari passu.* He stresses the dual nature of the events he describes, often through the use of carefully balanced verbal pairs: conflicts between faiths were also contests between secular powers pursuing political goals. Describing the almost continuous insurrection of barbarian peoples against Byzantine authority in late antiquity, for instance, he explains: "Therefore, it was possible for any enemies of *both the empire and the faith* who wished to do so, to reject *the imperial yoke and religion;* with the result that once the *faith and power* of the [independent] princes were united, the powers of *both* grew stronger throughout the world."[63]

Likewise, Muhammad's new religion imbued the Arabs with courage and passion, Biglia says, and yet the actual stimulus to their rebellion was mundane: a group of Arab mercenaries in the Byzantine army were denied their pay, provoking outrage in the entire Arab nation.[64] These malcontents attacked Byzantine territory not to proselytize or persecute Christians but rather to declare their independence and seize lands for themselves. As Biglia describes the initial eruption of the Arabs from their desert homeland, their capture of Damascus and Antioch, and their forays into Anatolia, Egypt, and Persia, he continues to stress the twin factors of religious fervor and political pride. The strength of their faith was an important element in their campaigns,[65] but at the same time they wished to shake off Byzantine rule because it was an affront to their political dignity which they could no longer endure. After defeating their Byzantine overlords, "spurred by both anger and religious zeal, they proclaim the liberty of their name."[66]

Here Biglia introduces an issue which recurs frequently in his analysis of Eastern history: the nature of political authority and, closely linked to it, the significance of political nomenclature. In his view, the authority of a political power stands or falls almost entirely by the willingness of its subjects to obey it. Some powers are more inherently worthy of authority than others: it is unfortunate that Byzantium lost so much of its empire, for instance, and equally lamentable that Persia, with its ancient and honorable heritage, fell to a tribe of desert brigands. Nevertheless, once subject peoples grow impatient with their rulers, little can be done to keep their allegiance. A key feature of this model of authority is the significance of the particular names nations and peoples choose for themselves. For Biglia, *nomen* is more than just a descriptive label; the term incorporates concepts of national and ethnic identity, political autonomy, and moral authority.[67] At times Biglia uses the word as no more than a synonym for *imperium* or *auctoritas,* but on several occasions he maintains that there is real significance in the actual name that a people or state claims for itself. The rebellious barbarians, as we have seen, took offense that the weakened Byzantine Empire "should still be called Roman." Later, after the Arab Empire itself begins to decline, the subject peoples of Asia Minor—the Phrygians, Dardanians, and Teucrians—will throw off the Saracen yoke and reclaim their ancient names.[68] Meanwhile, the Western empire limps on, ruled by Germans whose authority Biglia clearly doubts, arguing from the sheer oddness of their Christian names: when Henrys, Ottos, Conrads, and Ludwigs ruled the Roman Empire, "there was nothing Roman about it."[69]

These comments represent more than the usual humanist snobbery over the legitimate or illegitimate use of ancient names by contemporary states and peoples. In fact, Biglia's concern with names suggests that as a historian he was aware, as few previous Western authors had been, of the historical fluctuations of states, dynasties, and empires in the East. Biglia recognized that although the medieval East had seen a series of empires rise and fall, the land was actually populated by relatively stable local populations who were subjected by, or who transferred their allegiance to, a changing array of political ruling classes. It is this historical process—the rise and fall of political states—which Biglia charts when he records the names Eastern peoples choose and use for themselves.

Among these ancient populations, the seventh-century Arabs were insolent upstarts. Biglia had already belittled their nomadic way of life and condemned their rebellion against Heraclius. Another mark of shame was the name they used for themselves: "Although they could have been called by a more distinguished name, the Arabs did not hesitate to call themselves Saracens, after the ancient *Saraceni*, a name that was lowly and almost everywhere totally fallen out of use and despised."[70] Instead of glorying in the ancient and well-attested title of *Arabes*, they deliberately chose an obscure name (*Saraceni* came into use by Latin authors only in late antiquity)—a choice which Biglia finds inexplicable and shocking.

Biglia does not deny the power of Islam as a religion, nor the atrocities its followers committed in the name of religious zeal.[71] But he does not dwell on these topics, hinting that they are inappropriate for his purposes: "Such things should matter to a man saying his prayers, not to one writing history."[72] Instead he charts the territorial conquests of the Arabs, identifying both secular and religious motives at work in their exploits. The first Arab incursion into Asia Minor, he explains, was led by "pseudo-prophets and heralds of Muhammad" who hoped to win converts.[73] Likewise, the Arabs rejoiced at the capture of Jerusalem because of their veneration of the Old Testament patriarchs,[74] and conquered Egypt and Libya because the people there were inspired by the new "superstition."[75] But they launched naval attacks on Cyprus, Rhodes, and Constantinople for purely strategic political reasons.[76]

When it comes to the fall of Sassanian Persia, Biglia interprets the event as roughly parallel to the decline of Byzantium: political discord compounded by religious heterodoxy sapped the state of its strength. Earlier, he denigrated the Arabs as a nation hardly worthy of notice compared to the ancient and glorious Persians. Here he adds that at the time of the Arab invasions, some Persians had even accepted Christianity, and within the Persian Empire, the rights of Christians were safeguarded by law.[77] But, fatally, the Persian Christians were inclined to heresy and schism, and they lacked the will to retain their faith.[78] At the same time, the Persian king Absterothus (the last Sassanian, Yazdgerd III, Hetoum's *Asdaiorth*) had lost all authority over his subjects and could not compete with the growing power of the Arabs. As they advance on Persian territory, the Arabs temper their usual ferocity, hoping to ingratiate themselves with the local lords. Abandoned by his subjects, Absterothus tries frantically to summon allies from further afield. These include the *Turcimani*—the Turkic people who play such an im-

portant role in Hetoum's account. The Persian king's appeals are not successful. The Arabs descend on his depleted forces and he is killed in the fray.
Shortly thereafter, the first caliph is installed in Baghdad.[79]

Biglia derived most of these details from Hetoum, but his interpretation of
the significance of Persia's fall was entirely new. Earlier Western historians
took varying views of the role of Persia in the Arab conquests. Sigebert of
Gembloux claimed that the Persian Empire simply became Saracen—Persia
converted to Islam and was governed by Arabs but retained its ancient political function as the Eastern challenger to the authority of Rome. Hetoum allowed Persia less political autonomy, beginning his history with its "rebellion" against Rome, but like Sigebert, he believed that when the Arabs
conquered Persia, they inherited its antagonistic place in the ancient rivalry
with Rome. Biglia, by contrast, presents ancient Persia as an independent,
civilized, and possibly even Christian nation, one which together with Rome
had helped to anchor a relatively stable political world order. In his view, the
Arabs did not merely infiltrate the Persian government or assume the mantle of Persian authority; rather, they completely destroyed both the empire
and the stability it had maintained in the East for centuries. Thus the crime
of the Arabs was not only to have persecuted Christians and promoted apostasy but also to have destroyed ancient civilizations, Christian and pagan
alike: "That Machometan superstition had rendered people so senseless that
they seemed to have entirely rejected humanity. All memory of the ancients, *whether Greek or Persian,* perished, so that not even a trace of the virtue once known there survived."[80]

Later Biglia adds Egypt to the list of ancient civilizations the Arabs swept
away. Medieval Muslims had no recollection "of Dariuses or Ptolemies or
other such names; among them the name of the Persians themselves and of
Egypt was scarcely known."[81] Biglia's humanist fondness for antiquity is
such that he sees the fall of any ancient empire, Roman, Greek, or otherwise, as a cause for regret.

Toward the end of Book I, Biglia notes the first signs of weakness in the
Arab Empire and of a renewed resistance among Christians in both the East
and the West. A series of powerful French kings drive the Muslims out of
Spain[82] while the situation of the Christians in Asia begins to improve. Here
Biglia offers an extraordinary assessment of the nature of the Arab Empire:
the Arabs had not eliminated, supplanted, or even outnumbered the populations they conquered; the government of the Middle East was Arab, but
the people were not. The authority of the caliphate therefore rested entirely

on the willingness of its subjects to remain loyal to it and to Islam. Although the credulous peoples of the East at first succumbed to Muslim heresy and the Arab political yoke, deep down they retained a sense of their ancient political and cultural dignity, which at last began to stir. "The empire of the Saracens lasted in Asia for as long as there was faith in their superstition . . . [but] because the character of the people was too great to allow themselves to be ruled by an empire of Arabs, a sense of indignation and regret for the obsequiousness which they had until then shown to this ignoble race gradually took hold in their hearts."[83] Political tensions were beginning to turn local Arab rulers against one another and enfeeble the caliphate. The Greeks were in no position to capitalize on these divisions, for the emperors had grown corrupt, politically weak, and heterodox.[84] The vacuum of power would be filled by two new forces: Christian crusaders from Europe and local populations of Turks. Postponing his discussion of the crusades for the moment (they are the subject of Books X and XI), Biglia begins Book II of his *Commentaries* with a discussion of the origins and character of the Anatolian Turks.

This book, treating the rise and fall of the Seljuk sultanates, is much shorter than Biglia's first, and modeled much more closely on the corresponding text in Hetoum's *Flos*. The two works differ on one crucial point of interpretation, however: the origins of the Seljuks. Hetoum identified them as descendants of the central Asian Türkmens who entered the Middle East in the final days of the Persian Empire and lived quietly under Arab rule until the eleventh century, when they rebelled and established their own state.[85] Biglia, however, sees no connection between the Türkmens and the Seljuks. Instead he identifies the latter as the remnants of the ancient indigenous peoples of Asia Minor: Dardanians, Phrygians, and Teucrians.

As he brings his history forward into the second millennium A.D., Biglia begins to track the revival of ancient political traditions among these peoples of medieval Asia Minor. After four long centuries of Arab domination, he says, "In Asia, now, both empires and names were changing. Those who could be called Dardanians or Phrygians were ashamed to have been known for a while as Saracens; now indeed they are called Teucrians (or, in common parlance, 'Turks')."[86] Around the year 1000, these ancient peoples decided to take advantage of the dissent tearing the Arab Empire apart and declare their independence. Hetoum, no admirer of the Seljuks, had portrayed the Turks as usurpers of Arab authority who "seized" dominion over Asia and, in the course of their invasion, "assaulted and expelled" the Saracens.

Hetoum also stated very clearly that these rogue invaders came from the East, entering Persia from "beyond Khorasan."[87] Biglia, however, imagines that the Turks were indigenous to Asia Minor, descendants of peoples who had participated in and known the benefits of Hellenic civilization. Their territory included some of the most glorious cities and sites of the ancient East: Nicea, Nicomedia, Nicopolis, Mount Olympus, and "all of that ancient Greece of which both the poets and the historians speak."[88]

That an Italian humanist should grant the Turks such a distinguished pedigree is extraordinary. Biglia does not seem to be trying to identify the Turks with Trojans in particular, despite using Virgilian tags such as "Dardanian" and "Phrygian" and even admitting that the names *Teucri* and *Turci* are interchangeable. Nowhere in his work does he specifically mention the fall of Troy or claim that the revival of "Teucrian" power which the Turks represent was aimed at exacting revenge on the Greek sackers of that city. Instead Biglia sees the Turks as heirs to a greater *Hellenic* civilization (*illa vetus Grecia*), claiming for themselves the historic patrimony which their sometime governors, the irresponsible Byzantines, had lost.

Biglia's Turks now begin to take the lead in a sort of homegrown Anatolian liberation movement. Their first ruler, Saboch (Hetoum has *Salioch*, that is, Seljuk), dreams of conquering the rest of Asia, while his successor Virogrissa (Hetoum's *Dolcrilssa*, the historical Toghril Beg) intends to "liberate" the land and make himself its king.[89] Biglia cannot pretend that these reborn Teucrians also returned to any form of ancient religion, but he suggests that the people remained faithful to Islam for fairly superficial reasons.[90] The leadership, moreover, declared for Islam for purely political ends, in order to win the support of the caliph. Once again Biglia suggests that the proud Turks were freeing themselves from shameful political oppression: they promised the caliph that they would not change anything about Islam; it was just that "they did not wish the name of the Saracens to predominate in Asia."[91]

Biglia also modifies Hetoum's account of the early growth of the Seljuk Empire in order to square it with his own claim that the Turks were indigenous Anatolians. Hetoum wrote, somewhat vaguely, that Seljuk's successor Dolcrilssa captured many cities from the Greeks (he did not specify where Dolcrilssa was based or from where he launched these attacks) and granted to his son, "Artot," whatever he could conquer in "Mesopotamia."[92] In reality, Toghril Beg ruled from Baghdad; he captured Greek cities in eastern Anatolia and sent his son on campaign against Syria. Biglia retells this story somewhat differently. In his account, "Virogrissa" first captures many cities from the Greeks *in Bithynia* (that is, in northwest Anatolia, within the borders of ancient Phrygia) before sending his son "Archotus" *east* to carve out a kingdom for himself in Syria. In Biglia's scheme, the Seljuk conquests are an offensive launched *from the West* against barbarous Arabs in the East.

Biglia's insistence that the Turks are the descendants of the ancient inhabitants of Asia Minor was not really intended as a compliment to them. His main concern was to portray the Arabs as an ignoble race who had overturned the political order of the ancient world. It makes sense, therefore, to portray the fall of their empire as an act of restoration achieved by one of the renowned nations of antiquity. At times his vision of the Turks as a Western nation falters: the next event reported by Hetoum was the order given by the Great Seljuk sultan Malik Shah, whom he styled the "emperor of Persia," to his vassal sultans that they should capture Antioch.[93] Here Biglia follows Hetoum's model for the political organization of the Seljuk Empire quite closely, presenting the ruler of Persia as the supreme leader of the Turks and the civil war which consumed "Persia" after the failure of their campaign against Antioch as a catastrophe for the entire Turkish nation. Nevertheless, toward the end of this account Biglia begins to suggest once again that Persia was not really the center of Turkish power. He draws a distinction between, on the one hand, Malik Shah and his successors, whom he calls Persians, and, on the other, the mass of Turks whom they led into battle.[94] Hetoum had the Turks return "home" to Persia after their defeat at Antioch, and reported that after the later collapse of the Great Seljuk sultanate in Persia, mercenaries from Malik Shah's armies fled into Anatolia to form an inconsequential rump Turkish state which remained until the Mongol invasions.[95] Biglia, by contrast, says that the Turks who left Persia "returned home" to Asia Minor. After their arrival, alongside numerous other refugees of other nationalities, "the power of the sultan of the Turks grew incredibly and remained secure from external disasters."[96] Biglia does not mention, as Hetoum did, that this Turkish state would be swept away in the Mongol invasions.[97] Instead he suggests that it had remained intact and powerful up to the present day.

Biglia's Book III treats the Mongol invasions. His main source is still Hetoum; he begins with a sketch of the unrest that overtook the region after the invasions of the central Asian Khwarazmians, which Hetoum also described as a prelude to the arrival of the Mongols.[98] Biglia echoes the view that the Khwarazmians weakened the peoples of the East, leaving them ill-prepared to confront the more serious threat to come. But he characterizes this disorder according to his own humanistic criteria: political discord and religious heresy combined to make people careless of the common good, lacking in virtue and *humanitas*, heedless of their ancient heritage, self-indulgent and ignorant even of how uncivilized they had become. At this point, Biglia seems almost ready to introduce the Mongols as a welcome change. He suggests that they, not unlike the Persians and the "Teucrian" Turks before them, had noble political aspirations and some awareness of Christianity and *humanitas*.[99] At the same time, however, he also rehearses a more traditional view of the Mongol hordes—as beastly savages from the far north, beyond the Caspian Sea, whom the world had heard little about since an early defeat at the hands of Alexander the Great.[100] In the end, Biglia opts for this conventionally negative view of the Mongols. And it is not just their barbarity that he decries; the ease of their conquest also demonstrates how far the East itself had declined both politically and spiritually.

We can get further insight into Biglia's thinking on these points from a reading of Books X and XI, his survey of the crusades, where on several occasions he recapitulates the main points of his earlier books. Close to the start of Book X, for instance, he again discusses the significance of the Mongol invasions, explaining their place in the context of earlier Eastern history:

> Heraclius had attacked the rebel Persians somewhat, so that afterwards they were less ready to withstand the Saracens. The empire of the Saracens lasted until the Phrygians, having thrown off their yoke, ruled in Asia. Afterwards, as we have reported, the Tartars . . . filled all of Scythia. But the name of Machomet still prevailed everywhere, although that plague raged more fiercely in the south; thus the greater part of the world yielded to them . . . Moreover, there was no virtue, no humanity in all the world; all were turned into barbarians, whom neither law nor religion constrained.[101]

Despite mentioning, briefly, the "Phrygian" Turks and their moment of liberation, Biglia is clearly more interested in maintaining that the East has been steadily sinking into disorder for centuries, right up to the cataclysmic moment the Mongols arrived. His theory that the Turks launched a revival of ancient virtues in the middle of such decline, useful as it had been for explaining the eclipse of the Arabs, would not fit well with the argument he develops here. Later, in Book XI, he discusses the Mongol invasions again and makes clear that they were a divine scourge directed against the "Saracens"—one evil sent to afflict another.[102]

Biglia's noble Turks have little part to play in his moralizing interpretation of the Mongol invasions. But they do not disappear from his work for good. Books VIII and IX treat the life of Timur, the rapacious conqueror of Asia who claimed to be heir to the old Mongol khans. Timur died in 1405, close enough to Biglia's own time to convince him, ever the pessimist, that the chaotic spirit of Mongol barbarity was still abroad in the world. Nor did he have to stretch his material much to present Timur as the true heir to Genghis Khan: the sack of Damascus and the rout of the Ottoman army at Ankara in 1402 were among the most notorious events in recent Middle Eastern history.

After leveling Damascus, Biglia explains, Timur turned his attention north to Phrygia, where "Baysitus" (the Ottoman emir Bayezid I) ruled as king of the Teucrians. In Biglia's account of Timur's attack, Baysitus is a sympathetic and tragic figure, hampered by disloyal generals nursing ancient grudges and deserted by his guards in the heat of battle. Wounded, he is taken before Timur, who keeps him as a living trophy, chained like a dog. The conqueror goes on to capture all of Phrygia, even the city of Smyrna, which Baysitus himself had never been able to win—for which failure Timur mocks him cruelly. After many more such insults, he orders the execution of the "silent and trembling" Turk.[103] Biglia then eulogizes the murdered emir: "As much as is possible for an infidel, he was endowed with a modicum of *humanitas;* he did not pursue with zeal the rites of the pagans or the very faith of the Saracens; he was a friend to any Christians who came to trade in that region. For the ships of the Venetians and Genoese fill that sea, on whose shores the Teucrians possess much land . . . and they likewise love the Visconti [of Milan], because they say they were descended from Aeneas the Trojan."[104]

The death of such a man is, for Biglia, the final act in the long decline of the East.[105] Timur continues marauding through Asia Minor, leaving destruction in his wake, although he never repeats the atrocities committed at Damascus. Such severity may not have been necessary in the country of the Turks, Biglia muses, because "of all the people on that shore, the Teucrians are considered most humane."[106] With a brief account of Timur's death and some remarks on the meaning of his name, Biglia brings his history of the East to its chronological end.

This is not, however, the end of the work. In Books X and XI, Biglia returns to the reign of Heraclius and retraces the entire history of the East once again, this time focusing on how the Roman Empire and its successor states had failed to stop the twin forces of Islamic heresy and disorder from spreading through the world. Biglia's civilized Teucrian Turks do not appear in these final chapters. Indeed, it would be a mistake to attribute too much significance to them in the overall scheme of his work. Ultimately, Biglia believed that the problems of the East originated in the flaws and failings of Western Christendom; the region's troubles were only compounded by the evils of Islam. The decline of political dignity, culture, and *humanitas* in the East—virtues all embodied in Biglia's quite unreal "Teucrian" Turks—is for him a symptom of this affliction rather than its cause. His vision of the Turks as the preservers of ancient civilization in the East is in fact rather hard for him to sustain. In certain passages, where he follows his sources closely and pays less attention to the moral conclusions he can draw, he calls the Turks *Turci*, not *Teucri*, and they appear no more virtuous than any other Saracen people.[107]

It seems hard to imagine, on the face of it, why Biglia should lay so much emphasis on the cultural and political character of the nations of the Islamic East when his work purports to treat the history of the Christian faith. Here, a reading of Leonardo Bruni's *History of the Florentine People* may be helpful. Bruni's innovative theories about the decline and revival of ancient Italian civilization, articulated in Book I of his *History*, may well have inspired—and can certainly help to make sense of—Biglia's idiosyncratic model of the decline of Christianity in the East.

Biglia had met Bruni during his stay in Florence (1418–1423),[108] and Bruni's *History* was circulating in manuscript, not just in Florence but elsewhere in Italy as well, by 1429.[109] By the early 1430s, Biglia knew the text, for he modeled his *Milanese History* (1431–1434) closely on Bruni's work: in it, he expresses a similar interest in military and diplomatic history and, like Bruni, adopts the language and style of Livy to do so.[110] Bruni's historiographical innovations—his interest in secular, political history and his concern with identifying human action rather than divine intervention as the main causal agent in the course of events—seem to have exercised a similarly fundamental influence on Biglia's *Commentaries*.[111] One can see the effects of Bruni's work on a very basic level, for instance, in Biglia's insistence that the growth of Islam was a political as well as a religious phenomenon, not a providential scourge but the product of a political, military, and cultural crisis that overtook the Eastern empire in the early seventh century.

Likewise, Biglia's theory that the peoples of the ancient East possessed inherent character traits (a love of liberty, a sense of political dignity, a certain innate *humanitas*) which Islam suppressed but which were still capable of re-

vival seems to owe much to Bruni's theories about the changing fortunes of
the Italian people from antiquity through the Middle Ages. Bruni begins his
History with the assertion that Florence was founded by veterans of Sulla—
not, as medieval tradition held, by Caesar—and so should be considered a
republican rather than an imperial enterprise.[112] Later, however, he traces
the history of Tuscany back much earlier, to the civilization of the ancient
Etruscans. Here he expresses a low opinion of Rome, both republican and
imperial, proudly identifying Florence as the heir of the Etruscan city-states
which dominated northern and central Italy for centuries before the impo-
sition of Roman rule. Bruni's enthusiasm for Etruscan political culture is
clearly related to his estimate of the strengths and virtues of contemporary
Florence and its growing network of Tuscan client cities. The Etruscan towns
were independent, self-governing polities which lived in harmony with one
another. As a result, they enjoyed enormous wealth and power as well as an
impressively advanced culture. In fact, Bruni says, Rome in its earliest years
borrowed and imitated much from the Etruscans, including religion, political ceremony, letters, and learning.[113]

After centuries of war, the Etruscans fell victim to internal dissension and
finally capitulated to the rising power of Rome.[114] Thereafter, the great cities
of ancient Etruria grew small and weak; worse still, the Etruscan character
itself began to decay. Rome imposed idleness on the Etruscans, removed opportunities for advancement, and stifled the healthy competition among cities that had fostered political growth and cultural creativity.[115] For seven
centuries, Bruni concludes, Rome kept Tuscany in a state of impotent limbo,
until at last the empire fell apart, clearing the way for a Tuscan revival that
began in the early Middle Ages and culminated in the triumphant rise of
Florence.[116] This notion—that political liberty and cultural character are in-
extricably linked, each dependent on and necessary for the other—is also an
important element in Biglia's interpretation of Eastern history: once the
peoples of Asia surrendered their liberty to the Arabs, Biglia believed, their
humanitas and sense of common good quickly declined as well. But the rise
of the Seljuk Turks, like that of Bruni's Tuscans, marked a restoration of
those ancient liberties and cultural values.

Bruni's ideas about how exactly Rome fell also seem to have influenced
Biglia's thinking. Bruni identifies the immediate cause of the empire's decline as the barbarian invasions of the fourth and fifth centuries A.D. But, he
says, Rome's problems began long before. Just as the Etruscans surrendered
to Rome and thus brought about their own debilitation, so too the Roman

people lost both liberty and *virtus* when they yielded their sovereignty to princes.[117] From Tiberius on, most were insane and bloodthirsty tyrants who badly betrayed the public trust placed in them. Worst of all was Constantine's decision to remove the seat of empire from Italy altogether, leaving the peninsula open to assaults by tyrants and barbarians.[118] This is a key point: in Bruni's view, the barbarians were not an invincible or unstoppable force; rather, Roman power declined to the point where Italy could no longer defend itself. Internal decay preceded and made possible the damages of external assault.[119] Bruni refuses to condemn the Goths, Huns, Vandals, and Lombards as particularly bloodthirsty or barbarous; instead he points out how incompetent Roman leaders failed to take appropriate action to contain them, fought among themselves, and otherwise provoked the calamities that ultimately befell them.[120] The disaster was total: after the overthrow of Romulus Augustulus, the Western empire simply ceased to exist. When Italian fortunes began to revive around the ninth century, he concludes, it was not because the (largely absentee) Carolingian and Ottonian emperors at last reasserted imperial authority, but rather because the Italians began to cultivate their own success.[121] In short, the growth and prosperity enjoyed by contemporary Italian city-states were the result of a revival of the ancient, indigenous Tuscan spirit, freed from the authority of an empire that had proved unworthy to rule it.[122]

This highly original interpretation of Italian history has its parallels in Biglia's work. Biglia, too, imagined a landscape populated by ancient civilizations—Dardanians, Mysians, Phrygians, and Teucrians—who had been badly betrayed by the Roman emperors supposed to rule and protect them. Like Bruni, he placed great significance on Constantine's desertion of Rome: the decline of the empire began with this one act, which separated religious and secular authority, weakened both, and so made the Arab conquests possible. Biglia also believed that the Arabs, like Bruni's Goths and Huns, were not invincible conquerors but merely very lucky to have picked the target they did. Rome let them win. As a result of imperial negligence, the proud peoples of ancient Asia had to bow to a barbarian power. Both authors, finally, suggested that after centuries of subjugation, these indigenous peoples were able to reclaim their ancient independence. When the rule of the invaders (Germanic or Arab) began to falter, the indigenous locals established new states, not Roman but in one case Etruscan/Tuscan and in the other Teucrian/Turkish.

Here the two accounts diverge. In Bruni's scheme, the reborn cities of

Tuscany grow ever stronger, leading up to the triumphant moment in which the author himself writes; but the localized "Teucrian" revival Biglia describes ultimately falters because Christian Europe fails to support it. The Latin crusaders allow the Mongols to overwhelm the civilized Teucrian Seljuks, just as Byzantium had allowed the Arabs to overwhelm the Greek cities of Asia six centuries before. Biglia, of course, wrote his work as a critique rather than a celebration of the political institutions he set out to describe, so he did not transfer Bruni's model of Tuscan decline and revival wholesale to the history of the East. Nevertheless, the two works share several common themes: the primacy of secular political history, the importance of liberty and self-determination among peoples, the idea that historical continuities unite those peoples from antiquity to the present day. More specifically, the total failure of imperial Rome, as embodied in Constantine's epoch-making decision to move the seat of empire away from Italy, functions in both works as a fundamental turning point in the course of world history, an act whose ill effects can be detected across the whole of the known world down to the present day.

With the resurgence of Ottoman imperial ambitions in the 1440s under Murad II and Mehmed II, Biglia's optimistic view of Turkish accomplishments, past and present, could not be sustained for long. A brief look at Flavio Biondo's account of some of the same currents in Islamic history (in his *Decades*, completed by 1444) shows how rapidly attitudes changed. Biondo was, like Biglia, an enthusiastic admirer of Bruni's historiographical principles. And like Biglia, he tried to trace the history of Islam in the context of late antique and medieval Byzantine politics. He, too, laid much more stress on the Turks' participation in the cultural and political world of medieval Islam than did those humanists who emphasized only their Scythian origins. But—crucially—his interpretation of the role the Turks had played in that world was already far more negative than that which Biglia had proposed only a decade earlier.

The topic of historical decline and rebirth, which Bruni sketched at the start of his Florentine history, became the major theme of Biondo's antiquarian and historical writings, especially his *Decades* of history *ab inclinatione Romanorum imperii*.[123] Like Biglia, however, Biondo chose a much broader topic than Bruni: the history of all Italy (with occasional notices on the rest of the former Roman Empire) in the centuries after the barbarian invasions. In Biondo's work, no one city or region plays the heroic role that

Bruni assigned to Florence. Instead Biondo suggests that the papacy, the independent city-states, and the larger principalities of Italy are the joint heirs
of ancient Rome, all of them now busily reviving, after centuries of struggle,
the glories of their shared imperial past. It is in the context of his belief that
Italy as a whole continues Rome's ancient mission that Biondo's account of
Islamic history should be understood.

Biondo, like the medieval historians on whose works he drew, interpreted
the rise of Islam as a continuation of the ancient struggle between Persia and
Rome.[124] In his account of the religion's origins, he begins with the figure
of Muhammad (who, he says, may have been Persian by birth).[125] Then, relying on Theophanes, he describes the eruption of the Arabs from their
desert homeland in the 620s A.D. After capturing Damascus and Egypt, he
claims, they almost immediately conquered Persia: Biondo dates this event
to shortly after the death of Chosroes II, several years earlier than it actually
happened. (In reality, after Chosroes was murdered by his son in 628, Persia
was ruled by a series of short-lived pretenders to the throne and did not fall
to the Arabs until the late 630s. The last king, Yazdgerd III, maintained the
remnants of a government in exile until his death in 651.) Biondo condenses these events into what seems a much shorter space of time:

> This kind of fire [that is, of Islam] spread more widely than had at first been
> believed. The Arabs, seduced by Muhammad's tricks, decided first to pray
> that the Persians would accept their law; but when the Persians revealed
> themselves to be unwilling, they then attacked them, pursuing the threat-
> ened war with the greatest effort. The king of Persia, Syrochus, who had
> died in the first year of his reign, had been succeeded by his son Adhaeser.
> After he had likewise died in his first year of rule, the Persians on their own
> chose Hormisdas as their king. After the Arabs had defeated and killed
> Hormisdas in battle, the Persians were conquered by the Saracens.[126]

Some of the inaccuracy in Biondo's account stems from errors in his
source.[127] But Biondo also adds further details not found in Theophanes,
which confuse the order of historical events even more:

> The Persians accepted the rule of this Muhammad, and at his order they
> gave up the original and ancient name of their nation, and began for the
> first time to call themselves "Saracens" instead of Persians. And these Per-
> sians, turned into "Saracens," led a campaign against the city of Antioch,
> which was at that time subject to the Byzantine Empire, and captured it.

> When Heraclius heard of this, he sent to Jerusalem and ordered that the
> Holy Cross be brought to Constantinople. Immediately after their capture of
> Antioch, the Saracens proceeded to Jerusalem and likewise took possession
> of that city very quickly.[128]

The Persians were actually quite slow to accept Arab rule and certainly did
not participate in, much less lead, the Arab campaigns of conquest against
Byzantium in the way that Biondo suggests.[129] There were precedents for
the general idea Biondo expresses—that the imperial authority of Persia
was transferred intact to the "Saracen" Arabs. Theophanes himself seems
to suggest that Persia somehow continued to exist as a political entity after the Arab conquest, with the Arabs simply replacing the last Sassanian
ruler as governors of the empire.[130] And in the twelfth century, Sigebert of
Gembloux (another of Biondo's sources) argued that the Arab conquest of
Persia amounted to little more than a change of name; the old empire, now
known as "Saracen," continued to play its traditional role as the dominant
power in the East. Biondo takes this idea one step further by attributing to
the Persians two major conquests—Jerusalem and Antioch—which in reality were conquered by the Arabs alone, at least a year or two before they
even began their assault on Persia. Like Sigebert before him, Biondo elides
the historical roles of the Persians and Arabs in order both to keep his story
simple and to emphasize the historical continuities which he believed were
inherent to its logic.

Biondo's account of the emergence of the Turks in the following century
reveals the same urge to simplify the political history of the region and
thereby reinforce his theme of *translationes imperii*. Once again this leads him
away from a strict recounting of the facts. Biondo presented the emergence
of the Turks from the Caucasus in the 750s as evidence of a general crisis
gripping the Eastern Roman Empire, Italy, and the papacy: at the precise
moment when the Byzantine emperor failed to intervene to save Italy and
the pope from Lombard depredations, the Turks appeared in the East, a further symptom of imperial weakness. Having introduced the Turks at such an
early date, however, Biondo then confronted the same problem Sagundino
and Aeneas Sylvius would later face: what to do with them over the ensuing
centuries, when no historical evidence could be found for their whereabouts
or activities. Biondo's solution recalls his earlier transformation of the Persians into Arabs: he makes the Turks disappear, for the moment, by turning
them, together with the Arabs, back into Persians: "The onslaught of the

Turks was so violent that the Saracens could not make peace with them by any other means than by restoring the ancient name of the Persian Empire, which they had suppressed in favor of their own during the reigns of Phocas and Heraclius, as I have shown. For the Turks did not mind subjecting themselves to the Persians, a people of great renown; they were not, however, willing to tolerate the Saracens as superiors in a land that was not their own."[131]

In Biondo's view, Persia remained the primary locus of power in the East. The Saracen Arabs embarked on their campaigns of conquest not only to spread their religion but also because they had assumed Persia's role as the ancient political rival of Rome. The Turks appeared on the scene—significantly, at a moment when both Byzantine and Roman authority were at a low ebb—but instead of establishing an empire in their own name, they eagerly adopted a Persian identity. Biondo does allow that the Turks were ferocious and, by associating them with Alexander's enclosed nations, suggests that they appeared as a providential scourge, but ultimately he prefers to integrate the Turks into his larger narrative of Rome's ancient struggles in the East.

Biondo interprets the Turks' next appearance in the historical record—the arrival of the Seljuks in the eleventh century, their conquest of Persia and Syria, and the Western response in the form of the First Crusade—as a further extension of the ancient contest between East and West, Persia and Rome. By now, Biondo argues, Latin Christendom, not Greek Byzantium, had come to embody the old Roman *imperium*, with the pope, not the emperor, at its head. Accordingly, barbarian problems in the East were now something for the pope, not the Byzantine emperor, to confront. Pope Urban II launched the First Crusade not just as a Christian pilgrimage but also as a campaign of Roman imperial *recuperatio*.

Biondo's ideas are perhaps best expressed in his remarkable recreation of Urban II's sermon at the Council of Clermont. Here the pope's words reflect the concerns and preoccupations of the fifteenth century to a far greater degree than they do the eleventh. Urban II, speaking Biondo's words, first defines the crusade as a campaign to liberate Jerusalem. But he goes on to say that the expedition is necessary in order to reestablish throughout the East the ancient authority of the Roman Empire, to which the papacy is the rightful heir. In recent years the nation of Hagarenes, made up of both Turks and Saracens, has come from Persia to capture not only Jerusalem and the Holy Land but also "all those lands which once were subject to the Roman

Empire, and afterwards to the Roman pope."[132] Though Byzantium used to defend Europe from such Asiatic incursions, recently the Eastern empire has grown so weak that not only the Mediterranean lands but even the countries of eastern Europe lie in danger. (The idea that the Seljuk Turks threatened Hungary, Poland, Bohemia, and Germany is perhaps the most obvious example of Biondo's reading contemporary concerns back into the eleventh-century past.)[133] Therefore, Urban concludes, in the absence of effective imperial authority, the Roman pope must take up the task of defending and restoring Christendom—an entity which was once, and should still be, coterminous with the boundaries of the ancient empire—against an enemy who attacks not only the Christian religion but also the political integrity of Rome.[134]

Biondo's claim for continuity between ancient and medieval Eastern empires thus underscores his larger theme: that the medieval Italians, led by the medieval Church, together preserved and defended Rome's imperial legacy in the centuries after the empire's fall. Like Bruni and Biglia before him, Biondo is really interested in the history of Rome itself: he investigates Islamic history for its potential to illustrate the decline of (East) Roman political and religious authority in the early Middle Ages and its (Italian) revival around the turn of the first millennium. And like his humanist predecessors, Biondo believes that historical continuities link the ancient and medieval worlds: the structures of the ancient political economy have survived, in one form or another, down to the present day.

All three historians take a remarkably similar view of the significance of barbarian invasion (for Bruni, that of the Goths and Huns; for Biglia, the Arabs; for Biondo, the combined forces of Persians, Arabs, and Turks) as events that threatened the survival of those ancient structures. Indeed, in the accounts by Biglia and Biondo, the assaults of Eastern barbarians continue throughout the Middle Ages, continually challenging "Rome"—or its heirs in Italy—to revive ancient virtues and mount a proper resistance.[135] While Biglia identifies the Mongols and the Mamluks as the contemporary embodiment of the ancient barbarian threat (with the Turks appearing as their virtuous adversaries), in Biondo's work it is the Turks themselves who threaten Roman authority. For both Biondo and Biglia, however, these new barbarians are ultimately no worse than those who came before. Nor is there much that is new in their articulation of Christian-Islamic conflict as a continuation of ancient Roman-Persian hostility, or as part of a larger East-West conflict. This is an interpretation that had been circulating since at least the

time of Guibert of Nogent and Sigebert of Gembloux. If anything, the interpretation lost popularity among the Italian humanists of the generation after
Biglia and Biondo, who preferred to stress the Turks' alien barbarity and
thus severed the links between the Turks and their Persian and Arab predecessors which previous historians had tried to forge.

The Empires of Islam after 1453

The humanistic interpretation of Islamic history which flowered so briefly in
Biglia's and Biondo's works quickly disappeared from view in the later fifteenth century. In a few texts from this later period, scholars such as Filelfo
and Aeneas Sylvius borrowed information from Biglia and Biondo in order to affirm the place of the Turks in the history of the medieval Middle
East. But these later authors exploited the historiographical insights of their
predecessors for strongly polemical purposes: when they did choose to acknowledge the Turks' longstanding adherence to Islam and their centuries
of residence in the lands of the caliphate, they used this information as further grounds for attacking the Turks, adding another dimension to their hostile portrait of them as uncivilized and bloodthirsty barbarians. The more objective and better-informed approach to medieval Islamic history adopted by
Biglia and Biondo would not be taken up again by European scholars until
close to the end of the fifteenth century.

Filelfo, for instance, drew information on the early history of the Arabs
and Turks directly from Biglia but dismissed altogether his argument that
the "Phrygian" Turks were a particularly virtuous Eastern people. Instead he
reworked Biglia's material in order to present the Turks as an especially
wicked and barbarous race, far worse than other Muslim nations of previous
centuries or the present day.

Evidence for Filelfo's thorough reading of Biglia's *Commentaries* comes
from a manuscript notebook in the Vatican Archive headed "Ex fragmentis
F. filelphi."[136] Three quarters of the booklet is taken up with extracts from
Biglia's Books I–V.[137] The notes are not dated, but Filelfo must have made
them before he wrote his crusade letter to Charles VII of France, dated 17
February 1451, for here he quotes from Biglia's work in several places.[138]

Filelfo's letter to Charles is his longest essay on the Turkish question, a
somewhat disorganized combination of historical erudition, strategic analysis, and no small amount of shameless flattery, all aimed at persuading the
French king to support a new crusade. His pretext for writing to Charles was

the recent death of Murad II and the succession of the eighteen-year-old Mehmed II. Now was the ideal moment, Filelfo argued, for Christendom to strike a blow against the Ottomans.[139] Filelfo was also, as ever, searching for a new patron and may have had hopes of moving to the French court.[140] Critics have derided the letter as an unedifying display of humanist pedantry and self-promoting bombast.[141] Yet the ideas Filelfo expresses here about the historical origins of the Turkish problem represent yet another turning point in the Renaissance history of Islam.

One major theme Filelfo develops in the letter is the French monarchy's traditional association with crusading. He refers to the long line of Charles's illustrious forebears—among them Charlemagne, Godfrey of Bouillon, and St. Louis—who had triumphed over Muslim armies in centuries past.[142] Accordingly, he also tries to establish historical connections between the present-day Ottoman Turks and their "Saracen" predecessors, in order to argue that the French should likewise continue their ancestral commitment to the crusade. Instead of emphasizing the Turks' origins in the barbarous Caucasus (although he does not abandon this idea completely), Filelfo here integrates the Turks into a larger narrative of Islamic history. He does so in a lengthy excursus, from Muhammad's career to the early Arab forays into the Mediterranean world, the conflicts between crusaders and Saracens in the twelfth and thirteenth centuries, and finally the more recent assaults of the Ottomans on eastern Europe and the Mediterranean.[143] Filelfo bases this account on a creative reading of Biglia's *Commentaries* as well as information from other, earlier sources and a certain degree of outright invention. In essence, he suggests that the Turks have *always* been the main protagonists of Islamic history, from the seventh century down to the present day. Therefore they, and not the Arabs or anyone else, have always been and still remain the primary foes of the most Christian kings of France.

This is not a claim Filelfo is able to sustain with complete consistency. At the start of his letter, he identifies the Saracens and the Turks as two different races who have both, in the past as well as at present, attacked and insulted Christendom. The Saracens started out as an ignominious rabble who "stole" the three richest provinces of the Byzantine Empire, Egypt, Syria, and Palestine, while the Turks were fugitive Scythian slaves who broke out of the Caucasus to attack Persia. In the present day, moreover, the Saracens (whom he now seems to identify with the Mamluks of Egypt) continue to assail Christian islands in the Mediterranean, while the Turks occupy great stretches of territory in Europe as well as Asia.[144] In the historical excursus itself, however, Filelfo rejects the idea that the two nations have had parallel and roughly similar histories. Instead he suggests an early transfer of power from the Saracen Arabs, who dominated only the very first years of Islamic history, to the Turks, who quickly overshadowed them.

Filelfo begins the excursus by rehearsing the traditional polemical biography of Muhammad: his early years as a camel trader and marriage to a wealthy widow; his epilepsy and feigned conversations with the angel Gabriel; the promulgation of his scurrilous "law," which aped Christian and Jewish theology; the converts he won by mounting impressive stunts (like receiving divine messages from a tame dove and a trained cow) and by promising men the freedom to indulge in whatever carnal pleasures they desired.[145] Then, probably relying on the notes he had taken on Biglia's work, Filelfo recounts how Arab mercenaries rebelled against their Byzantine paymasters and, led by Muhammad, launched their first attack on Antioch.[146] Immediately afterward, they invaded Persia. Filelfo's account of this episode is even more obscure and puzzling than Biglia's or Biondo's, and demonstrates his very flexible use of historical sources:

[Muhammad] now made war against the neighbouring Persians, who greatly frightened him. At that time the ruler of Persia was Chosroes, who had himself become quite deranged and had ordered that divine honors be accorded him. He hired the Turks, who were the tributaries—practically the slaves—of the Scythians and dwelled within the defiles and very rugged crags of the Caucasus, and with them he confronted the Saracens. The battle was begun . . . Many on each side were wounded, captured or killed. In the midst of much slaughter, Muhammad was finally overpowered and, having received a disfiguring wound to his face, took flight. Muhammad was overpowered and wounded by these Turks, I say, whose descendants now venerate him greatly.[147]

The story Filelfo tells is hardly accurate. Muhammad never invaded Persia, nor did any of the Arabs during his lifetime. The Arab invasion of Persia took place after his death, and long after the death of Chosroes II in 628. The Arabs, moreover, were victorious in this campaign; finally, no Turks were involved. No single historical source recounts the story as Filelfo tells it here, but several texts can be identified from which he may have borrowed details.

Filelfo's frequently repeated claim that the Turks were tributaries or slaves of the Scythians probably derives from a remark about the origins of the

Parthians by Trogus. The story that they entered Persia from the Caucasus derives from Theophanes' account of the Khazar Turks' invasion of Armenia, undertaken after they struck their alliance with Heraclius—we have seen Biondo retail nearly the same claim. But Filelfo contradicts much of what Theophanes has to say about the Khazars: although the Byzantine historian records them coming out of the Caucasus in the 620s, within Muhammad's lifetime, he describes how they fought *against* Chosroes and does not involve the Arabs in the story (Theophanes dates the Arab invasion of Persia to the 630s, during the reign of "Hormisdas"). Filelfo's claim that the Turks came to protect Chosroes rather than attack him probably reflects his reading of Biglia—specifically, the latter's account of how Chosroes's ultimate successor, Yazdgerd III, requested help from the Eastern Türk "Turcomans" against the Arabs in the 640s. That appeal was unsuccessful, as Biglia (following his source, Hetoum) explains, and as Filelfo, too, understood; in his notebook he paraphrases Biglia's account of the incident fairly accurately.[148] In the letter to Charles VII, however, Filelfo takes the basic outline of the story—that "Turks" were summoned by a Persian king to fight the Arabs within a few years of the foundation of Islam—and changes the outcome, now presenting the Turks rather than the Arabs as the victors in the battle.

Finally, Filelfo's claim that the Turks triumphed not just over the Arabs but over Muhammad himself, inflicting a "disfiguring wound" to his face in the process, derives from yet another historiographical tradition. Several medieval crusade histories, including the widely circulated *Historia orientalis* of Jacques de Vitry, record that Muhammad was struck in the jaw and lost several teeth during a disastrous battle in Arabia, fought early in his career. Some historians put the incident, erroneously, at a later date, including it in accounts of Arab attacks on Byzantium.[149] But "Turks" never figure in these medieval accounts; this appears to be Filelfo's invention.

In reality, neither Persians nor Turks had anything to do with the injury Muhammad suffered. Filelfo took that incident and transposed it to Persia, where the Prophet never went, and credited it to the Turks, whom he never fought. He did so to exaggerate the importance of the Turks in the early years of their history. By putting the Turks into battle against Muhammad and by making them win that battle, Filelfo promoted them to a position of political prominence in the medieval Middle East which they would not historically occupy for several more centuries. Filelfo's account here seems to contradict completely the usual humanist portrayal of the Turks as Scythian barbarians who never achieved any honest victories in war—an argument he himself was capable of making.[150] But in writing to Charles VII, his creative interpretation of seventh-century history serves a special purpose: he uses it to show that it was the Turks, not the Arabs, who had led the tide of Muslim expansion down through the ages—and against whom French kings had always gone out to fight.[151]

Having introduced the Turks as conquerors at such an early date, Filelfo in effect removes the Arabs from the historical scene. Turks and Arabs continued to dwell side by side in Persia until the year 1000, he says, but it was clear whose star was in the ascendant. At last the Turks rose up and ejected the "Saracens" from Asia altogether. Drawing again on Biglia, he explains:

> The Turks, not long after the year 1000, began to attack [the Arabs] more violently than they had before, in open warfare . . . They created a king by the name of Saboch,[152] who thought constantly about conquering Asia. So that he might accomplish this more easily, he pretended to be a worshipper of Muhammad, doing this not so much out of fear of God as of other men, whom he wanted to win over to his cause. Therefore he attested to the Caliph, whom they venerate above all others like a pope, that he would change nothing whatsoever concerning the doctrine of Islam, but that he did not want the shameful name of the Saracens to predominate in Asia. Thereupon the Turks very quickly expelled all the Saracens, who are Arabs, from Asia.[153]

The claim Filelfo makes here about the Turks' commitment to Islam is especially interesting. Elsewhere in the excursus, he stresses that Islam is a religion based on trickery and carnal licentiousness—familiar topics of medieval anti-Islamic polemic. He reviews the events of Muhammad's life and the implausible aspects of his "law," for instance, in order to portray both Arabs and Turks as ridiculously credulous. And elsewhere he states that the Turks chose to convert to Islam—even though they had soundly defeated Muhammad in battle—because they found the sensual pleasures it promised to be irresistibly attractive: "It was not, therefore, out of religious devotion (which the Turks have never possessed) nor out of superstition (which the Turks feel even less than religion, for they are a people who care neither for God nor for the soul and know neither fear nor rational thought) that the Turks finally converted to the nefarious sect of Mahomet, even after they had destroyed his forces in Persia and inflicted a shameful wound to his face; it was, instead, for the sake of [Islam's] very lax manner of life."[154]

Here, however, in his account of Seljuk's career, Filelfo suggests that the Turks converted for purely political reasons. Once again he changes Biglia's account in a subtle but significant way. Biglia said the Turks converted to Islam shortly after they came to Persia in the sixth century; later, Seljuk struck a deal with the caliph, promising him that he would do no harm to the religion of Islam but needed his support in order to overthrow the Arabs in Asia.[155] Biglia even made this seem a positive thing for the Turks to do: a canny strategic maneuver undertaken by the "Teucrians" in order to restore their ancient political independence. Filelfo, however, says that Seljuk promised the caliph that his followers would *convert* to Islam. Having already condemned the Turks for their credulity and hedonism, he now charges them with hypocrisy, because they pretended to adopt a new religion solely for political gain. In either case, he seems to suggest, the Turks were worse than the Arabs, who had at least embraced their faith sincerely.

The Turks also posed a far greater political and military threat. After their expulsion from Asia, the Saracens retreated meekly to the deserts of Arabia and North Africa, where "they returned to their original way of life, namely brigandage, in which they continue to excel above all others even to the present day."[156] Of course, they did not all cling to this shiftless Bedouin existence: later in the letter Filelfo admits that one group of Saracens, the Mamluks, still exercised political power in Egypt, at least. But they were a heterogeneous mix of Arabs and formerly Christian slaves who could cause Christendom little trouble—unlike the Turks, who remained a dangerous menace.

In Filelfo's view, Saboch's Turks had not only seized power over all of Asia in the year 1000 but had retained it down to the present day. The Turks, not the Arabs or anyone else, had ruled the East in the crusade period; they had challenged Frankish might over the centuries; they alone of all Muslim peoples were the true adversaries of France. Filelfo even suggests that these medieval Turks were *Ottomans:* he claims that Saladin, the Kurdish commander who led an army out of Egypt in 1187 to recapture Jerusalem, was not only "emperor of the Turks" but founder of the Ottoman dynasty:

> And that Saladin, who was a Turk and an Ottoman and was carried away by his great victory which had been so unfortunate for the Christians, made such a name for himself and assumed so much importance that he alone was the first of the Ottoman family to be made king (or emir, as they call him) by an incredible degree of consent among all the Turks; and he won

such a place in the hearts of those barbarians that even to this day they will endure no one else of their race to be their emir, but insist on an Ottoman.[157]

The crusaders' defeat at Hattin was not one of the last episodes in France's medieval adventure in the East. It was, rather, the first act of aggression by the new Ottoman dynasty, which would thereafter remain the chief agent of Muslim aggression against the Christian West.[158] The loss of Jerusalem was a crime whose perpetrators remained unpunished, but Charles VII could avenge it now by leading a crusade against the Ottoman Turks.

Aeneas Sylvius was the fifteenth century's most impassioned and prolific proponent of the theory that the Turks were barbarous Scythians lacking a distinguished record of political achievements. But on occasion he too tried to integrate the Turks into the history of the Islamic world. He drew on the works of both Biglia and Biondo to do so; like Filelfo, he was chiefly interested in portraying the Turks in as poor a light as possible.

In his oration at the Congress of Mantua in 1459, for example, Aeneas adopted a tone far closer to that of the medieval crusade sermon than he had used in previous exhortations (the occasion practically required such a rhetorical move). Consequently, his account of the Turks' historical origins also emphasized their adherence to Islam rather than their cultural barbarity. Aeneas may have decided that, given his position as the head of the Church, some of the arguments he had most relied on in previous orations were no longer appropriate. At Mantua he neither flattered the princes he addressed nor encouraged them to imitate ancient heroes, nor did he condemn the Turks as enemies of classical culture. Instead he lectured his audience on their spiritual obligations and suggested, by frequent reference to the sacred authority with which he now spoke, that he no longer meant to plead for a crusade but instead would command one.

Throughout the oration Aeneas places particular stress on the religious character of the proposed crusade, its necessity, and the spiritual benefits it will bring to participants. After a solemn prayer to God to look favorably on the endeavor he proposes, he laments "what we have lost, what injuries the Turks have done to us and to our God."[159] Here, instead of recounting how the Turks destroyed ancient Roman cities and Greek books (as he did in his letters of 1453), he retells the story of the rise of Islam and the simultaneous decline of Christianity in the East. In its first few centuries, Aeneas explains, the Christian religion spread so quickly that by the time of Constantine, believers could be found from India to Spain. Now, however, the Gospel is hardly known in Africa or Asia, and Christians huddle in the tiny corner of Europe to which they have been confined. This long retreat was forced by the combined activities of the Turks and the Saracens, starting with the appearance of Muhammad in the seventh century.[160] But Islam by itself, at least as it was first practiced by the Arabs, did not cause much damage to Christendom, Aeneas maintains. The real crisis occurred only when the Turks appeared on the scene:

> This disaster [that is, Islam] began during the reign of Heraclius. For, after the way of salvation had lain open to all through Christ the son of God . . . the Devil, filled with hatred for the human race and unable to bear it that Christ should reign everywhere, raised up a pseudo-prophet in Arabia called Mahomet . . . Among the Greeks, the empire had already grown weak, and Roman virtue had languished after being transferred to a different place [Constantinople] . . . nevertheless, a large number of Christians remained in Asia up to the time of Pepin, king of the Franks . . . At that time the Turks came out of Scythia and occupied Cappadocia, Pontus, Bithynia, the Troas, Cilicia and all of Asia Minor, and having grown powerful thanks to our negligence, not only drove true Christians out of Asia, but crossed the Hellespont in boats and invaded Macedonia, Thrace, Attica.[161]

Aeneas could have derived such a general account of Islamic history from any number of sources, but his reference to the transfer of imperial power to Constantinople and the consequent failure of Roman *virtus* points to Biglia as a likely source of information.[162] He also follows Biglia in claiming that the decline of Roman power and virtue was what allowed the rise of the Arabs (though he also credits a spiteful Satan for their success). Unlike Biglia, however, Aeneas does not portray the Arabs as a particularly potent force of barbarism or heresy; indeed, "a large number of Christians" in Asia still kept their faith, despite the Arabs' best attempts to convert them. It was only when the Scythian Turks emerged on the scene that Christianity really faltered in the East—because, he seems to imply, the Turks were simply much more violent and wicked than any other Eastern people.

Aeneas goes on to suggest that the Turks were responsible for instigating almost every act of violence or apostasy subsequently committed against Christendom. After they emerged from Scythia and began their attacks on Eastern Christians, he says, other infidels also began to threaten Christendom from other directions. Berbers and Moors in Spain and the Mediterranean, pagan Lithuanians on the borders of Poland, Tartars in Russia, and "half-human" tribes in the northern reaches of Scandinavia all started to encroach on European territory—following the lead of the Turks.[163] The result was the sorry state of present-day Christendom: "These are your borders, Christians, thus you are surrounded, thus you, once the most powerful lords and masters of the world, are confined in a corner."[164] Most lamentable of all was the loss of the Holy Land, "the land of milk and honey, where the first buds of our faith appeared."[165]

Like Filelfo, Aeneas apparently was incapable of taking a moderate view of Turkish history. Either the Turks were an anarchic barbarian rabble fresh from Scythia, or—if their longstanding residence in the Islamic world was to be admitted—they were the most fearsome of all Muslims, the canniest and best organized, with the longest and most impressive record of violence against Christians. Biglia's positive view of the Turks and of their history and culture must have struck Aeneas as grossly unacceptable. The only element in Biglia's account he found worth preserving was the association of the rise of Islam with a moment of Roman weakness.

Even Biondo's more neutral portrayal of the Turks as the latest in a series of Eastern challengers to Roman authority seemed to Aeneas to be far too mild—as we can tell from the epitome he made of Biondo's *Decades* in the early 1460s.[166] In his summaries of the two passages by Biondo examined above (recounting the Arab conquest of Persia in the seventh century and the Turkish "invasion" a hundred years later), Aeneas rejects Biondo's suggestion that the Turks somehow perpetuated the rule of ancient Persia. In the first passage, he preserves Biondo's statement that the Persians "became" Saracens after capitulating to them.[167] But in the second account, where Biondo describes how the Turks defeated the Saracens and both nations agreed to call themselves Persians again, Aeneas rather illogically maintains that although the two peoples agreed to restore the Persian Empire, the Turks nevertheless continued to be called by their own name.[168] The Saracens and Turks, far from continuing the tradition of Persian rule, actually obliterated it.

Platina, who used Aeneas's *Epitome* of Biondo as a source for his *Lives of the Popes*,[169] tells a version of this same story in which details are reversed yet again. Platina says that the Turks agreed to be called Saracens, not Persians. "After much mutual slaughter, after the Turks and Saracens at last agreed to peace," he explains, "it was decided that those Turks who were living in Persia should henceforth be known as Saracens. It was for this reason that the Saracens did not mind allowing the Turks to rule in Asia." There is not much point in the story as Platina tells it—did he mean to imply that this was a shameful choice for the Turks to have made, or was he just confused? Whatever the case, he concludes on a negative note: the Arabs "also saw that the Turks would soon accept the superstition of Muhammad, so ready were their hearts for evil."[170]

Aeneas and Platina both refused to accept Biondo's model of Eastern history as the continuing story of ancient Persian aggression against the West. In another text from the period of Aeneas's pontificate, however, this idea is enthusiastically developed, although with a completely different interpretation, which is once again particularly prejudicial to the Turks. This is a letter written in late 1463, addressed to Pius II in the name of Francesco Sforza and expressing his commitment to the coming crusade. It is entirely possible that the letter was composed by Filelfo, then employed as one of the duke's secretaries, though this is only conjecture. In the letter "Sforza" claims that his crusaders will have no trouble conquering the Turks, for their innate ferocity was long ago tempered by the softness of the Persians with whom they had intermingled. Although the Persians themselves had a long history of attacking the West, their adventures had always ended in defeat—the author cites ancient Persian campaigns against Scythia, Athens, Macedon, and Rome.[171] The Turks, of course, were a different and much more dangerous race, but in truth the enemy the crusaders set out to fight could hardly be considered Turkish: "For when those ancient Turks mingled with [the Persians], the mildness and the old customs and habits of that country rendered them so soft and effeminate, that only the name of the Turks remained among them; in a generation, their strength was extinguished."[172]

In recent years these "Persian" Turks had lost more battles than they had won. As proof, one need look no further than Timur, who had within living memory overwhelmed the Turkish army and subjected the sultan to the most painful humiliations. If the Ottomans now rampaged through Europe with impunity, Christendom had only itself to blame.[173]

Other anti-Turkish texts of the period sometimes portray the Turks as effeminate Asiatics.[174] But rarely is there proposed, as here, a historical justification for the claim. The author of this letter clearly knew something about the movement of Turks into medieval Persia—whether as recounted by Biglia, Biondo, or some other authority is unclear. But he interpreted the story in an entirely original way. He did not claim, as Biondo did, that the

Turks assumed the important political role the Persians had played in the ancient contest between East and West, nor that they brutally overwhelmed and obliterated Persia, as Aeneas and Platina maintained. Rather, the Turks had been infected by Persian softness and so ceased to pose any real threat to the West.

The letter from Sforza is also unusual in that it associates the Turks and Persians with one another while introducing Timur as the leader of a different nation altogether. It was far more common for authors of the period to identify Timur as a Persian and to explain his crushing victory over the Turks at Ankara in 1402 as the resurgence of the ancient enmity that had long held between those two distinct Asian nations, as the next chapter shows.

The texts we have examined in this chapter hardly present a consistent view of the role of the Turks in the medieval Middle East or their relations with their Persian and Arab predecessors. This is perhaps the most important point to be made about them. Biglia and Biondo compiled detailed accounts of Islamic history in which Persians, Arabs, and Turks all had important roles to play. Aeneas Sylvius, Filelfo, and Platina took this material out of its original context and manipulated it in order to support a range of rhetorical positions—each different from the next but all meant to support the contemporary political movement for a crusade against the Ottomans. Thus the ferocious medieval Turks had overwhelmed and destroyed the imperial glories of ancient Persia, or they had been softened and corrupted by barbarous Persian vices. They had driven the Saracens out of Asia and back into Bedouin obscurity, or they had eagerly transformed themselves into Saracens, "since their hearts were ready for evil." They were lusty and sensual devotees of Islam, or they were cynical political operators who exploited the loyalties of sincere Muslims for political gain. Timur was a new barbarian conqueror, throwing the decadent East into greater disarray, or his conquests were the first moves of a revived, imperial Persian offensive that might yet redraw the geopolitical map and restore Asia to its ancient glories. Whatever conclusions the humanists reached, they had little to do with the historical reality of what had happened, or was happening, in the Islamic East—or even with what their sources told them of such matters.

One thing the variety of their conclusions does indicate is that humanist historians of the second half of the fifteenth century were hardly committed to a Herodotean antithesis between monolithic East and West. A handful of medieval chroniclers (Sigebert of Gembloux, Guibert of Nogent, Hetoum) had toyed with such a concept, and their early humanist readers—Biglia and Biondo—made some efforts to promote it. But historians writing after 1453 directed their energies to portraying the Turks as fundamentally different from and far worse than their Persian or Arab predecessors. In their view, the Arabs, while not harmless, had been a minor political thorn in the side of the Byzantine Empire. And Persia (the quintessentially barbarous enemy in the eyes of classical Greek authors) came to seem to them a rather civilized place, the seat of an ancient empire and the cradle of an impressive civilization which various Islamic empires had almost—but not entirely—destroyed. As the humanists of Aeneas Sylvius's circle used the events of Islamic history to denigrate the early history of the Turks and their contemporary Ottoman descendants, so too did they exploit these same narratives to lionize other contemporary Islamic peoples, states, and kings.

CHAPTER 5

Wise Men in the East

The humanist habit of distinguishing the Turks from other Muslim polities extended to the interpretation of current affairs in the East. Just as the Turks had always been (and therefore continued to be) far worse than other Islamic nations, so those other nations (both past and present) were now understood to have played a positive role in the history of the region. As the humanists demonized the Turks, they romanticized the histories of other Islamic dynasties and burnished the biographies of their princes, especially those ruling to the east of the Ottoman Empire, in the territories of classical Persia. Humanist biographers of Timur, for example, developed a politically useful and inspiring portrait of the conqueror as an Oriental champion, imperial Persia's answer to Europe's barbarian Turkish troubles. This romanticized interpretation of Persian history and its latter-day rulers in turn shaped Renaissance responses to later Islamic empires arising on the Ottomans' eastern frontier.

Tamerlane: Humanist Hero

In the decade between 1395 and 1405, the warlord Timur (often styled Timur Lenk or "Timur the Lame" and known to European posterity as Tamerlane) transformed the political landscape of the medieval Middle East. From his native Transoxania, he led armies south and west to conquer first the Iranian plateau, then Mesopotamia, and finally Mamluk Syria and vast stretches of Ottoman Anatolia. Famously, he captured the Ottoman emir Bayezid I at the Battle of Ankara in 1402, throwing the Ottoman state into an anarchic interregnum that lasted nearly two decades.

In an effort to establish the legitimacy of Timur's imperial conquests, his court historians claimed for him a political inheritance from the Chagatai Mongols, and even hinted at direct descent from Genghis Khan.[1] European observers, however, had rather different ideas about his lineage and character. In the north, chroniclers celebrated Timur as a crypto-Christian champion in the mold of Prester John. In Italy, by contrast, early observers of Timur's campaigns vacillated between admiration for his victories over the Muslim populations of the Levant and horror at the cruelty with which he pursued them. Within a generation, however, Italian humanists were casting Timur in a range of more abstract, moralizing roles: the conqueror was either a scourge of sinful and corrupt civilizations or a morally neutral example of the unpredictability of fortune. After the Ottoman capture of Constantinople in 1453, Timur's reputation underwent yet another transformation. As Italian concern over the Ottoman threat increased, Timur came to be valorized as a sympathetic hero, a warrior with Christian Europe's best interests at heart, a sign of God's providential concern for his people. That the European image of a Muslim conqueror could change in light of later historical developments is no great surprise: European historians had revised their estimates of almost every Asiatic empire (whether Persian, Arab, Turk, or Mongol) once it ceased to pose a threat to Christian interests or once a new and more aggressive dynasty arose to replace it. What is interesting about Timur's treatment at the hands of the Italian humanists is *how* they chose first to demonize him and then later to celebrate his achievements.

The complex Italian response to Timur is all the more intriguing when compared to reactions in northern Europe. When the conqueror burst onto the Middle Eastern scene in the closing years of the fourteenth century, northern European observers were eager for news of any challenge to Ottoman might, however brutal. The crusading armies of France, Burgundy, and Hungary had suffered a humiliating defeat at the hands of the Turks at Nicopolis in 1396. Reports that a triumphant Asiatic conqueror had avenged this defeat by destroying the Ottoman army at Ankara were greeted with enormous enthusiasm. The conqueror had not only captured the Turkish emir Bayezid I, it was said, but also subjected him to a satisfying gauntlet of humiliations: he had bound the Turk in chains, kept him confined in an iron cage, mocked him for his failures, forced him to eat the scraps beneath his table, made him crouch and serve as his mounting block. He was said to treat the Christians in his domains, by contrast, with great kindness, and it was thought he might soon convert to Christianity, if he had not already done so.

Of course, the idea that a distant Oriental champion might appear on the Eastern horizon, ready to help Christendom overthrow the forces of Islam, was not new. Spurious letters from Prester John, the legendary Christian emperor of India, had been circulating in Western Europe since the late twelfth century.[2] And in the early fourteenth century (prompted in part by propagandists like Hetoum), the French crown had negotiated with Mongol princes in western Asia in an effort to envelop the Muslim states of the Levant in a war on two fronts.[3] Moreover, there were grains of truth to the stories that were told of Timur. After the battle of Ankara (where Bayezid I *was* taken captive, though he seems to have been treated with respect), Timur dispatched letters to several European princes announcing his victory and inviting the Christian powers to establish commercial and diplomatic relations. Sending congratulations in reply, the governments of England, France, and Castile all explored the possibility of formal alliances with him.[4] In 1403 the Dominican bishop Jean of Sultaniyya traveled from Syria to present the French court with a vivid (at times even gruesome) report on the conqueror's military might, together with an optimistic account of his intentions toward the most Christian king.[5] In 1406 his Castilian counterpart Ruy González de Clavijo brought similar tidings back to Spain. Such reports led the traditional crusading powers to entertain hopes (for a brief while, at least) that the Tartar lord might join them in a coordinated attack against the empires of Islam. At least one English chronicler imagined that Timur, on capturing Jerusalem, had not only converted to Christianity but also taken up the crusader's cross—a deliberate echo of the sort of tales that had been told of Prester John and the Mongol khans in an earlier age.[6]

Adam Knobler has shown that it was only centuries later, in the colonial era, that northern European authors transformed Timur into a barbarian savage, demoting the Asiatic conqueror "from the status of ally to that of enemy."[7] But few scholars have examined how Timur's image developed in quattrocento Italy.[8] There, the process seems to have been almost exactly the reverse, with fear and contempt coming first, admiration and approval only later.

The initial enthusiasm of northern European observers seems not to have extended to Italy. The *Chronicle* of Adam of Usk, a Welshman resident in Rome in 1402 when news of Timur's Syrian conquests broke, reflects a more ambivalent stance. The unnamed "son and heir" of the king of Persia had defeated the Turkish sultan and thus brought relief to the beleaguered Christians of eastern Europe, Adam wrote, but he had gone on to raze Jerusalem to the ground, "and this has posed grave difficulties for Christian pilgrims to the region."[9] Indeed, to many Italian observers, Timur's violence toward Turks and other Muslims, though gratifying, was overshadowed by the threat of disruption to Mediterranean pilgrim routes and Levantine trade. Early reports of Timur's depredations in southern Russia prompted the Venetian Senate to search for ways to resist him, not court his favor.[10] (When the Venetian merchants of Tana did approach Timur to ask for protection, he responded by plundering their goods.) The Genoese got further in their negotiations, going so far as to raise his standard for a time over their colony at Pera and publicly rejoicing at his victory over Bayezid, but even they were under no illusions as to his character: "a very cruel man and the worst sort of traitor, who by his treachery has conquered many nations."[11]

Italian observers could gloat at Timur's assault on the Muslim Levant for only so long before thoughts turned to their own survival. The Venetian captain Giovanni Cornaro, manning a galley in the Dardanelles in the summer of 1402, at first rejoiced at the news of Timur's victory at Ankara. But his satisfaction turned to horror as crowds of panicked Turkish refugees began swarming the shore and begging for passage across the straits. Their pleas, he wrote in a letter home, left him with a growing sense of unease: "You've never seen such a pitiful collection of men as has gathered in these parts; the whole coast is packed with people. They've lost everything. They are hiding in caves . . . I don't know how things will turn out . . . In effect, we've fallen out of the frying pan and into the fire [*siamo esciti da un laberinto e siamo in un'altro*]. We await the arrival of Timur."[12]

Cornaro's nervously ambivalent response to Timur's victory over the Turks is reflected in several Italian histories of the early quattrocento. Their authors do sometimes follow their northern colleagues in calling the Tartar conqueror a divine scourge, sent by a benevolent God to punish the Muslims for their arrogance and cruelty toward Christians. But these same authors still confess themselves appalled by the fury of his campaigns. One anonymous Venetian chronicler, writing before 1415, marked Timur's arrival as an event of cosmic gravity. In 1402, he wrote, a comet appeared in the night sky, portending the death of great princes; shortly afterward the twin enemies of Venice—the Ottoman Bayezid I and Giangaleazzo Visconti, duke of Milan—were both dead.

So an Italian observer could interpret the appearance of Timur, like the comet itself, as a sign of the divine protection that Venice enjoyed. But Timur's conduct—specifically, his habit of arranging his enemies' skulls in macabre towers in the center of each conquered city—prompted the anonymous chronicler to grieve for his victims and to worry more generally for the safety of the civilized world.[13] Likewise, the d'Este chronicler Jacopo Delaito (writing after 1409) thanked divine providence for sending Timur against Bayezid but expressed dismay at his behavior during the sack of Damascus in 1401, "that great, important, and famous city, which he laid waste and turned over to fire and sword, wickedly capturing or cruelly murdering anyone in his way."[14] The Damascenes were Muslims, but even so, Timur's treatment of them was outrageous and frightening. The Sienese merchant and historian Beltramo de' Mignanelli felt much the same way: "Even though the people of Damascus were a very bad lot, I am forced to grieve for their destruction."[15]

Mignanelli was one of the few Italian authors to witness the effects of Timur's work at first hand. A longtime traveler and trader in the Levant, Mignanelli was in Jerusalem when Timur sacked Damascus in the winter of 1400–1401. As a friend and admirer of the Mamluk sultan Barquq, he was already disposed to think poorly of the invading Timur; his opinion only grew worse after he was forced to flee Jerusalem before the conqueror's approach in the spring of 1401. Taking refuge in Mamluk Egypt, he made his way in the fall of 1402 to Damascus, where he was shocked by the devastation of the city and further dismayed to hear news of Bayezid's defeat at Ankara. He returned to Europe a few years later. In 1416 he served as an interpreter for various Eastern delegations at the Council of Constance; it was there that he composed his *Vita Tamerlani*, describing Timur's Syrian and Anatolian campaigns.[16]

Mignanelli's portrait of Timur is unrelentingly negative: "a most wicked man," "a powerful and vile man," "that cursed man," Timur stormed through the Levant at the head of an invincible army. He did not conquer Damascus by force of arms nor display any great valor in the field. Rather, Mignanelli describes how, in a series of agonizing interviews with the city fathers, Timur bullied, threatened, and extorted every last coin from the population. Each time he promised to leave on receipt of his tribute, only to return and demand yet more concessions from the beleaguered citizens. At last, when there was neither money nor merchandise left to extract, he broke faith with his victims entirely and ordered his men to storm the walls. The carnage lasted for days: "With all humanity put aside they entered Damascus . . . they seized their possessions and then tortured them with whips, knives, and fire. The tale is unbelievable to tell and was more pitiable to see . . . Thus (it pains me to say it!) the whole of this great and broad city was reduced to a mountain of ash."[17]

In closing, Mignanelli tempers his lament for Damascus with some fairly

caustic comments on the wickedness of its citizens, among whom he had
lived for several years. They had cheated him and made his life a misery,
throwing obstacles in his way at every turn; in some respects, then, they deserved the terrible punishments that Timur inflicted. But Mignanelli expresses no such ambivalence over Timur's conquest of Turkey. Unlike the
wily citizens of Damascus, the Turks were an honest and noble people (*non
sunt . . . diabolici ut illi Damasci*) and hardly deserved the torments they suffered. Bayezid's death was particularly to be mourned, for he was a wise and
prudent ruler. True, he was sometimes cruel to Christians. But this was because his hand had been forced by political circumstances beyond his control. For the most part, his policy toward Christian traders had been respectful, his reign tranquil, and he himself deserving of the highest praise.[18] This
was an opinion voiced again (apparently independently) almost two decades later by the Genoese chronicler Giorgio Stella, who portrayed Bayezid
as a decent and just ruler who granted free passage to Christian traders in his
domains. Timur, by contrast, was a murderous usurper.[19]

The economic and diplomatic interests of the Italian republics were so
closely bound up with those of the Muslim states of Anatolia and Syria in
the early fifteenth century that Italian observers took any disruption to
that world very seriously. Their relations with the Ottoman and Mamluk administrations may not have been perfect, and their distrust of the Muslims among whom they dwelled and did business was often profound. But
Timur's sudden and devastating attacks, his relentless destruction of people
and goods, and his mercurial and often treacherous temperament could
hardly be considered improvements on the status quo. Thus Italian writers
like Cornaro (1402), Delaito (1409), Mignanelli (1416), and Stella (1435)
adopted a stance of wary pessimism toward the conqueror. Unlike their
counterparts in the crusading kingdoms north of the Alps, they had seen
and heard too much of Timur to entertain fantasies of a new Prester John, a
crypto-Christian Oriental champion prepared to deliver Jerusalem back into
the hands of his Christian friends.[20]

Timur's biography underwent a series of subtle transformations in Italy in
the decades after his death. Four humanist authors writing between the
1420s and 1440s considered Timur's life and career not in strictly descriptive
historical accounts but rather in the course of broader moral reflections on
the nature of power and the passage of time. For these authors, Timur
served as a useful example to illustrate various ethical or historical principles. As the humanists appropriated and adapted Timur's biography for

these ends, some of the less attractive aspects of his character began to fall from view.

Mignanelli's *Vita Tamerlani* was a key source for Andrea Biglia's account of Timur's career (described in Chapter 4), but Biglia puts Mignanelli's information to a very different use. Focusing rather less on the particulars of Timur's monstrous conduct, Biglia finds the Asiatic conqueror's career useful for illustrating a larger point: the generally sorry state of political culture, civilization, and *humanitas* in the formerly Roman East. In his *Commentaries*, Biglia reproduces not only specific details from the *Vita Tamerlani* but also Mignanelli's more general conviction that Timur was a sadistic fiend, a scourge of nations. Biglia even elaborates on the conqueror's Tartar ancestry, glossing Mignanelli's statement that he came from lands "beyond the Tartars" with a more elaborate and sinister account of origin: Timur, in Biglia's view, was descended from the same unclean and exiled nations whom Alexander the Great had locked away behind the Caspian Gates. He shared their supernatural viciousness and fury. And yet, despite this unfortunate pedigree, Biglia's Timur is a less distinct and also less frightening character than Mignanelli's; he functions primarily as a distressing sign of a world gone out of kilter.

There is a similar sense of moral abstraction at work in the contemporary account of Andrea Redusio, chancellor of Treviso and author of a world chronicle to 1428.[21] Redusio, like Biglia, had his eyewitness sources: in his case, a group of Venetian merchants from the Black Sea colony of Tana, which Timur stormed in 1395. From the stories they told him, Redusio developed an astonishing and blackly comic portrait of the conqueror, at once more vividly drawn and yet rather less repulsive than any previous historian's account.

Redusio introduces his Timur in a lengthy, digressive meditation on the unpredictability of human fortune, inserted into his chronicle in the year 1402. This year saw the fall of two great and terrible princes, Redusio explains: Giangaleazzo Visconti, duke of Milan, and Bayezid the Turk. Both had aimed at hegemony. Visconti (whom Redusio, as chancellor of Treviso, had special reason to despise) sought to conquer all of northern Italy, while Bayezid conquered Greece, threatened Hungary, and dared to plan an assault on Rome. But as these twin tyrants prepared to realize their violent designs, fate intervened: a comet appeared in the night sky to signify the imminent death of the Milanese duke, and Christ took pity on his flock in the East and sent Timur to Ankara to bring the Great Turk low.

Redusio expands considerably on the traditional list of Bayezid's humiliations. After seeing his army destroyed on the Anatolian plain, the emir is dragged to the conqueror's camp in chains and subjected to a series of painful insults. Timur, after making his captive wait outside his tent while he finishes his game of chess, finally emerges to berate the Turk ("You son of a bitch, how dare you challenge me?"),[22] bind a golden chain around his neck, and thrust him into an iron cage. He has this carried with him around Anatolia while he reduces the rest of Bayezid's empire to his control. When they reach Smyrna, the last redoubt of the Christian Hospitallers, Redusio has Timur mock the Turkish emir for failing to take the city himself (this is a story also told by Biglia). In Redusio's version, Timur not only needles the emir ("You swine, how could you leave your enemies encamped in your kingdom till now?") but also ridicules him with a display of his own phenomenal powers of command. "I want you to see the difference between you and me," he sneers, before announcing to his officers that he is going hunting and will return at sundown, when he expects to see the city razed to the ground. Timur's men dare not fail him; immediately they fill the harbor, scale the walls, and take the citadel. As the sun sets, Timur returns from the chase to find Smyrna a smoking ruin.[23]

Redusio then shifts his focus to discuss the contemporaneous fall of Giangaleazzo Visconti, another conqueror brought low by the intervention of fate. It is clear that for Redusio, Timur's own actions and career matter less than his symbolic significance: like the comet that heralds the duke of Milan's death, Timur's treatment of Bayezid marks him as a supernatural agent of divine retribution, a sign that no king, however mighty, is safe from fortune's blows.

Redusio comes back to this point a little later in the digression, when he juxtaposes another two anecdotes freighted with heavy moral significance, both relating to Timur's campaigns around the remote Venetian colony of Tana, at the mouth of the River Don. Redusio's Timur is a ruthless, formidable, and grandiloquent commander. He travels everywhere surrounded by his enormous army; his personal guard alone numbers in the thousands. His camp is ringed by vast concentric palisades; at the center stands his magnificent tent, lined with precious carpets and golden silks, embroidered with pearls and gems, and surmounted by a golden tree whose jeweled leaves make music in the breeze. Here the conqueror is attended by his eunuchs and his harem—each concubine, clad in the costume of a Persian queen, more beautiful than the next. Three hundred of them together can barely satisfy their master's enormous lusts.

To this fabulous Oriental court, the Italian traders of Tana dispatch an anxious peace delegation. Prostrating themselves on the conqueror's carpets, they hail him as "King of Kings and Lord of Lords" and beg him to spare their lives and merchandise. Timur, warmly assuring their safety, sends them home with one of his most trusted officers. But here the Tartar's treachery is revealed: the escort is a spy, who reports back to his master on the defenses of the city and the extent of its wealth. Within days Timur has plundered it all: "And thus the barbarian showed the worth of his barbarous word."[24]

Redusio uses this story to do more than simply underscore Timur's treachery. He sets the tale of the deluded merchants of Tana in artful counterpoint to another story, with which he closes the whole digression, concerning Giovanni Miani, the Venetian *podestà* of Treviso, who lost 12,000 ducats in the sack of Tana and whose three sons were taken captive by Timur. Redusio reports (apparently at first hand) that when news of this disaster reached Treviso, everyone around Miani was thrown into despair, but the *podestà* himself remained impassive—as he did when his three sons finally returned, miraculously spared, to Treviso. Throwing themselves at his feet, the sons bewailed the loss of the ducats, but the father calmly replied, "If you are sons of mine, you can make the money again." For Redusio, the entire episode of the fall of Tana is useful for pointing out the folly of excessive attachment to worldly goods. Far better to remain indifferent to their destruction: "What constancy in the man," he concludes, "whom neither good nor bad fortune can shake!"[25]

Contrasting the craven greed of the merchants of Tana with the stoic indifference of Miani, Redusio brings his excursus back around to his larger theme of fortune and its vicissitudes. It might seem that he recounts these vivid tales in order to stress Timur's general faithlessness and villainy, much as Mignanelli did in his account of 1416. But Redusio's concerns are both larger and more abstract. He uses the digression on Timur to explore several favorite humanist topics: the rise and fall of princes, the folly of ambition, the unpredictability of human affairs. The moral is not that Timur was particularly bad, nor that his victims deserved his wrath; rather it is that no one—neither kings, nor merchants, nor loving fathers for that matter—can control his fate. All should be prepared for the turn of fortune's wheel. Timur's appearance on the historical scene simply serves to illustrate this larger truth.

Redusio does offer a few more specific political lessons to be learned from

Timur's career. These have to do with the moral capacity of his own compatriots to withstand fortune's violent assaults—a sort of geopolitical corollary to the tale of the *podestà*'s plundered ducats. He dwells on Timur's ruthless efficiency in order to show up the weakness and vacillation of those whom he attacks, Turks and Christians alike. The conqueror is appalled to see how Bayezid let the Hospitallers keep a foothold in Turkey, for example; later, he declares that Christians, too, demean themselves by trafficking with their foes. As he watches Genoese, Catalan, Greek, and Venetian ships swarm to the coast to rescue Turkish refugees and transport them (at a high price) to safer shores, Timur splutters, "Have I come from the ends of the earth to destroy the King of the Turks, the enemy of the Christians, only to see them now rescue their enemies for the sake of profit? If I did not have to return to my own lands, I would do worse to the Christians than I have done to the Turks!"[26]

Here Redusio, like Biglia, casts Timur as a scourge of weak and sinful nations, whatever their religion. The same circumstances that provoked pity in earlier commentators—Bayezid's tolerance of Christians and Christian compassion toward Turkish refugees—serve Redusio as examples of the global decadence that Timur has come to punish. Once again, Timur's own career is not really the point; rather, he serves to cast a harsh light on the nations he invades, exposing greed, moral decay, and negligence wherever he goes. As two Florentine chroniclers writing at midcentury noted, the very mention of Timur's name struck fear in the hearts of all who heard it, for "it seemed he had come to punish the sins of the entire world."[27]

As memories of Timur's conquests began to fade, however, the conqueror gradually came to seem less like the swaggering agent of fate and rather more like its victim. The most famous humanist to examine his career, Poggio Bracciolini, sketched a portrait of Timur in the first book of his dialogue *De varietate fortunae* (1447–1448), which sets him very much on the receiving end of fortune's slings and arrows.

Poggio introduces Timur in a densely textured passage which treats not only the unpredictability of fate but also the nature of fame and its relationship to history writing. Perched atop the Capitol hill, inspired by the ruins of the Roman Forum laid out before them, Poggio and his interlocutor, Antonio Loschi, discuss the relentless passage of time and the frailty of human achievements. After running through the stock classical examples, they turn to discuss the deeds of modern princes. Are there any even worth recording? Poggio, convinced of the decline of contemporary civilization, believes not, but Loschi wonders whether this is because the princes themselves are unworthy or because they have yet to find historians who can glorify their deeds. Is modern statesmanship or modern stylistics to blame? Many of fortune's recent favorites could have held their own against the heroes of antiquity, Loschi says, but for want of a decent historian their exploits have fallen into oblivion.[28] He offers two arguments to support his claim: on the one hand, some ancient conquerors were probably not as admirable as their talented biographers made them out to be. On the other, could any ancient historian offer a story to compare with the achievements of the modern "Tambellanus," the all-powerful emperor of Asia?

Poggio then has Loschi review Timur's remarkable achievements. His point is to underscore the importance of historians, whose works alone can preserve the ephemeral conquests of kings, but the digression also stresses the larger themes that define the dialogue on fortune as a whole. Timur was a private citizen (*quondam privatum virum*), not born to power. By his bravery, prudence, cunning, and luck he managed to triumph in spectacular style—a true favorite of fortune. He started small, conquering neighboring warlords in Parthia, Persia, and Scythia. Soon he advanced against the kingdoms of Media and Armenia; then he crossed the Euphrates, sacked Damascus and Smyrna, overthrew the Mamluks, and triumphed over the lord of Turkey, casting him into a cage. Everywhere he went he sacked cities and put kings to flight. His army was vast, ferocious, and formidably disciplined. His camp was as large as a city but more orderly and better run, and his men would do anything he asked. A brilliant tactician, a shrewd negotiator, a charismatic leader of men, "he had everything one expects in a great commander."[29] At last he returned to Parthia, loaded down with captives and spoils, to the city of Samarkand, which he had founded to serve as the capital of his empire. His conquests could rival those of Alexander or Xerxes. What better subject for history? And yet because no one had immortalized Timur's achievements in decent prose, nowadays hardly anyone even remembered his deeds.

In Poggio's dialogue, Timur plays three stock humanist roles at once—the commoner who wins a crown (the self-made man, the master of fortune), the conqueror whose empire cannot last (the victim of fortune), and the prince who is nothing without a scribe at his side (proof that in the long run words will always trump deeds). Along the way he has grown into a lion-hearted hero almost unrecognizable from previous portraits, a paragon of military virtue and—certainly a first in European accounts—an object of humanist admiration, compassion, even regret.

The Sicilian Dominican Pietro Ranzano's life of Timur amplifies the tone of admiration even further. A polymath compiler of histories, biographies, and geographical texts, Ranzano includes an extensive review of Timur's career in his manuscript *Omnium temporum annales,* most likely composed in the late 1440s or 1450s.[30] Ranzano's Timur is a charismatic superman: virtuous, talented, admired by all, a "most powerful king" renowned for his "most famous deeds," easily the equal of Alexander, Xerxes, Caesar, or any other emperor of antiquity. Like Poggio (whom he cites as a source), Ranzano charts Timur's rise from private citizen to leader of a world empire. But unlike Poggio, who focuses on Timur's military exploits, Ranzano also stresses his patient and lawful acquisition of political power, his tolerance for Christianity, and what might be termed his cultural attainments. Timur starts out as a humble shepherd, joins the Persian army, is made an officer, then a provincial governor, and at last becomes king of Persia. He ascends the ranks not so much by tricks or schemes (as earlier authors often say) but by the exercise of virtue, careful political maneuvering, and the acclaim of his fellow men. By adding a political dimension to Poggio's portrait of the world conqueror, Ranzano rounds out Timur's character into that of a more completely humanist hero. And where Poggio stresses only Timur's military discipline and seriousness, Ranzano adds intellectual and social gifts. Timur was a good and loyal friend, and extraordinarily respectful of women. He declared himself a monotheist but had little regard for Muslims (on account of their sexual perversions) and absolutely despised Jews; by contrast, the various bishops who attended his court convinced him to treat Christians well.[31] He had great respect for learning and generously rewarded the efforts of astronomers, physicians, and astrologers whom he welcomed to his entourage.[32] His claims to authority were reinforced, finally, by the judgment of his Persian forebears, issued in the form of a supernatural endorsement from beyond the grave. Wherever he went on campaign, Ranzano says, Timur used "magic arts" to divine the location of caches of coins left buried by the ancient kings of Persia: Xerxes, Artaxerxes, Cyrus, and Darius. These discoveries fueled his conquests; the land of Persia literally offered up its treasure to him. Altogether, Ranzano's Timur is a paragon of humanist virtues: steadfast, loyal, capable, intelligent, cultured, and utterly in command. Despite all this (or perhaps because of it), Ranzano is not really interested in Timur's particular significance for world history. He expresses no opinion on whether his rise to power boded well or ill for Christendom. Though he portrays the Ottoman Bayezid as Timur's victim, he neither mourns nor gloats over his defeat. Rather, Bayezid plays a neutral role: another impressively powerful Asian king, he was the "only man who might have stopped Timur, had Fortune allowed." But fortune does not allow: at Ankara, a tremendous clash of empires, with epic losses and great exploits on both sides, Timur emerges the victor, proof positive of fortune's favor. Ranzano takes little interest in the larger political significance of the battle; it is important simply as a final illustration of Timur's marvelous and admirable achievements, the culmination of a virtuous career worthy of humanist celebration. Ranzano concludes with a review of Timur's sons' careers after his death; unable to live up to their father's achievements, they fall victim to squabbling and civil strife—highlighting, by their lack of them, the extraordinary confluence of virtues that fortune placed in the heart of one great man.

By the middle of the century, Italian historians had found various ways to use the figure of Timur in their meditations on the nature of power, virtue, and fame. But as the Ottoman Turks returned to the offensive in the 1440s, and especially after the fall of Constantinople in 1453, crusade propagandists found yet other significances in the story of his brief and brilliant reign. In the 1450s and '60s, Aeneas Sylvius Piccolomini and the circle of humanists around him—including Francesco Filelfo, Flavio Biondo, Niccolò Sagundino, and Platina—revised the Italian estimate of Timur once again. First a monstrous scourge, then a morally neutral example of fortune's ferocious power, he now emerged as a positively valorous example of God's providential concern for Christendom, a divinely sent warrior whose noble exploits foretold the final doom of the Turks.

Flavio Biondo pursued this line in an oration on the fall of Constantinople addressed to King Alfonso of Aragon in the summer of 1453. The only correct response to the recent disaster, Biondo argued, was a new crusade against the Turks. History showed that European states from ancient Greece to medieval France had always triumphed in Asia, but Asiatic invaders had never managed to succeed on European soil. Xerxes' armies had perished in the wilds of Thrace, and who could forget the sorry reign of Bayezid I? The moment he led his armies across the Hellespont into Europe, disaster struck in the form of "Timerbeus," king of Parthia, who destroyed the Ottoman army at Ankara and cast Bayezid himself into a cage "like a leopard or a dog."[33] Now, as Bayezid's grandson Mehmed II renewed the Turkish threat to Christendom, it was time for Alfonso to prove once again that Asiatic kings who overstepped their bounds faced certain defeat in Europe. On the surface, this would seem a radically secular interpretation of the history of

Christian-Islamic conflict, as a perennial struggle between East and West dating back to antiquity and having little to do with matters of faith. But in positioning Alfonso and Timur under the same rubric—as two great kings who know how to keep Asiatic barbarians in their place—Biondo does not revive a classical model of East-West relations so much as transform it.

First he posits the existence of good as well as bad Asiatic (indeed, Muslim) princes; Bayezid may be another Xerxes, but the Oriental Timur is firmly aligned with Europe. Furthermore, Biondo restates Timur's historical significance. No longer an exemplar of fortune's random and inescapable caprice, Timur appears here as a force for good, one who works to keep the world and its people in their proper order. The subtext is most important: Biondo intimates that there *is* an order to the world, and that virtuous kings are set on earth to preserve it. His providential convictions mark a shift in discussions of Timur from the less teleologically charged reflections of earlier humanist commentators like Redusio, Poggio, and Ranzano.

As ever, Filelfo could be relied on to push this new interpretation to its rhetorical limits. In crusade texts written in the 1450s, Filelfo referred to Timur in grandiose terms (styling him "Thomyris the Massagete") as a divinely sent agent of salvation whom the princes of Christendom, to their eternal shame, had failed to embrace. In a historical excursus in his oration at the Congress of Mantua in 1459, Filelfo reviewed the steady and inexorable rise of Turkish power from its barbarous beginnings to the present day. Each warlord, petty prince, and emir had left the Ottoman nation stronger than he had inherited it, and Bayezid I was the most fearsome of all. He destroyed a vast army of European crusaders at Nicopolis and went on to lay siege to Constantinople itself:

> Then and there, the worship of Christ—indeed Christianity itself—was very nearly destroyed. If Jesus Christ had not suddenly deigned to punish one set of his enemies with another, sending Thomyris the Massagete (known as Tamerlane) . . . with a vast and powerful army, then the new Rome itself would have lain captive and despoiled from that time up until this. But omnipotent God chose not to suffer such an indignity then. Rather, He chose that moment to declare to the world the vanity of all human schemes that lack His favor. And so Bayezid, that horrible "Thunderbolt," was defeated and captured by Thomyris Tamberlane . . . Dear God, what miraculous providence! What incomprehensible, boundless power! Oh, the infinite mercy with which you embraced us! But still we wretches did not understand, still we paid no heed![34]

Filelfo does not exactly praise Timur; he portrays him as yet another enemy of the Christian Lord, a pernicious tyrant made to serve his ends.[35] But he suggests that his appearance on the historical stage was a good thing—and here he and all his contemporaries part ways with the first generation of Italian writers on Timur, who expressed far more ambivalence about his brutal achievements. Filelfo saw no reason to recoil from Timur's record of violence. The only horror he expressed was at the inertia of the Christian princes, who failed to capitalize on his appearance and thus turned down a gift from God.

Two decades later, the papal historian Platina followed this line—though in an altogether more specific and rather petty context—using Timur's sudden appearance in the East as a stick with which to beat Pope Boniface IX, one of two rivals to the papal throne in the year 1402. The Roman pope was too busy throwing benefices at his nephews, Platina remarked, to notice the great opportunity to rescue Eastern Christendom that Timur provided. What greater indication could there be of the depravity and godlessness of those dark, schismatic times?[36]

Platina completely reverses the judgment of earlier humanist historians: while Biglia and his reform-minded contemporaries viewed Timur as a symptom of all that had gone wrong in their world, by the 1470s it was not Timur but Europe's failure to embrace him that provoked outrage and dismay. Now Timur was considered a heaven-sent champion, dispatched by Christ himself to rescue his people. It is remarkable how late the humanists were to come to this romantic notion, after decades of more realistic appraisals from eyewitnesses and chroniclers. The image that took root right away in northern Europe—at courts still reeling from the shock of Nicopolis and inflamed by the desire for a new Eastern ally to avenge it—developed in Italy only after 1453. The point is not that the Italians were belatedly influenced by their northern predecessors, but rather that in each case it was a devastating Turkish victory—at Nicopolis or Constantinople—that suddenly cast Timur, the Ottoman nemesis, in an attractive political light. In Italy there was time for Mignanelli's horror to give way first to Poggio's distant and slightly patronizing reflections and then, only at midcentury, to the unqualified admiration and praise of Biondo, Filelfo, Aeneas Sylvius, and their contemporaries.

As the humanists effected their rehabilitation of Timur, they also endowed him with a new national identity. Early reports identified him as either a "Tartar" lord or as coming from some even more remote and uncivilized country.[37] In his *De varietate fortunae,* however, Poggio styled Timur a

"Parthian" prince. Poggio may simply have wanted to keep his prose within the bounds of correct Latinity (just as Filelfo tried to recast Timur as a classical "Thomyris"). But "Parthian" was an ethnicity that humanists sympathetic to Timur became increasingly eager to assign him. In the hands of humanist geographers, historians, and political theorists, "Parthian" and "Persian"—like "Scythian"—were heavily weighted terms.

The elevation of Persia to a country of noble princes was a dramatic step. In the Middle Ages, it was often the *Turks* who were identified as latter-day rulers of Persia. Medieval historians like Sigebert of Gembloux traced the succession of power in Asia from the Assyrians and Babylonians (oppressors of Israel) to the Persians (enemies of Greece and Rome) to the Saracens and Turks of more recent memory. But quattrocento historians preferred a different genealogy and narrative of national identity for the Turks, maintaining that they were descended from the Scythians of central Asia. Far from inheriting the mantle of imperial Persian despotism, the Scythian Turks in the Renaissance imagination were inherently barbarous, beyond the pale of any civilization, European or Asiatic.

As the humanists demoted the Turks from imperial Persian oppressors to cannibalistic wild men, they simultaneously upgraded the notion of Persian identity. This is a move that at first glance seems almost inexplicable for Renaissance enthusiasts of classical civilization to have made. Modern critical readings of classical authors like Herodotus and Aeschylus emphasize how the ancient Greeks viewed the kings of Persia as paragons of Asiatic despotism, barbarity, concupiscence, decadence, and irrationality.[38] But in the Renaissance revival of Greek literature and culture, this particular classical model of Persian barbarity does not seem to have resurfaced. The humanists were inspired not by Herodotus but by Xenophon, whose *Cyropaedia* presented the Persian king Cyrus as a consummate philosopher-prince, a paragon of royal wisdom, virtue, piety, and political savvy. The *Cyropaedia*—which Xenophon wrote for expressly pedagogical purposes—had long been a favorite text of humanist educators and political theorists, who (following Cicero) took from the text an image of imperial Persia as a school of princely virtue.[39] Gradually, over the course of the fifteenth century, Persia came to be seen as one of many ancient civilizations from whom Christian Europe might hope to learn, a fount of "alien wisdom" on a par with ancient Egypt, India, and Babylon, home to magi, sybils, astrologers, and other visionary seekers of truth.[40] In the intellectual circles arrayed around the Renaissance papacy in particular, where the classics had not been revived in the service of a republican ideology inherently suspicious of kingship and its claims, it became almost axiomatic to argue that *all* monarchies (even those that were pagan) were respectable and in some way divinely ordained; this was especially true of those monarchies whose authority rested on ancient foundations. (Francesco Filelfo made precisely this claim in the dedicatory letter to Pope Paul II with which he prefaced his translation of Xenophon's *Cyropaedia:* ancient history teaches that monarchy has always been the best sort of government, and kings of all nations, from Cyrus to Hannibal to the Caesars, could offer exemplary inspiration to a modern prince like Paul II.)[41] In this context, it makes sense that humanist commentators who went out of their way to deny the Ottoman Turks any sort of respectable, legitimate, or ancient claims to political authority should also seek to endow any possible opponents of Ottoman power (even if Islamic) with precisely such traits. Making Timur a Persian accomplished this.

The change in Timur's (and Persia's) status came about rather quickly. In the early 1440s, Flavio Biondo tried to explicate the history of "Persia" after the fall of Rome by arguing that first the Saracens and later the Turks had assumed the ancient mantle of Persian hegemony in Asia. Each in turn took up classical Persia's role as the chief obstacle to Roman authority in the East. This made Persia an evil (or at least contrary and fractious) empire, and contrary and fractious modern nations like the Saracens and Turks were to be identified as somehow fundamentally "Persian." But Biondo's thoughts on Persia—and what Persian identity signified—changed after 1453. By then, humanist consensus had settled on the identification of the Turks as Scythian barbarians hailing from beyond the bounds of any imperial civilization. Biondo's earlier attempt to assign the Turks a Persian heritage was now unworkable. And as the Turks came to seem "unfit" to be called Persian (Aeneas Sylvius argues precisely this in his earliest letter on Turkish origins, from 1453),[42] being Persian came to be seen as something not altogether bad. In his 1453 oration to Alfonso of Aragon, in which Biondo praised Timur for keeping the barbarous arrogance of Bayezid I in check, the historian expressly identified his hero as the "King of Parthia or, as some prefer, Persia."[43]

A wholesale historiographical realignment was under way. Originally cast as Rome's "old enemy" in the East, Persia now came to seem more like Rome's partner in imperial rule, possessing equivalent status and legitimacy and plagued by the same violent northern barbarians. How this realignment played out can best be understood by a glance at Aeneas Sylvius's own later writings on Persian history. In the chapter of his *Asia* (1462) devoted to the geography and history of Parthia, Aeneas relies on the account in Biondo's *Decades* of the Arab conquest of Sassanian Persia. But he completely repudiates Biondo's idea that the rule of ancient Persia had somehow survived in later Saracen and Turkish incarnations. In *Asia,* Aeneas maintains that after the Arab conquests, all the ancient nations of the East lost their identity and became Saracen. While Biondo claimed that in the eighth century, after the first Turkish invasion, the name of the Persian Empire was restored, Aeneas expressly asserts that the barbarous Arabs had suppressed the name of the Parthians—sometime rulers of Persia—for over 750 years. In his view, it was only in recent times, with the rise of Timur, in fact, that Persian/Parthian fortunes at last began to revive.[44]

Aeneas recounts the "Parthian" Timur's sweeping conquest of the East in some detail. He takes almost all his information from Poggio's *De varietate fortunae,* but he puts the older scholar's anecdotes to very different use. Poggio, marveling at the speed and vast extent of Timur's conquests, used these to meditate on the unpredictable vicissitudes of fortune. By contrast, Aeneas's interest in Timur is political, not philosophical. He reduces Poggio's portrait to its bare narrative essentials: Timur came from nowhere, seized the throne of Parthia, and then proceeded on a dizzying campaign of conquest across the medieval Middle East. While Poggio described the military discipline of Timur's camp and the efficiency of his sieges in order to argue that he was, despite being a barbarian, fit for historians to write about, Aeneas recounts the same details simply to reinforce his account of a ruthlessly efficient, Muslim-slaying war machine. He then adds three other anecdotes. The first describes a clever trick Timur used to despoil the merchants of Caffa of their gold; the second recounts his terrible practice (later made famous by Marlowe) of pitching a different-colored tent on each day of a siege—first white, to signal clemency for all who surrendered; then red, to signal death for the head of each household; and last black, to signal that the city was condemned to fire and sword.[45] The third anecdote describes how one city's leaders, having failed to surrender before the white tent came down, hoped to prevail on the conqueror's clemency by sending their children to greet him, dressed in white and waving olive branches; Timur's response was to send his cavalry to trample the children to death. Remarkably, Aeneas does not condemn these horrifying deeds (imagine what a Mignanelli or Redusio might have done with this material). Rather, he professes himself impressed by the stern resolve and unrelenting energy of the conqueror, whose soldiers never rebelled, who ran a shipshape camp, who "would tolerate rapacity in no one but himself," and who—an extraordinary achievement for a Renaissance prince from East or West—remained miraculously untouched by the hostile blows of fate.

Finally, Aeneas recounts how, at the end of his life, having laid waste to all of Asia from the Don to the Nile, Timur returned home to the east, loaded down with captives and spoils, to establish an imperial capital for himself at Samarkand. Here Aeneas stops following Poggio and returns to the larger trajectory of his own narrative, concerning the fortunes of Parthia in world history. For a brief moment, Aeneas concludes, Timur restored the ancient empire of the Parthians; but, fatally, the dissipation and quarreling of his sons prevented a complete revival. This is a failure which Aeneas seems to regret.[46]

By the early 1460s, Aeneas and the humanists in his circle were agreed that Persia was not a barbarous place but in fact a rather civilized and possibly even Christian dominion. (Aeneas enthusiastically collected reports from traveling friars and missionaries on the presence of Christians in "Persia" in the early 1460s. His informants were most likely reporting on the Christian kingdoms of Georgia, but when an ambassador representing one of these princes appeared in Rome, the pope received him as a representative of the "King of Persia.")[47] The briefly mooted theory that the Turks represented a revival of ancient Persian despotism had fallen almost entirely from favor. The exception is found in the context of rhetorical analogy: a Turkish sultan might still be described as thinking and acting *like* a new Xerxes, just as he was *like* a new Hannibal or Pyrrhus or Attila.[48] But when humanists left the realm of analogy and tried to write about real geography or history, "Persia" now served as a generally positive political construct: a good empire, powerful, orderly, intellectually advanced, with political traditions dating back to antiquity and rulers deeply sympathetic to Christianity. It was around this time, in the late 1460s or early '70s, that Platina found in the early medieval text of Paul the Deacon the curious story of Caesarea, crypto-Christian queen of Persia (see Chapter 3), which he introduced into his papal history as dramatic proof of imperial Persia's early submission to Christianity and short-lived triumph over the anarchy of Islam.

Aeneas's glowing portrait in *Asia* gave a powerful boost to the "Persian" Timur's reputation, which continued to improve over the closing decades of the fifteenth century. Jacopo Foresti da Bergamo repeats Aeneas's account more or less verbatim in his world history of 1483; so, too, does Hartmann Schedel in the *Nuremberg Chronicle*, alongside a woodcut depicting "Tamerlane the Great, King of Tartary or Parthia" as a strapping young knight in gleaming armor, with pale, flowing locks and a handsome plume.[49]

By the early sixteenth century, Timur was celebrated as an admirable and successful character, fortune's favorite, and rightful ruler of a great empire. In 1506, Raffaele Maffei recorded Timur's exploits in his geographical encyclopedia, in an extended excursus on the history of Persia. From Cyrus and

Figure 8. Tamerlane, king of Tartary or Parthia. Hartmann Schedel, *Liber cronicarum* (Nuremberg: Anton Koberger, 1493), fol. 237r. Photo Warburg Institute, London

Xerxes to the Magi and down to the present day, Persia had been a fount of wise and formidable kings. Two years earlier, Petrus Crinitus led off his collection of anecdotes *De honesta disciplina* with the dreadful story of Timur's multicolored tents, which in Crinitus's view demonstrated an approach to waging war that combined firmness with justice. What could be more rational than to declare one's intentions to the enemy, to allow him to surrender while there was time, and then to follow through on one's threats without hesitation? Here was a strategic model worthy of emulation.[50] The Genoese historian and former doge Battista Fregoso likewise insisted on Timur's virtues. In his 1509 collection of lives of famous men (in which, like Crinitus, he arranges his subjects according to the moral lessons their biographies suggest), Fregoso lists Timur, "King of Persia," under the rubric of "men who have risen from humble origins to great fame." His companions include such other rags-to-riches characters as King David, St. Peter, John the Baptist, Francesco Sforza, and Popes Nicholas V and Sixtus IV![51] Fregoso gives no indication that Timur's achievements were at all transitory; in his brief life of the conqueror (the details are borrowed from Antoninus Florentinus),[52] it is implied that the king of Persia, like his illustrious companions, not only rose to glory but remained there.

This was not an outrageous claim for a historian of the early sixteenth century to make. Indeed, a series of dynastic upheavals in eastern Anatolia, Mesopotamia, and Iran in the latter half of the fifteenth century made it possible to imagine that Timur's "Persian" empire had not simply dissolved at his death but had continued to thrive—and to pose a threat to the Ottomans in the East—down to the present day.

Zancassanus and the Sophy: Renaissance Kings of Persia

On the first of March 1473, the last Monday of Carnival, Cardinal Pietro Riario held a banquet in his palace at SS. Apostoli, to which he invited several of his fellow cardinals, foreign ambassadors, curial officials, Roman nobles, and some of the city's more celebrated courtesans. The evening's entertainment began as an imperious figure took his seat on a magnificent throne, dressed in lavish robes and headgear *alla grechescha*, with a placard identifying him as "King of Macedon." The king and his retinue presided over the banquet for more than three hours, until an ambassador of the Turkish sultan suddenly entered the hall, bearing letters challenging the king's claim to the territories of Macedon, which rightfully belonged to the

Great Turk. After an acrimonious dialogue, the two sides agreed to settle their dispute in combat. The next day the party reconvened in the piazza, where the actors and their retinues staged an elaborate mock battle, culminating in the triumph of the king of Macedon, the shameful retreat of the humiliated ambassador, and the forced conversion and baptism of the "Turkish" followers he left behind.[53]

The story of this theatrical spectacle, pieced together from contemporary letters and diaries, is intriguing for the light it sheds on public entertainments and political theater in fifteenth-century Italy, and on the nighttime activities of cardinals and their associates in Renaissance Rome. It is perhaps most fascinating for what it reveals about how Renaissance Italians imagined not only the Ottoman threat but also possible sources of redress against it. The event had plenty of classical flavor. By conjuring up a "Macedonian" champion against overweening Ottoman aggression, the pageant framed the Ottoman Turks as the latest in a long line of Asiatic barbarians: just as Alexander had conquered the empires of the ancient East, what was needed now to combat the Ottoman threat was a new Alexander, a new imperial conqueror to battle the barbarians and lead Europe to victory in Asia once again.

And yet in this particular pageant, the Christian champion, the "king of Macedon," was not meant to evoke the figure of the ancient Alexander alone. Guests at the event referred to the character by a variety of outlandish names—"Zuncassanus," "Oxon Cassan," "Ussoncussan"[54]—revealing that their thoughts had been directed not just back in time to the ancient Macedonian conqueror of Persia but also, simultaneously, to a much more current figure holding sway over the same Eastern lands. This was Uzun Hasan, lord of the Aqqoyunlu, or "White Sheep" Türkmens, of eastern Anatolia.[55] His name sounded to Western ears like "Zuncassan" or, in Latin, "Zuncassanus."

Timur's empire had collapsed quickly and spectacularly in the decades after his death in 1405. But the disruption and devastation he inflicted on Syria, Anatolia, and Iran opened the way for a series of smaller, local dynasties to emerge, many of them expanding up to and even across the eastern fringes of Ottoman power. The Aqqoyunlu were among the most prominent to pose a challenge to Ottoman rule, and their leader, Uzun Hasan, soon came to the attention of Christian Europe. His territories spread from eastern Anatolia across the mountains of Armenia and Azerbaijan to the northern Iranian plateau. As early as 1457, Pope Calixtus III sent a message east to the prince, seeking an alliance against the Turks in the wake of the fall of Constantinople.[56] Uzun Hasan was already thinking along the same lines. That same year he contracted a marriage alliance with the empire of Trebizond, thereby joining a coalition of eastern principalities, some Christian and some Muslim, united against Ottoman expansion in the East. In 1458, after hearing of this alliance, Pius II sent the Franciscan friar Ludovico da Bologna to try to find Uzun Hasan.[57] Fra Ludovico returned to Rome in December 1460 with a delegation of Asiatic ambassadors, including one purporting to represent Uzun Hasan, whom Pius greeted with great enthusiasm. (During this episode, the Christian king of Georgia was hailed as the king of Persia, while Pius recognized Hasan as the "king of Mesopotamia.")[58] Aeneas hoped to form a grand alliance with these Eastern lords, but his trust in Fra Ludovico as their intermediary may have been misplaced. It remains unclear whether any of the exotic legates Ludovico produced was a genuine representative of an Asian prince, and the pope died attempting to muster a crusader fleet at Ancona in 1464, before he could send an envoy to the East to pursue the matter. What is certain, though, is that the pope expressed both interest in and respect for Uzun Hasan as a possible Christian ally.

Uzun Hasan remained a tantalizing prospect for European diplomacy against the Turks. In the later 1460s and '70s, the papacy and the governments of Venice, Hungary, and Poland all sent embassies to his peripatetic court, trying to woo him into an intercontinental alliance that would strike at the Ottoman Empire simultaneously from east and west. During these years several genuine "Persian" emissaries were received with honorable pomp in both Venice and Rome.[59] Little known he may be today, but the Türkmen chief was a fairly respectable figure in the political economy of the late medieval Middle East. His wife, a princess of the house of the Komnenoi and daughter of the last emperor of Trebizond, had a sister who had married into a prominent family of Venetian merchants, putting both Greek and Venetian contacts at his disposal. The leader of one of the early Venetian embassies to Hasan's court, Caterino Zeno, was a son of Hasan's Greek sister-in-law and thus his nephew by marriage. When Zeno arrived at the king's summer quarters in the highlands of Azerbaijan in 1472, he found him negotiating to marry his daughter to the king of Poland; it was rumored that he had promised to have her baptized a Catholic.[60]

Excited by the prospect of an alliance with this powerful prince, Italian policy-makers and propagandists alike tended to play down Hasan's Muslim beliefs while magnifying his political stature and assimilating him to their own models of kingship, civilization, and culture. (This even though at the time, the upstart Türkmen prince's main concern was to improve his status in the eyes of neighboring Muslim states by making war on local Christian populations and sending elaborate embassies to Mecca.)[61] By the early 1470s, it was no longer the Christian king of Georgia but Uzun Hasan himself whom European commentators identified as the king of Persia. A king of kings, a worthy successor to the Achaemenid rulers of ancient Persia, he too might be a mighty imperial commander, another Xerxes or Darius, or a second Cyrus, steadfast friend to the chosen people of God. In Venice, Doge Pietro Mocenigo referred to him not as an "infidel," "heretic," or "pagan," all standard terms for Muslim believers, but simply as a stranger to the Christian religion, by no means its enemy.[62] Pius II also noted that Hasan was, "though not a Christian himself, a friend to Christians," while Sixtus IV praised him unreservedly as "a distinguished prince, a friend of Christians."[63] Like Prester John, that medieval object of geographical fantasy and political desire, Uzun Hasan seemed to have appeared on the global stage to offer Christian Europe a providential rescue from the forces of barbarism and unbelief. Some Italians styled the king not "Zuncassanus" (nor "Sumcassianus," "Osomcassan," or any other of numerous permutations seen elsewhere) but "San Cassano," thus seeming to promote him, whether intentionally or not, to the company of Christian saints.[64]

And Christian sympathies were not his only virtues. In 1464 an ambassador from Uzun Hasan made a speech before the Venetian Signoria, which the Venetian diarist Domenico Malipiero records in some detail. (How much of this the ambassador actually said and how much is Malipiero's embroidery is impossible to say; what matters here is what the Venetian observer made of the event.) Malipiero noted that the "Signor della Persia" boasted an impressive pedigree, including descent from Timur, with whom he shared a hatred of the Turks:

> The Ambassador representing Uzun Hasan recalled how Tamberlan (whom he called the grandfather of his lord) once captured Baisit, father of that Mehmed who reigns today, and kept him in a cage under his dinner table, and led him about wherever he went, until he wretchedly ended his life. And he said that he reminded them of Tamberlan's victory in order to inform the Signoria of his lord's hostility toward the Turk, and in concluding, he begged the Signoria to have full faith in that which he had revealed in the name of his lord.

The ambassador and his promises were both impressive. So too was his rhetorical skill:

> And then he suggested, by way of example, that even a great tree, which stands firm against the wind and cannot be weakened no matter what comes against it, needs nothing more than a little worm to get inside its roots and gnaw away, until the wind can knock it to the ground with ease. The worm, he said, was his lord, who would so gnaw away at the great tree (the Turk), that the wind of the Signoria's fleet could then destroy it completely.[65]

Such was Uzun Hasan: a valiant, eloquent, and generous commander, and charmingly modest to boot. He was also, as Malipiero noted elsewhere, the very model of an ideal Renaissance prince, "de bellissimo corpo, liberal, cortese, e benigno."[66]

In 1472, Venice made public the details of the secret treaty which Caterino Zeno and other ambassadors had negotiated between the Serene Republic and the Crown of Persia.[67] Venetian galleys were to deliver artillery, including harquebuses and heavy cannon, to an Aqqoyunlu fortress on the Gulf of Iskenderun; afterward, Hasan would proceed overland against the Ottoman frontier in Cilicia while the republic's fleet provided cover from the sea. News of the alliance caused great excitement across Italy.[68] Francesco Filelfo, who like Aeneas frequently lamented Christendom's failure to capitalize on Timur's previous attacks on the Turks, hailed the new alliance as evidence that Europe might yet take advantage of the "Persian" threat to the Ottoman rear. Filelfo congratulated his Venetian friends on what he called their "wonderful," "splendid," and "holy" alliance, which divine providence had made possible and which was sure to bring about a change in Christian fortunes.[69] Less than three years before, in a letter written after the fall of Negroponte, Filelfo had darkly condemned all Muslims as untrustworthy and villainous;[70] now, however, he was willing to make allowances for Uzun Hasan. The prince was a Muslim, but he was also a Persian, and it was on the basis of this supposed Persian ethnicity that Filelfo found it acceptable for Western powers to deal with him. Filelfo recognized great qualities in the Persian prince—generosity, wisdom, culture, crypto-Christian sympathies. These extended to his subjects as well. Describing the enmity between Turks and Persians, Filelfo explained in November 1473: "Although both sides follow the same impious Muslim religion, all right-thinking people nevertheless would prefer to hear of a Persian victory, not a Turkish one, inasmuch as

the Turks both threaten us more closely and are of a far more savage character than the Persians . . . What else can you expect from a bunch of rude
shepherds and brigands, but affronts and destruction? Yet if we look at history, we find that the Persians spring from a most noble race and are in no
way wild or uncivilized."[71]

Good King Hasan, Filelfo concluded, would be eager to repay Venetian
kindnesses, since it was an ancient Persian belief that ingratitude is the
worst of all vices.[72] This last aphorism derives directly from Xenophon's
Cyropaedia,[73] a text which Filelfo knew very well. A lifelong enthusiast of the
text and its author (he had even named his first son Senofante), Filelfo had
completed a Latin translation of the work in 1467 and in the early 1470s was
negotiating to have the text printed at Rome.[74]

The conviction that Uzun Hasan was a Persian king, with all the positive
characteristics that identity now entailed, spread rapidly through Italy along
with news of the Venetian alliance. A portrait medal of the prince circulated
among Roman collectors,[75] and he figured on at least one Florentine *cassone*
of the period.[76] In 1477 an Italian ballad celebrating Hasan's victories circulated in print, trumpeting the virtues of the "Re di Persia," a figure "mag-
nanimo, eloquente . . . valloroso e degno," who had converted to Christianity and forced every Turk whom he defeated to do the same.[77] Marvelous
portents were associated with his rise to power: a pamphlet printed in 1472
explained that the comet then appearing in the night sky over Naples was a
sign of the king of Persia's impending victories.[78] Giovanni Pontano, writing
some years after the event, explained that the comet traversed the heavens
from the east to the north, presaging the momentous campaign of "Ussonus
Cassanus" against the king of the Turks in the summer of 1473.[79]

In November of that year, a spurious collection of letters addressed from
and to Mehmed II appeared in print in Rome. Composed in fact by the
humanist Laudivio Zacchia, the collection was destined to become one of
the early bestsellers of European publishing. The so-called *Epistolae Magni
Turci* begin with a letter from Mehmed (originally written in his native
"Scythian" tongue, so the editor claims) to Zancassanus, "King of Persia." As
in the rest of the collection, the exchange follows a set pattern: angry, men-
acing boasts from the sultan, followed by a reply from the threatened party
which parries the worst of the bluster and thus rhetorically disarms the
Turk. So Mehmed first tells the king of Persia to stay on his side of the Euphrates River; his raids into Ottoman territory brand him as an outlaw, a
scandal to law-abiding people. To this, Zancassanus coolly replies that he

does not seek his enemy's approval, just victory. The Turk writes again: he awaits Zancassanus at the Cilician Gates, where Darius of Persia was vanquished by Alexander. If the new king of Persia dares to meet him in battle, he will meet a similar fate at the hands of the only conqueror ever to equal the glory of the Macedonian king. To this, Zancassanus replies that the Turk may aspire to Alexander's "glory," but he, Zancassanus, has already conquered Alexander's empire; Bactria, Media, Persia, Armenia, and Parthia all lie beneath his sway. He alone, after Alexander, has conquered Asia. Mehmed, if he likes, can keep the Cilician Gates.[80]

The rhetorical maneuvering in these letters is complex: by putting boastful claims to the legacy of Alexander in the sultan's mouth, the text recalls the charges of presumption made by other Italian authors, who mocked the sultan for claiming a Trojan pedigree for himself. Mehmed's claim to Macedonian authority here is likewise meant as a sign of his grandiose delusions. But the claim seems to mean something quite different in Zancassanus's case; as in the Carnival fete of the same year, the two Asiatic princes bicker over the Macedonian legacy, but Zancassanus is clearly understood to be the true and proper heir. The audience is invited to respect *this* Macedonian, not mock him as a pretender. There is some irony in the fact that in both the letter book and the Carnival fete, it is the king of Persia (the empire Alexander overthrew) who now lays claim to the conqueror's authority. But in Renaissance courtly contexts, descent from Darius apparently conferred legitimacy, not shame, especially since the hotheaded, "Scythian" Turk was a demonstrably less worthy contender for the imperial prize. To Italian minds in 1473, at least, the traditional Greco-Roman assessment of Alexander as the champion of Western civility against the despotism of the East sat perfectly comfortably with a more recent preference for southern monarchy (Greek, Persian, or otherwise) against the barbarity of the anarchic North. So the king of Persia was enlisted as Christendom's champion against the Scythian fury of the Turks.

Despite the best efforts of Italian propagandists, theatrical impresarios, and gunrunners, European hopes for Uzun Hasan were not to be realized. After a spectacular victory over the Ottomans at Erzincan in August 1473, a battle much celebrated in Europe, the Türkmen prince suffered a punishing defeat at the hands of Mehmed II only a week later, near the Anatolian town of Bashkent. His entire baggage train was lost, and the scattered remnants of his armies retreated home to the east.[81] By 1476, Hasan was wearily dismissing European ambassadors from his court; he had learned the hard way that taking on the Ottomans was neither in his interests nor to his liking, and he regretted he could offer his Christian friends no further support.

Nevertheless, his image in the West was hardly tarnished.[82] How did Italian historians interpret his career? Mattia Palmieri, continuing the *Chronicle*

Figure 9. Sumcassianus (Uzun Hasan), king of Persia. Hartmann Schedel, *Liber cronicarum* (Nuremberg: Anton Koberger, 1493), fol. 249v. Photo Warburg Institute, London

of Eusebius and his followers to the year 1481, records that the comet of 1472 was followed closely by the rise of "Hazoncassan" to power in Persia. At the battle of Erzincan, he triumphed over the Turks, slaughtering some 30,000 Ottoman troops. Palmieri explains away the defeat at Bashkent, by contrast, as a merely tactical retreat, a prudent move after the loss of the Persian baggage train.[83] The hardiness of Hasan's reputation is perhaps best witnessed by the illustrated encomium published by Hartmann Schedel in the *Nuremberg Chronicle* in 1493. "Sumcassianus" had been a great man (so his very name revealed), highly learned, great-hearted, and a formidable commander. His felicitous reign brought peace to the lands of the Persians; he had inflicted terrible losses on the Turks at Erzincan (Bashkent, again, is not mentioned). He had been a friend of popes and a great scourge of infidels.[84]

Uzun Hasan's literary afterlife recalls that of Prester John, who, even after repeated failures to ride to the rescue of Christendom, remained an object of serious political speculation in the Christian West, as well as that of Timur, whose Italian reputation steadily improved in the decades after his death, as we have seen.[85] Toward the end of the fifteenth century, the Genoese biographer Battista Fregoso portrayed Hasan as a formidable (but virtuous) character, a paragon of paternal severity.[86] In 1504, Marcantonio Sabellico rehearsed with approval the history of papal and Venetian relations with Hasan, making much of the latter's humble beginnings and phenomenal rise to power.[87] By contrast, Raffaele Maffei stressed Uzun Hasan's imperial pedigree; he discussed his reign in the chapter of his universal history dedicated to Persia, beginning with the astrologers of Babylon, proceeding through the reigns of Cyrus and Xerxes, the Magi, the caliphs of classical Islam, the Ghaznavids, and culminating in the reigns of Timur and Uzun Hasan—all of them, in Maffei's view, distinguished figures worthy of historical respect. Despite Hasan's failures at the end of his reign, Maffei concluded, there was reason to hope that the imperial house of Persia might yet produce a new challenger to rescue Europe from the barbarous Ottoman regime.[88]

In 1501, some twenty-three years after the death of Uzun Hasan, a new prince appeared on the Persian horizon. Hasan's teenage grandson, Shah Ismail Safavi, stormed out of his power base on the shores of the Caspian Sea, murdered his Aqqoyunlu cousins in the capital, Tabriz, and proclaimed himself shah of Iran. By 1510 he had captured Baghdad, established his rule over Iraq as well as western Iran, and was dispatching belligerent threats to the Ottoman sultan Bayezid II.[89]

At first news of Ismail's rise to power was greeted in Italy with an enthusiasm reminiscent of the craze for Uzun Hasan. In December 1501 the Venetian diarist Marino Sanudo recorded a garbled version of his exploits, details of which would become only somewhat clearer in the following months. A new prophet had arisen in the East, Sanudo wrote; he was a descendant of Muhammad, who claimed to be either God himself or his anointed messenger. His followers adored him, but he was merciless to his foes. He had crushed his rivals, seized the throne of Persia, and now commanded an army of 150,000 men.[90] Most exciting of all, he was a sworn enemy of the Ottoman Turks and their faith, for he intended to replace Islam with his own cult. As a result, he was inclined to treat with the nations of Christian Europe.

In Venice, the early trickle of reports on this intriguing new prince and potential ally soon grew to a flood. The Signoria had instructed its agents in the Levant to forward any information that they came across regarding his actions and intentions. Sanudo notes more than a hundred reports on the young king's activities which reached Venice between 1501 and 1504, culminating with the thrilling news that Ismail had advanced as far west as Baghdad.[91] The Turks were said to be terrified by the apparition of this imperial challenger on their eastern frontier.

The timing of this news could not have been better for Venice. The Republic's Second Ottoman War (1499–1503) had gone badly from the start;[92] in 1501, it was not hard for Venetians both in the Levant and at home to imagine that providence had sent them a savior from the East—one endowed, moreover, with all the best qualities of a prince of the West. By mid-1502, Sanudo was able to give the new prophet a name: "Ismail Sophy"—a title derived either from his family name, Safawi, or from his religious role as head of a powerful Sufi order of mystics.[93] The ambiguity was fortuitous, for Sanudo and other Italian observers tended to stress both Ismail's impressive dynastic pedigree *and* his idiosyncratic religious ideas as evidence that Christian Europe might rely on him as a champion against the Ottomans, the self-appointed defenders of orthodox Sunni Islam. Many noted that the Sophy, in addition to possessing great wisdom, an ancient pedigree, and profound religious authority, was kind and tolerant (though an implacable enemy of the Turks), as well as keenly aware of his imperial heritage. In 1508 a Venetian merchant praised him as "studiosissimo et doctissimo in letere, et non lascivo al solito de' persi; homo de grande justitita e senza alcuna avidità, et molto più liberal de Alexandro":[94] "Since Xerxes and Darius, there has never been a king of Persia, neither so adored, nor so loved by his people, nor so bellicose, nor with such a great army, nor so graced with fortune . . . [he has subdued] all of Persia in such a way that Alexander himself could not have rivalled."⁹⁵

Note once again the conflation of ancient models: the Sophy combines the best attributes of Alexander *and* the Achaemenids. What was more, the merchant wrote, the Sophy seemed quite sympathetic to the Christians he met, granting privileges to Armenians in his conquered territories and going out of his way to accord more honor to Christian emissaries than to those who came from the Turk.⁹⁶ "He is a natural leader," another observer announced. "His ancestors are of the royal house of Persia; . . . this Sufi, in his faith, is very Catholic."⁹⁷ Venice had only to reach out to this courtly prince and the two states together would crush the Ottomans between them.

Positive reports on Ismail continued to flow into Europe through the first decade of the sixteenth century. About 1504, Giovanni Rotta, a Venetian agent in Aleppo, sent Doge Leonardo Loredan a lengthy report on the origins, career, and recent activities of Ismail, the first such text to find its way into print. The letter focuses in turn on Ismail's family origins—his descent, via Ali, from the princely house of Muhammad on his father's side, and, via Uzun Hasan on his mother's side, from the royal house of ancient Persia; the story of his rise to power; and his remarkable personal characteristics. Like previous written reports, this was a story designed to make Ismail look good to Italian Renaissance readers: the Sophy's father, Rotta said, had been *litteratissimo* in various sciences, especially astrology, and had lived a life of honest and virtuous poverty; he had instructed his son "in various decorous habits, in the liberal arts [*bone littere*] . . . and had kept him from ever tasting the decadent delights of the court." Ismail was a man of such upright probity that he was now making a tour of his domains to redistribute wealth from the rich to the poor. His actions were attracting hordes of grateful followers, who would fight for him "as we do when on crusade, that is, *senza stipendio*."⁹⁸ What was more, Rotta said, Ismail was enormously sympathetic to Christians and might even secretly harbor Christian beliefs. Unlike most Muslims, he drank wine and ate pork. He even kept a pet pig, which he liked to take with him on campaign. He had named the animal Bayezid, after the reigning Ottoman sultan, a grave and deliberate insult.⁹⁹ He eagerly wished the Venetians would join him in an alliance against the Turk.

Ismail was a topic of great interest in France as well. In 1508, a short pamphlet, attributed to a Knight of Rhodes by the unlikely name of "Monolitricon Manoflundino," was published in Poitiers.[100] Manoflundino claimed recently to have traveled to Shah Ismail's court in the company of four Franciscan friars. The party had been warmly received by the shah, who declared his desire to convert to Christianity, was duly baptized by the friars, and then delivered a lengthy harangue (this is reproduced in the pamphlet in direct speech) excoriating the Turks for their heretical attachment to Islam and inviting the princes of Christian Europe to join him in a crusade to defeat the infidel.

The response to Shah Ismail was not the same at all levels, however. While in previous decades Italian scholars had joined their contemporaries in enthusing over the "kings of Persia" and their heroic exploits, by the early 1500s a new attitude of skepticism seems to have taken hold. Learned scholars writing in the first decade of the sixteenth century expressed rather more guarded opinions about the rise of Shah Ismail—a development which brings us close to the end of our story.

Marcantonio Sabellico concludes his *Enneads* of world history (1504) with an account of contemporary events in Italy and abroad. Among them, he mentions the early rumors of Ismail's rise to power, which circulated in Venice in 1501:

> Around this time a rumor spread that a new prophet had emerged in Persia—not a preacher, nor a miracle worker, but a man who trafficked in fear. His appearance threw the entire East into disarray. Reports of his far-off wars soon began to resound in the West, and in Italy there was talk of courting the favor of the new Sophy (for so he was called) against the Turks, whose borders he threatened. This Terror had advanced as far as Tabriz when he suddenly—by his own volition and for no apparent reason—pulled his forces back. And the whole affair receded into legend.[101]

Sabellico concludes with a bit of moralizing reflection: what was wrong with contemporary Italians, he wondered, that they could waste their energies on such sensational and improbable rumors even as real and pressing matters of public concern—such as the clash of foreign arms on Italian soil—went unremarked: "Thus, even as the most terrible and bloody war was breaking out in the very heart of Italy, the thought of this phantom warrior completely captivated the minds of men."[102]

Here the familiar tropes of reform are turned on their head. Where Filelfo, for example, asked how Europeans could have been so blind as to fail to recognize the heaven-sent blessing of Timur, Sabellico criticizes his contemporaries for placing too *much* faith in an Eastern warlord. His skepticism suggests a certain elitist scorn for popular opinion. But he might as well have directed his distaste backward in time toward his own humanist predecessors, those quattrocento authors who inflated the reputation of Timur and Uzun Hasan with similar enthusiasm.

As he dismisses the Venetian crowd that runs wild after any rumor, no matter how fantastic, Sabellico asserts his own determination to examine the situation with clear-eyed objectivity. The Sophy posed a threat to the Turks, it was true, but he was neither a divinely inspired visionary nor a particularly reliable commander in the field. There was no reason to indulge in excessive excitement over his rise to power.

Two years later, the Volterran humanist Raffaele Maffei included in his *Commentaria urbana* (1506) some similarly ambiguous notes on Ismail's ambitions and achievements: "Recently, in the year 1502, there appeared in Persia a certain ignorant cowherd [*idiota et bubulcus*], who calls himself a prophet of God, and speaks in oracles, and veils his face like Moses when he speaks to his people, and has led a great army against the countries around him, especially the Ottomans from whom he has taken a great deal of territory."[103] Like Sabellico, Maffei moderates his enthusiasm: the Sophy inflicts damage on the Turks, and that is all to the good, but he can claim no distinguished pedigree. If the countries of Christian Europe wish to treat with him, they should do so for tactical reasons (he conquers Turkish territory), not because of any pretended genealogy or claims to ancient imperial authority. Maffei's Sophy heralds neither the resurgence of an ancient civilization in Persia nor a reawakening of the Christian faith in Asia.

In 1507 the Augustinian reformer Cardinal Egidio da Viterbo took an even more negative line, in a celebrated public sermon delivered before Pope Julius II. The emergence of the Sophy was a divine blessing, the cardinal claimed, but only because it meant that *two* heretic nations in the East—the Persians and the Turks—would expend their energies destroying each other, leaving the way open for Julius to lead a victorious crusade:

How can the multitude of our enemies be conquered by so few? Listen to Isaiah . . . *I will feed your enemies with their flesh* [Is. 49:26]. This is clearly fulfilled in your own time, when the ruler of the Turks and another, who has initiated a new heresy and whom they call Sophi in the vernacular, battle each other with savage and cruel weapons. Each fights against an enemy of religion; each acts without knowing your own purpose; and while each believes he wages war for himself, he actually wages war, by God's will, for your republic. Victory may never be hoped for with greater certainty and ease than when enemies suffer internal dissent.[104]

Egidio's dismissive stance toward the "king of Persia" recalls the earliest Italian appraisals of Timur, as a fearsome conqueror, divinely sent and to be welcomed because of it but hardly the equal of European princes.

What, then, should we make of these early sixteenth-century reports? On the one hand, the skepticism Sabellico and Maffei express about Ismail and his dynastic claims suggests we may have reached a turning point in humanist history writing on Islam. Neither author was willing to slot Ismail into the expected, traditional categories; rather, each assessed the Iranian prince in pragmatic terms: a brilliant but erratic thorn in the Ottomans' side; a military genius but still a Muslim; a friend to Christian powers but not a completely reliable one.

Nevertheless, the comments of these authors hardly signifies an overnight transformation in European thinking on Persia. Maffei, for one, still thought it was possible that Ismail might be an imperial champion; he mentions him in the context of his survey of Persian history. After reviewing the glories of ancient Babylon and Achaemenid and Arsacid Persia, Maffei lists modern princes of the realm, from Timur to Uzun Hasan to Ismail. The humanist compulsion to invent ancient pedigrees for enemies and friends alike remained a powerful factor in Maffei's work. In the end, he left the tension in his work unresolved: was Shah Ismail a charlatan or a scion of the Achaemenids? Cardinal Egidio's comments, moreover, underscore the persistence of yet another element in humanist thinking on the empires of Islam: the continuing appeal of providential history. Perhaps Ismail was not, after all, a crypto-Christian champion, but he was nonetheless divinely sent. His significance in world history could best (perhaps only) be understood in terms of God's plan for his Christian people. His appearance should be interpreted by good Christians as a divinely sanctioned spur to reform and a call to action: now was the moment of Christian triumph, if the pope would only seize the opportunities that the Lord had arrayed before him. This too is a familiar trope.

Maffei's curiously indecisive stance on Shah Ismail brings us to the threshold of the sixteenth century and to a new phase in Renaissance writing on Islam, one that would increasingly strive to balance the dictates of tradition against both the evidence of empirical experience and the unpredictability of emerging events. In the epilogue, I note some early milestones in this cinquecento transition from history writing to ethnography and political reportage. By contrast, the quattrocento humanist response to "Persia"— whether Timurid, Aqquyunlu, or Safavid—tended toward assimilation, toward fitting new developments in Islamic politics into older paradigms. Just as historians imagined the Turks were descendants of Alexander's unclean nations, so they pictured the Safavid shah as a long-lost heir of Cyrus, the Magi, and Prester John. Monstrous races and wise men still haunted the humanist map, suggesting the remarkable persistence of medieval tradition in Renaissance intellectual culture.

Epilogue

In the meantime, what of the Turks? European writing on Turkish history certainly proliferated in the years when Sabellico and Maffei wrote. But there were no radical changes to the narrative of Turkish origins those humanists developed, even after the turn of the century. Previous humanist findings were accepted, reconciled where necessary, and reproduced largely without question in a growing body of Latin and vernacular historical works. But even as the humanist narrative of origins—that the Turks came originally from Scythia—remained unchallenged, the larger project of history writing on the Ottoman Empire did change in important regards. As in European writing on the revival of imperial Persian might in Safavid Iran, new sources of information (especially eyewitness reports on the contemporary Ottoman Empire) and new attitudes toward the subject of study (including a markedly more evenhanded, dispassionate, and at times even skeptical tone) gradually came to bear on traditional assumptions about the content and significance of Turkish history.

Friar Felix Fabri wrote the narrative of his pilgrimages to the Holy Land in 1484. The *Evagatorium* was meant to be a personal account, but, as he proudly claimed, he also ornamented his text with erudite citations from earlier historical and geographical authorities.[1] Near the end of his work Fabri pauses, as his pilgrim ship lies anchored off the Troas, to give an account of the origins and early history of the Turks, whose coastline he sees in the distance. Citing Antoninus of Florence, the friar explains how Turcus led his band of Turks from Troy into Asiatic Scythia. There they lost their civilized habits and became rustic shepherds; later some of them came under the rule of the king of Persia. Around the year 900, they overthrew their rightful lord, elected a king for themselves, and went on to conquer all of Asia and no small part of Europe. Fabri also cites Foresti of Bergamo to show that while dwelling in the "Hyperborean regions," the unclean Turks were shut up by Alexander the Great, alongside the Jews, behind giant gates in the mountains. It was not clear when they broke out of this mountainous prison: Otto of Freising dated their escape to the year 758, when they entered into a fierce battle with the Avars; St. Jerome seemed to describe their eruption in the late fourth century; other chronicles put it instead in the reign of Heraclius. Whenever the Turkish invasion occurred, Fabri concludes, it was an infernal catastrophe. The Turks soon joined forces with the "devil incarnate" Muhammad against the Christian faith, a campaign which the Saracens and Turks together continued up to the present day.[2]

In compiling his account, Fabri relied on traditional scholastic chronicles, but all of the tales he pieced together in 1484 had also been rehearsed by Italian humanists in the preceding decades, in the context of what purported to be authoritative, critical accounts of the historical origins of the Turks. Throughout this book, I have stressed the debts that humanist historians owed to the medieval chronicle tradition. Equally important are the operations they performed on this material. Although nearly all the details in their accounts can be traced back to historical texts of late antiquity or the Middle Ages, the humanists extracted each piece of information they found from its original context, refashioning it along moralizing lines and assembling it with others to create seemingly authentic but in fact highly polemical accounts. Their method was, in this sense, not all that different from the piecemeal approach of Friar Felix. Ultimately, the humanists took little interest in the accuracy or even the historical plausibility of the narratives of Islamic history they constructed.

In the last two decades of the fifteenth century, European historians of the Turks continued to work in this conservative but eclectic vein, often drawing their citations not from scholastic compendia, as Fabri had done, but from the works of Renaissance humanists. Foresti of Bergamo, whom Fabri cites, pieced his account of Turkish origins together from Aeneas Sylvius's geographical writings and Biondo's *Decades*.[3] In 1488 the Hungarian bishop Janos Thuroczy reproduced notes from Foresti along with information on the truculent Scythian Turks taken directly from Aeneas's *Asia* or *Europa*.[4] In the *Nuremberg Chronicle*, published in 1493, Hartmann Schedel quoted information from Biondo (some of it taken directly from the *Decades* and some from Platina's citation of Aeneas's *Epitome*) as well as passages of Aethicus, Otto of Freising, and Sagundino borrowed from Aeneas's *Asia*; in an early chapter on Troy, Schedel also cited Vincent of Beauvais on the Trojan exile Turcus.[5] Like Fabri, Schedel tried to reconcile the disparate stories of the Turks' Trojan, Scythian, and Saracen past; two years later, Sebastian Brant repeated Platina's version of Biondo's notice on the Turks (via Schedel?)

in his history of Jerusalem.[6] By contrast, the Venetian historian Marino Barlezio dismissed the Trojan theory out of hand (yet another instance of *anasceua*), then drew on Aeneas Sylvius, Sagundino, Biondo, and Filelfo to create a résumé of Turkish origins at the start of his history of the 1474 Ottoman siege of Scutari, published in 1504.[7]

The same year saw publication of the second volume of Marcantonio Sabellico's *Enneads* of universal history. Sabellico, as we have seen, took a skeptical view of historical anecdotes, no matter how authoritatively sourced, if they seemed too good to be true. He doubted both the ancient tale of Caesara, Christian queen of Persia, and the messianic claims his contemporaries were making for her distant heir, Shah Ismail Safavi. His *Enneads* also mark a turning point in Renaissance history writing on the Ottoman Turks.[8] In his excursus on Turkish origins, Sabellico introduced new material to the debate in the form of a long extract from the Greek historian Laonicus Chalcocondyles's *Demonstrations of Histories*, a text that had reached Venice sometime in the 1490s.[9]

Chalcocondyles's history provided Sabellico with important new information about the birth of the Ottoman dynasty in Bithynia (including the name of Osman's father, Ertoghrul, and his relationship to the last of the Seljuks), as well as the Seljuks' own early history in Persia. Sabellico still believed that the original Turks had been Scythians—*European* Scythians, he specified, from around the River Don. To support this claim he cited ancient reports by Pomponius Mela alongside Otto of Freising on their emergence from the Caucasus. He also included a brief account of relations between the Turks, Arabs, and Persians in the seventh century, derived from Biondo and Hetoum (perhaps via Filelfo or even Biglia), and a description of the Seljuk conquest of Anatolia taken from the fourteenth-century chronicle of the Venetian doge Andrea Dandolo.[10] But Sabellico paid equal attention to their later history (it was here that Chalcocondyles's work proved especially useful). The wide range of sources Sabellico drew on, and in particular his use of Chalcocondyles, is noteworthy. But, as in his discussion of Persian affairs, what truly sets Sabellico's work apart from that of his predecessors is its tone. He raises no alarms. Sabellico recounts the Turks' origins in Scythia and early campaigns of conquest, but he draws no inferences or moralizing conclusions. His Turks are not the base, ignoble, violent, or treacherous creatures the quattrocento humanists so routinely described, nor does he suggest that their history should strike his readers as particularly worrisome. (They may originally have been Scythians, but they were not necessarily still *barbarians*.) It was this neutral stance that allowed Sabellico to exploit in such detail the reports by Chalcocondyles and Dandolo on the Turks' medieval history. His concern was not to find the source of their terrible behavior but simply to tell their story. His (relatively) objective stance also allowed him to admit the possibility of other, less prejudicial accounts of their origins—for instance, that they might have come from Arabia or Syria, or were the descendants of Parthians named for their home city of "Turcis."

Sabellico's work was followed by a series of sixteenth-century excursuses *de origine Turcorum* by such authors as Johannes Adelphus (1513), Gian-Maria Angiolello (after 1514), Giovanni Battista Cipelli (called Egnatius, 1516), Johannes Spiessheimer (called Cuspinianus, 1517), Ludovico Tuberone (c. 1527), and Andrea Cambini (published 1528 but composed well before). All reveal the same relatively detached interest in reconstructing medieval Seljuk history, often relying on Chalcocondyles or even earlier accounts by Byzantine historians such as Theophanes, Zonaras, Skylitzes, and Bryennius along with (it appears) the Latin tradition of Hetoum, and in relating these sources to the origins of Osman and his family.[11] The idea of the Turks' Scythian origins—while still almost universally accepted as the proper way to begin an account of Turkish history—is far less central to these narratives, and the moralizing points earlier historians drew from the story of their conquests are not as frequently raised.

What accounts for the change? As European contacts with the Ottoman East grew in the sixteenth century, information about contemporary Turkish politics, institutions, and customs began to circulate more widely in the West and—just as important—to be considered appropriate material for inclusion in learned books of history. Compared to the vivid, sometimes titillating tales of Ottoman dynastic intrigues, court ceremonials, and social customs retailed by, say, midcentury historians like Francesco Sansovino and Paolo Giovio, the origin and early history of the Turks may no longer have seemed the most colorful material for an author to recount. Interest in lurid details of their primordial barbarity died down. Moreover, this new information began to gain not just in popularity but also in authority. Sabellico, for example, qualifies the last discussion of Turkish affairs in his history with a telling comment: "Throughout this work, much has been said about the origins of the Turks and their culture [*ritus*], but here it will not be amiss to add a little about their military organization, and the ranks of soldiers that nation now employs."[12] He goes on to provide a detailed and fairly accurate appraisal of the modern Turkish way of doing war.

As Sabellico's comments suggest, European anxieties about the Turks hardly subsided in the sixteenth century. What changed is that the fear and fascination Westerners continued to feel regarding the "Turkish menace" found new expression in accounts of their contemporary culture and institutions rather than in the traits of character their origins had supposedly left ingrained in them. Put another way, confronted by an avalanche of new information, especially information on new or at least recent events, narratives of origin began to lose their claim to be the most authoritative source of information on a foreign people or state.

A second early sixteenth-century work, Raffaele Maffei's encyclopedic *Commentaries* (1506), also reveals certain shifts in thinking which would come to characterize sixteenth-century Turcica. If Sabellico, in his *Enneads*, followed Biondo's example of a humanistic survey of universal history, Maffei took as his model Aeneas Sylvius's cosmography. Like Aeneas, Maffei set out to survey the countries of the world (traveling east from Spain and Britain, across Europe and the Levant to, in his twelfth book, Africa, East Asia, and the islands newly discovered by Spain in the Western Ocean), tracing the history of each from its origin to the present day. Unlike Aeneas, Maffei made good his promises regarding contemporary history, quoting sources to illuminate the most recent events in each part of the world. His history of the Turks begins with a résumé of earlier authorities that surpasses even Sabellico's in its breadth. Maffei quotes Pliny, Pomponius Mela, Ptolemy, Theophylactus Simocatta, "Scilix" (that is, Skylitzes, from Gaza's treatise), and Otto of Freising on the Turks' origins in Scythia.[13] These are followed by some notes on the early Seljuk conquests in Iran, Iraq, and Anatolia which appear to derive from Hetoum or possibly Biglia.

Maffei then turns to the history of the Ottomans. He explains that they were but one of four Turkish families who came out of Persia to occupy Anatolia. The others included the dynasty of Karaman, whose ambassadors approached Pius II in an attempt to negotiate an alliance against the Ottomans, and the family of the Assembeci, most recently led by their lord Usuncasanus, who had inflicted great damage on the Ottomans in the 1470s before his final defeat at their hands. For details of Uzun Hasan's early victories over both Mehmed II and Timur's son and successor Shah Rukh, Maffei quotes from reports by the Venetian envoy Caterino Zeno and a letter from a Genoese merchant, one "Maestro Seguranza," sent to Sixtus IV from the peripatetic Aqqoyunlu court.[14] He then goes on to describe recent popular reports on the new prophet (or was he just a cowherd?) in Persia, Shah

Ismail. The boy seemed to have tricked his compatriots into revering him as a divine messenger, but his campaigns against the Ottomans were nonetheless brilliant and impressive.

Maffei's work differs from those of his humanist predecessors in several regards. First, he draws careful distinctions among the Islamic powers of recent Eastern history (Ottoman, Aqqoyunlu, Karamanli, Timurid, Safavid), recognizing each as an independent political entity, with an independent and rational approach to foreign policy. None of these Islamic states can be characterized as totally bad, or indeed as entirely good. Periodic skirmishes between Ottomans and Karamanli, or Ottomans and Aqqoyunlu for that matter, did not represent for Maffei the resurgence of a global struggle between civilized, southern Persia and the barbarous Scythians of the north. He recognized the essentially local character of their disputes. (Indeed, in his scheme, the Ottomans and the Aqqoyunlu were closely related kin.) Maffei's approach also allowed for historical change: dynasties might rise and fall; tribal identities and policies could change. The idea of nations as homogenetic groups, each enjoying direct and unbroken descent from a primordial race of founding fathers and marked by inborn and unchanging traits of character, had been a mainstay of the fifteenth-century approach to the question of Turkish and "Persian" origins, but it found little purchase in Maffei's work.

Last, like Sabellico, Maffei based some of his account on contemporary reports—in fact, it was probably information from travelers and ambassadors that allowed him to understand the complex political situation in the East as well as he did. Taken together with Sabellico's, Maffei's work signals the start of a new chapter in Western writing on the empires of Islam. Sixteenth-century editions of Turcica regularly offer scholarly historical investigations into Turkish and Persian history alongside ambassadorial *relazioni*, practical crusade treatises, journalistic reports of recent battles, and the exciting tales of escaped captives and prisoners of war.[15] Frequently, as in Maffei's case, such material is integrated directly into the learned scholar's own work. Humanists of the previous generation had little regard for—or even awareness of—literature of this type. They ignored important sources for Asian ethnography, such as the reports of Marco Polo and the mendicant missionaries. And though they were fascinated by Uzun Hasan, they very rarely repeated details about him garnered by contemporary travelers and diplomats, preferring to raid favorite classical texts like Xenophon to fuel their speculations. Quattrocento authors approached the question of Eastern peoples—

whether friends or foes—by focusing almost entirely on the past. Who the Ottomans, Mamluks, Timurids, or Aqqoyunlu had been originally and where they had come from told them what they needed to know.

Indeed, in contrast to authors like Sabellico and Maffei, quattrocento historical writing on the empires of Islam reflected the continuing influence of three long medieval traditions: repetition of authorities, the formulaic description of northern barbarians, and hopeful praise of Oriental kings. The humanists distinguished themselves from their medieval predecessors by striving for at least an appearance of critical objectivity and authenticity. Few were prepared to assert that the Turks were vengeful Trojans, for instance. The majority argued that the Turks were savage Scythians, a people with an ancient and barbarous pedigree. But even so, this was a narrative of origins rooted not so much in classical ethnography as in misinterpretations of medieval chronicles and the wilder fringes of Christian apocalyptic. The legend of Alexander's gates may not have been invoked explicitly, but it lurked close beneath the surface. The idea that the Turks, like other Muslim nations of Asia, could lay claim to at least a few chapters of distinguished imperial history was rarely entertained.

Likewise, few quattrocento writers claimed that the "kings of Persia" wielded the magical powers of Prester John. Timur, Uzun Hasan, and Shah Ismail had no supernatural gifts; their kingdoms held no marvels, no miraculous relics or virtuous stones. Instead, humanist biographers burnished their images by endowing them with ancient political pedigrees and admirable traits of character. Even so, their portraits owe less to the canons of classical biography than to medieval convictions about the divinely ordered institution of kingship and the medieval compulsion to discover Christian champions in the East. It was important to make these Eastern dynasties "Persian," but only if Persia was understood as an empire that had long respected (if not outright embraced) the salvific virtues of Christianity.

For humanists writing in the decades after Constantinople's fall, the empires of Islam offered stories of moral and political rather than scholarly significance. But for modern readers, Renaissance narratives of Islamic history can best (and perhaps only) be understood in the context of the history of scholarship. Humanist attempts to reconstruct the origins of the Turks, the "Saracens," and the Persians can tell us something about early modern Orientalist images of East and West, it is true. But the material reveals far more about the methods of the authors who made it. The epistemological conflicts in these scholars' work in particular cast a vivid light on larger tensions in the intellectual culture of the period: between classical and medieval ways of thinking about foreign peoples and their place in world history, and between both learned traditions and the challenges of modern empirical experience.

Renaissance Europe's halting attempt to come to grips with the history of a faith other than its own is a story that has yet to find an ending. "We," the humanists' heirs, still do not know quite what to make of Islam, or how to tell its story outside our longstanding discourses of alterity, expertise, and reform. In this sense, the intellectual struggles and subterfuges of scholars five hundred years ago can serve to illustrate yet another narrative of origins, one that remains highly contested and is in many ways still under construction: that of the modern discipline of history itself. In the humanist pursuit of origins we discern, as in a sort of infinite regress, the origins of our own modern fascination with origins—ethnic, political, religious, intellectual, or otherwise. Historians still wrestle with the ancient saw "Origin defines essence."[16] The importance of the past for the present derives from a fundamentally rhetorical model of history, one long in the making and one which continues to be used—to praise, to instruct, to inspire, and also to blame.

APPENDIX

ABBREVIATIONS

NOTES

ACKNOWLEDGMENTS

INDEX

The Caspian Gates

The term *Kaspiai pulai* or *Caspiae Portae* originally referred to an area of mountain passes running through the Elburz Mountains south of the Caspian Sea, near ancient Rhagae and some fifty miles southeast of modern Tehran. In antiquity, the Caspian Gates marked the boundary between ancient Media in the west and the satrapies of outer Iran (Parthia, Hyrcania, Bactria) in the east; they served as a cardinal point from which distances in Asia were measured.[1] According to Pliny the Elder, the pass derived its name from the Caspii tribe, who lived in the area and who also gave their name to the Caspian Sea and the Elburz Mountains (as *Montes Caspii*).[2] The association of Alexander the Great with these Iranian Caspian Gates is quite justified: he traversed them in his final pursuit of Darius in the summer of 330 B.C., and this passage marked the start of his long expedition through outer Iran, Bactria, Sogdiana, and India.[3] Pliny mentions firsthand campaign reports (now lost) which plot all the cities and countries of the East that Alexander subsequently explored in terms of their distance from the Iranian Caspian Gates.[4]

Pliny also mentions, however, that by his time there was some confusion regarding the exact location of the Caspian Gates. Some thought they actually lay in the Caucasus, west of the Caspian Sea, instead of in the Elburz, to its south. Several factors contributed to this confusion.

After passing through the Caspian Gates, Alexander traveled to Hyrcania, southeast of the Caspian Sea. Over the next year he led his army farther east into Aria and Arachosia, up over the Hindu Kush, down into the desert plains of Bactria, north across the Oxus, and through Sogdiana to its northern boundary, the Jaxartes River. Local resistance and revolts kept him campaigning in Sogdiana and Bactria for more than two years before he finally turned south again to invade India.[5]

Alexander had traveled much farther east than any Greek before him. There is evidence to show, however, that in the course of his Sogdian campaign, neither he nor his followers had a clear idea of where in the world they actually were. The patchy state of existing Greek geography, and the equally confusing information supplied by local sources, convinced them that they were much farther west, much closer to familiar ground, than was the case.[6] They believed, for example, that the Oxus and Jaxartes drained not into the Aral Sea but into the Caspian, to its west.[7] And it was believed that the Caspian Sea itself might be part of the Black Sea or the Maeotic Lake, connected by either an open strait of water or an underground channel.[8] Some thought the Jaxartes was actually the Tanais (the European Don) and so discharged directly into the Maeotic Lake. Because the Don was the traditional boundary between Europe and Asia, Alexander and his followers believed that the northern bank of the Jaxartes (deep in central Asia) was actually European soil: the trees on the far bank were "European" firs, and the tribes who came across to meet them were "European" Scythians.[9]

This erroneous view of the local geography sometimes colored the conduct of the campaign. For example, Alexander discussed with the king of Chorasmia, on the lower reaches of the Oxus, the possibility of a joint expedition against the Amazons of Colchis, on the eastern end of the Black Sea, which the king said was within easy reach.[10] Similarly, when Alexander met a group of mounted warrior women in Hyrcania, south of the Caspian Sea, his chroniclers reported it as a visit by Amazons from the River Thermodon, which flows into the Black Sea south of Colchis.[11]

After the collapse of Alexander's empire and the resurgence of an independent Persia, Greco-Roman geographical knowledge of central Asia grew even vaguer. Histories of Alexander described his apparent encounters with Amazons from near Colchis, in the Caucasus, and the River Tanais (Don) to its north; the assumption was almost inevitable that Alexander had actually traveled through the Caucasus itself, taking the direct route, as it were, to these Scythian adventures.[12] Since Alexander's passage through the Caspian Gates was considered (quite accurately) to have marked the start of these far-flung exploits, it followed that when his adventures were transferred in popular imagination to the country beyond the Caucasus, the gates themselves should be imagined as a pass running through that mountain range.

Various Locations of the Caucasus

Another factor which lay behind this geographical confusion was the uncertainty prevailing in Greek geography over the location and size of the Caucasus itself. Greek geographers had from very early times conceived of Asia as a continent divided by a single mountain range running east to west, from the Taurus Mountains of southwest Asia Minor through the Antitaurus in Armenia, the Elburz in Iran, the Hindu Kush and Pamirs in Bactria, and finally the Himalayas north of India.[13] The range as a whole was usually called Taurus, and the Iranian Caspian Gates were considered a break in this massive chain.[14] The Caucasus, by contrast, was considered a separate range of mountains, far to the north.

Strabo relates that during Alexander's crossing of the Hindu Kush from Arachosia to Bactria and Sogdiana in the winter or spring of 329 B.C.,[15] he or his followers began to call the Hindu Kush (usually known as Paropamisus and considered part of the Taurus chain) by the name "Caucasus" and named the city they established there "Alexandria ad Caucasum."[16] Strabo says this was a deliberate attempt to associate Alexander with those gods and heroes of Greek myth who had also had adventures in the East, among them Prometheus, Hercules, and Jason. Their exploits had taken place in the Caucasus, and Alexander, despite having traveled much farther afield, wanted to be known as an explorer of the same region.[17]

Gradually the two Caucasuses (the true Caucasus, between the Black and Caspian Seas, and the false one, in reality the Hindu Kush) were joined up in ancient geography. The process began with the inclusion of the true Caucasus in the list of mountains which were part of the great continental Taurus chain. Pliny explains, for example, that the course of the Taurus does not follow a straight line but rather curves north and south, avoiding the inlets of various seas, and so includes mountains which lie north and south of the main axis. He then calls the Caucasus the *highest* of all the mountains in the range, and we know he means the true Caucasus because he mentions the Paropamisus separately.[18] Quintus Curtius Rufus actually calls the whole range "Caucasus," while the Taurus, according to him, is another range, lower than the Caucasus, running parallel to it across Asia.[19] By the early Middle Ages, the term "Caucasus" is used (by, for example, Isidore of Seville) to describe the entire chain as well as the highest mountain in it, while "Taurus" denotes only a subsidiary peak at its western end.[20]

Thus, thanks to a particular conceit of Alexander the Great, the term "Caucasus" came to be used in antiquity to describe not only the true Caucasus but also the scene of Alexander's campaigns in the Paropamisus or Hindu Kush. Following the collapse of Alexander's empire, Greek and Latin geographical knowledge of Asia grew so vague that the name "Caucasus" came to be applied to the *whole* mountain range that was supposed to cut across the continent, of which both the true Caucasus and the false one were now imagined to be a part.

Various Locations of the Caspian Gates

This confusion over the geography of the Caucasus, together with uncertainty about the location of Alexander's Sogdian exploits, was directly responsible for the transfer in popular imagination of the Caspian Gates from the Elburz to the Caucasus—the true Caucasus, that is, between the Black and Caspian Seas. This part of the world had its own mountain passes, which were also usually described as the "gates" to one area or another: Caucasian Gates, Albanian Gates, Sarmatian Gates, and so on. It is not surprising, then, that at least one of these passes should attract to itself the name of the famous Caspian Gates of Iran. The fact that the mountains of the Caucasus were sometimes called the "Caspian" Mountains must also have contributed to the error. Describing the Caucasus, Pliny comments on the misunderstanding:

> [Next] one comes to the Gates of the Caucasus, which many very erroneously call the Caspian Gates, an enormous work of Nature, who has here suddenly rent the mountains asunder. Here gates have been placed, with iron-covered beams, under the centre of which flows a river emitting a horrible odor; and on this side of it on a rock stands the fortress called Cumania, erected for the purpose of barring the passage of the innumerable tribes. At this spot, therefore, the world is divided by gates into two portions.[21]

Later Pliny distinguishes explicitly between the false and the true Caspian Gates. He states that the true pass is the one in Iran, which is associated with Alexander's campaigns; he also hints at the source of the confusion:

> In this place we must correct a mistake made by many people, even those who recently served with Corbulo in the war in Armenia. These have given the name of Caspian Gates to the pass in Hiberia, which, as we have stated, is called the Gates of the Caucasus, and maps of the region sent home from the front have this name written on them. Also the expedition threatened by the emperor Nero was spoken of as intended to penetrate to the Caspian Gates, whereas it was really aimed at the pass that gives a road through Hiberia to Sarmatia, the mountain barrier affording scarcely any access to the Caspian Sea. There are however other Caspian Gates adjoining the Cas-

pian tribes; the distinction between the two passes can only be established by means of the report of those who accompanied the expedition of Alexander the Great.[22]

Nero had tried, once or possibly twice, to send a legion to the "Caspian Gates," in an attempt to emulate the deeds of Alexander the Great.[23] We know his goal was the Caucasus, and not the Iranian Caspian Gates, both because Pliny explains that the expedition was aimed at "Hiberia" (Georgia) and because Tacitus, who describes how the soldiers chosen for this campaign ended up loitering dangerously in Rome, says that Nero had directed them against the Albani, a Caucasian tribe: "[In Rome at the time of Nero's death] there were, in addition, many Germans, Britons and Illyrians, because after Nero himself had selected them and sent them to the Caspian Gates, to the campaign he was preparing against the Albani, he had recalled them for the purpose of crushing the rebellion of Vindex."[24]

Suetonius gives a slightly different account of the same plan (possibly indicating another attempt altogether), in which Nero's emulation of Alexander is made clear: "He even planned an expedition to the Caspian Gates, with a new legion made up of Italian men, all six feet tall, which he called the Phalanx of Alexander the Great."[25]

It is impossible to say whether Nero, in his vanity, was solely responsible for transferring the name "Caspian Gates" from Iran to the goal of his campaign in the Caucasus, thereby making himself seem like a second Alexander, or whether the notion that the Caspian Gates were located in the Caucasus was already current in Nero's time, based on the mistaken view that Alexander's Sogdian campaign had taken him close to the Don and the Maeotic Lake, and on the confusion over which Caucasus Alexander really crossed, the true one or the Hindu Kush.[26] Whatever the case, from the first century A.D., the term "Caspian Gates" was used in both Greek and Roman literature to describe a pass through the true Caucasus, now considered the scene of some adventures of Alexander the Great.[27]

One such adventure, which enjoyed great fame in late antique and medieval literature in both the East and the West, involved Alexander in the construction of actual gates across the pass in the Caucasus erroneously known as the Caspian Gates.[28] Exactly how and when the legend developed is unclear. Pliny, in a passage quoted above, indicates that in his day the geographical Caspian Gates of the Caucasus were guarded by real "gates . . . with iron-covered beams . . . erected for the purpose of barring the passage of the innumerable tribes." A few decades later, the Jewish historian Josephus noted that the king of Hyrcania controlled an iron gate which had been built by Alexander, through which the barbarian Alans of the Caucasus wished to pass in A.D. 72.[29]

Josephus's text is the first extant reference to a gate constructed by Alexander; he does not, however, give a precise indication of its location. Hyrcania is not in the Caucasus but on the southern shore of the Caspian Sea, not far from the original, Iranian Caspian Gates. Josephus may have meant to refer to a gate in the Caucasus—perhaps the one Pliny described—in which case he erred both in assigning its construction to Alexander (who never was in that part of the world) and in attributing control of the gate to the Hyrcanians. If so, then we should consider Josephus the unsuspecting victim of a misunderstanding already current in the time of Nero. A. B. Bosworth, however, suggests that Josephus's story is accurate as it is written: that he correctly refers to the Alans invading through Hyrcania and so means to refer to the Iranian Caspian Gates, which were historically associated with Alexander (even if even there he did not build a gate).[30] According to Bosworth's hypothesis, the Alans, inhabitants of the northern Caucasus, planned a surprise attack on Hyrcania from an unexpected quarter: by circling the long way around the Caspian Sea, rounding its northern and eastern coasts, they invaded from the east, through the *real* Caspian Gates. If Bosworth's guess is right (we have no conclusive evidence for how the Alans actually invaded), then their surprise attack on Hyrcania may actually have played an important part in the transfer of the name of the Caspian Gates—and their association with Alexander—to the Caucasus in the first place. Later writers reading of the exploit in Josephus may have assumed that the obvious place for an Alan invasion to erupt would be from the Caucasus, and so imagined that the "gate built by Alexander" which Josephus says they wanted to force was one constructed across a Caucasian pass.

By the end of the fourth century, the existence of Alexander's gates in the Caucasus seems to have become common knowledge. Jerome, for example, identified the Huns who invaded the Holy Land by way of the Caucasus in 395 as the barbarian tribes whom Alexander had excluded. In a letter describing their violent incursions, Jerome first compared them to the Scythian raiders mentioned by Herodotus (who invaded Media by the same route in the seventh century B.C.) and then associated them with Alexander's tribes: "Behold, suddenly . . . great swarms of Huns, flying this way and that on their swift horses, filling the whole world with terror and death, have erupted from amongst the monstrous tribes of Massagetes on the far shore of the Maeotic Lake, around the frozen Don, where the gates of Alexander confine wild peoples within the crags of the Caucasus."[31]

From the fourth to the seventh century, the barbarians behind Alexander's Caucasian gates were mentioned frequently in Latin and Greek historical and geographical literature.[32] At the same time, the exploit of building the gates began to feature in the growing collection of prose romances retailing Alexander's fantastic adventures at the ends of the earth.[33] A final development in the story was the identification of the tribes Alexander confined behind the gates with the biblical nations of Gog and Magog—the terrifying, horse-riding northerners whom Old Testament prophecy and the Book of Revelation predicted would overwhelm the world in the last days.

Several older traditions contributed to this idea. Josephus, in the late first century A.D., identified the Scythians in general as descendants of Magog.[34] Christian writers in the fourth century identified the Goths and the Huns with Gog and Magog, often playing on the similarity between the names "Goth" and "Gog," or "Massagetae" (an ancient Scythian tribe whose name was often used for the Huns) and "Magog," and commenting on the cataclysmic nature of their sudden arrival in the Mediterranean world.[35] The association of these biblical tribes with Alexander, however, was a late development, the innovation of a group of Syriac Christian authors writing in the mid-seventh century. They were inspired by the invasion of another barbarian people, which took place two centuries after the incursions of the Goths and the Huns: the Turkic Khazars, who made raids on Armenia and Media through the Caspian Gates of the Caucasus in the late 620s A.D.

A Syriac homily entitled *Neshana d'Aleksandros* (*History of Alexander*), composed shortly after the Khazar invasion, contains the first known reference to the peoples behind Alexander's Caspian Gates as Gog and Magog, together with the idea that their eruption through that barrier meant that the end of the world was at hand.[36] The Khazar incursions had obviously made a powerful impression on the local Syrian population in the lands south of the Caucasus. The story was repeated in several other Syriac texts of the mid-seventh century. Around 690 it appeared again in the apocalyptic *Revelations* of ps.-Methodius,[37] which was translated, first into Greek and then into Latin, by 700.[38]

The lines of transmission between these texts have not always been understood correctly. Because the apocalyptic legend also appears in some recensions of the Greek and Latin *Alexander Romances*, a tradition which probably dates back to the third century A.D., some critics have concluded that the apocalyptic form of the legend was just or nearly as old as the oldest elements of the *Romance*—that it was a Greek story which only later passed into Syriac Christian writings.[39] Similarly, because some of the Syriac texts that repeat the story were once thought to predate the *Neshana*, the significance of the Khazar invasions to the development of the legend has not always been recognized.[40] It now seems established beyond doubt, however, that the apocalyptic form of the legend did not develop until the early seventh century, in a Syriac Christian milieu.[41]

Afterward, it quickly passed, via the Greek and Latin translations of ps.-Methodius, into several traditions of the Greek ps.-Callisthenes *Alexander Romance* and its Latin counterpart, the *Historia de preliis,* and thence into an enormous range of medieval Latin and vernacular poetry, romances, and encylopedic compendia.[42] The entire collection of motifs—the gates built by Alexander, the identity of the barbarians as Gog and Magog, their cannibalism and other unclean habits—was invoked by historians seeking to explain the appearance not only of the Khazars but also, much later, of the Mongols.[43] Though he dismissed the eschatological significance of the terrible "Tartars," Roger Bacon, for instance, still drew on the tradition as enshrined in the *Cosmographia* of Aethicus:

> Ethicus the philosopher therefore states that about the time of Antichrist there will be a race of the stock of Gog and Magog . . . [in] the North around the Black Sea, the worst of all the nations, which in company with the worst seed of those shut up behind the Caspian Gates of Alexander will cause a great devastation of this world, and will meet Antichrist and will call him God of gods . . . The race of the Tartars has come forth from those places, as we know, since they dwelt behind those gates to the northeast, shut up in the mountains of the Caucasus and of the Caspian.[44]

The same tradition, with its roots in ancient geographical lore but profoundly transformed by its passage through medieval Christian apocalyptic, also had an enormous, if often sublimated, influence on Renaissance humanist accounts of the origins of the Ottoman Turks.

Abbreviations

AHR	*American Historical Review*
BMC	*Catalogue of Books Printed in the 15th Century,* now in the British Museum (London, 1908–)
Briefwechsel	*Der Briefwechsel des Eneas Sylvius Piccolomini,* ed. R. Wolkan, 3 vols. (Vienna, 1912–1918)
BSOAS	*Bulletin of the School of Oriental and African Studies*
BT	G. Moravcsik, *Byzantinoturcica,* 2d ed., 2 vols. (Berlin, 1958)
Caduta	A. Pertusi, *La caduta di Costantinopoli. Le testimonianze dei contemporanei,* 2 vols. (Verona, 1976)
CHEIA	*The Cambridge History of Early Inner Asia,* ed. D. Sinor (Cambridge, 1990)
CHI	*The Cambridge History of Iran,* eds. W. B. Fisher and J. A. Boyle (Cambridge, 1968–)
Clauser	*Laonicus Chalcocondyles, De origine et rebus gestis Turcorum libri decem,* trans. C. Clauser (Basel, 1556)
CMH	*The Cambridge Medieval History,* eds. J. B. Bury et al., 8 vols. (Cambridge, 1911–1936)
CQ	*Classical Quarterly*
DBI	*Dizionario biografico degli Italiani* (Rome, 1960–)
DGM	W. Wattenbach, R. Holzmann, and F.-J. Schmale, *Deutschlands Geschichtsquellen im Mittelalter,* 3 vols. (Darmstadt, 1967–1971)
DLMV	*Die deutsche Literatur des Mittelalters: Verfasserlexicon,* 2d ed., eds. W. Stammler et al. (Berlin, 1977–)
EI2	*The Encyclopaedia of Islam,* 2d ed., eds. H.A.R. Gibb et al. (Leiden, 1960–)
GW	*Gesamtkatalog der Wiegendrucke* (Leipzig, 1925–1940; Stuttgart, 1971–)
Hain	L. Hain, *Repertorium bibliographicum,* 2 vols. (Stuttgart, 1826–1838)
HC	*A History of the Crusades,* 2d ed., eds. K. M. Setton et al., 6 vols. (Madison, Wis., 1969–1989)
IGI	*Indice generale degli incunaboli delle biblioteche d'Italia,* eds. T. M. Guarnaschelli, E. Valenziani, et al., 6 vols. (Rome, 1943–1981)

Iter Italicum   P. O. Kristeller, *Iter Italicum: A Finding List of Uncatalogued or Incompletely Catalogued Humanistic Manuscripts of the Renaissance in Italian and Other Libraries*, 6 vols. (London, 1963–1997)

JMRS   *Journal of Medieval and Renaissance Studies*

JRAS   *Journal of the Royal Asiatic Society*

JWCI   *Journal of the Warburg and Courtauld Institutes*

MGH   *Monumenta Germaniae historica* (Hanover, 1826–)

OCD   *Oxford Classical Dictionary*, 3d ed., eds. S. Hornblower and A. Spawforth (Oxford, 1996)

ODB   *Oxford Dictionary of Byzantium*, ed. A. P. Kazhdan, 3 vols. (New York, 1991)

ODP   J.N.D. Kelly, *Oxford Dictionary of Popes* (Oxford, 1986)

PG   *Patrologiae cursus completus, series graecolatina*, ed. J.-P. Migne, 161 vols. (Paris, 1857–1866)

PL   *Patrologiae cursus completus, series latina*, ed. J.-P. Migne, 221 vols. (Paris, 1844–1864)

P-W1   *Paulys Real-Encyclopadie der classischen Altertumswissenschaft*, eds. G. Wissowa et al., 1st ser. (A–Q), 24 vols. (1894–1963)

P-W2   *Paulys Real-Encyclopadie der classischen Altertumswissenschaft*, eds. G. Wissowa et al., 2d ser. (R–Z), 19 vols. (1914–1972)

RHC Occ   *Recueil des historiens des croisades. Historiens occidentaux*, 5 vols. (Paris, 1844–1895)

RHC Arm   *Recueil des historiens des croisades. Documents arméniens*, 2 vols. (Paris, 1869–1906)

RHGF   *Recueil des historiens des Gaules et de la France*, eds. M. Bouquet et al., 24 vols. (Paris, 1738–1833)

RIS1   *Rerum Italicarum scriptores ab anno aerae christianae quingentesimo ad millesimum quingentesimum*, eds. Ludovico Muratori et al., 25 vols. (Milan, 1723–1751)

RIS2   *Rerum Italicarum scriptores. Raccolta degli storici italiani dal cinquecento al millecinquecento*, eds. G. Carducci and V. Fiorini (Città di Castello, 1900–)

RQ   *Renaissance Quarterly*

SCJ   *Sixteenth Century Journal*

Testi inediti   A. Pertusi, *Testi inediti e poco noti sulla caduta di Costantinopoli. Edizione postuma*, ed. A. Carile (Bologna, 1983)

Notes

Introduction

1. Aeneas Sylvius Piccolomini to Nicholas of Cusa, *Briefwechsel*, 3:209–210. Unless otherwise noted, all translations are my own.
2. On the political and professional usefulness of origin myths in early modern Europe, see R. Bizzocchi, *Genealogie incredibili: Scritti di Storia nell'Europa Moderna* (Bologna, 1995); M. Rothstein, "Etymology, Genealogy, and the Immutability of Origins," *RQ* 43 (1990): 332–347; P. Burke, "Foundation Myths and Collective Identities in Early Modern Europe," in *Europe and the Other and Europe as the Other*, ed. B. Stråth (Brussels, 2000), 113–122.
3. See the differing interpretations of H. A. Gibbons, *The Foundation of the Ottoman Empire* (Oxford, 1916); W. L. Langer and R. P. Blake, "The Rise of the Ottoman Turks and Its Historical Background," *AHR* 37 (1931–1932): 488–505; M. Fuad Köprülü, *The Origins of the Ottoman Empire* [1935], trans. G. Leiser (Albany, N.Y., 1992); P. Wittek, *The Rise of the Ottoman Empire* (London, 1938). In recent decades these works—in particular, Wittek's theory that the early Ottomans were fervent champions (*gazis*) of Islamic holy war—have been the subject of intense critical scrutiny: H. Inalcik, "The Question of the Emergence of the Ottoman State," *International Journal of Turkish Studies* 2 (1981–1982): 75–79; R. Lindner, *Nomads and Ottomans in Medieval Anatolia* (Bloomington, Ind., 1983); R. C. Jennings, "Some Thoughts on the Gazi-Thesis," *Wiener Zeitschrift für die Kunde des Morgenlandes* 76 (1986): 151–161; C. Imber, "The Ottoman Dynastic Myth," *Turcica* 19 (1987): 7–27; idem, "Who Was Osman Gazi?" in *The Ottoman Emirate (1300–1389)*, ed. E. A. Zachariadou (Rethymnon, 1993), 67–76; C. Heywood, "Wittek and the Austrian Tradition," *JRAS* (1988): 7–25; idem, "'Boundless Dreams of the Levant': Paul Wittek, the *George-Kreis*, and the Writing of Ottoman History," *JRAS* (1989): 30–50. More recently, see C. Kafadar, *Between Two Worlds: The Construction of the Ottoman State* (Berkeley, Calif., 1995), esp. 1–59 and 166n56, opening a new round in the debate as the first recent scholar to support, with qualification, Wittek's *gazi* thesis.
4. Kafadar, *Between Two Worlds*, 29–32.

5. N. Daniel, *Islam and the West: The Making of an Image* (Edinburgh, 1960); J. V. Tolan, *Saracens: Islam in the Medieval European Imagination* (New York, 2002), 135–169.

6. A. Momigliano, "Ancient History and the Antiquarian," *JWCI* 13 (1950): 285–315, at 286–292; D. Hay, *Annalists and Historians: Western Historiography from the Eighth to the Eighteenth Centuries* (London, 1977), 110.

7. J. Burckhardt, *The Civilization of the Renaissance in Europe,* trans. S.G.C. Middlemore (New York, 1987), 98.

8. This interpretation has been sustained in general surveys of European historiography over the past century—E. Fueter, *Geschichte der neueren Historiographie* (Munich, 1936, repr. New York, 1968), 1–14; R. G. Collingwood, *The Idea of History,* rev. ed., ed. J. van der Dussen (Oxford, 1994), 57–58; H. F. Butterfield, *The Origins of History* (New York, 1981); E. Breisach, *Historiography: Ancient, Medieval, and Modern,* 2d ed. (Chicago, 1994), 153–156; M. T. Guilderhus, *History and Historians: A Historiographical Introduction,* 3d ed. (Englewood Cliffs, N.J., 1996), 29–31; D. R. Kelley, *Faces of History from Herodotus to Herder* (New Haven, 1998), 138–141—as well as in specialist studies of the Renaissance art: B. Ullmann, "Leonardo Bruni and Humanist Historiography," *Medievalia et Humanistica* 4 (1946), 45–61; W. K. Ferguson, *The Renaissance in Historical Thought: Five Centuries of Interpretation* (Cambridge, Mass., 1948), 1–28; F. Gilbert, *Machiavelli and Guicciardini: Politics and History in Sixteenth-Century Florence* (Princeton, 1965); D. J. Wilcox, *The Development of Florentine Humanist Historiography* (Cambridge, Mass., 1969); E. H. Fryde, *Humanism and Renaissance Historiography* (London, 1983), 3–31; J. Soll, "The Uses of Historical Evidence in Early Modern Europe," *Journal of the History of Ideas* 64 (2003): 149–157, at 152–153.

9. See the important remarks of E. Cochrane, *Historians and Historiography in the Italian Renaissance* (Chicago, 1981), xi–xiii. My own methodology has been informed by Cochrane's nuanced and skeptical view, as well as by the critical observations of L. Martines, *Power and Imagination: City States in Renaissance Italy* (New York, 1979), 262–300; P. Burke, *The Renaissance Sense of the Past* (London, 1969); A. Grafton, *Forgers and Critics: Creativity and Duplicity in Western Scholarship* (Princeton, 1990); and G. Ianziti, *Humanist Historiography under the Sforzas: Politics and Propaganda in Fifteenth-Century Milan* (Oxford, 1988).

10. With the possible exception of the Venetian state historians, especially Marcantonio Sabellico at the very end of the century: F. Gilbert, "Biondo, Sabellico, and the beginnings of Venetian Official Historiography," in *Florilegium historiale: Essays Presented to Wallace K. Ferguson* (Toronto, 1971), 275–293.

11. For Florence, Ullman, "Leonardo Bruni," and Wilcox, *Development;* for Milan, Ianziti, *Humanist Historiography;* for Rome, M. Miglio, *Storiografia pontificia del quattrocento* (Bologna, 1975) and (a particularly useful case study) Aeneas Sylvius Piccolomini, *De gestis Concilii Basiliensis commentariorum libri II,* eds. D. Hay and W. K. Smith, 2d ed. (Oxford, 1992).

12. C. Ginzburg, "Lorenzo Valla on the 'Donation of Constantine,'" in his *History, Rhetoric, and Proof* (Hanover, N.H., 1999), 54–70; see also Aeneas Sylvius's hostile rewriting of conciliar history in his *De gestis Concilii Basiliensis.*

13. In his account of Ottoman governance in *The Prince,* Chapter 4.

14. S. Chew, *The Crescent and the Rose: Islam and England during the Renaissance* (New York, 1937); F. L. Baumer, "England, the Turk, and the Common Corps of Christendom," *AHR* 50 (1944); C. D. Rouillard, *The Turk in French History, Thought and Literature 1520–1600* (Paris, 1938); F. Babinger, *Mehmed the Conqueror and His Time,* ed. W. Hickman and trans. R. Mannheim (Princeton, 1978).

15. R. Schwoebel, *The Shadow of the Crescent: The Renaissance Image of the Turk* (Nieuwkoop, 1967), 148; F. Cardini, "La crociata, mito politico," *Il Pensiero Politico* 8 (1975): 3–32, esp. 31–32; J. Hankins, "Renaissance Crusaders: Humanist Crusade Literature in the Age of Mehmed II," *Dumbarton Oaks Papers* 49 (1995): 111–207, at 123–124, 141–142, and 145–146; K. Fleet, "Italian Perceptions of the Turks in the Fourteenth and Fifteenth Centuries," *Journal of Mediterranean Studies* 5 (1995): 159–172, at 167, 169; N. Bisaha, "New Barbarian or Worthy Adversary? Renaissance Humanist Constructs of the Ottoman Turks," in *Western Views of Islam in Medieval and Early Modern Europe: Perception of Other,* eds. D. R. Blanks and M. Frassetto (New York, 1999), 185–205; M. Soykut, *Image of the "Turk" in Italy: A History of the "Other" in Early Modern Europe, 1453–1683* (Berlin, 2003); N. Bisaha, *Creating East and West: Renaissance Humanists and the Ottoman Turks* (Philadelphia, 2004).

16. E. Said, *Orientalism* (New York, 1978).

17. E. Hall, *Inventing the Barbarian: Greek Self-Definition through Tragedy* (Oxford, 1989); *The Birth of the European Identity: The Europe-Asia Contrast in Greek Thought, 490–322 B.C.,* ed. H. A. Khan (Nottingham, 1994); Tolan, *Saracens;* D. H. Strickland, *Saracens, Demons, and Jews: Making Monsters in Medieval Art* (Princeton, 2003); *Western Views of* Islam, eds. Blanks and Frassetto; P. Springborg, *Western Republicanism and the Oriental Prince* (Austin, 1992); Bisaha, *Creating East and West;* Soykut, *Image of the "Turk";* N. Matar, *Turks, Moors, and Englishmen in the Age of Discovery* (New York, 1999); D. J. Vitkus, *Turning Turk: English Theater and the Multicultural Mediterranean, 1570–1630* (New York, 2003); M. Dimmock, *New Turkes: Dramatizing Islam and the Ottomans in Early Modern England* (Ashgate, 2005).

18. This concern was not unique to Renaissance humanists. Fifteenth-century theologians were also eager to break out of the confines of scholastic discourse: see the study by D. Hobbins, "The Schoolman as Public Intellectual: Jean Gerson and the Late Medieval Tract," *AHR* 108 (2003): 1308–1337.

19. M. Meserve, "Italian Humanists and the Problem of the Crusade," in *Crusading in the Fifteenth Century: Message and Impact,* ed. N. Housley (London, 2004), 13–39.

20. N. Iorga, "Notes et extraits pour servir à l'histoire des croisades au XVe siècle," *Revue de l'orient latin* 8 (1900–1901): 267–310, followed by *Notes et extraits pour*

servir à l'histoire des croisades au XVe siècle, 6 vols. (Paris, 1901–1916); K. Setton, *The Papacy and the Levant (1204–1571),* 4 vols. (Philadelphia, 1976); F. Babinger, "Die Aufzeichnungen des genuesen Iacopo de Promontorio-de Campis über den Osmanenstaat um 1475," *Sitzungsberichte der bayerische Akademie der Wissenschaften,* philos.-hist. (Klasse, 1958), Heft 8; idem, *Johannes Darius (1414–1494), Sachwalter Venedigs im Morgenland, und sein griechischer Umkreis* (Munich, 1961), 9–52. See M. Philippides, "The Fall of Constantinople 1453: Bishop Leonardo Giustiniani and his Italian Followers," *Viator* 29 (1998): 189–225, at 189–197. Babinger's contempt for humanist crusade rhetoric was palpable: "It is hard to think of anything sillier or more degrading" (*Mehmed the Conqueror,* 198); idem, "Mehmed II., der Eroberer, und Italien," *Byzantion* 21 (1951): 127–170; "Maometto II il Conquistatore e gli umanisti in Italia," in *Venezia e l'Oriente fra tardo Medio Evo e Rinascimento,* ed. A. Pertusi (Florence, 1966), 433–449.

21. For scholarship on European-Turkish contacts and commerce, see *Crusading in the Fifteenth Century,* ed. Housley, esp. 3–8; D. M. Vaughan, *Europe and the Turk: A Pattern of Alliances, 1350–1700* (Liverpool, 1954); P. Coles, *The Ottoman Impact on Europe* (London, 1968); P. Preto, *Venezia e i Turchi* (Florence, 1975); Setton, *Papacy and Levant;* C. A. Frazee, *Catholics and Sultans: The Church and the Ottoman Empire, 1453–1923* (London, 1983); N. Housley, *The Later Crusades, 1274–1580: From Lyons to Alcazar* (Oxford, 1992); *I Turchi, il Mediterraneo e l'Europa,* ed. G. Motta (Milan, 1998); D. Goffman, *The Ottoman Empire and Early Modern Europe* (Cambridge, 2002); E. Dursteler, *Venetians in Constantinople: Nation, Identity, and Coexistence in the Early Modern Mediterranean* (Baltimore, 2006).

22. Chew, *Crescent and Rose;* Baumer, "England"; O. Burian, "Interest of the English in Turkey as Reflected in the Literature of the Renaissance," *Oriens* 5 (1952): 209–229; C. A. Patrides, "The Bloody and Cruell Turke: The Background of a Renaissance Commonplace," *Studies in the Renaissance* 10 (1963): 126–135; B. H. Beck, *From the Rising of the Sun: English Images of the Ottoman Empire to 1715* (New York, 1987); S. Artemel, "'The Great Turk's Particular Inclination to Red Herring': The Popular Image of the Turk in Renaissance England," *Journal of Mediterranean Studies* 5 (1995): 188–208; Matar, *Turks, Moors, and Englishmen;* L. Deitz, "Das Türkenbild in der englischen Literatur des 16. Jahrhunderts," in *Europa und die Türken in der Renaissance,* eds. B. Guthmüller and W. Kühlmann (Tübingen, 2000), 395–407.

23. R. Ebermann, *Die Türkenfurcht: ein Beitrag zur Geschichte der öffentlichen Meinung während der Reformationszeit* (Halle, 1904); H. J. Kissling, "Türkenfurcht und Türkenhoffnung im 15. und 16. Jahrhundert: zur Geschichte eines 'Komplexes,'" *Südost-Forschungen* 23 (1964): 1–18; J. W. Bohnstedt, *The Infidel Scourge of God: The Turkish Menace as Seen by the Pamphleteers of the Reformation Era* (Philadelphia, 1968); K. M. Setton, "Lutheranism and the Turkish Peril," *Balkan Studies* 3 (1962): 133–168; *Europa und die Türken,* eds. Guthmüller and Kühlmann, esp. J. Helmrath, "Pius II und die Türken," 79–138, who surveys recent work: 88n25.

24. W. Weintraub, "Renaissance Poland and Antemurale Christianitatis," *Harvard*

Ukrainian Studies 3–4 (1979–1980); M. B. Petrovich, "The Croatian Humanists and the Ottoman Peril," *Balkan Studies* 20 (1979): 257–273; J. Jankovics, "The Image of the Turks in Hungarian Renaissance Literature," in *Europa und die Türken*, eds. Guthmüller and Kühlmann, 267–273; B. Milewska-Wazbinska, "The Turks in the Renaissance Latin Poetry of Poland," ibid., 437–442.

25. Rouillard, *The Turk*; M. J. Heath, *Crusading Commonplaces: La Noue, Lucinge, and Rhetoric against the Turks* (Geneva, 1986); A. Mas, *Les Turcs dans la littérature espagnole du Siècle d'Or,* 2 vols. (Paris, 1967); A. Merle, *Le miroir ottoman: une image politique des hommes dans la littérature géographique espagnole et française (XVIe–XVIIe siècles)* (Paris, 2003).

26. C. Göllner, *Turcica: Die europäischen Türkendrucke des XVI. Jahrhunderts,* 3 vols. (Bucharest, 1961–1978). Further studies on this and related literature: A. N. Pippidi, "Knowledge of the Ottoman Empire in the Sixteenth and Seventeenth Centuries," Ph.D. dissertation, Oxford University, 1985; N. Pienaru, "Imagini si stereotipuri occidentale despre Otomani in veacul al XV-lea," *Revista de Istorie* 38 (1985): 498–509; K. M. Setton, *Western Hostility to Islam and Prophecies of Turkish Doom* (Philadelphia, 1992); *Europa und die osmanische Expansion im ausgehenden Mittelalter,* ed. F.-R. Erkens (Berlin, 1997); *Chrétiens et Musulmans à la Renaissance,* eds. B. Bennassar and R. Sauzet (Paris, 1998); *Islam and the Italian Renaissance,* eds. C. Burnett and A. Contadini (London, 1999); *Western Views of Islam,* eds. Blanks and Frassetto; *Europa und die Türken,* eds. Guthmüller and Kühlmann; *Osmanische Expansion und Europäischer Humanismus,* ed. F. Fuchs, *Pirckheimer Jahrbuch für Renaissance- und Humanismus-forschung* 20 (2000); A. Çirakman, *From the "Terror of the World" to the "Sick Man of Europe": European Images of Ottoman Empire and Society from the Sixteenth Century to the Nineteenth* (New York, 2002); L. Zilli, *L'Europa e il Levante nel Cinquecento,* 2 vols. (Padua, 2001–2004); *Crusading in the Fifteenth Century,* ed. Housley; G. Poumarède, *Pour en finir avec la Croisade: mythes et réalités de la lutte contre les Turcs aux XVIe et XVIIe siècles* (Paris, 2004); A. Servantie, ed., *L'Empire ottoman dans l'Europe de la Renaissance: idées et imaginaires d'intellectuels, de diplomates et de l'opinion publique dans les anciens Pays-Bas et le monde hispanique aux XVe, XVIe et début du XVIIe siècles* (Louvain, 2005).

27. M. Bataillon, "Mythe et connaissance de la Turquie en occident au milieu du XVIe siècle," in *Venezia e l'Oriente fra tardo Medio Evo e Rinascimento,* ed. A. Pertusi (Venice, 1966), 451–470; C. Dionisotti, "Le guerre d'Oriente nella letteratura veneziana del Cinquecento," in ibid., 471–493; J. P. Donelly, "The Moslem Enemy in Renaissance Epic," *Yale Italian Studies* 1 (1977); A. Cavallarin, "Umanesimo e i turchi," *Lettere italiane* 32 (1980); A. Comboni, "Alcune puntualizzazioni sulla tradizione delle rime del Cornazano con una canzone inedita sulla minaccia del Turco (1470)," *Bollettino storico piacentino* 76 (1985); P. Grendler, "Chivalric Romances in the Italian Renaissance," *Studies in Medieval and Renaissance History* 10 (1988); *Guerre in ottava rima,* 4 vols. (Modena, 1988–89), 4: *Guerre contro i Turchi (1453–1570),* eds. M. Beer and C. Ivaldi.

28. Pertusi was a pioneering figure in this regard. See *Caduta, Testi inediti,* and "Le epistole storiche di Lauro Quirini sulla caduta di Costantinopoli e la potenza dei Turchi," in *Lauro Quirini Umanista,* ed. V. Branca (Florence, 1977), 165–212. Also key are Schwoebel, *Shadow;* R. Black, *Benedetto Accolti and the Florentine Renaissance* (Cambridge, 1985), 226–241; Hankins, "Renaissance Crusaders"; Fleet, "Italian Perceptions"; Bisaha, "New Barbarian" and *Creating East and West;* A. Wunder, "Western Travelers, Eastern Antiquities, and the Image of the Turk in Early Modern Europe," *Journal of Early Modern History* 7 (2003): 89–119.

29. A. Pertusi, "I primi studi in occidente sull'origine e potenza dei Turchi," *Studi Veneziani* 12 (1970): 465–552 (a survey of Western literature on Ottoman origins which serves as an introduction to a 1480 treatise on crusade strategy addressed by Martino Segono, bishop of Dulcigno, to Sixtus IV); C. Göllner, "Legenden von der skythischen, trojanischen und kaukasischen Abstammung der Türken im 15. und 16. Jahrhundert," *Revue des études sud-est européens* 15 (1977): 49–61; idem, *Turcica,* 3:229–250; M. J. Heath, "Renaissance Scholars and the Origins of the Turks," *Bibliothèque d'humanisme et Renaissance* 41 (1979): 453–471; Hankins, "Renaissance Crusaders," 135–144.

30. V. J. Parry, "Renaissance Historical Literature in Relation to the Near and Middle East (with special reference to Paolo Giovio)," in *Historians of the Middle East,* eds. B. Lewis and P. M. Holt (London, 1962), 277–289. E. Cochrane, *Historians and Historiography in the Italian Renaissance* (Chicago, 1981), 324–337, surveys fifteenth- and sixteenth-century descriptions and histories of both Persia and Turkey.

31. Schwoebel, *Shadow,* 148, 153–154, repeated by Cochrane, Hankins, Bisaha, etc.

32. Cf. Schwoebel, *Shadow,* 148; Bisaha, "New Barbarian," 194. Filelfo did, however, make later use of it (cf. Pertusi, "Primi studi," 470).

33. Cf. Pertusi, "Primi studi," 473, who suggests that Chalcocondyles was the ultimate source for Sagundino and Aeneas Sylvius.

34. Preliminary source criticism in M. Meserve, "Medieval Sources for Renaissance Theories on the Origins of the Ottoman Turks," in *Europa und die Türken,* eds. Guthmüller and Kühlmann, 409–436; a theme also explored by A. Höfert, *Das Fremde durch die Brille des Eigenen: Das mittelalterliche Erbe im europäischen Türkenbild der Renaissance* (Istanbul, 1995).

35. Studies on ideas of origins and national character in other eras and cultures have been most useful in helping me frame my approach: first and foremost, R. Thomas, *Lands and Peoples in Roman Poetry: The Ethnographical Tradition* (Cambridge, 1982); also E. J. Bickerman, "Origines gentium," *Classical Philology* 47 (1952): 65–81; G. B. Ladner, "On Roman Attitudes toward Barbarians in Late Antiquity," *Viator* 77 (1976): 1–25; W. R. Jones, "The Image of the Barbarian in Medieval Europe," *Comparative Studies in Society and History* 13 (1971): 376–407; C. W. Connell, "Western Views of the Origin of the 'Tartars': An Example of the Influence of Myth in the Second Half of the Thirteenth Century," *JMRS* 3

(1973): 115–137; S. Vryonis, "Byzantine Attitudes toward Islam during the Late Middle Ages," *Greek, Roman and Byzantine Studies* 12 (1971): 263–286. On ideas about the origins of European nations, see D. Hay, *Europe: The Emergence of an Idea* (Edinburgh, 1957), esp. 43–51; A. Borst, *Der Turmbau von Babel: Geschichte der Meinungen über Ursprung und Vielfalt der Sprachen und Völker,* 4 vols. (Stuttgart, 1957–1963); Burke, *Renaissance Sense of the Past;* F. L. Borchardt, *German Antiquity in Renaissance Myth* (Baltimore, 1971); R. E. Asher, *National Myths in Renaissance France: Francus, Samothes and the Druids* (Edinburgh, 1993), esp. 9–35; W. Stephens, *Giants in Those Days: Folklore, Ancient History, and Nationalism* (Lincoln, Neb., 1989); P. G. Bietenholz, *Historia and Fabula: Myths and Legends in Historical Thought from Antiquity to the Modern Age* (Leiden, 1994); idem, *Desert and Bedouin in the European Mind* (Khartoum, 1963). On the image of the Turks in Arabic, Persian, and Chinese literature, see U. W. Haarmann, "Ideology and History, Identity and Alterity: The Arab Image of the Turk from the Abbasids to Modern Egypt," *International Journal of Middle East Studies* 20 (1988): 175–196; A. Al-Azmeh, "Barbarians in Arab Eyes," *Past and Present* 134 (1992): 3–18; D. Sinor, "The Greed of the Northern Barbarian," in *Aspects of Altaic Civilization II: Proceedings of the XVIII Permanent International Altaistic Conference,* eds. L. V. Clark and P. A. Draghi (Bloomington, Ind., 1978), 171–182.

36. For the early Turks' own theories of their beginnings, see "The Legendary Origin of the Turks," in *Folklorica: Festschrift for Felix Oinas,* eds. E. V. Zygas and P. Voorheis (Bloomington, Ind., 1982), 223–257. Debate over the historical origin of the Turks continues in modern Turkey, sometimes generating heated controversy: B. Lewis, "History-Writing and National Revival in Turkey," *Middle Eastern Affairs* 4 (1953): 218–227; also T. Özal, *Turkey in Europe* (Nicosia, 1991); S. Vryonis, *The Turkish State and History: Clio Meets the Grey Wolf* (New York, 1993); U. Freitag, "A Turkish Vision of History and a Greek Answer," *Storia della Storiografia* 26 (1994): 125–135.

37. Türkü, Tou-kiue, or T'u-chüeh: D. Sinor, "The Historical Role of the Türk Empire," *Cahiers d'histoire mondiale* 1 (1953): 427–434; idem, "The Establishment and Dissolution of the Türk Empire," in *CHEIA,* 285–316, 478–483. The classic account of primary sources for the Western Türks remains E. Chavannes, *Documents sur les Tou-kiue (Turcs) Occidentaux* (St. Petersburg, 1903). For Western Türk history in Islamic Central Asia, see C. E. Bosworth, "Islamic Frontiers in Africa and Asia: Central Asia," in *The Legacy of Islam,* 2d ed., ed. J. Schacht with C. E. Bosworth (Oxford, 1974), 116–129.

38. Sinor, "Establishment and Dissolution," 287–301.

39. Ibid., 301–305; C. A. Macartney, "On the Greek Sources for the History of the Turks in the Sixth Century," *BSOAS* 11 (1944): 266–275; *BT,* 1:70–81; M. Whitby, "Greek Historical Writing after Procopius: Variety and Vitality," in *The Byzantine and Early Islamic Near East. I: Problems in the Literary Source Material,* eds. A. Cameron and L. I. Conrad (Princeton, 1992), 25–80, at 39–45.

40. "Khazars," *ODB,* 2:1127; D. M. Dunlop, *A History of the Jewish Khazars* (Princeton, 1954); P. B. Golden, *Khazar Studies: An Historico-Philological Inquiry into the*

Origins of the Khazars (Budapest, 1980); idem, "Peoples of the Russian Steppes," 263–270; *BT,* 1:81–86.

41. P. B. Golden, *An Introduction to the History of the Turkic Peoples: Ethnogenesis and State-Formation in Medieval and Early Modern Eurasia and the Middle East* (Wiesbaden, 1992), 205–213; idem, "The Migrations of the Oğuz," *Archivum Ottomanicum* 4 (1972): 45–84; idem, "The Peoples of the South Russian Steppes" and "The Karakhanids and Early Islam," in *CHEIA,* 256–284 and 343–370; V. V. Bartold, "A History of the Turkmen People," in *Four Studies on the History of Central Asia,* (Leiden, 1962), 3: 75–170, esp. 91–108; and "Ghuzz," *EI2,* 2:1106–1110. The Oğuz arrived at the Aral Sea in the 780s, probably driven by the collapse of the Eastern Türks in Mongolia in the 740s, but their ethnic composition and the chronology and specific details of their movements are far from clear: Golden, "Migrations," 54–58.

42. Inalcik, *The Ottoman Empire,* 5–8; C. Cahen, *Pre-Ottoman Turkey,* trans. J. Jones-Williams (London, 1968), 1–32; idem, "The Turkish Invasion: The Selchükids," in *HC,* 1:135–176, esp. 135–146; "Saljukids," *EI2,* 8:936–978; C. E. Bosworth, *The Ghaznavids: Their Empire in Afghanistan and Eastern Iran, 994–1040* (Edinburgh, 1963), 205–268; idem, "The Early Ghaznavids," in *CHI,* 4:162–197, and "The Political and Dynastic History of the Iranian World (AD 1000–1217)," ibid., 5:1–202, esp. 1–23; I. Kafesoğlu, *A History of the Seljuks: Ibrahim Kafesoğlu's Interpretation and the Resulting Controversy,* ed. and trans. G. Leiser (Carbondale, Ill., 1988), 21–45; Y. Bregel, "Turko-Mongol Influences in Central Asia," in *Turko-Persia in Historical Perspective,* ed. R. L. Canfield (Cambridge, 1991), 53–77.

1. The Rise and Fall of the Trojan Turks

1. Aeneas Sylvius, *Europa,* in *Opera omnia* (Basel, 1551), 394. Similar comments can be found in his *Asia* (ibid., 383); *Oratio de Constantinopolitana clade* (ibid., 681); and letter to Nicholas of Cusa, 21 July 1453, in *Briefwechsel,* 3:209.

2. F. L. Borchardt, *German Antiquity in Renaissance Myth,* (Baltimore, 1971), 44–45 and *ad indicem* s.v. "anasceua."

3. E.g., A. Pertusi, "I primi studi in occidente sull'origine e potenza dei Turchi," *Studi Veneziani* 12 (1970): 480–481.

4. A. Eckhardt, "La Légende de l'origine troyenne des Turcs," *Körösi Csoma Archivum* 2 (1926–1932): 422–433; T. Spencer, "Turks and Trojans in the Renaissance," *Modern Language Review* 47 (1952): 330–333; idem, *Fair Greece, Sad Relic* (London, 1954), 8–12; R. Schwoebel, *The Shadow of the Crescent: The Renaissance Image of the Turk,* (Nieuwkoop, 1967), 31–32, 148, 188–189, 204; Pertusi, "Primi studi," 480–484; S. Runciman, "Teucri and Turci," in *Medieval and Middle Eastern Studies in Honor of Aziz Suryal Atiya,* ed. S. A. Hanna (Leiden, 1972), 344–348; C. Göllner, "Legenden von der skythischen, trojanischen und kaukasischen Abstammung der Türken im 15. und 16. Jahrhundert," *Revue des études sud-est européens* 15 (1977): 51–54; M. J. Heath, "Renaissance Scholars

and the Origins of the Turks," *Bibliothèque d'humanisme et Renaissance* 41 (1979): 453–456; J. Hankins, "Renaissance Crusaders: Humanist Crusade Literature in the Age of Mehmed II," *Dumbarton Oaks Papers* 49 (1995): 136–141; N. Bisaha, "New Barbarian or Worthy Adversary? Renaissance Humanist Constructs of the Ottoman Turks," in *Western Views of Islam in Medieval and Early Modern Europe: Perception of Other,* eds. D. R. Blanks and M. Frassetto, (New York, 1999), 195–196; idem, *Creating East and West: Renaissance Humanists and the Ottoman Turks,* (Philadelphia, 2004) 56, 58, 77–78, 89–92; A. F. D'Elia, "Genealogy and the Limits of Panegyric: Turks and Huns in Fifteenth-Century Epithalamia," *SCJ,* 34 (2003): 973–991, esp. 985–990; J. Harper, "Turks as Trojans, Trojans as Turks: Visual Imagery of the Trojan War and the Politics of Cultural Identity in Fifteenth-Century Europe," in *Translating Cultures: Postcolonial Approaches to the Middle Ages,* eds. A. J. Kabir and D. Williams (Cambridge, 2005), 151–179.

5. E. Gibbon, *Decline and Fall of the Roman Empire,* ed. J. B. Bury, 7 vols. (London, 1909–1914), 7:202n87.
6. Schwoebel, *Shadow,* 148–149, 204.
7. Hankins, "Renaissance Crusaders," 139–142. Harper, "Turks as Trojans," 156–157, argues that the theory of the Trojan origins "rendered the early Ottoman successes less transgressive in the European imagination." I argued much the same point in my article "Medieval Sources," 410–411, but have reconsidered my views.
8. Heath, "Renaissance Scholars," identifies the shift from the Trojan theory to belief in Scythian origins as the major development in historical scholarship on the Turks in the fifteenth century.
9. Spencer, "Turks and Trojans," 331; Runciman, "Teucri and Turci," 345.
10. Coluccio Salutati to Tvrtko I of Bosnia, 20 October 1389, in *Thesaurus anecdotorum novissimus,* ed. B. Pez and P. Hüber, 6 vols. (Augsburg, 1729), 6.3:89. The battle which Salutati congratulates the king for winning was the infamous clash of Kosovo Polje (15 June 1389). Early reports on its outcome varied widely; it was only much later that Western Europeans realized how grave a setback the Christian peoples of the Balkans had suffered. See T. A. Emmert, "The Battle of Kosovo: Early Reports of Victory and Defeat," in *Kosovo: Legacy of a Medieval Battle,* ed. W. S. Vucinich and T. A. Emmert (Minneapolis, 1991), 19–40.
11. Salutati to Josse, margrave of Moravia, 1397, in *Epistolario,* ed. F. Novati, 4 vols. (Rome, 1891–1911), 3:208; also in Hankins, "Renaissance Crusaders," 136.
12. E.g., his letter to Alfonso of Aragon, February 1455, in Poggio, *Lettere,* ed. H. Harth, 3 vols. (Florence, 1984–1987), 3:322–327; letter to Emperor Frederick III, 1455/56, ibid., 381–387; *De varietate fortunae,* ed. O. Merisalo (Helsinki, 1993), 150–151; "Oratio in funere Iuliani de Caesarinis," in *Opera omnia,* ed. R. Fubini, 4. vols. (Turin, 1969), 2:732–733; "De nobilitate," ibid., 1:69; "De miseria conditionis humanae," ibid., 88–89.
13. Poggio, *Lettere,* 3:286.
14. Ibid.

15. Ibid.
16. Hankins, "Renaissance Crusaders," 136.
17. *Caduta,* 2:20–26, and *Testi inediti,* 58.
18. Hankins, "Renaissance Crusaders," 179–186.
19. Runciman, "Teucri and Turci," 345, from *Thesaurus novus anecdotorum,* ed. E. Martene and U. Durand, 5 vols. (Paris, 1717), 1:1744 (Emperor Sigismund, letter to the pope, c. 1412).
20. Jean de Lastic, grand master of the Knights of St. John, letter to Charles VII of France, 1448, noted by Runciman, "Teucri and Turci," 345; text in L. d'Achery, ed., *Spicilegium sive collectio veterum aliquot scriptorum,* 3 vols. (Paris, 1723), 3:777; idem, letter to Frederick, margrave of Brandenburg, June 1453, in *Testi inediti,* 54–57.
21. Sigismund's letter to the pope is actually a long complaint against Venice, whose encroachments on imperial territory in the Balkans have forced him to make a truce with the Turks—an embarrassing fact he seeks to excuse.
22. *Caduta,* 2:20–26, and *Testi inediti,* 58.
23. Bartolomeo da Giano, "Epistola de crudelitate Turcarum," in *PG,* 158:1062.
24. A great many of these texts are collected in *Caduta* and *Testi inediti,* from where much of the material in the following pages is drawn. See also D.R.M. Jones, *The Siege of Constantinople 1453: Seven Contemporary Accounts* (Amsterdam, 1972), and M. Philippides, *Mehmed II the Conqueror and the Fall of the Franco-Byzantine Levant to the Ottoman Turks: Some Western Views and Testimonies,* in *Medieval Renaissance Texts and Studies* (Phoenix, forthcoming). For descriptions of the literature, see L. R. Loomis, "The Fall of Constantinople Symbolically Considered," in *Essays in Intellectual History Presented to James Harvey Robinson* (New York, 1929), 243–258; Schwoebel, *Shadow,* 1–23; A. Pertusi, "Ripercussioni della caduta di Costantinopoli," in *3e Congrès international d'Etudes du sud-est européen* (Bucharest, 1974), 1–83; M. Philippides, "The Fall of Constantinople 1453: Bishop Leonardo Giustiniani and his Italian Followers," *Viator* 29 (1998).
25. Spencer, "Turks and Trojans," 331; Runciman, "Teucri and Turci," 345; Hankins, "Renaissance Crusaders," 136–137.
26. Isidore of Kiev to Nicholas V, 6 July 1453, in *Caduta,* 1:58; to Doge Francesco Foscari, 26 July 1453, ibid., 100. In his letter to Duke Philip of Burgundy, 22 Feb. 1455, ibid., 106–110, Isidore also calls the Turks "Teucri" and Mehmed II "rex Teucrorum."
27. Isidore of Kiev "universis Christianis," 8 July 1453, ibid., 82.
28. Isidore of Kiev to Cardinal Bessarion, 6 July 1453, ibid., 64 ("Turci," "Turcopolis"); "universis Christianis," 80–90 ("Turchorum princeps et dominus," "Turchi"); to Nicholas V, 15 July 1453, ibid., 92–100 ("Turchi"). Further letters in *Testi inediti,* 12–21, display the same flexibility.
29. Leonard of Chios to Nicholas V, 16 August 1453, in *PG,* 159:923–944; see also *Caduta,* 1:120–123; Philippides, "Bishop Leonardo." Cf. Runciman, "Teucri and Turci," 345; Spencer, *Fair Greece,* 9.
30. Leonard of Chios to Nicholas V, in *PG,* 159:925. The reference is to Isaiah 54:11. The providential role of the "Teucri" is emphasized again at col. 927.

31. Excerpts and commentary in *Caduta* 1:198–212; also Schwoebel, *Shadow,* 17–18, and H. J. McGann, *"Haeresis castigata, Troia vindicata:* The Fall of Constantinople in Quattrocento Latin Poetry," *Studi umanistici Piceni* 4 (1984): 137–145.

32. Puscolo, *Constantinopolis,* 1.13–14, in McGann, *"Haeresis castigata,"* 141 (a passage not in *Caduta*): Constantinople has been captured by the *Teucri,* whom the Greeks themselves once conquered.

33. See, e.g., his hostile description of the Greek policy of appeasement of the Turks, pursued until the very end of the siege (*Constantinopolis,* 3.204–214, in *Caduta,* 1:202).

34. Ibid., 3.502.

35. Hankins, "Renaissance Crusaders," 136.

36. Marsilio Ficino to Sixtus IV, 1478, in *Opera omnia,* 2 vols. (Basel, 1576), 1:808. See also his letter to Sixtus IV, 25 December 1478, ibid., 814.

37. Ficino to Matthias Corvinus of Hungary, 1 October 1480, in *Opera omnia,* 1:721–722.

38. Angelo Giovanni Lomellino (*podestà* of the Genoese colony at Pera in 1453), in *Caduta,* 1:42–50; Franco Giustiniani, in *Caduta,* 2:100–107 (in both, the Turks are *Teucri*); also Antonio Ivani, letter to Federico da Montefeltro (sometimes entitled *Expugnatio Constantinopolitana*), c. 1453–1454, in *Testi inediti,* 146–165 (Turks as *Teucri,* Mehmed as *rex Teucrorum*). The term is often used in Italian chronicles of the fifteenth century—e.g. Andrea Redusio, *Chronicon Tarvisinum,* in *RIS1,* 19; Giorgio Stella, *Annales Genuenses,* in *RIS1,* 17—but these chroniclers likewise do not refer to the Trojan ancestry or identity of these "Teucrians."

39. Giustiniani in *Caduta,* 2:102.

40. Aegidius Calerius, *De morte Iuliani Caesarini* (1447), in É. Baluze, *Miscellanea novo ordine digesta et non paucis ineditis monumentis. . . aucta,* ed. J. D. Mansi, 4 vols. (Lucca, 1761–1764), 3:301–302: "Teucrorum, seu Turcorum, rex. . ."

41. E.g., in a letter from the Knights of St. John (see n. 20 above), Murad II is "magnum Teucrorum sive Turchorum regem." For other texts see nn. 19 (Sigismund) and 28 (Isidore) above.

42. Henricus de Soemmern, *Qualiter urbs Constantinopolis . . . a Turcis depredata fuit et subiugata,* in *Caduta,* 2:82–97. Also known as Henricus de Zoemeren, he eventually entered Bessarion's circle; see J. Monfasani, *Fernando de Cordova: A Biographical and Intellectual Profile* (Philadelphia, 1992), 93.

43. Niccolò Sagundino, oration to Alfonso of Aragon, 1454, in *Caduta,* 2:128–141. Early in the oration, Sagundino calls Mehmed II "rex ipse Theucrorum" (128), but later he is "rex Turcus" (136).

44. For instance, some manuscript copies of Sagundino's oration use *Turci* throughout, some use *Teucri,* and some (like that used by Pertusi for his edition) use both interchangeably. At least some of Isidore of Kiev's letters were composed by him in Greek and translated into Latin by an amanuensis (Philippides, "Bishop Leonardo," 193n14), so it is impossible to say who was responsible for using the term *Teucri* when it appears in his letters.

45. Schwoebel, *Shadow,* 4, 25, and 31.

46. Adam de Montaldo, *De Constantinopolitano excidio,* in *Testi inediti,* 190–209.

47. Giorgio Fieschi, *Eubois* [Naples: Sixtus Riessinger, late 1470 or early 1471], *IGI* 3977.
48. Lauro Quirini, letter to Nicholas V, 15 July 1453, in A. Pertusi, "Le epistole storiche di Lauro Quirini sulla Caduta di Costantinopoli e la potenza dei Turchi," in *Lauro Quirini Umanista*, ed. V. Branca (Florence, 1977), 226. Similar comparisons in Quirini, letter to Pius II, 1 March 1464, ibid., 242; and Isidore of Kiev, letter to Nicholas V, in *Caduta* 1:98.
49. Nestor-Iskander, *The Tale of Constantinople (of Its Origin and Capture by the Turks in the Year 1453)*, trans. W. K. Hanak and M. Philippides (New Rochelle, N.Y., 1998), 92–95; an Italian translation of the same text is in *Caduta*, 1:267–298. I am grateful to W. F. Ryan for the translation (based on the medieval Russian text reproduced in Hanak and Philippides) quoted here.
50. Laonicus Chalcocondyles, *De origine et rebus gestis Turcorum libri X*, in *PG*, 159:397. Chalcocondyles's work is not dated; he began it shortly after 1453 but was still writing after 1487. See Laonikos Chalkokondyles, *A Translation and Commentary of the Demonstrations of Histories (Books I–III)*, trans. N. Nicoloudis (Athens, 1996), 75, where a date around 1490 is suggested.
51. See Quirini's letter in n. 48 above. Isidore of Kiev and Leonard of Chios also likened the fall of the city to the fall of Jerusalem to the Assyrians (Isidore, letter to Nicholas V, 98; Leonard, text in n. 30 above), while Nicola Loschi calls Mehmed "the Assyrian" under whose rule Christ has been humiliated (Nicola Loschi, *Constantinus supplex*, c. 1463, in *Testi inediti*, 272–279, at line 53). Another popular comparison was with the sack of Rome by the Goths (Niccolò Tignosi, *Expugnatio Constantinopolitana*, before Nov. 1453, in *Testi inediti*, 102).
52. Hieronymus Guarino, *Contra Magni Turchi Maumethi Othman impetum cohortatio ad Nicolaum V* (1 August 1454), in Hankins, "Renaissance Crusaders," 187–192, compares the Turks to these enemies of Rome; also Tignosi, *Expugnatio Constantinopolitana*, 102 (Mehmed II as Hannibal) and 108 (Caesar, Augustus, Caligula); Jacopo Tedaldi, *Informationes*, in *Caduta*, 1:186–187 (Caesar, Nero); Quirini, letter to Pius II, 248 (Nero) and 256 (Pharaoh); Guarino, in Hankins, "Renaissance Crusaders," 188 (Caesar, Hannibal) and 191–192 (Pharaoh); Ficino, text in n. 37 above (Pharaoh); A. Comboni, "Alcune puntualizzazioni sulla tradizione delle rime del Cornazzano con una canzone inedita sulla minaccia turca," *Bolletino storico piacentino* 80 (1985), 195–209, at 206 (Xerxes and Pontius Pilate!). Comparisons of Mehmed and Alexander were by far the most frequent: e.g., Quirini, letter to Nicholas V, 229.
53. Tignosi, *Expugnatio Constantinopolitana*, in *Testi inediti*, 118.
54. In the 1490s, the French poet Johannes Angelus de Leonessa ventured a similar theory of autochthony in his Christian allegorical poetry, discussed below.
55. Spencer, "Turks and Trojans," 331; Runciman, "Teucri and Turci," 345; Schwoebel, *Shadow*, 204. The letter of Morbisanus should not be confused with the collection of spurious letters composed by the Ligurian humanist Laudivius Zacchia under the title *Epistolae Magni Turci* (cf. Heath, "Renaissance Humanists," 455; see Chapter 5 below), which consists of brief letters purportedly sent

by the Turkish sultan to various Eastern and Western princes and states, together with their equally spurious replies. The enormous late medieval corpus
of spurious correspondence addressed from rulers of Turkey, Egypt, Ethiopia,
and even more remote Oriental countries to Western princes awaits a system-
atic survey, though Bettina Wagner's recent article, "Sultansbriefe," in *DLMV*
11:1462–1468, is extremely helpful. See also F. Babinger, "Laudivius Zacchia,
der Erdichter der 'Epistolae Magni Turci,'" *Sitzungsberichte der bayerische
Akademie der Wissenschaften,* philos.-hist. (Klasse, 1960), Heft 13; D. C. Waugh,
*The Great Turkes Defiance: On the History of the Apocryphal Correspondence of the Otto-
man Sultan in Its Muscovite and Russian Variants* (Columbus, Ohio, 1978); G. Constable, "Forged Letters in the Middle Ages," in *Falschungen im Mittelalter,* 5 vols.,
in *MGH, Schriften,* 33.1–5 (Hanover, 1988), 5:11–37; B. Wagner, *Die "Epistola
presbiteri Johannis" lateinisch und deutsch: Überlieferung, Textgeschichte, Rezeption
und Übertragungen im Mittelalter* (Tübingen, 2000), esp. 667–668.

56. Pius II, *Lettera a Maometto II (Epistula ad Mahumetem),* ed. G. Toffanin (Naples,
    1953), 181–182. More recent editions include *Epistola ad Mahomatem II (Epistle
    to Mohammed II),* ed. and trans. A. R. Baca (New York, 1990); *Il Corano e la ti-
    ara: l'epistola a Maometto di Enea Silvio Piccolomini (papa Pio II),* ed. L. D'Ascia (Bo-
    logna, 2001); *Epístola a Mehmet II/Eneas Silvio Piccolomini,* ed. D. F. Sanz (Madrid,
    2003). See also the discussion by Hankins, "Renaissance Crusaders," 128–130;
    N. Bisaha, "Pius II's Letter to Sultan Mehmed II: A Reexamination," *Crusades* 1
    (2002): 183–200.

57. The first dated edition of the letter was printed at Treviso by Gerardus de Lisa,
    12 August 1475 (*IGI* 7765); followed by Rome: Bartholomaeus Guldineck,
    about 1477, *IGI* 7766; Rome: Eucharius Silber, c. 1485, *IGI* 7767; Rome:
    Stephan Plannck, 1488–90, *IGI* 7768. On *IGI* 7764, see n. 74 below.

58. Toffanin believes it is a genuine letter from Mehmed (*Lettera a Maometto II,* xix–
    xxi); see also H. Pfefferman, *Die Zusammenarbeit der Renaissancepäpste mit den
    Türken* (Schwarzenburg, 1946), 77–81. A. Linder, "'Ex mala parentela bona
    sequi seu oriri non potest': The Troyan Ancestry of the Kings of France and the
    Opus Davidicum of Johannes Angelus de Legonissa," *Bibliothèque d'humanisme et
    Renaissance* 40 (1978): 497–512, at 500, suggests that the letter was composed
    in Istanbul by an Italian humanist in the sultan's service. Runciman, "Teucri
    and Turci," 345, and Schwoebel, *Shadow,* 204, suggest that it was composed by
    a French opponent of Pius's crusade; Heath ("Renaissance Scholars," 455)
    maintains that it was written in the pontificate of Nicholas V; Hankins ("Re-
    naissance Crusaders," 140) attributes it to a German author active in the
    1470s.

59. F. Gaeta, "Alcune osservazioni sulla prima redazione della 'Lettera a
    Maometto'," in *Enea Silvio Piccolomini Papa Pio II: Atti del convegno per il quinto
    centenario della morte,* ed. D. Maffei (Siena, 1968), 177–186, at 179; F. Babinger,
    "Pio II e l'oriente maomettano," ibid., 1–14, at 9; *Epistola ad Mahomatem II,* ed.
    Baca, 7.

60. N. Iorga, "Notes et extraits pour servir à l'histoire des croisades au XVe siècle,"

Revue de l'orient latin 8 (1900–1901): 298–299; idem, *Notes et extraits,* 3:333–334; also F. Gaeta, "Sulla 'Lettera a Maometto' di Pio II," *Bulletino dell'Istituto storico per il Medio Evo e Archivio Muratoriano* 77 (1965): 127–227 at 130–131.

61. E.g. MS Florence, Biblioteca Medicea-Laurenziana, Ashburnham 1182, fols. 51v–53r, letter from "Morbosiano" to Clement VI, dated 1345: *Iter Italicum,* 1:95. A version of the letter in Italian, attributed to "Morbasiano" and dated 1346, is reproduced without indication of the source in *Prose antiche di Dante, Petrarcha, Boccaccio et di molti altri nobili et virtuosi ingegni,* ed. A. F. Doni (Florence, 1547), 15–16.

62. K. Setton, *The Papacy and the Levant (1204–1571),* 4 vols. (Philadelphia, 1976), 1:182–194.

63. A small sample: MS Vienna, Österreichische Nationalbibliothek, lat. 4764, fols. 168r–169v, letter of "Morbosanus" to Eugenius IV (in Latin), dated 1444: *Tabulae codicum manuscriptorum . . . in bibliotheca Palatina Vindobonensi asservatorum* (Vienna, 1869), 3:380; MS Florence, Biblioteca Nazionale Centrale, Landau 13, fols. 34r–35r, letter from "Marbassion" to an unspecified pope (in Italian), dated 1445: *Manoscritti Landau Finaly della Biblioteca Nazionale Centrale di Firenze,* eds. G. Lazzi and M. Rolih Scarlino, 2 vols. (Florence, 1994), 1:47; MS Leiden BPL 2010, "Literae transmissae summo pontifici a Morbosano Teucro domino magno." For more, see Wagner, "Sultansbriefe," 1464; idem, *Die "Epistola,"* 667n16.

64. Tedaldi, who escaped to Negroponte after the capture of Constantinople, dictated his story to a Frenchman, who either translated the account into French or perhaps composed it himself. Tedaldi's story was then sent to the cardinal of Avignon (Alain de Coëtivy, appointed by Calixtus III in 1455 to raise support for a crusade in France and Burgundy), along with various other anti-Turkish texts, such as a crusade plan and an appeal for Christian unity, all written in French. This was probably the point at which the letter of "Morbisanus" was added to the collection. See M.-L. Concasty, "Les *Informations* de Jacques Tedaldi sur le siège et la prise de Constantinople," *Byzantion* 24 (1954): 95–110; *Caduta,* 1:172–174.

65. MS Paris, Bibliothèque Nationale, lat. 9635.3: see Jean Chartier, *Chronique de Charles VII,* ed. Vallet de Viriville, 3 vols. (Paris, 1858), 3:36; MS Munich, Bayerische Staatsbibliothek, Cgm. 317 ("Morbosanus an Papst Nicholas V").

66. MS Würzburg, Franziskanerkloster, I.90 (destroyed in World War II): letter of Mehmed II to Nicholas V, *Iter Italicum,* 3:739. The contents of this letter have not been recorded; it may in fact have been a version of a different German letter, also purportedly sent by Mehmed II to the pope, which does not mention the common Trojan ancestry of the Turks and the Romans (text in Iorga, *Notes et extraits,* 4:126–127; see also Wagner, "Sultansbriefe," 1465–1466), though it does identify the sultan as "Kunig aller ander und Hector von Troy . . . Kunig von Troyen." This letter was sometimes addressed to Philip of Burgundy (*Chroniken der deutschen Städte vom 14. bis ins 16. Jahrhundert* [Leipzig, 1872], 11:212–213).

67. Jacques du Clercq, continuing Enguerran de Monstrelet, *Chronique*, 3 vols. (Paris, 1512), 3:223v; Jean Chartier, *Chronique de Charles VII*, 36–39; Mathieu d'Escouchy, *Chronique*, ed. G. du Fresne de Beaucourt, 3 vols. (Paris, 1863–1864), 2:58–61. For other chronicles still in manuscript which contain the letter in French, see Concasty, "Les Informations," 96. Spencer, "Turks and Trojans," 331–332, notes citations of the letter of "Morbisanus" by Innocent Gentillet (writing in 1576) and Montaigne (1580).

68. Morbisanus, Hebraeus et Gessius, *Epistola ad Clementem V Papam* [Rome: Ulrich Han, c. 1473]: K. Haebler, *Einblattdrucke des XV. Jahrhunderts* (Halle, 1914), no. 1018.

69. Filippo da Rimini, letter to Francesco Barbaro, c. 1453–1454 (also entitled *Excidium Constantinopolitanae urbis*), in *Testi inediti*, 128–141, at 138. See 139 for other versions of the tale, which do not make a connection with the rape of Cassandra; also Schwoebel, *Shadow*, 12–13.

70. An Italian version of Filippo's story is found in a collection of various accounts of Constantinople's fall compiled by an unknown author and interpolated into the *Cronaca* of Zorzi Dolfin (written after 1478). This text appears, incorrectly attributed to the Venetian scribe Giacomo Languschi, as *Excidio e presa di Constantinopoli nell'anno 1453*, in *Testi inediti*, 169–180, with the revenge described at 176. On Languschi, who appears to have died in 1453, see M. C. Davies, "An Enigma and a Phantom: Giovanni Aretino and Giacomo Languschi," *Humanistica Lovaniensia* 37 (1988): 1–29, esp. 16–17.

71. Adam de Montaldo, *De Constantinopolitano excidio*, 204.

72. Timoteo Maffei, *Epistola qua cunctos Italiae principes exhortatur quo copiis suis in Turcam quamprimum contendant*, in *Thesaurus anecdotorum novissimus*, ed. B. Pez and P. Hüber, 6 vols. (Augsburg, 1729), 6.3:367; Iorga, *Notes et extraits*, 4:74–75; Schwoebel, *Shadow*, 31–32; H. Rüben, *Der Humanist und Regularkanoniker Timoteo Maffei aus Verona (ca. 1415–1470)* (Aachen, 1975).

73. Giovanni Luigi Toscani, *Declamationes in Turcum* [Rome: Ulrich Han (Udalricus Gallus), 1470–1471], *IGI* 9896; Cornazzano, "Ad italicos principes pro Turci adventu," line 17, ed. A. Comboni, "Alcune puntualizzazioni . . . ," 206.

74. The first half of the exchange, a poem attributed to Pius, appears under the title *Pius II in Maumethem perfidum Turchorum regem* at the end of Cugnoni's edition of Pius's collection of elegiac poems, the *Cynthia*: Pius II, *Opera inedita*, ed. J. Cugnoni (Rome, 1883), 368, reprinted in *Poeti latini del Quattrocento*, eds. F. Arnaldi, L. Gualdo Rosa, and L. Monti Sabia (Milan, 1964), 156–158; a new edition is in Aeneas Sylvius Piccolomini, *Carmina*, ed. A. van Heck (Vatican City, 1994), 157–159. The poem does not, however, appear in any manuscripts of the *Cynthia* collection; Cugnoni knew of it from two manuscripts: the miscellany of *Carmina epaenetica* dedicated by various humanists to Pius (R. Avesani, "Epaeneticorum ad Pium II pont. max. Libri V," in *Enea Silvio Piccolomini. Atti del convegno per il quinto centenario*, ed. D. Maffei [Siena, 1968], 15–97, at 35), and a sixteenth-century collection of verses among which it is the only one associated with Pius (see Cugnoni's note at 368). Avesani records a further ten

MSS. The poem was also printed once in the fifteenth century (see below). I have doubts about the attribution to Pius, although the historical material treated in it clearly derives from his researches on the Turks, discussed in Chapter 2. The *Responsio Magni Turci,* Mehmed's purported poetic reply, appears directly after *In Mahumetem* in an incunable assigned to Leonardus Achates of Padua before 1474 (wrongly catalogued by *IGI* (7764) as another edition of Pius's *Epistola ad Mahumetem* with the reply of "Morbisanus"; see Hain 178 for a more accurate description. Mehmed's reply is also edited by Hankins, "Renaissance Crusaders," 206–207.

75. "Responsio Magni Turci," in Hankins, "Renaissance Crusaders," 207.

76. Ibid., 207, line 37.

77. Ibid., 207. A similar idea is expressed, although less explicitly, by Elisio Calenzio in a poem entitled *Hector.* Calenzio, in an apparent comment on the contemporary Turkish threat, offers a poetic vision of the Trojan hero returned to life and striding across the Mediterranean, intent on punishing the Greeks (including the "Danai" of southern Italy and, somewhat less logically, Rome and the rest of Europe) for destroying his city and his people. Cited by Hankins, "Renaissance Crusaders," 141, from Elisio Calenzio, *Opuscula* (Rome, 1503), sig.a1r.

78. Florentinus Liquenaius Turonensis, *De destructione Constantinopolitana sive de ultione Troianorum contra Graecos* (Paris, 1500?), sig. a1r.

79. Ibid., sig. a2v.

80. Ibid., sig. a5r.

81. Ibid., sigs. a5v–b5v.

82. Giovanni Mario Filelfo, *Amryis,* ed. A. Manetti (Bologna, 1978), 69 (1.463–465).

83. Ibid., 70 (1.472–484).

84. Ibid., 152 (3.566–76).

85. Othman Lillo Ferducci, "Ad illustrissimum et invictissimum Turcorum Amyram . . . praefationem in Amyridos codicem," ibid., 40–48.

86. Ibid., 22. G. M. Filelfo continued to produce anti-Turkish rhetoric for other events and contexts: D'Elia, "Epithalamia," 987–988.

87. Translation from D'Elia, "Epithalamia," 986, with the reference to "Amorbassanus" at 990.

88. Ibid., 988, and see D'Elia's comments on similar genealogical inventions in other wedding orations, ibid., 973–985.

89. Critoboulos, *History of Mehmed the Conqueror,* trans. C. T. Riggs (Princeton, 1954), 181–182.

90. Herodotus, *Histories,* 7.43; Arrian, *Anabasis,* 1.12.1–5; Lucan, *Pharsalia,* 9.950–999.

91. Annius of Viterbo, *De futuris Christianorum triumphis in Turchos et Saracenos* (Genoa: Baptista Cavalus, 8 Dec. 1480), *IGI* 585, sig. f7r. His mention of Apulians at Troy probably refers to the forces of the Greek warrior Diomedes, who was reputed to come from Apulia. On this work and Annius in general, see A. Grafton, *Defenders of the Text: The Traditions of Scholarship in an Age of Sci-*

ence, 1450–1800 (Cambridge Mass., 1991), 76–103, esp. 85, with further bibliography. Whatever Annius may have thought about the Turks' Trojan origins, he also identified them with the Beast of the Apocalypse: D. Weinstein, *Savonarola and Florence: Prophecy and Patriotism in the Renaissance* (Princeton, N.J., 1970), 89–90.

92. See Linder, "'Ex mala parentela.'" The *Opus Davidicum* is known from a single manuscript, which Linder describes and excerpts in this article.

93. Quoted by Linder, "'Ex mala parentela'," 509n77. Like Biglia and Poggio before him, Johannes Angelus believed the Turks were the direct descendants of those defeated Trojans who stayed in the Troas after Troy's fall and that they were thus indigenous to Asia Minor.

94. An early example of such a claim, actually predating the Ottoman conquest of Asia Minor, is in Robert de Clari's history of the Fourth Crusade. A French knight justifies the capture of Constantinople from the Byzantines as the reclamation of his Trojan patrimony. Cited by Eckhardt, "Légende," 429.

95. Salutati, letter to Charles of Durazzo, in *Epistolario*, 2:24.

96. Filelfo, letter to Charles VII, in *Epistolae* (Venice, 1502), fol. 59v. In 1464, Aeneas Sylvius made a similar crusade appeal to Duke Charles the Bold of Burgundy and his dynasty, "cuius originem ab Ilio repetunt"; *Commentarii rerum memorabilium*, ed. A. van Heck, 2 vols. (Vatican City, 1984), 2:756.

97. Publio Gregorio Tifernate, *Vaticinium cladis Italiae*, c. 1453, in *Testi inediti*, 246–249 (lines 33–36).

98. Jean Lemaire de Belges, *Illustrations de Gaule et Antiquitez de Troye* and *Epistre du Roy à Hector de Troye*, in *Oeuvres*, ed. J. Stecher, 3 vols. (Louvain, 1882–1891), 1:138–139.

99. Ibid., 1:15.

100. Ibid., 3:72.

101. Text in *Chronicarum quae dicuntur Fredegarii Scholastici libri IV cum continuationibus*, ed. B. Krusch, *MGH, Scriptores rerum Merovingicarum*, 2 (Hanover, 1888), 1–193. The *Chronicle* breaks off in A.D. 642. It was compiled by an anonymous monastic author or authors around 660; the attribution of the work to the otherwise unknown "Fredegar" is a sixteenth-century invention. See J. M. Wallace-Hadrill, *The Long-Haired Kings and Other Studies in Frankish History* (London, 1962), 71–94; W. Goffart, "The Fredegar Problem Reconsidered," *Speculum* 38 (1963): 206–241; R. Collins, *Fredegar* (Aldershot, 1997). Though the identities of the *Chronicle*'s authors are unknown, I follow convention in calling them collectively "Fredegar."

102. Fredegar, *Chronicarum . . . libri IV*, 45–46. At various points in the *Chronicle* the nation is called *Torci, Turqui,* and *Turchi*.

103. Ibid., 46.

104. Isidore of Seville defines Scythia Inferior as the area between the Danube and Ocean: *Etymologiae*, 14.4.3.

105. Fredegar, *Chronicarum . . . libri IV*, 46. The same story is told in a slightly different redaction later in the *Chronicle* (ibid., 93).

106. W. Wilmanns, *Beiträge zur Geschichte des älteren deutsche Literatur*, 4 vols. (Bonn,

1885–1887), 2:107–135; G. Kurth, *Histoire poétique des Mérovingiens* (Paris, 1893), 505–516; E. Faral, *La Légende arthurienne,* 3 vols. (Paris, 1929), 1:263–293; A. Eckhardt, *De Sicambria à Sans-Souci. Histoires et légendes franco-hongroises* (Paris, 1943); Wallace-Hadrill, *Long-Haired Kings,* 79–82; Collins, *Fredegar,* 82–83.

107. Wilmanns, *Beiträge,* 2:111–118; also Eckhardt, "Légende," 424.

108. Fredegar, *The Fourth Book of the Chronicle of Fredegar with its Continuations,* ed. and trans. J. M. Wallace-Hadrill (London, 1960), 39.

109. Fredegar elsewhere preserves a report of the most famous incursion of the Western Türks into the Byzantine world, that of their vassals the Turkic Khazars through the Caucasus in the 620s, but he calls them neither "Khazars" nor "Turks": *Fourth Book,* 54–55. Even if we allow that more than one author may have contributed to the text, it is most unlikely that the *Chronicle* would refer to the same Central Asian people as "Turks" in this passage but anonymously there.

110. C. Cahen, "Frédegaire et les Turcs," in *Économies et sociétés au Moyen Âge. Mélanges offerts à Édouard Perroy* (Paris, 1973), 24–27.

111. N. Wagner, "Die Torci bei Fredegar," *Beiträge zur Namenforschung* 19 (1984): 402–410, at 405–406.

112. Ibid., 407–410.

113. E. Ewig, "Le mythe troyen et l'histoire de France," in *Clovis: histoire et mémoire. Le Baptême de Clovis, l'événement,* ed. M. Rouche (Paris, 1997), 817–847, at 824–825 and 845–847.

114. P. B. Golden, *An Introduction to the History of the Turkic Peoples: Ethnogenesis and State-Formation in Medieval and Early Modern Eurasia and the Middle East* (Wiesbaden, 1992), 97–113; also *BT,* 2:320–327.

115. Bruno Krusch, the first modern editor of the text, thought that the whole story was nothing more than a disastrous misreading of a passage in the source text (Jerome, *Eusebii Chronicon libri interprete Sancto Hieronymo,* in *PL,* 27:399–400), where Alexander and Philip, Pompey and the Roman consul Manlius Torquatus are all mentioned in quick succession: B. Krusch, "Die *Chronicae* des sogenannten Fredegar," *Neues Archiv der Gesellschaft für altere deutsche Geschichtskunde* 7 (1882): 247–351, 421–516, at 455 and 473–475. Krusch's theory is accepted by the latest editor of the *Chronicle,* A. Kusternig (*Chronicarum quae dicuntur Fredegarii libri quattuor,* in *Quellen zur Geschichte des 7. und 8. Jahrhunderts,* ed. H. Wolfram [Darmstadt, 1982], 84–85). Elsewhere, G. Schnürer (*Die Verfasser der sogenannten Fredegar-Chronik* [Freiburg, 1900], 180–183) proposes that *Torci* is a corruption of *Thuringi,* a solution which at least agrees with the geographical and historical situation of the Franks and their German neighbors. Another plausible suggestion is that the name is a corruption of *Teucri,* who would have been included in the story for the same reason as the Macedonians: to make the Franks appear a nation as ancient and noble as two of the most renowned of antiquity. See Eckhardt, "Légende," 424–425; Wagner, "Die Torci bei Fredegar," 405.

116. In this version, the Franks, led jointly by Priam and Antenor, flee Troy and sail across the Black Sea and up the Don, where they build a city called Sicambria. Later, after serving Emperor Valentinian as mercenaries and helping him defeat the rebel Alans in the Maeotic Lake, they migrate west to establish an independent state on the Rhine under the leadership of their dukes Marcomir, Sunno, and Pharamond. See *Liber Historiae Francorum*, ed. B. Krusch, *MGH, Scriptores rerum Merovingicarum* 2 (Hannover, 1888), 241–243. Eckhardt, *Sicambria*, suggests a number of historical and poetical sources which may have contributed to the genesis of the story.

117. Freculph, *Chronica*, in *PL*, 106:964.

118. Aimoin, *Historia Francorum*, in *PL*, 139:639.

119. On the manuscript tradition, see Cahen, "Frédégaire et les Turcs," 25–26.

120. Hugh of St. Victor, *Excerptionum priorum libri XXIV*, in *PL*, 176:275–276. Hugh's source may be the *Chronica ecclesiastica* of Hugh of Fleury (c. 1109), one of the earliest works to report extensively on the Muslim peoples encountered by the crusaders in the Holy Land. On his use of Hugh of Fleury, see W. V. Green, "Hugo of St. Victor, *De tribus maximis circumstantiis gestorum*," *Speculum* 18 (1943): 484–493.

121. William of Tyre, *Chronicon*, ed. R.B.C. Huygens (Turnhout, 1986); also *A History of Deeds Done beyond the Sea by William Archbishop of Tyre*, trans. E. A. Babcock and A. C. Krey, 2 vols. (New York, 1943); A. C. Krey, "William of Tyre: The Making of an Historian in the Middle Ages," *Speculum* 16 (1941), 149–166; A. V. Murray, "William of Tyre and the Origin of the Turks: On the Sources of the *Gesta Orientalium Principum*," in *Dei Gesta per Francos: Etudes sur les croisades dédiés à Jean Richard. Crusade Studies in Honour of Jean Richard*, ed. M. Balard, B. Z. Kedar, and J. Riley-Smith (Aldershot, 2001), 217–229. Born and raised in Frankish Palestine, William knew Latin, French, Greek, Arabic, and some Hebrew. In writing his *Chronicon* he consulted works of Arabic history in the royal library in Jerusalem. He also began a separate history of the Muslim principalities of the East, entitled *Gesta orientalium principum;* the work, which was never completed and has not survived, probably formed the basis for his account of Turkish history in the *Chronicon*.

122. William of Tyre, *Chronicon*, ed. Huygens, 114–115.

123. Murray, "William of Tyre," explores some interesting literary elements in the tale as told by William; he suggests echoes, probably unconscious, of legends of origin developed among earlier European peoples.

124. For its wide diffusion, see Krey, "William of Tyre," 165–166.

125. Murray, "William of Tyre," 222.

126. Rigord, *De gestis Philippi Augusti Francorum Regis*, in *RHGF*, 17:17; R. E. Asher, *National Myths in Renaissance France: Francus, Samothes and the Druids* (Edinburgh, 1993), 12.

127. Vincent of Beauvais, *Speculum historiale* 2.66, in *Speculum maius*, 4 vols. (Douai, 1624), 4:68; Martin of Troppau, *Chronicon expeditissimum* (Antwerp, 1574), 219.

128. E.g., Rigord, *De gestis Philippi Augusti*, 17: "Atque ex eo *quidam tradunt* duos

populos sumpto nomine Francos et Turchos usque hodie vocari" (italics mine).
An exception is the cosmographical poet Fazio degli Uberti (c. 1360), who
maintains without reservation that Franco's companion "Turco" was the epon-
ymous founder of Turkey (Fazio degli Uberti, *Il Dittamondo e le Rime*, ed. G.
Corsi [Bari, 1952], 4.18, lines 34–35: "Turco fu l'uno pel quale al presente/
Turchia è detta").

129. Rigord, *De gestis Philippi Augusti*, 17.

130. For a similar and possibly related legend of national origin involving tension
with the pagan nations of northeastern Europe, compare the Saxon legend of
origin described in n. 161 below.

131. *Les Grandes Chroniques de France (Chroniques de Saint Denis)*, in *RHGF*, 3:155;
Eckhardt, *Sicambria*, 28–31; Asher, *National Myths*, 12.

132. Guillelmus Armoricus (alias Guillelmus Brito), *De gestis Philippi Augusti*, in
RHGF, 17:63.

133. Ekkehard Uraugiensis/Frutolf of Michelsberg, *Chronica*, in *PL*, 154:523;
Sigebert of Gembloux, *Chronica*, in *PL*, 160:59–60; Otto of Freising, *Chronica de
duabus civitatibus*, ed. A. Hofmeister (Hanover, 1912), 56–57. All these authors
discuss the origins of the Turks elsewhere in their works, without reference to
Troy.

134. Hugh of Flavigny, *Chronicon*, in *PL*, 154:108; *Historiae regum Francorum
Monasterii Sancti Dionysii*, ed. G. Waitz, *MGH, Scriptores*, 9 (Hanover, 1851), 395.

135. See n. 116 above.

136. Godfrey of Viterbo, *Pantheon* (Basel, 1559), col. 195.

137. Ibid., col. 511; also col. 162.

138. L. Meyer, *Les Légendes des Matières de Rome, de France, et de Bretagne dans le "Pantheon" de Godefroi de Viterbe* (Paris, 1933), 9, 43–55; Borchardt, *German Antiquity*,
235–238.

139. Brunetto Latini, *Li Livres dou Trésor*, ed. F. J. Carmody (Berkeley, 1948), 46–47.

140. Giovanni Villani, *Cronica*, in *Croniche di Giovanni, Matteo e Filippo Villani*, ed. A.
Racheli (Trieste, 1857), 12.

141. *Manipulus Florum*, in *RIS1*, 11:545.

142. Likewise, the Erfurt chronicler Gobelinus Persona (writing c. 1418–1422) follows Godfrey in tracing the origins of the Franks back to the Trojans of Italy. He
rehearses the story of the Trojan Franks no less than three times but does not
mention Turcus or his Turks: Gobelinus Persona, *Cosmodromium*, ed. H. Meibom
(Frankfurt, 1599), 57–58, 154, 158.

143. Giovanni Boccaccio, *Genealogiae deorum gentilium libri*, ed. V. Romano (Bari,
1951), 1:307, cited by Linder, "'Ex mala parentela,'" 498. Boccaccio does not
mention the claim of the Turks to Trojan origins; presumably it seemed beneath consideration.

144. Matthew Paris, *Chronica majora*, ed. H. R. Luard, 7 vols. (London, 1872–1883),
1:16 and 170.

145. Ranulph Higden, *Polychronicon*, ed. J. R. Lumby, 9 vols. (London 1865–1886),
5:232.

146. Bartholomaeus Anglicus, *De proprietatibus rerum* (Frankfurt, 1551), 653.

147. *Rudimentum novitiorum* (Lübeck: Lucas Brandis, 5 August 1475), Hain 4996*, fol. 85r.

148. *Gesta Francorum et aliorum Hierosolymitanorum*, ed. B. A. Lees (Oxford, 1924), 20; Eckhardt, "Légende," 429–431; Spencer, "Turks and Trojans"; Runciman, "Teucri and Turci."

149. Cf. Eckhardt, "Légende," 429, who believes that this statement indicates that the Turks were aware of Fredegar's claims regarding their Trojan ancestry. Eckhardt does not attribute any great antiquity to the legend among the Turks, suggesting they had learned of it only recently, most likely from the crusaders. Runciman likewise suggests that the statement attributed to the Turks in the *Gesta* reflects knowledge of the Fredegar tradition (*HC*, 1:187). In "Teucri and Turci," he suggests that the story may have reached the Turks via Icelandic mercenaries in Byzantine service (the Fredegar legend is repeated in at least one Icelandic saga). There is no evidence, however, that the Turks themselves ever claimed descent from the Trojans: Cahen, "Frédégaire et les Turcs," 25n10.

150. *Gesta Francorum*, ed. Lees, 20.

151. Ibid., 19.

152. Ibid., 20. Murray, "William of Tyre," 223–224, makes a similar point.

153. Runciman, *HC*, 1:327–341, esp. 329–330.

154. Guibert of Nogent, *The Deeds of God through the Franks: A Translation of Guibert de Nogent's* Gesta Dei per Francos, trans. R. Levine (Woodbridge, Suffolk, 1997), 68, from *Dei gesta per Francos*, ed. R.B.C. Huygens (Turnhout, 1996), 158–159.

155. Baudri of Dol, *Historia Jerosolymitana*, in *RHC Occ.*, 4:35.

156. Vincent of Beauvais, *Speculum historiale*, 1036.

157. Hector and Troilus were both sons of King Priam of Troy. Jean de Paris, *Memoriale historiarum*, in *Historiae Francorum scriptores coaetani, ab ipsius gentis origine ad nostra usque tempora*, ed. A. du Chesne (Paris, 1636), 130.

158. See nn. 95 and 96 above.

159. Aeneas Sylvius, *Europa*, in *Opera*, 433. He traces the Trojan origins of the Romans through Aeneas, the Venetians through Antenor, and the French through Francus.

160. Francesco Filelfo, *Odes* 3.1: *Odae* ([Brescia]: Angelus Brittanicus, 4 July 1497), *IGI* 3879, sigs. e7v–f2v, at f1r:
    > Nam meminit Teucrona olim et Francona potentes
    > Iliacos, venisse duces cum fortibus armis
    > Danubii primum fluuii campique iacentis
    > Danubium iuxta multa cum laude colonos.

161. Werner Rolewinck, *Fasciculus temporum* (Cologne: Arnold Ther Hoernen, 1474), *BMC* 1: 204, sig. [b]8v. See K. Colberg, "Werner Rolewinck," *DLMV*, 8:153–158. Rolewinck's chronicle was printed in thirty-two editions, including translations into Dutch, French, and German: A.G.W. Murray, "The Edition of the 'Fasciculus temporum' printed by Arnold ther Hoernen in 1474," *The Li-*

brary, 3rd ser., 4 (1913): 57–71. Borchardt, *German Antiquity,* 292 (and, following him, Hankins, "Renaissance Crusaders," 140) maintains that Rolewinck borrowed from the early fifteenth-century jurist Dietrich of Nieheim an entirely different theory about the origins of the Turks, namely, that they were pagan Saxons descended from soldiers left by Alexander the Great to guard the Caspian Gates in the Caucasus. While some of these "Macedonian" Saxons accepted Christianity after migrating to Europe, those who did not fled back into Asia to become the ancestors of the Turks. The legend of the Macedonian Saxons is well documented and dates back at least to the twelfth-century *Chronica* of Frutolf of Michelsberg, but neither Dietrich nor Rolewinck mentions anything about their later development into Turks. Borchardt seems to have confused statements in both authors to the effect that those Saxons who did not accept Christianity fled east to join the pagan Lithuanians, Livonians, and Prussians of the Baltic coast. Dietrich of Nieheim, "Privilegia aut iura imperii circa investituras episcopatum," in *De iurisdictione, auctoritate et praeeminentia imperiali ac potestate ecclesiastica,* ed. S. Schard (Basel, 1566), 802; Werner Rolewinck, *De laude antiquae Saxoniae nunc Westphaliae dictae* [Cologne: Arnold Ther Hoernen, c. 1477–1484], *BMC* 1:209, sig. e5r.

162. Hartmann Schedel, *Liber cronicarum* (Nuremberg: Anton Koberger, 12 July 1493), *IGI* 8828, fol. 37r. When Schedel returns to the subject of the Turks, he offers a long digression about their origins in Scythia (ibid., fol. 165r).

163. MS Leeds University Library, Brotherton Collection 100 (*Genealogie de la bible,* c. 1461–1483). Illustrations 16–17d show scenes of the fall of Troy and the flight, in separate ships, of Aeneas, Priam, Turcus, and Helen (N. Ker, *Medieval Manuscripts in British Libraries* [Oxford, 1969], 3.60–62); MS Manchester, John Rylands Library Fr. 99 (*Chronicle Roll,* s xv2), illustrations 17–21, of the same scenes (Ker, *Medieval Manuscripts,* 446–448); MS Cambridge, Fitzwilliam 176 (*Chronicle of the World in roll-form,* c. 1450), illustrations 19–23, of the same scenes (M. R. James, *A Descriptive Catalogue of the Manuscripts in the Fitzwilliam Museum* [Cambridge, 1895], 381–383: "a fair specimen of a very numerous class"). It is intriguing that both James and Ker read the name of the Trojan exile as "Turtus," not "Turcus."

164. G. Huppert, "The Trojan Franks and their Critics," *Studies in the Renaissance* 12 (1965): 227–241, at 229–230; idem, *The Idea of Perfect History. Historical Erudition and Historical Philosophy in Renaissance France* (Urbana, Ill., 1970), 12–14; Asher, *National Myths,* 15. Gilles's *Annales* may have been printed as early as 1492; the first extant edition is dated 1525.

165. Nicole Gilles, *Les tres elegantes et copieuses Annales des tres preux, tres nobles, tres chretiens et tres excellens moderateurs des belliqueuses Gaules* (Paris, 1534), fol. 6v.

166. Ibid., fol. 8v.

167. E.g., the texts of Rigord, Guillerumus Armoricus, Hugh of Flavigny, and the Latin and French version of the *Grand Chroniques,* discussed above.

168. The *fortuna* of the legend has been the subject of much study: in addition to the works listed in n. 106, see J. Barzun, *The French Race: Theories of Its Origins and*

Their Social and Political Implications prior to the French Revolution (New York, 1932); M. Klippel, *Die Darstellung der Fränkischen Trojanersage in Geschichtsschreibung und Dichtung vom Mittelalter bis zur Renaissance im Frankreich* (Marburg, 1936); R. Kliger, "A Renaissance 'Controlled Etymology': *Frank= Phrygian*," *Romance Philology* 4 (1950–1951): 276–280; A. Bossuat, "Les Origines troyennes: leur rôle dans la littérature historique du XVe siècle," *Annales de Normandie* 8 (1958): 187–197; Huppert, "Trojan Franks"; idem, *Perfect History*, 72–87; Borchardt, *German Antiquity*, 195–197; B.L.O. Richter, "Trojans or Merovingians? The Renaissance Debate over the Historical Origins of France," in *Mélanges à la mémoire de Franco Simone*, 4 vols. (Geneva, 1983), 4:111–134; Asher, *National Myths*, 9–35; A. R. Brown, "The Trojan Origins of the French: The Commencement of a Myth's Demise," in *Medieval Europeans: Studies in Ethnic Identity and National Perspectives in Medieval Europe*, ed. A. P. Smyth (London, 1988), 135–179; P. Cohen, "In Search of the Trojan Origins of French: The Uses of History in the Elevation of the Vernacular in Early Modern France," in *Fantasies of Troy: Classical Tales and the Social Imaginary in Medieval and Early Modern Europe*, eds. A. Shepard and S. D. Powell (Toronto, 2004), 63–80.

169. Robert Gaguin, *Compendium de originibus et gestis Francorum* (Lyons: Johannes Trechsel, 24 June 1497), *IGI* 4120, fol. 1r.

170. Ibid; Asher, *National Myths*, 15. Gaguin attributes this information to Aimoin (whom he calls Annonius), but Aimoin does not mention the Thorgori. I have not found any historical reference to "Thorgori" in Macedonian service.

171. On Riccio and Raffaele Maffei (discussed below), see P. Gilli, "L'Histoire de France vue par les italiens à la fin du quattrocento," in *Histoires de France, Historiens de la France. Actes du colloque international, Reims (14–15 mai 1993)*, ed. Y. M. Bercé and P. Contamine (Paris, 1994), 73–90. Brown, "Trojan Origins," argues persuasively that none of these historians succeeded in demolishing the story entirely.

172. The text is extant in a later translation: Michele Riccio, *De re di Francia libri III*, trans. G. Tatti (Venice, 1543), fol. 3r.

173. Raffaele Maffei, *Commentariorum urbanorum libri XXXVIII* (Rome, 1506), fol. 21v.

174. Nevertheless, the Italian historians Marcantonio Sabellico (*Rapsodie historiarum enneades*, first published 1504; I rely on the Paris, 1513, edition, 2:296r) and Paolo Emilio (*De rebus gestis Francorum libri VII* [Paris, (1520)], fol. 3r) still accept the Trojan origins of the Franks, although with varying degrees of reservation. But neither discusses the Turks in this context.

175. On Annius, see n. 96 above, and A. Grafton, *Forgers and Critics: Creativity and Duplicity in Western Scholarship* (Princeton, 1990), 104–109; for Trithemius, see N. L. Brann, *The Abbot Trithemius (1462–1516): The Renaissance of Monastic Humanism* (Leiden, 1981).

176. Annius of Viterbo, *Auctores vetustissimi* (Rome: Eucharius Silber, 1498), *IGI* 584, sig. Z7r ("Manetho" on Francus, and commentary); Asher, *National Myths*, 44–50.

177. Johannes Trithemius, *Compendium . . . de origine regum et gentis Francorum* (Mainz, 1515), sig. A1r.
178. Text in Andrea Dandolo, *Chronica per extensum descripta,* ed. E. Pastorello, in *RIS2,* 12.1 (Bologna, 1942), 9–327. The *Chronica* was written between 1344 and 1347: ibid., iii–lxxvii; G. Ravegnani, "Dandolo, Andrea," *DBI,* 32:432–440. For his use of the *Historia satyra* of Paulinus Minorita, bishop of Pozzuoli (d. 1344), see Pastorello, xxxii–xxxiii.
179. Dandolo, *Chronica,* 87.
180. Antoninus Florentinus, *Chronica,* 3 vols. (Nuremberg: Anton Koberger, 31 July 1484), *IGI* 608, vol. 1, fol. 18r.
181. Ibid., fol. 195v.
182. H.F.M. Prescott, *Jerusalem Journey: Pilgrimage to the Holy Land in the Fifteenth Century* (London, 1954), 13 and 69–70.
183. Felix Fabri, *Evagatorium in Terrae Sanctae, Arabiae et Egyptii peregrinationem,* ed. C. D. Hassler, 3 vols. (Berlin, 1849), 3:237–239.

2. Barbarians at the Gates

1. R. Schwoebel, *The Shadow of the Crescent: The Renaissance Image of the Turk* (Nieuwkoop, 1967), 7–13, summarizes several accounts. Details were immediately picked up and reworked by humanist commentators across Europe. For three independent reactions written within a week of each other by humanists in Italy (Bessarion), Austria (Aeneas Sylvius), and Crete (Quirini), see Cardinal Bessarion to Doge Francesco Foscari, 13 July 1453, in L. Mohler, *Kardinal Bessarion als Theologe, Humanist und Staatsman,* 3 vols. (Paderborn, 1923–1942), 3:475–477; Lauro Quirini to Nicholas V, in A. Pertusi, "Le epistole storiche di Lauro Quirini sulla caduta di Costantinopoli e la potenza dei Turchi," in *Lauro Quirini Umanista,* ed. V. Branca (Florence, 1977), 226; Aeneas Sylvius to Nicholas of Cusa, in *Briefwechsel,* 3:207, and to Nicholas V, 12 July 1453, ibid., 3:199. See also n. 24, Chapter 1.
2. For the formulaic repetition of such stories by later Western propagandists, see L. F. Smith, "Pope Pius II's Use of Turkish Atrocities," *Southwestern Social Science Quarterly* 46 (1966): 407–415.
3. E.g., Aeneas Sylvius, oration at the Diet of Regensburg, in *Briefwechsel,* 3:542: "This is not an enemy to be taken lightly . . . he is driven to persecute Christians by a kind of instinctive hatred, rising from deep-seated wickedness and an inborn thirst for blood."
4. N. Daniel, *Islam and the West: The Making of an Image* (Edinburgh, 1960), 109–114, 123–127; idem, "Crusade Propaganda," in *HC,* 6:39–97, esp. 53–62; J. V. Tolan, *Saracens: Islam in the Medieval European Imagination* (New York, 2002).
5. N. Bisaha, "New Barbarian or Worthy Adversary? Renaissance Humanist Constructs of the Ottoman Turks," in *Western Views of Islam in Medieval and Early Modern Europe: Perception of Other,* eds. D. R. Blanks and M. Frassetto (New York, 1999), 189–192.

6. Leonardo Bruni, *Epistolarum libri VIII*, ed. L. Mehus (Florence, 1741), 193, cited by Bisaha, "'New Barbarian,'" 190.

7. Quirini to Nicholas V, in Pertusi, "Le epistole storiche," 227.

8. Aeneas Sylvius to Nicholas V, in *Briefwechsel*, 3:200; to Nicholas of Cusa, ibid., 209; and oration at the Diet of Regensburg, ibid., 3:540.

9. Marsilio Ficino to Matthias Corvinus, in *Opera omnia*, 2 vols. (Basel, 1576), 722.

10. Schwoebel, *Shadow*, 11–14.

11. For the arguments from advantage and honor, see ps.-Cicero, *Rhetorica ad Herennium*, 3.2.3. For a particularly good example of the honor topos, see the opening lines of Filelfo's letter to Wladyslaw of Poland and Hungary, *Epistolae* (Venice, 1502), fol. 37r.

12. Bessarion to Doge Foscari, in Mohler, *Kardinal Bessarion*, 3:475.

13. Quirini to Nicholas V, in Pertusi, "Le epistole storiche," 225–226: "This ancient city, noble, wealthy, once the seat of the Roman Empire, mistress of all the Orient, now captured by such savage barbarians . . . Constantinople, imperial city . . . alas! she lies in misery, cruelly captured and pitiably sacked."

14. The wording is important here (ibid., 227): "Gens barbara, gens inculta, nullis certis moribus, nullis legibus, sed fusa, vaga, arbitraria vivens, perfidiarum fraudumque plena."

15. Filelfo, oration at Congress of Mantua, *Orationes* [Milan: Leonardus Pachel and Uldericus Scinzenzeler, 1483–1484], *IGI* 3905, sig. H2v: "Eo enim omnis indignitas ducenda est indignior, quo ab indignioribus infertur hominibus; si homines quidem potius quam efferatae prorsus et truculentissimae quaedam belluae Turci sunt appellandi, cum nihil in se humanitatis habeant praeter hominis figuram, et eam sane ob flagitiossimam turpitudinis foeditatem depravatam ac nequam." For an ancient parallel, see the imperial historian Velleius Paterculus's comment on Germanic tribes (*Historia romana*, 2.117.3: "Varus . . . concepit esse homines qui nihil praeter vocem membraque haberent hominum"). Filelfo would not have known this particular text, however, which was recovered in Germany only in 1515.

16. Isidore of Kiev to Nicholas V, 6 July 1453, in *Caduta*, 1:98.

17. Aeneas Sylvius to Nicholas of Cusa, 21 July 1453, in *Briefwechsel*, 3:209.

18. Aeneas Sylvius to Nicholas V, 199–200; to Nicholas of Cusa, 207.

19. Aeneas Sylvius, *Oratio de Constantinopolitana clade*, in *Opera omnia* (Basel, 1551), 681: "Scytharum genus est ex media Barbaria profectum, quod ultra Euxinum . . . ad septentrionalem Oceanum sedes habuit; gens immunda et ignominiosa, fornicaria in cunctis stuprorum generibus, quae . . . montes Caspios exivit, ac longo itinere in Asiam se recepit, ibique post hac morata est."

20. Ibid., 681: "Et quamvis sub miti coelo et mundiori terra per tot saecula parumper excultam se praebuerit, sapit tamen adhuc multum pristinae deformitatis, neque omnem barbariem detersit." Aeneas made a similar point in his letter to Nicholas of Cusa of the previous year, 207 ("Sapiunt igitur adhuc aliquid originis sue. . ."), and returned to the topic again in the closing chapter of his *Asia*, in *Opera omnia*, 384–385.

21. Filelfo to Wladyslaw III of Poland and Hungary, 5 November 1444, *Epistolae*, fols. 37r–38r, at 37r.

22. Publio Gregorio Tifernate, *Vaticinium cladis Italiae*, c. 1453, in *Testi inediti*, 246: "Barbara gens Italos venit eversura penates/Et magnum a gelido panditur axe malum."

23. Nicola Loschi, *Constantinus supplex*, c. 1463, in *Testi inediti*, 274 (". . . Si Scythico iuveni tantarum pondera rerum/excussisse datum est?") and 276 ("Caspia gens").

24. Antonio Cornazzano, *Vita di Cristo* [Venice?: Printer of Cornazzano], 1472), *IGI* 3198, fol. 70v: "contra Caucaseas tueamur origine tigres."

25. Paolo Marsi, *Lamentatio de crudeli Europontinae urbis excidio* [Rome: Printer of Silius Italicus, about 1471], *IGI* 6202, fols. 1v and 6r. A similar invocation of "Caucasian" bondage can be found in Cornazzano, *Vita di Cristo*, fol. 71v.

26. Tifernate's lines (see n. 22 above) recall Jeremiah 1:14: "Ab aquilone pandetur malum super universam terram."

27. *Airs, Waters, Places*, 18–23, in A. O. Lovejoy and G. Boas, *Primitivism and Related Ideas in Antiquity* (Baltimore, 1935), 316–321.

28. Herodotus, *Histories*, 4.1–142; Lovejoy and Boas, *Primitivism*, 321–322; F. Hartog, *The Mirror of Herodotus: The Representation of the Other in the Writing of History*, trans. J. Lloyd (Berkeley, 1988); J. Redfield, "Herodotus the Tourist," *Classical Philology*, 80 (1985): 97–118; B. D. Shaw, "'Eaters of Flesh, Drinkers of Milk': The Ancient Mediterranean Ideology of the Pastoral Nomad," *Ancient Society* 13–14 (1982–1983): 5–31, at 9–13; S. Greenblatt, *Marvelous Possessions: The Wonder of the New World* (Chicago, 1991), 124–128.

29. Herodotus, *Histories*, trans. A. de Sélincourt, 3d ed. (London, 1996), 4.28 (weather); 4.47 (horses); 4.2 and 4.19 (nomadism); 4.46 (lack of towns); 4.32–35 (Hyperboreans); 4.110–117 (Amazons); 4.26 (Issedones). Quotation from 4.106, p. 249. See also 4.18.

30. Ibid., 4.46, 62, 64–66, 103. More on human sacrifice at 4.71–72.

31. Ibid., 1.106, trans. de Selincourt, 44; see also 1.103–105 and 4.1, 12–13. Cimmerian incursions south out of the Caucasus are recorded c. 722–715 B.C. Scythian raids into Media may have begun as early as the 670s; the occupation Herodotus describes occurred about 652–625: I. M. Diakonoff, "Media," in *CHI*, 2:91–119.

32. Lovejoy and Boas, *Primitivism*, 287–369, with an extensive anthology of texts; J. S. Romm, *The Edges of the Earth in Ancient Thought: Geography, Exploration and Fiction* (Princeton, 1992), esp. 67–77.

33. Jeremiah 1:13–15, 4:6 ("For I will bring evil from the north and a great destruction"), 6:1, 6:22–23 ("A people cometh from the north country, and a great nation shall be raised from the sides of the earth. They shall lay hold on bow and spear, they are cruel, and have no mercy, their voice roareth like the sea, and they ride upon horses, set in array as men for war."), 31:8, 50:3; also Isaiah 14:31. Ezekiel 38–39, esp. 38:1–7 and 15–16. Magog first appears as one of the sons of Japheth in the table of nations (Genesis 10:2), but in Ezekiel,

Magog is the name of a country whose ruler is Gog. Both Gog and Magog appear again, now as two nations rising up against Israel in the last days, in Revelations 20:7–10. For the historical northerners Gog and Magog may represent,
see G. von Rad, *Genesis: A Commentary,* trans. J. H. Marks (London, 1972), 139–
145; W. Eichrodt, *Ezekiel: A Commentary,* trans. C. Quinn (London, 1970), 519–
523; J. L. Myres, "Gog and the Danger from the North," *Palestine Exploration
Fund Quarterly Statement for 1932,* 213–219, esp. 214–215; A. Lauha, *Zaphon: der
Norden und die Nordvolker im Alten Testament,* Annales Academiae Scientiarum
Fennicae 49 (Helsinki, 1943); J. P. Tanner, "Rethinking Ezekiel's Invasion by
Gog," *Journal of the Evangelical Theological Society* 39 (1996): 29–45.

34. Shaw, "'Eaters of Flesh'"; D. Sinor, "Central Asia," in *Orientalism and History,*
ed. D. Sinor (Cambridge, 1954), 82–103, esp. 82–83; idem., "The Greed of the
Northern Barbarian," in *Aspects of Altaic Civilization II: Proceedings of the XVIII Permanent International Altaistic Conference,* eds. L. V. Clark and P. A. Draghi
(Bloomington, Ind., 1978).

35. Aristotle, *Politics,* 1.3 (1256a29–b8); discussed by Shaw, "'Eaters of Flesh,'" 16–
20.

36. D. B. Saddington, "Roman Attitudes to the 'Externae Gentes' of the North,"
Acta Classica 4 (1961): 90–102, esp. 94–95; also Y. Dauge, *Le Barbare: Recherches
sur la conception romaine de la barbarie et de la civilisation* (Brussels, 1981).

37. Pliny the Elder, *Historia naturalis,* 4.80–84, 88; 6.30, 33, 53; Pomponius Mela,
De situ orbis, 2.2–15; 3.36–45, 59–60; Solinus, *Collectanea rerum memorabilium,*
15.1–31; 17.3–11.

38. Justin, *Epitome in Pompeium Trogum,* 41.1–2.

39. Lovejoy and Boas, *Primitivism,* 362–367.

40. Virgil, *Georgics,* 3.349–383, esp. 376–383. See R. Thomas, *Lands and Peoples in
Roman Poetry: The Ethnographical Tradition,* (Cambridge, 1982), 51–52.

41. Texts reproduced in Lovejoy and Boas, *Primitivism,* 325–333.

42. Justin, *Epitome in Pompeium Trogum,* 2.1.1–4; 2.2.7, 10–15.

43. Ibid., 2.2.3–10.

44. Ibid., 2.2.14–15; translation from Justin, *Epitome of the Philippic History of
Pompeius Trogus,* trans. J. C. Yardley (Atlanta, 1994), 27.

45. Excerpts from Ammianus Marcellinus, *Res gestae,* 31.2.1–12. On the formulaic
aspects of this and other descriptions of the Huns, see O. Maenchen-Helfen,
The World of the Huns: Studies in their History and Culture (Berkeley, 1973), 1–15;
Shaw, "'Eaters of Flesh,'" 25–26.

46. Coluccio Salutati to Josse, margrave of Moravia, 1397, In *Epistolario,* ed. F.
Novati, 4 vols. (Rome, 1891–1911), 3:208–209. The stoic *patientia* of the barbarian is an ancient topos: Thomas, *Lands and Peoples,* 20–21.

47. Ibid., 209.

48. Ibid., 211.

49. One example, however, is Poggio's comment on the martial valor of Turks and
Tartars: "De nobilitate" (*Opera omnia,* 1:69).

50. Quirini to Nicholas V, 227.

51. Filelfo to Wladyslaw, *Epistolae,* fol. 37r.
52. Niccolò Sagundino, *De origine et rebus gestis Turcarum,* Clauser, 186.
53. Herodotus, *Histories,* 4.46; defense of Scythia: 102–142.
54. Justin, *Epitome in Pompeium Trogum,* 2.1.1–4; 2.3.1–18. Another positive account of Scythian history is Diodorus Siculus, *Bibliotheca historiarum,* 2.43–44.
55. Jerome, Epistola 77, in *PL,* 22:695–696.
56. The origins of this legend in ancient geography and history, its development between the first and fourth centuries A.D., and its later ramifications in medieval literature are extraordinarily complex. I review the main sources and secondary literature in the Appendix, to which reference should be made for the material in the following paragraphs.
57. Jerome, *Epistola* 77, col. 695.
58. Sigebert of Gembloux, *Chronica,* in *PL,* 160:63.
59. Ibid., col. 64. The quotation is from Jeremiah 1.14.
60. Flavio Biondo, *Historiarum ab inclinatione Romanorum imperii libri XXXI* (hereafter cited as *Decades*) (Basel, 1531), 151: "Fueruntque et ipsi Turci Scythae ex iis quos Alexandrum Macedonem intra Hyperboreos montes, ferreis clausisse repagulis, quum alii tradunt scriptores, tum beatus Hieronymus affirmat." Biondo also quotes Jerome's letter in his account of the arrival of the Huns themselves: *Decades,* 6.
61. Platina, *Vitae pontificum* ([Venice]: Johannes de Colonia and Johannes Manthen, 11 June 1479), *IGI* 7857, sig. k6r; Jacopo Filippo Foresti, *Supplementum chronicorum* (Venice: Bernardinus Benalius, 23 August 1483), *IGI* 5075, 83; Hartmann Schedel, *Liber cronicarum* (Nuremberg: Anton Koberger, 12 July 1493), *IGI* 8828, fol. 165r.
62. He lists these in no particular order: Androphagi (*Asia,* in *Opera omnia,* 287: "gentem asperrimam et efferatam") and Seres (ibid.: "inter se mites et quietissimos"); Massagetes (289: "foeda gens et brutis simillima") and cannibal Essedones (ibid.); Armiphaeans (291: "Hyperboreis similes Armiphaeos esse dicunt, Asiaticos Scythicos qui . . . nullum laedunt, quietem amant") and Albani (297: "simplex mortalium genus"). For a fuller treatment, see M. Meserve, "From Samarkand to Scythia: Reinventions of Asia in Renaissance Geography and Political Thought," in *Pius II: el piu expeditivo pontifice. Selected Studies on Aeneas Silvius Piccolomini (1405–1464),* eds. Z.R.W.M. von Martels and A. Vanderjagt (Leiden, 2003), 13–39.
63. Diodorus's Greek text was translated into Latin by Poggio Bracciolini in 1449 and revised shortly thereafter by Pier Candido Decembrio: E. Fryde, *Humanism and Renaissance Historiography* (London, 1983), 27–28.
64. Aeneas Sylvius, *Asia,* in *Opera omnia,* 305–306.
65. Justin, *Epitome,* 2.3.5: "Romanorum audivere, non sensere arma."
66. Aeneas Sylvius, *Asia,* 306. See Meserve, "From Samarkand to Scythia," 24.
67. Ibid., 306–307.
68. Ibid., 307.
69. Filelfo to Wladyslaw, *Epistolae,* fols. 37r ("agreste Turcorum vulgus, ex

humillimis pastoribus ac famellicis et fugitivis Scytharum servis"), 37v ("adversus Turcos, adversus pastores et fugitivos. . ."); to Charles VII, fols. 55v ("Turci . . . qui fugitivi Scytharum servi"), 57r ("Turcis, qui tributarii et tanquam servi Scytharum"), 59v ("Bellum tibi omne futurum est cum agrestibus incultisque hominibus, cum latronibus, cum fugitivis, cum vaenalibus abiectissimisque servis. . .").

70. Justin, *Epitome*, 41.1–2.

71. Ibid., 41.3–6.

72. Filelfo to Wladyslaw, *Epistolae*, fol. 37r.

73. Foresti, *Supplementum chronicorum*, 8. Also in Schedel, *Liber cronicarum*, fol. 18r.

74. Foresti cites Augustine, *De civitate dei*, 18.3, as his source for the Scythians' antiquity; the chapter in Augustine, however, treats the history of the Sicyonians of archaic Greece.

75. Aeneas also mentions Lombards, Goths, and Hungarians in his chapter on Scythia in the *Asia;* however, he says that the first two nations were not Scythian in origin but German, while the Hungarians were Scythian but renounced their barbarous ways when they embraced Christianity: *Asia,* 307–308.

76. Foresti, *Supplementum chronicorum*, 8.

77. Werner Rolewinck, *De laude antiquae Saxoniae,* sig. a8v, derived from the anonymous *Rudimentum novitiorum* (Lübeck, 1475), 107r.

78. Foresti, *Supplementum chronicorum*, 8.

79. On Filelfo's life and works, see C. De Rosminis, *Vita di Francesco Filelfo Tolentino,* 3 vols. (Milan, 1808); L. A. Sheppard, "A Fifteenth-Century Humanist, Francesco Filelfo," *The Library,* 4th ser., 16 (1935): 1–26; R. G. Adam, "Filelfo at the Court of Milan," Ph. D. dissertation, Oxford University, 1974; P. Viti, "Filelfo, Francesco," *DBI,* 47:613–626. L. Gualdo Rosa, "Filelfo e i Turchi: un inedito storico dell'Archivio Vaticano," *Università di Napoli. Annali della facoltà di lettere e filosofia* 2 (1964–1968): 109–165, deals primarily with a single manuscript containing notes made by Filelfo on Islamic history but at 111–114 gives a partial list of his other crusade writings; also Schwoebel, *Shadow,* 150–152.

80. D. Robin, *Filelfo in Milan: Writings, 1451–1477* (Princeton, 1991), traces Filelfo's persistent search for patronage and financial security; also Sheppard, "Filelfo," 4–6.

81. Dozens of these, from 1427 to 1473, are in his 1502 *Epistolae.* Some of his Greek letters are published in *Cent-dix lettres grecques de François Filelfe,* ed. E. Legrand (Paris, 1892); a larger but still incomplete collection of Latin and Greek letters from 1427 to 1477 is preserved in MS Milan, Biblioteca Trivulziana, 873. I am preparing a study of Filelfo's crusade letters in the context of his search for patronage and employment both in Italy and north of the Alps, forthcoming in *Osiris* 25 (2010).

82. E.g., Burckhardt's dismissive comments on Filelfo's worth as a historian in general (*The Civilization of the Renaissance in Italy,* trans. S.G.C. Middlemore [London, 1990], 157). For his approach to Turkish affairs, see Sheppard, "Filelfo,"

20; Schwoebel, *Shadow,* 150–152; and Babinger's frequent and rather harsh criticism in *Mehmed the Conqueror,* 67–8, 118, 169, 237–238, 250, 304, 322.

83. Filelfo to Wladyslaw, *Epistolae,* fol. 37r.

84. Ibid.

85. Ibid., fol. 37v.

86. Ibid., fol. 37r.

87. Ibid., fol. 37v.

88. "Cimmerian" Bosporos (so called to distinguish it from the Thracian Bosporos connecting the Black Sea and the Sea of Marmara) was the ancient name for the strait between the Black Sea and the Maeotic Lake; it was also the Byzantine name for the ancient city of Pantikapaion, in the Crimea, which guards the western side of the strait: "Bosporos," *ODB,* 1:313. For its sack by Bokhan, see *CMH,* 4:479; D. Sinor, "Establishment and Dissolution," in *CHEIA,* 304.

89. It is clear that the *Suda* was Filelfo's source, not only because of the erroneous date which he reproduces but also because many years later he advised his friend Theodore Gaza that information on Bokhan could be found in the lexicon (see Chapter 3). For his copy of the *Suda,* see A. Calderini, "Ricerche intorno alla biblioteca e alla cultura greca di Francesco Filelfo," *Studi italiani di filologia classica* 20 (1913): 204–424, at 397–398. M. J. Heath, "Renaissance Scholars and the Origins of the Turks," *Bibliothèque d'humanisme et Renaissance* 41 (1979): 463, unaware of Filelfo's reliance on the *Suda,* suggests that he refers to a later, completely unrelated Byzantine dispute with the Khazars during the reign of Justinian II.

90. Suidas, *Lexicon,* ed. A. Adler, 5 vols. (Leipzig, 1928–1938), 1:481, 492; 2:199. *Bōkhanos* is possibly a transliteration of the Old Turkic title *Bugha-qan (BT,* 2:108), in which case the *Suda*'s gloss (*onoma kurion*) is entirely accurate.

91. Menander Protector, *History,* ed. R. C. Blockley (Liverpool, 1985), 178 (Fragment 19.1).

92. Filelfo, *Orationes,* sig. H3r: "Primum Iustiniani temporibus ad Hellespontum usque clandestinis insidiis impetum facientes, eodem ductore et collatrone perditissimo Bochano urbem opulentissimam Bosphorum repentina vi captam diripuerunt."

93. Filelfo to Wladyslaw, *Epistolae,* fol. 37v. Filelfo repeats the story—without dating it to the reign of Heraclius—in his letter to Charles VII of France, ibid., fol. 55v. Here he also omits the story of Bokhan.

94. Filelfo, *Orationes,* sigs. H2v–3r: "Quis unus omnium Turcos ignoret fugitivos esse Scytharum servos eosque pastores, qui ex ergastulis illius vasti et inhospitabilis montis Caucasi . . . in Persida ac Mediam latrocinatum descendissent nullumque certum incolerent domicilium praeter obsoleta lustra et horrentes sylvarum latebras?"

95. Text in Theophanes, *Chronographia,* ed. C. de Boor, 2 vols. (Leipzig, 1883). Translations from *The Chronicle of Theophanes Confessor: Byzantine and Near Eastern History,* A.D. *284–813,* trans. C. Mango and R. Scott (Oxford, 1997). On

Theophanes and his place in Byzantine historiography, see Mango and Scott, xliii–xcv; H. Hunger, *Die hochsprachliche profane Literatur der Byzantiner,* 2 vols. (Munich, 1978), 1:334–339; G. Ostrogorsky, *History of the Byzantine State,* 2d ed., trans. J. Hussey (Oxford, 1968), 87–92; C. Mango, "Who Wrote the Chronicle of Theophanes?" *Zbornik radova Vizantoloskog Instituta* 18 (1978): 9–17; idem, "The Tradition of Byzantine Chronography," *Harvard Ukrainian Studies* 12/13 (1988/1989): 360–372, esp. 367–370; R. Scott, "The Byzantine Chronicle after Malalas," in *Studies in John Malalas,* eds. E. Jeffreys, B. Croke, and R. Scott (Sydney, 1990), 38–54, esp. 40–42. For the issues treated here in particular, see *BT,* 1:531–537; A. S. Proudfoot, "The Sources of Theophanes for the Heraclian Dynasty," *Byzantion* 144 (1974): 367–439.

96. Anastasius Bibliothecarius completed his translation in the early 870s. As *Chronographia tripartita,* it is published in Theophanes, *Chronographia,* ed. de Boor, 2:33–346; also in *PG,* 108:1187–1428. See G. Arnaldi, "Anastasio Bibliotecario," *DBI,* 3:25–37; Ostrogorsky, *History,* 88–89; *ODP,* 106–107 (Anastasius was illegitimately elected pope in 855; once deposed, he turned to a life of scholarship). On the later *fortuna* of Anastasius's text, see A. Pertusi, *Storiografia umanistica e mondo bizantino* (Palermo, 1967), 8–9.

97. Theophanes' *Chronographia* treats world events from Creation to the year A.D. 813; the text is the only substantial Greek source for Byzantine foreign relations in the seventh and eighth centuries, with first Persia, then the emerging Arab Empire, and last the khaganate of the Turkic Khazars. Theophanes derived his material from earlier Byzantine and Syriac sources, most of which are now lost: Scott, "Byzantine Chronicle," 41; *BT,* 1:534–535; Mango, "Byzantine Chronography," 367–368.

98. Byzantine authors, always conservative and classicizing in the terms they used to describe barbarians, at first called both the Western Türks and the Khazars by generic terms like *Skuthai* ("Scythians") and *Hounnoi* ("Huns"). In the seventh century, however, the term *Tourkoi* was adopted as the name not only for the Western Türks but also for their political heirs, the Khazars: *BT,* 2:279–283, 320–327, 335–336.

99. Ostrogorsky, *History,* 92–112; A. A. Vasiliev, *History of the Byzantine Empire,* 2d ed. (Oxford, 1952), 193–200; J. F. Haldon, *Byzantium in the Seventh Century: The Transformation of a Culture* (Cambridge, 1990), 41–53; A. N. Stratos, *Byzantium in the Seventh Century,* 5 vols., vol. 1 (602–634), trans. M. Ogilvie-Grant (Amsterdam, 1968), and vol. 2 (634–641), trans. H. Hionides (Amsterdam, 1972).

100. Stratos, *Byzantium,* 1:197–203; D. M. Dunlop, *A History of the Jewish Khazars* (Princeton, 1954), 28–30.

101. Ostrogorsky, *History,* 103; Golden, *Khazar Studies,* 50–51. Stratos questions whether the Khazar desertion really took place (*Byzantium,* 1:206–210).

102. Ostrogorsky, *History,* 103; Vasiliev, *History,* 197–199.

103. Theophanes dates his chronicle entries with a complicated listing of years elapsed since Creation, indiction cycles, regnal years of emperors and patriarchs, etc.:. Mango and Scott, lxiii–lxxiv. His tabulation is frequently out by

several years. In this and the following citations, I reproduce the year given in the text rather than the correct historical date, since this allows me to trace how later Latin chroniclers transferred information from Theophanes into their own annals.

104. Theophanes, *Chronicle,* trans. Mango and Scott, 446–447, from *Chronographia,* ed. de Boor, 315–316.

105. Ibid., 447, from *Chronographia,* ed. de Boor, 316.

106. Ibid., 448, from *Chronographia,* ed. de Boor, 317.

107. Ibid., 563, from *Chronographia,* ed. de Boor, 407.

108. Ibid.

109. Ibid., 567, from *Chronographia,* ed. de Boor, 409.

110. Theophanes is a year or two behind in his dating. With reference to entry 3: in 730, a Khazar army marched south through the Caspian Gates and defeated the Arabs led by Jarrah ibn-'Abdullah al-Hakami (Theophanes' "Garachos"), who was killed during the fighting (Dunlop, *Jewish Khazars,* 69–71). Entry 4: in 731, Jarrah's replacement, Maslamah ibn-'Abd-al-Malik (Theophanes' "Masalma"), led another Arab army deep into the Caucasus but, on hearing of a large Khazar army nearby, retreated again. Contrary to Theophanes, there was no battle (ibid., 76–78). Entry 5 may refer to the disastrous campaign of Maslamah's replacement, Marwan ibn-Muhammed (the future caliph Marwan I), who led an Arab army into the Caucasus in late 732, became bogged down in mud, and was forced to retreat; or it may refer obliquely to the fact that in late 731 Maslamah, before leaving the campaign, captured the fortress at Derbend, which guards one of the two Caucasian passes known as the Caspian Gates, and stayed there to supervise fortifications rather than launch another invasion into Khazar territory (ibid., 80).

111. Ibid., 61–84.

112. Theophanes, trans. Mango and Scott, 600, from *Chronographia,* ed. de Boor, 433.

113. Ibid., 602, from *Chronographia,* ed. de Boor, 435.

114. Although material from Theophanes is found in numerous Latin chronicles, his information on the alliance between Heraclius and the Khazars was not always repeated; an alternate account from the *Chronicle* of Fredegar was sometimes preferred: M. Meserve, "Medieval Sources for Renaissance Theories on the Origins of the Ottoman Turks," in *Europa und die Türken,* eds. B. Guthmüller and W. Kühlmann (Tübingen, 2000), 432–434.

115. R. Fubini, "Biondo, Flavio," *DBI,* 10:536–559, esp. 573–574; D. Hay, "Flavio Biondo and the Middle Ages," *Proceedings of the British Academy* 45 (1960): 97–128; E. Cochrane, *Historians and Historiography in the Italian Renaissance* (Chicago, 1981), 34–40. For his use of Anastasius, see P. Buchholz, *Die Quellen der* Historiarum Decades *des Flavius Blondus* (Naumberg, 1881), 52–53; Pertusi, *Storiografia umanistica,* 19n27.

116. Hay, "Flavio Biondo," 103–105.

117. *ODP,* 91–92.

118. See the opening lines of the book (*Decades,* 150): "Scribentem hactenus decimo

volumine non magis Romanorum imperii inclinationem, quam ipsius urbis Romae atque Italiae desolationem, ad quam superius eas ostendimus perductas, saepe moestitia, saepe pavor invasere. Nunc tanquam ipse in periculi parte versor, horreo consyderare atque recensere, quam gelido trementique corde, Romani et suarum partium Itali regis Aistulfi saevitiam formidabant."

119. Biondo, *Decades,* 151.

120. Hay, "Flavio Biondo," 120, citing Biondo, *Decades,* 163–164 and 166; Fryde, *Humanism and Renaissance Historiography,* 8–9.

121. B. Nogara, *Scritti inediti e rari di Biondi Flavio* (Rome, 1927), CXLIX–CLVI.

122. Flavio Biondo, *Roma triumphans* (Basel, 1531), 1: "Exciti enim a te ingentes Italiae, Galliarum, Hispaniarum, Germaniae, populi in magnam praeclaramque expeditionem quam paras in Turcos . . . Nonnulla in ipso opere edocebuntur, aliquando alias simile in rerum difficultate gesta, ut ipsa priscorum virtutis imitatio . . . sit ad rem capessendam stimulos additura." See also his long meditation on the subject at 217, discussed by A. Mazzocco, "Rome and the Humanists: The Case of Flavio Biondo," in *Rome in the Renaissance: The City and the Myth,* ed. P. A. Ramsey (Binghamton, N.Y., 1982), 185–195, at 191–192.

123. Biondo, *Decades,* 207–209, a passage discussed further in Chapter 4.

124. Biondo quotes from Anastasius repeatedly over the years 602–806: Buchholz, *Quellen,* 113–117.

125. Biondo repeats the whole account in his *De origine et gestis Venetorum* of 1454 (*Opera omnia,* 274–275).

126. E.g., Filelfo, oration at Mantua, sig. H2v: "[Turci] qui ex ergastulis illius vasti et inhospitabilis montis Caucasi . . . descendissent."

127. Platina, *Vitae Pontificum,* sig. k6r.

128. The fullest biographies remain G. Voigt, *Enea Silvio de' Piccolomini als Papst Pius der Zweite und sein Zeitalter,* 3 vols. (Berlin, 1856–1863), and G. Paparelli, *Enea Silvio Piccolomini: L'umanesimo sul soglio di Pietro* (Bari, 1950). In English, see briefer surveys by R. J. Mitchell, *The Laurels and the Tiara: Pope Pius II, 1458–1464* (London, 1962); J. G. Rowe, "The Tragedy of Aeneas Sylvius Piccolomini," *Church History* 30 (1961): 288–313. For Aeneas's commitment to a new crusade and his writings in support of the project, see R. Eysser, "Papst Pius II und der Kreuzzug gegen die Türken," in *Mélanges d'histoire générale,* ed. Constantin Marinescu, 2 vols. (Bucharest, 1938), 2:1–134; E. Hocks, *Pius II und der Halbmond* (Freiburg, 1941); A. Matanic, "L'idea e l'attività per la crociata anti-turca del papa Pio II (1458–1464)," *Studi Francescani* 61 (1964): 362–394; Schwoebel, *Shadow,* 57–81; F. Babinger, "Pio II e l'oriente maomettano," in *Enea Silvio Piccolomini Papa Pio II: Atti del convegno per il quinto centenario della morte,* ed. D. Maffei (Siena, 1968); J. Helmrath, "Pius II und die Türken," in *Europa und die Türken,* eds. Guthmüller and Kühlmann, with extensive review of earlier scholarship and a list of his major crusade writings (89–99); N. Bisaha, "Pope Pius II and the Turks," in *Crusading in the Fifteenth Century: Message and Impact,* ed. N. Housley (London, 2004), 39–52.

129. Aeneas's oration on the fall of Constantinople, delivered at the Diet of Frankfurt in 1454 (*De Constantinopolitana clade*), was printed three times in the fifteenth century (Hain, 250–252); two later crusade orations from 1455 and
1459 were each printed once (W. A. Copinger, *Supplement to Hain's
Repertorium Bibliographicum*, Part I [London, 1895], no. 208) and M. L.
Polain, *Catalogue des livres imprimés au quinzième siècle des bibliothèques de Belgique*,
5 vols. [Brussels, 1932–1978], no. 2918, the latter a collection of crusade orations including two by Filelfo). His bull proclaiming the crusade of 1464 was
printed twice, once in Latin and once in German (Hain, 261 and 263). Perhaps
most influential of all were his two geographical treatises, *Asia* and *Europa*,
completed during his pontificate, each of which was printed once in the fifteenth century (Copinger, *Supplement*, 1:257–258). These had an immediate
and profound effect on the writing of geography and history in Europe, especially in the north; both contain extensive descriptions of the Turks and Turkish history.

130. So argues Rowe, "Tragedy," 290–291, although Voigt, *Enea Silvio*, 2:90–91,
identifies the fall of Constantinople as the event that truly confirmed his commitment to a new crusade. Aeneas certainly felt great respect for the papal legate, Cardinal Cesarini, who helped organize and lead the crusade of Varna:
see scattered comments in letters from 1443to 1444 in *Briefwechsel*, 1.1: 165,
281–283; 321–322; 323–324; 487–490; 565–567 (the last two letters on the
battle and Cesarini's death). Official letters written from the imperial chancery
in this period, which Aeneas helped to draft, express support for Cesarini's crusade and more generally stress the need for a united German, Hungarian, and
Polish response to Ottoman incursions: *Briefwechsel*, 1.2 *passim*.

131. Aeneas was ordained in 1446, appointed bishop of Trieste in March 1447 and
of Siena in January 1451, made cardinal of Santa Sabina in December 1456,
and elected pope in August 1458.

132. Aeneas Sylvius, *Oratio coram sanctissimo senatu cardinalium, imperatore coronato,
pontifice, et eius nomine ad passagium inducendum* (1452), in *Opera omnia*, 928–
932, at 929: "Tria sunt quae Caesarem passagii cupidum reddant:
commiseratio, utilitas, atque honestas rei."

133. Ibid., 929.

134. Ibid.: "Sed quid Graecia literarum mater? Inventrix legum, cultrix morum, et
omnium artium bonarum magister? Quem non miseret gentis illius afflictae
oppressae pessundatae?"

135. Ibid., 930: "O nostram maximam negligentiam! O tempora! O mores!"

136. Ibid.

137. Ibid., 929–930: "Quem non miseret gentis . . . cuius imperium non sub
Alexandro Macedone solum suisque successoribus, sed sub Atheniensibus,
Thebanis ac Lacedaemonibus olim florentissimum et potentissimum fuit. Nunc
ubilibet effoeminatis Turcis servire coacta est."

138. Ibid., 931: "Novit maiestas imperatoria Turcorum, Assyriorum,
Aegyptiorumque gentem, imbelles, inermes, effoeminati sunt, neque animo,

neque consilio martiales . . . Quis truncatos mitratosque Turcos, aut brachatos timeat Aegyptiacos?"

139. Ibid.

140. Ibid.: "Martiales enim et feroces Europae populi nescientes quiescere; nisi adversus exteros praelientur, in se minus vertunt."

141. Aeneas Sylvius to Nicholas V, *Briefwechsel*, 3:189–202. The first portion of the letter deals with unrelated events; Aeneas heard of the capture while he was writing, and his comments on the event begin at 199: "Sed quid illud horribile novum modo allatum de Constantinopoli?"

142. Ibid., 199: ".Proh pudor ab effeminatis Turcis inclitam urbem Constantinopolim capi permittimus." In his later orations, Aeneas still occasionally described the Ottomans as effeminate or weak—usually when arguing that a new crusade would be easy as well as honorable and advantageous for Europeans (he would say, for instance, that although the Turkish army was enormous, it was made up of untrained soldiers, compelled to fight out of fear of the sultan rather than true desire for victory). For examples, see Helmrath, "Pius II," 105–106. But he never again made the claim in the context of establishing their origins, history, or national character, which from this point on he consistently identified as Scythian and therefore warlike and violent.

143. Aeneas Sylvius to Nicholas V, *Briefwechsel* 3:199–200.

144. Aeneas Sylvius to Nicholas of Cusa, ibid. 3:209–210.

145. Letter to Troster in *Opera omnia*, 915; oration at Frankfurt, ibid., 681; oration at Wiener Neustadt, in *Orationes politicae et ecclesiasticae*, ed. J. D. Mansi, 3 vols. (Lucca, 1755–1759), 1:308; oration to Callixtus, in *Opera omnia*, 926; *Commentaries*, eds. M. Meserve and M. Simonetta (Cambridge, Mass., 2003), 208–209; *Europa*, in *Opera omnia*, 394; oration at Mantua, ibid., 906; *Asia*, ibid., 307, 383–385.

146. Aeneas Sylvius, oration at the Council of Basel, November 1436, quoted by Helmrath, "Pius II," 89.

147. See *Briefwechsel*, 1.2, ad indicem s.v. *Teucri*. For chancery practice, see Chapter 1.

148. Oration at Frankfurt, *Opera omnia*, 681; oration at Wiener Neustadt, *Orationes*, ed. Mansi, 1:308; oration to Callixtus, *Opera omnia*, 926; *Europa*, ibid., 394. In a first draft of his letter to Nicholas of Cusa, Aeneas put the point that the Turks could not be Trojans because they were inherently barbarous even more starkly: "haberent enim humanitatis aliquid si soboles horum [Teucrorum] essent" (*Briefwechsel*, 3:209n4).

149. There was some speculation in medieval and early humanist historiography that the Turks were the heirs, if not the descendants, of the ancient Persians (discussed in Chapter 4), and Aeneas himself associated the Turks with other nations of Asia (the Assyrians and Egyptians) in his oration of 1452. But he did not repeat this denial of their Persian ancestry in any of his later writings, where he preferred to introduce and refute only the claim that they were Trojans.

150. I am not sure whether Aeneas knew their works at this time. The text of Biondo's *Decades* had been circulating since 1444, and Aeneas knew Biondo personally; in the early 1460s he made an epitome of the *Decades*. Filelfo had taught Aeneas in Siena in his youth, and they continued to correspond during this period. I have found no proof, however, that Aeneas read either scholar's account of the origins of the Turks before he began to develop his own version in the months after the fall of Constantinople.

151. Aeneas Sylvius to Nicholas of Cusa, *Briefwechsel* 3:209–210. See n. 20 above for other texts where Aeneas makes a similar point.

152. Oration at Frankfurt, in *Opera omnia*, 681: "Carnes adhuc equorum, vesontium, vulturumque comedit."

153. *Europa*, ibid., 394–395: "Turcae (ut Ethicus philosophus tradit) ultra Pyrenaeos montes et Taracontas insulas contra aquilonis ubera, id est, ad septentrionalem oceanum sedes patrias habuere, gens truculenta . . . Comedit quae caeteri abominantur: iumentorum, luporum et vulturum carnes, nec abortivis hominum abstinet." Repeated more or less verbatim in *Asia*, ibid., 307 and 383–385.

154. For the relationship between the distant and the monstrous/unclean in medieval geographical literature, see M. B. Campbell, *The Witness and the Other World: Exotic European Travel Writing 400–600* (Ithaca, N.Y., 1988), 52–53.

155. "Romanorum imperium audivit magis quam sensit, quamvis Octaviano Augusto in auro littorio censum dedit": Aeneas Sylvius, *Europa*, 394–395, and again in *Asia*, 307 and 383–385. The sentence is from Justin, *Epitome*, 2.3.5; but elsewhere in *Asia*, Aeneas strongly disagrees with this statement (see above). The inhabitants of Georgia, in the Caucasus, were renowned in antiquity for their practice of using sheepskins ("golden fleece") to pan for gold in the mountain streams of Colchis: D. Braund, *Georgia in Antiquity* (Oxford, 1994), , 20–21.

156. Aethicus, *Die Kosmographie*, ed. O. Prinz, *MGH, Quellen zur Geistesgeschichte des Mittelalters*, 14 (Munich, 1993).

157. *Kosmographie*, ed. Prinz, 1–84; K. Hillkowitz, *Zur Kosmographie des Æthicus* (Frankfurt-am-Main, 1973), 1–19.

158. See Prinz's remarks in Aethicus, *Kosmographie*, 25–44.

159. Aethicus, *Kosmographie*, 119–120, 121–122.

160. Ibid., 122–123.

161. Ibid., 25. The debt of the passage just quoted to the apocalyptic text of ps.-Methodius is confirmed by Aethicus's use of the phrase *ubera aquilonis* ("breasts of the north"), which J. Trumpf proved must derive from the original, late seventh-century Syriac text of the *Revelations*. See the Appendix.

162. The precise location of the country of the Turks described by Aethicus is not clear: he places it at the far end of the Black Sea, bordered by "Birrichean" mountains and the islands of Taraconta. These places are not mentioned in any ancient or medieval geography of the Caucasus I know. Pertusi suggests that the "Pyrrenean" mountains and city of Tarragona, in Spain ("Iberia"), have somehow been transplanted to Caucasian Georgia (also "Iberia"): A. Pertusi, "I

primi studi in occidente sull'origine e potenza dei Turchi," *Studi Veneziani* 12 (1970): 476n29. Braund, *Georgia in Antiquity,* 20–21, notes parallels drawn in antiquity between the Iberian peninsula and Iberia in the Caucasus. On the other hand, the "Birrichean" mountains may reflect the fortified city of Biraparakh in the Caucasus, where a Byzantine garrison guarded the pass of Dariel: ibid., 270. This was one of the main Caucasian passes and was at various times known as both the Caspian and the Caucasian Gates. Whatever the case, Aeneas certainly interpreted his text as indicating the Caucasus and the territories beyond it: in the *Asia,* he glosses Aethicus's information with the words "Asiatica Scythia" and also, probably relying on information from Pliny, corrects Otto of Freising's phrase "Caspian Gates" to "Caucasian Gates." This was, according to ancient geographers, the correct name of the pass of Dariel in the Caucasus, which was mistakenly known as the "Caspian Gates." The true Caspian Gates lie in Persia. Aeneas seems to be taking special care to ensure that his readers understand that the Turks came from north of the Caucasus and not Persia.

163. Cf. Prinz's suggestion (Aethicus, *Kosmographie,* 18) that Aethicus's portrait of the "Turchi" derives not from any literary text but from firsthand knowledge of the "turkstämmigen" Avars. This cannot be right: though the Avars, by the eighth century, occupied territory in central Europe and were well known to Carolingian authors, their ethnic origins are far from clear, and there is no evidence that they ever called themselves, or were called by others, "Turks"; even the suggestion that they may have spoken a Turkic language has not been proved: S. Szádecky-Kardoss, "The Avars," in *CHEIA,* 206–228, at 221–225.

164. An analogous case is the ninth-century exegete Christian of Stavelot, who, clearly influenced by the ps.-Methodian tradition, identifies the Khazars with Gog and Magog, but unlike ps.-Methodius also explicitly calls them "Khazars" (*Gazari*). This suggests that other information about them was circulating in Europe at the time: L. S. Chekin, "Christian of Stavelot and the Conversion of Gog and Magog: A Study of the Ninth-Century Reference to Judaism among the Khazars," *Russia Mediaevalis* 9 (1997): 13–34. Thanks to Peter Golden for the reference.

165. Aeneas Sylvius, Oration at the Diet of Frankfurt, 681: "[Turcorum gens] ut tradit vester Otto Frisingensis episcopus, non futilis autor, regnante apud Francos Pipino, montes Caspios exivit, ac longo itinere in Asiam se recepit, ibique posthac morata est," and again in his oration to Callixtus, *Opera omnia,* 926, and in the *Commentaries,* 208–209.

166. *Asia,* 307: "Otho historicus, qui Phrisingensis fuit episcopus, tradit Turcas, imperantibus Graecis ac regnante apud Francos Pipino, annis ab hinc supra sexcentis, Caspias portas egressos, cum Avaribus ferocissima pugna, multis utrinque desideratis, conflixisse." Similarly at the end of the *Asia* (*Opera omnia,* 383–385) and in the *Europa* (ibid., 394–395). For Aeneas's use of Otto's text, see B. Schürmann, *Die Rezeption der Werke Ottos von Freising im 15. und frühen 16. Jahrhundert* (Stuttgart, 1986), 17–27; R. Avesani, "Un codice di Ottone di

Frisinga appartenuto a Pio II e i suoi nipoti Giacomo e Andrea," *Bulletino senese di storia patria* 71 (1964): 160–166.

167. Otto of Freising, *Chronica de duabus civitatibus,* ed. A. Hofmeister (Hanover, 1912), 253: "[A.D. 758] Ea tempestate Turci a Caspiis portis egressi cum Avaribus multis utrobique profligatis conflixere."

168. See Meserve, "Medieval Sources," 425–434. B. Z. Kedar, *Crusade and Mission: European Approaches toward the Muslims* (Princeton, 1984), 33–34 and 206–207, traces a similar transmission of information on the life and career of Muhammad from Theophanes via Anastasius to Landulphus and Frutolf.

169. Landulphus Sagax, *Historia Romana,* ed. A. Crivellucci, 2 vols. (Rome, 1912–1913), 2:117–118; 118–119; 197 (twice); 199; 223; 225.

170. Frutolf's *Chronica* was written about 1101; it was revised and continued by Ekkehard, abbot of Aura, to whom the entire work was attributed until the late nineteenth century: F.-J. Schmale, "Frutolf von Michelsberg," *DLMV,* 2:993–998; *DGM,* 2:491–507. Text in Ekkehardus Uraugiensis, *Chronica,* in *PL,* 154: 841: "Turci egressi a Caspiis portis, cum Avaribus bellum inierunt, multique ex utrisque perierunt."

171. Anastasius, *Chronographia tripartita,* 286: "Exierunt iterum Turci ad Caspias portas et Hiberiam; quibus cum *Avaribus* bellum ineuntibus ex utrisque perierunt multi" [my italics], from Theophanes, *Chronographia,* ed. de Boor, 435.

172. Landulphus Sagax, *Historia Romana,* 2:225.

173. Cf. Heath, "Renaissance Scholars," 464, who maintains that Otto's remark correctly reflects the "inveterate hostility between Turk and Avar." The Western Türks and the Avars were bitter enemies in the sixth century, a fact recorded by Menander Protector but unknown in the Renaissance; the dispute mentioned by Anastasius and Otto (and repeated by Aeneas) is the product of a spelling mistake and no more. N. Casella, "Pio II tra geografia e storia: La 'Cosmografia,'" *Archivio della Società Romana di Storia patria* 95 (1972): 35–112, at 56n68, also takes "Avaribus" as genuine.

174. Aeneas Sylvius, *Europa,* in *Opera omnia,* 394–395: "Haec gens, teste Othone historico et imperatoris Frederici patruo, regnante apud Francos Pipino, a Caspiis portis egressa, cum Avaribus (quos Hungaros nostra vocat aetas) feroci pugna, multis utrobique desideratis conflixit." There was a long tradition of associating the Hungarians with earlier tribes of Scythia—most commonly the Huns, on etymological as well as historical grounds. The Avars, too, were considered a Hunnish people. See Aeneas's comments linking the Huns with the Avars in his *Epitome* of Biondo's *Decades,* ibid., 161; and his comments on the Scythian ancestry of the Hungarians in *Asia,* ibid., 307.

175. Franz Babinger, *Johannes Darius (1414–1494), Sachwalter Venedigs im Morgenland, und sein griechischer Umkreis* (Munich, 1961) 9–52; idem, "Nicolaos Sagundinos, ein griechischer-venedischer Humanist des 15. Jahrhunderts," *Charistērion eis Anastasion Orlandon,* 3 vols. (Athens, 1964), 1:198–212; P. D. Mastrodemetres, *Nikolaos Sekoundinos (1402–1464), Bios kai Ergon* (Athens, 1970), esp. 241–248.

176. Paparelli, *Enea Silvio,* 121–123.

177. Sagundino, *De origine et rebus gestis Turcarum;* the text is dated July 1456 in a

copy made by Hartmann Schedel: Babinger, *Johannes Darius,* 23–25. Pertusi, "Primi studi," 471–475, discusses the text; see also *Caduta,* 2:126–127; Mastrodemetres, *Nikolaos Sekoundinos,* 168–183.

178. *Liber de familia Authmanorum id est Turchorum,* an unsigned incunable assigned to Chelmno, ca. 1473–1474: E. Szandorowska, "A Dutch Printing-Office in Fifteenth-Century Poland," *Quaerendo* 2 (1972): 162–172; Mastrodemetres, *Nikolaos Sekoundinos,* 169–170.

179. MS Venice, Biblioteca Marciana, lat. XIV, 265 (4501), fol. 115r–v: letter of Marino Sanudo to Pietro Bembo, 1503: "In Nicolai Sagundini viri doctissimi de Othomani stirpis origine ac imperio brevem sed ellegantem libellum incidi, quem ad te mittendum et tibi nominatim dicandum censui . . . Sub tui igitur nominis ac numinis patrocinio, expolitam pagellam hanc comendamus eruditissimo ac virtutis fonti uberimo Aldo Romano studiosoque nobilium monimentorum instauratori, cuius emendatis typulis adiutus Sagundinus prodibit, legetur, amabitur."

180. E.g., Johannes Cuspinianus and Andrea Cambini, quoted by Pertusi, "Primi studi," 471n17. Pertusi lists four sixteenth-century editions. A transcription of the text from MS BAV, Vat. lat. 5109, is in Aeneas Sylvius Piccolomini, *Carmina,* ed. A. van Heck (Vatican City, 1994), 217–225.

181. Babinger, *Johannes Darius,* 25: "der erste europäische Versuch eines Abrisses *De familia Autumanorum . . .* und verdient also solcher besonderer Beachtung."

182. Pertusi, "Primi studi," 472–473.

183. N. Nicoloudis, *Laonikos Chalkokondyles: A Translation and Commentary of the "Demonstration of Histories" (Books I–III)* (Athens, 1996), 75. See also n. 150 in Chapter 1.

184. Schwoebel, *Shadow,* 148.

185. Sagundino, *De origine et rebus gestis Turcarum,* 186: "Primo per Pontum et Cappadociam transgressi, ad reliquas inde finitimas partes sensim illapsi sunt."

186. See, e.g., references to a Caucasian homeland in accounts of the origins of the Seljuks in Nicephorus Bryennius, *Historiae,* in *PG,* 127:48, and Johannes Zonaras, *Annales,* in *PG,* 135:220.

187. Sagundino, *De origine et rebus gestis Turcarum,* 186.

188. Skylitzes's account of Seljuk origins and early history is discussed in Chapter 3. Bryennius starts with an excursus on Seljuk activities up to the battle of Manzikert derived partly from Skylitzes (*Historiae,* cols. 48–66) and includes details of later Seljuk history throughout his work; also Zonaras, *Annales,* cols. 220–224. For the importance of Manzikert in Byzantine historiography, see S. Runciman, *History of the Crusades,* 3 vols. (London, 1951), 1:64.

189. Sagundino, *De origine et rebus gestis Turcarum,* 190.

190. Aeneas Sylvius, Oration at the Diet of Frankfurt, 681.

191. Aeneas Silvius, Oration to Callixtus, *Opera omnia,* 926: "[Turci] qui regnante apud Francos Pipino in Asiam migravere eamque *pedetentim* provinciam sui iuris fecere" (italics mine). Filelfo used similar terms (*sensim atque paulatim*) when describing how the Ottomans later occupied the Balkans in his letter to Wladyslaw of 1444, *Epistolae,* fol. 37v.

192. Mastrodemetres, *Nikolaos Sekoundinos*, 124–223.

193. The only complete edition of the oration, delivered on 25 Jan. 1454, is in V. V. Makushev, *Monumenta historica Slavorum Meridionalium vicinorumque populorum* (Warsaw, 1874), 295–306. A more accurate but abridged edition is in N. Iorga, *Notes et extraits pour servir à l'histoire des croisades au XVe siècle*, 6 vols., (Paris and Bucharest, 1901–1916), 3:316–323; reproduced in part in *Caduta*, 2:128–140. See also Babinger, *Johannes Darius*, 16–20. Pertusi, "Primi studi," 472, says Sagundino developed most of his ideas on Turkish history in this oration, which he then simply reworked in his 1456 treatise for Aeneas Sylvius; in fact, the two texts are completely different.

194. The standard humanist portrait of Mehmed II (as a proud emulator of Alexander and Caesar, a bold and hardy soldier, etc.) was as formulaic as the list of atrocities that accompanied descriptions of his campaigns. For examples, see Schwoebel, *Shadow*, 1, 5, 48.

195. Mastrodemetres, *Nikolaos Sekoundinos*, 216. It was a ubiquitous humanist commonplace to compare the Turks to ancient enemies of Greek and Roman civilization, whether Persians, Scythians, Gauls, Huns, or Goths. Analogies with Macedon were less common, although in 1471 Cardinal Bessarion translated this same oration and added a marginal commentary on its applicability to the contemporary threat posed by the Ottomans: Bessarion, *Orationes contra Turcos*, in *PG* 161:670–676, but without the marginal comments, which appear in early manuscript copies and the *editio princeps: Epistolae et orationes contra Turcos*, [Paris: Ulrich Gering, Martin Crantz, and Michael Friburger, April 1471], *GW* 4184. Sagundino makes no such explicit comparisons in his translation; still, he may have seen its relevance to the situation in the Ottoman East.

196. MS Venice, Biblioteca Marciana, lat. XIII, 62 (4418), fols. 164r–165r (preface, addressed to Pietro Bembo) and 165r–v (translation). On the oracle, probably composed after the Turks destroyed the wall in 1423 and copied down by Ciriaco d'Ancona, see E. W. Bodnar, "The Isthmian Fortifications in Oracular Prophecy," *American Journal of Archaeology* 64 (1960): 165–171 (Bodnar is unaware, however, that Sagundino made a translation of the text).

197. Loschi, *Constantinus supplex*, 274.

198. "De Peloponnesiaca quondam Venetorum . . . ac Pii II Pontificis expeditione," in *Poesie inedite di Bartolomeo Pagello*, ed. F. Zordan (Tortona, 1894), 251–252:

> Oderuntque Scythae rigidum genus, unde profecti
> Turcarum dicuntur avi, quos egit Erinnys
> Discordes, atque hinc profugi, lateque vagantes
> Invasisse Asiam, traiectoque Hellesponto
> Threicias tenuisse oras, hoc littore magni
> Constantini urbem, possessaque moenia Grais
> Iampridem infando proles Ottomania bello
> Cepit, et hic sedem regni, soliumque locavit.

199. R. Avesani, "Epaeneticorum ad Pium II pont. max. Libri V," in *Enea Silvio*, ed. Maffei.

200. "In Mahumetem perfidum Turchorum regem" (also discussed in Chapter 1). The poem refers to "Pope Pius" in the third person. Although Aeneas employed this device in his *Commentaries,* it seems to me more likely that the poem was written by someone else, in an attempt to flatter Aeneas and his crusading project. A comparable case could be that of Leodrisio Crivelli, who composed an epitome in verse of Aeneas's *Historia Bohemica* in which he also rehearses the necessity of a crusade against the Turks: R. Bianchi, *Intorno a Pio II: un mercante e tre poeti* (Messina, 1988), 161–184. Crivelli also began work on a history of Pius's proposed crusade (*De expeditione Pii papae II adversus Turcos,* in *RIS2,* 23.5, ed. G. C. Zimolo [Bologna, 1950]), which likewise commences with a review of his patron's Scythian theory.

201. Edited in Aeneas Sylvius, *Carmina,* ed. van Heck, 157–159, at 158:
> Non hoc Dardanidum genus est nec sanguine Teucro
>> ducit avos: Scythica est tetraque barbaries;
> Pyrrhicheos montes et inhospita saxa colebat,
>> gens ignara Dei, gens inimica tibi.

202. This poem actually concludes the *Epaenetica* collection of verses dedicated to Pius (Avesani, "Epaeneticorum," 85–88). Edited as "Pro ingenii exercitatione," in Aeneas Sylvius, *Carmina,* 160–168, at 162:
> . . .sedibus unde
> dimissis venere truces, fera pectora Turchi
> Phaside transmisso Colchorum littora circum
> consedere, bonus Francis dum iura Pipinus
> diceret. Hinc terras nacti, quas influit Halys
> pascua Cappadocum, celsi de vertice Thauri
> qui cadit et domiti prorumpit in equora Ponti.
> Tum Galatas Venetumque patres, Paphlagones, et urbes
> Bithynie, tum tecta Phrygum, celebresque ruinas
> invasere. . .

203. Ludovico Carbone, *Epithalamium for Paula Strozzi and Zarabinus Turchus:* "Et quamvis ego in mea illa oratione ad pontificem dixerim non esse Turchos istos ex genere Teucrorum utque pontifici blandiri voluerim utque fortasse tunc ita senserim. . ." From A. F. D'Elia, "Genealogy and the Limits of Panegyric: Turks and Huns in Fifteenth-Century Epithalamia," *SCJ* 34 (2003): 986.

204. After describing the ceremony in his *Commentaries,* Aeneas immediately turned to a discussion of his hopes and plans for a new crusade: *Commentarii* 2.1.2, eds. Meserve and Simonetta, 208–209.

205. Aeneas Sylvius, Oration at Mantua, 26 Sept. 1459, in *Opera omnia,* pp. 905–914, at 906.

206. *Europa,* in *Opera omnia,* 387–403.

207. *Asia,* ibid., 305–308; see n. 77.

208. The description is in *Asia,* 323–383. On the composition of the work, see Casella, "Pio II"; Meserve, "From Samarkand to Scythia."

209. *Asia,* 383–386. Aeneas never completed the *Asia.* A second section of the text,

covering southern Asia, including the Holy Land, was projected; it seems likely
that it too would have ended with a lament for territories lost to the Muslims.

210. Quoted by L. Martines, *Power and Imagination: City States in Renaissance Italy*
(Harmondsworth, 1979), 268; see Aeneas Sylvius, *Opera omnia*, 224–225.

3. In Search of the Classical Turks

1. Theophylactus Simocatta, *Historiae*, ed. C. de Boor, rev. P. Wirth (Stuttgart,
1972), 5.10.13–15.

2. The captives were probably mercenaries hired by Bahram; their vague awareness of Christianity most likely derived from the activities of Nestorian Christian mercenaries in central Asia at the time: Sinor, "Establishment and Dissolution," in *CHEIA*, 306.

3. I.e., *Tourkia*, the "land of the Turks" in central Asia, not Asia Minor.

4. Theophanes, *Chronographia*, ed. C. de Boor, 2 vols. (Leipzig, 1883), 266–267;
The Chronicle of Theophanes Confessor: Byzantine and Near Eastern History, A.D. *284–
813*, trans. C. Mango and R. Scott (Oxford, 1997), 389.

5. Anastasius, *Chronographia tripartita*, ed. de Boor, 164; Landulphus Sagax,
Historia Romana, ed. A. Crivellucci, 2 vols. (Rome, 1912–1913), 2:79.

6. Sigebert used Landulphus's *Historia Romana* as a source elsewhere in his chronicle: J. Krimm-Beumann, "Sigebert v. Gembloux," *DLMV*, 8:1214–1231,
esp. 1214–1215; *DGM*, 2:726–737.

7. Sigebert of Gembloux, *Chronica*, in *PL*, 160:144: "Turci a Caspiis portis
erumpentes, Armeniam infestant. In quorum patria cum antiquo tempore
pestilentia orta fuisset, suasu Christianorum in modum crucis se totonderunt,
et quia per hoc signum salus patriae reddita fuerat, hunc ritum tondendi
tenuerunt." The first sentence is copied from Landulphus Sagax, *Historia
Romana*, 2:223. Compare Theophanes' entry 6, as numbered in Chapter 2.

8. M. C. Duchenne, "Un Historien et sa source: l'utilisation de la *Chronique* de
Sigebert de Gembloux par Vincent de Beauvais," *Spicae* 4 (1986): 31–79,
esp. 32–36 and 79; M. Schmidt-Chazan, "La Réception de Sigebert de
Gembloux dans les chroniques universelles françaises de la fin du XIIe au
début du XIVe siècle," *Vincent of Beauvais Newsletter* 13 (1988): 3–6.

9. Vincent of Beauvais, *Speculum historiale* 23.158, in *Speculum maius*, 4 vols.
(Douai, 1624), 4.955.

10. A. Dandolo, *Chronica per extensum descripta*, ed. E. Pastorello, in *RIS2*, 12.1 (Bologna, 1942): 86–87.

11. Ibid., 119. His direct source for the anecdote was the *Historia satyra* of the Italian chronicler Paulinus Minorita, a work based in part on Vincent's *Speculum
historiale*.

12. It does not even appear in the exhaustive résumé of information on the origins
of the Turks in Marcantonio Sabellico's *Enneads*, in which another, later notice
by Dandolo on the Turks is cited at length and with attribution ("Dandulus, qui
res Venetas scripsit, homo sacrae historiae non ignarus"): Sabellico, *Rapsodie
historiarum enneades*, 2 vols. (Paris, 1513), 2:217r–v.

13. J. B. Walker, *The "Chronicles" of Saint Antoninus: A Study in Historiography* (Washington, D.C., 1933), 3–33; P. Brezzi, "Gli scritti storici e l'azione politica di S. Antonio," in *Settimana di studio sulla vita e le opere di S. Antonino Pierozzi* (Florence, 1960), 63–77; E. Maurri, *Un fiorentino tra Medioevo e Rinascimento: Sant'Antonino* (Milan, 1989); E. Cochrane, *Historians and Historiography in the Italian Renaissance* (Chicago, 1981), 21–22.

14. B. Ullmann, "A Project for a New Edition of Vincent of Beauvais," *Speculum* 8 (1933): 312–326. Antoninus clearly imitated Vincent's model, composing the *Chronica* as an appendix to his massive and popular handbook of moral theology, entitled *Summa theologica* or *Summa moralis*. The *Chronica* integrates biblical history, the sayings of the saints, and "the deeds of pagan peoples from the beginning of the world up to the present day": Walker, *The "Chronicles*," 17.

15. Ibid, 111.

16. Antoninus Florentinus, *Chronica*, 3 vols. (Nuremberg: Anton Koberger, 31 July 1484), *IGI* 608, 2:130r. The entry appears, as in Sigebert and Vincent of Beauvais, under the twenty-first year of the Emperor Constantine V (i.e., A.D. 762).

17. Maurri, *Sant'Antonino*, 145–147.

18. Werner Rolewinck, *Fasciculus temporum* (Cologne: Arnold Ther Hoernen, 1474), *BMC*, 1:204), sig. [o]10r.

19. B. Platina, *Liber de Vita Christi ac omnium pontificum*, in *RIS2*, 3.1:108–109. Although Platina (and his followers) call the queen Caesarea, all previous latin sources give the name Caesara or Cesara.

20. See W. Baum, *Shirin: Christian—Queen—Myth of Love: A Woman of Late Antiquity: Historical Reality And Literary Effect* (Piscataway, N.J., 2004).

21. Fredegar, *The Fourth Book of the Chronicle of Fredegar with its Continuations*, ed. and trans. J. M. Wallace-Hadrill (London, 1960), 4.9. Johannes Biclarensis, in *Victoris Tunnunensis Chronicon, cum reliquiis ex Consularibus Caesaraugustanis et Iohannis Biclarensis Chronicon*, ed. R. Collins (Turnhout, 2001), 92, includes a much abbreviated account of the Persian king's conversion around this time.

22. Paul the Deacon, *De gestis Langobardorum*, in *PL*, 95:589.

23. *PL*, 95:1152; 132:34; 139:885; 148:1332; 154:837; 213:485.

24. Petrus de Vicentia (Pietro Menzi), *Oratio pro capessenda expeditione contra infideles* [Rome: Eucharius Silber, after 25 March 1490], *IGI* 7674, fol. 10v.

25. Sabellico, *Rapsodie historiarum enneades* 2:179r.

26. On Gaza, see E. Legrand, *Bibliographie hellénique des XVe et XVIe siècles*, 4 vols. (Paris, 1885–1906), 1:xxxi–xlix; L. Mohler, "Theodoros Gazes, seine bisher ungedruckten Schriften und Briefe," *Byzantinische Zeitschrift* 42 (1943–1949): 50–75; J. Irmscher, "Theodoros Gaza als griechischer Patriot," *Parola del Passato* 16 (1961): 161–173; D. J. Geanakoplos, "Theodore Gaza, a Byzantine Scholar of the Paleologan 'Renaissance' in the Italian Renaissance," *Medievalia et Humanistica* 12 (1984): 61–81, revised in his *Constantinople and the West* (Madison, Wis., 1989), 68–90; "Theodore Gazes," *ODB*, 2:825–826; C. Bianca, "Gaza, Teodoro," in *DBI*, 52:737–746; P.L.M. Leone, "Sulla corrispondenza di Teodoro Gaza," *Quaderni Catanesi di studi classici e medievali* 18 (1987): 419–449; idem,

"Le lettere di Teodoro Gaza," in *Dotti bizantini e libri greci nell'Italia del secolo XV,* eds. M. Cortesi and E. V. Maltese (Naples, 1992), 201–218; C. Bevegni, "Teodoro Gaza fra cultura greca e cultura latina," *Studi Umanistici Piceni* 12 (1992): 47–56.

27. *Peri arkhaiogonias tōn Tourkiōn (De origine Turcarum)* in *PG,* 161:997–1006. A more recent but not entirely reliable edition is T. Gaza, *Epistole,* ed. E. Pinto (Naples, 1975), 100–106, with Italian translation 151–156 and commentary 40–44. Another edition, which I have not seen, is T. Gaza, *Epistolae,* ed. P.L.M. Leone (Naples, 1990). The treatise is discussed briefly in the article "Theodore Gazes," *ODB,* 2:825–826, and by M. J. Heath, "Renaissance Scholars and the Origins of the Turks," *Bibliothèque d'humanisme et Renaissance* 41 (1979): 459; A. Pertusi, "I primi studi in occidente sull'origine e potenza dei Turchi," *Studi Veneziani* 12 (1970): 470; J. Hankins, "Renaissance Crusaders: Humanist Crusade Literature in the Age of Mehmed II," *Dumbarton Oaks Papers* 49 (1995): 138; and G. Moravcsik, "Byzantinische Humanisten über den Volksnamen Türk," *Körösi Csoma Archivum* 2 (1926–1932): 381–385.

28. "*Boēdromiōnos hebdomēi phthinontos*": Pinto (in Gaza, *Epistole,* 100) translates this as 8 October and supplies, without comment, the year 1470; Leone ("Sulla corrispondenza," 448–449) rejects this and argues that the letter cannot be dated precisely, as does L. Gualdo Rosa, "Filelfo e i Turchi: un inedito storico dell'Archivio Vaticano," *Università di Napoli. Annali della facoltà di lettere e filosofia* 2 (1964–1968): 114n27. None of them is aware of Moravcsik's article suggesting that Gaza wrote the treatise in reply to a letter from Filelfo dated 1 July 1472: "Byzantinische Humanisten," 381–382. It is possible to establish the date more firmly. Gaza's formula indicates the seventh day before the month of Boēdromiōn, the third Attic month, which fell in September/October. In his treatise of 1470 on the Greek months, however (T. Gaza, *Peri mēnōn,* in *PG,* 19:1167–1218; see M. V. Anastos, "Pletho's Calendar and Liturgy," *Dumbarton Oaks Papers* 4 (1948): 185–305, esp. 189–190 and 215–216), Gaza erroneously claimed that Boēdromiōn straddled the Roman months of August and September (col. 1193B) and, a little later, said its Roman equivalent was a month of thirty-one days (col. 1200A). Thus, he must have equated Boēdromiōn with August, putting the date seven days back into July: the 25th.

29. Filelfo to Gaza, in *Cent-dix lettres grecques de François Filelfe,* ed. E. Legrand (Paris, 1892), 163.

30. Although Filelfo queried his use of *Turkos,* Gaza in his treatise argues that the correct form is *Turkios.* The discrepancy suggests that Gaza may not have written the treatise specifically in reply to Filelfo's query.

31. Text in P. Arcudius, *Opuscula aurea theologica* (Rome, 1630), 685–699, with "*barbaroi*" on 693. Gaza's *Laudatio canis,* sometimes described as a satirical portrait of Mehmed II, is in fact a rhetorical exercise composed in praise of dogs. Gaza refers in passing to the Turkish sultan at the start of the piece but nowhere mentions "Turks": *Laudatio canis,* in *PG,* 161:985–998, with the reference to Mehmed at 985–988. J. F. Kindstrand, "Notes on Theodorus Gaza's *Canis Laudatio,*" *Eranos: Acta Philologica Suecana* 91 (1993): 93–105.

32. Leone, "Sulla corrispondenza," 428–429, 434–435, 446–447, and "Lettere di Teodoro Gaza," 210–211, 215–216; and Gaza, *Epistole*, 107 and 112.
33. R. P. Pierling, *La Russie et l'Orient. Mariage d'un tsar* (Paris, 1891), 48–49 and 54–55; L. Pastor, *The History of the Popes from the Close of the Middle Ages*, trans. F. I. Antrobus, 40 vols. (London, 1891–1953), 4:229–230.
34. K. Setton, *The Papacy and the Levant (1204–1571)*, 4 vols. (Philadelphia, 1976), 2:314–318.
35. E.g., the contemporary report by Jacopo Ammanati-Piccolomini, *Diario consistoriale*, ed. E. Carusi, in *RIS2*, 23.3 (Milan, 1904), 141–144.
36. See J. Monfasani, *George of Trebizond* (Leiden, 1976), 201–229 for the controversy in general and 208–212 for Gaza's contributions; also C. M. Woodhouse, *George Gemistos Plethon: The Last of the Hellenes* (Oxford, 1986), 357–373; J. Hankins, *Plato in the Italian Renaissance*, 2 vols. (Leiden, 1990), 1:208–216.
37. Plethon made his attacks on Aristotle in lectures at the Council of Florence in 1439, in his tract *De differentiis* (an account of these same lectures written in Greek), and in two further letters to Bessarion on the same subject from 1441. For Gaza's replies, see Geanakoplos, "Theodore Gaza," 69–70 and 79n49; J. W. Taylor, *Theodore Gaza's De Fato* (Toronto, 1925), 5–7; Monfasani, *George of Trebizond*, 208. Gaza and others continued to write against Plethon's ideas for decades after his death c. 1454.
38. "Sumbouleutikos pros ton despotēn Theodōron peri tēs Peloponnēsou logos," in *Palaiologeia kai Peloponnesiaka*, ed. S. Lambros, 4 vols. (Athens, 1912–1930), 4:113–135. Woodhouse, *Plethon*, 91–98; E. Barker, *Social and Political Thought in Byzantium* (Oxford, 1957), 206–212. Translations and further commentary in Plethon, *Politik, Philosophie und Rhetorik im spätbyzantinischen Reich*, trans. W. Blum (Stuttgart, 1988), 151–172; Plethon, *Tratado sobre las leyes. Memorial a Teodoro*, trans. F. L. Lisi and J. Signes (Salamanca, 1995), lviii–lxxi and 135–166.
39. Plethon, Oration to Theodore, ed. Lambros, 114–115.
40. The ancient sources are discussed in the Appendix.
41. Woodhouse, *Plethon*, 92n62, and Plethon, *Politik, Philosophie und Rhetorik*, trans. Blum, 169–170n2, claim that the Paropamisidae lived near the original Turkic homeland in Inner Asia. Even less convincingly, Barker, *Social and Political Thought*, 206n1, and Lisi and Segnes, *Memorial a Teodoro*, 137n6, maintain that Plethon's allusion is accurate because the primordial Turks really did come from the Hindu Kush, which is not the case.
42. MS Vienna, Österreichische Nationalbibliothek, Hist. gr. 113; H. Hunger, *Katalog der griechischen Handschriften der österreichischen Nationalbibliothek*, 1 (Vienna, 1961), 116–118. For Plethon's early activities extracting and commenting on classical authors, see the extensive lists of his MSS by L. Allatius, in *PG*, 160:773–794, esp. 779–780; B. Knös, "Gémiste Pléthon et son souvenir," *Bulletin de l'Association Guillaume Budé* n.s. 9 (1950): 97–184, at 107–108; Woodhouse, *Plethon*, 18–21.
43. Plethon's extract, on fols. 111v–112v of the Vienna MS, is of Arrian, *Anabasis*, 5.5.2–5.6.3. The crucial part of the text is 5.5.2–3 (trans. Brunt): "Mount

Taurus . . . joins Mount Paropamisus, which the Macedonians who served with Alexander called Caucasus, with a view (so it is said) of glorifying Alexander, to make out that Alexander actually reached the farther side of Mount Caucasus, victorious in arms."

44. A. Diller, "A Geographical Treatise by Georgius Gemistos Pletho," *Isis* 27 (1937): 441–451; idem, "The Autographs of Georgius Gemistus Pletho," *Scriptorium* 10 (1956): 27–41; idem, *The Textual Tradition of Strabo* (Amsterdam, 1975), 121–124; M. V. Anastos, "Pletho, Strabo and Columbus," *Annuaire de l'Institut de Philologie et d'Histoire Orientales et Slaves* 12 (1952): 1–18; Woodhouse, *Plethon*, 181–186; Knös, "Gémiste Pléthon," 108.

45. Gaza may well have used the manuscript owned by his friend Bessarion (MS Venice, Biblioteca Marciana, gr. 407), which contains four extracts from Skylitzes on various Turkic peoples, including the main passage Gaza relies on in his treatise: E. Mioni, *Codices graeci manuscripti*, 3 vols. (Venice, 1985), 2:160–161.

46. Gaza, *De origine Turcarum*, col. 997.

47. *BT*, 1:335–340; H. Hunger, *Die hochsprachliche profane Literatur der Byzantiner*, 2 vols. (Munich, 1978), 1:389–394; "John Skylitzes," *ODB*, 3:1914; "George Kedrenos," *ODB*, 2:1118; W. Seibt, "Ioannes Skylitzes: Zur Personen des Chronisten," *Jahrbuch der österreichischer Byzantinistik* 25 (1976): 81–85; Skylitzes, *Synopsis historiarum*, ed. H. Thurn (Berlin, 1973), vii–xi. Thurn's edition is the *princeps;* the *Compendium historiarum* of the twelfth-century chronicler George Cedrenus reproduces nearly the whole text of Skylitzes without interruption (in *PG*, vols. 121–122).

48. Skylitzes, *Synopsis historiarum*, 442: "Here begin the evils done by the Turks. . ." (*arkhetai de loipon ta apo tōn Tourkōn kaka*). The excursus is on 442–445. Few of Skylitzes's sources for eleventh-century history are known (*BT*, 1:336–337), but some of his material for the 1040s seems to derive from a lost biography, or autobiography, of the Byzantine general Catacalon Cecaumenos, who led the defense against early Turkish incursions into Armenia (J. Shepard, "Scylitzes on Armenia in the 1040s, and the Role of Catacalon Cecaumenos," *Revue des Études Arméniennes* 11 [1975–1976]: 269–311; idem, "A Suspected Source of Scylitzes' *Synopsis Historion:* the Great Catacalon Cecaumenos," *Byzantine and Modern Greek Studies* 16 [1992]: 171–181). The immediate context of his excursus on the Turks is an account of Cecaumenos's activities in the East.

49. Pinto, in his edition of Gaza's *Epistole*, fails to recognize Skylitzes as the source of Gaza's information. He suggests instead that Gaza means to invoke the authority of the fifth-century B.C. geographer Skylax of Carianda (42n47) and even emends the text of the treatise to fit this hypothesis: e.g., when Gaza says "Skylax" lived four hundred years before Plethon ("*tetrakosiois etesin*," *De origine Turcarum*, col. 1001), Pinto supplies "nineteen hundred years" ("*hennakosiois kai khiliois etesin*," 104, l.3).

50. Gaza, *De origine Turcarum*, col. 997. The citation is of Skylitzes, *Synopsis historiarum*, 442.

51. Skylitzes, ibid., 443, identifies him as "*arkhēgos Persidos kai Khōrasmiōn kai Ōrētanōn kai Mēdias huparkhōn Moukhoumet . . . ho tou Imbraēl.*" These details help confirm the identification: Mahmud controlled through a semi-independent governor the oasis state of the Kwarazmshahs (*Khōrasmiōn*), at the mouth of the Oxus on the Aral Sea; by "Oretani" (*Ōrētanōn*), Skylitzes probably means the *Ōreitai*, the fish-eating people whom Alexander encountered on his return from India in 325 B.C. (mentioned by all the historians of Alexander: "Oreitai," *P-WI*, 18:942–951; J. R. Hamilton, "Alexander among the Oreitai," *Historia* 21 (1972): 603–608). Their territory is modern Baluchistan, which the Ghaznavids controlled. For a brief time they also claimed parts of northern Iraq (ancient Media, Skylitzes's *Mēdias*). For Mahmud's career and the extent of his possessions, see C. E. Bosworth, *The Ghaznavids: Their Empire in Afghanistan and Eastern Iran, 994–1040* (Edinburgh, 1963), 27–44 and 54.

52. Bosworth. *Ghaznavids*, 234–235.

53. In Skylitzes, the defeat of al-Basasiri actually appears twice, in the passage discussed here and in the next section of text (445–446), following Toghril's capture of Baghdad in 1055, which is the proper place for it. Skylitzes may have used more than one source for his account of early Seljuk history.

54. *HC*, 1:91–92, 145–147; H. Bowen, "The Last Buwayhids," *JRAS* (1929): 225–245.

55. Skylitzes, *Synopsis historiarum*, 443–444: "*tēn Karbōnitin . . . erēmon.*" The Karakum lies southwest of the Oxus, between it and Khorasan. Bosworth notes that the Seljuks frequently used it as a convenient and unassailable base for launching raids against Ghaznavid territory: *Ghaznavids*, 245–252. The origin of the term *Karbōnitis* is unclear; it may be a translation of Turkic *Karakum* ("black sand"), deriving from *karbōn* or *karbōnion* ("charcoal": *A Patristic Greek Lexicon*, ed. G.W.H. Lampe [Oxford, 1961], s.v.).

56. Historically, Mahmud's son and successor Masud sent a large army against the Seljuks in the Karakum, which was routed in the desert near the city of Nasa: Bosworth, *Ghaznavids*, 242. Skylitzes, however, continues to call the Ghaznavid ruler "Muchumet."

57. Skylitzes, *Synopsis historiarum*, 445.

58. Skylitzes also condenses and conflates disparate events in later Seljuk history: Shepard, "Scylitzes on Armenia," 280–283.

59. Skylitzes, *Synopsis historiarum*, 443.

60. Aristotle, *Meteorology*, 1.13; see Appendix, n9; and "Araxes" and "Oxus," *OCD*, 137 and 1088; "Araxes," and "Oxos," *P-WI*, 2:403 and 18:2007–2008.

61. Herodotus, *Histories*, 1.205 and 3.36.

62. Compare the verbal similarities between Skylitzes's description of the bridge in n. 59 and Herodotus, *Histories*, 1.205. The bridge across the "Araxes" seems to have had a certain fame in antiquity; it appears—and still the Oxus is really meant—as one of the future conquests of Rome on the shield of Aeneas: "indomitique Dahae, et pontem indignatus Araxes," Virgil, *Aeneid*, 8.728.

63. Skylitzes, *Synopsis historiarum*, 445: "*kata to legomenon Aspakhan.*" Cf. *Aspadana*

(Ptolemy, *Cosmographia*, 6.4.4) and *Aspada* (Anonymous Ravennas, *Cosmographia*, 2.2), reproduced in Arabic as *Isbahan* and Persian as *Isfahan*: "*Aspadana*," *P-W1*, 2:1709; "Isfahan," *EI2*, 4:100–101. But Shepard ("Scylitzes on Armenia," 282n34) suggests that "Aspachan" is no more than a corruption of the place-name Dandanqan.

64. Skylitzes, *Synopsis historiarum*, 443: "*tōi tōn Arabōn arkhonti Pissasiriōi.*" On al-Basasiri's reliance on Arab troops: *HC*, 1:145–146. The "Arabs" here should not be taken as the inhabitants of the Arabian Peninsula proper but rather the ethnically Arab population spread throughout the medieval Middle East, including Palestine, Syria, Iraq, and western Iran.

65. Skylitzes, *Synopsis historiarum*, 445.

66. Gaza, *De origine Turcarum*, col. 1000.

67. Ibid., cols. 1000–1001.

68. Ibid., col. 1001. For the reference to Aristobulus, see n. 81 below.

69. Ibid.

70. Ibid.

71. Ibid., cols. 1001–1004.

72. Ibid., col. 1000.

73. Skylitzes, *Synopsis historiarum*, 75. For the events which took place in 838, see *CMH*, 4:710–711; "al-Mu'tasim," *EI2*, 7:776.

74. A further argument against the introduction of *Kourtoi* into this passage is that al-Mu'tasim was famous for recruiting large numbers of Turkish mercenaries, so a statement that he had ten thousand of these at his disposal would be entirely in keeping with his historical reputation: O.S.A. Ismail, "Mu'tasim and the Turks," *BSOAS* 29 (1966): 12–24; H. Kennedy, *The Prophet and the Age of the Caliphates* (London, 1986), 158–160; C. E. Bosworth, "Barbarian Incursions: The Coming of the Turks into the Islamic World," in *Islamic Civilisation, 950–1150*, ed. D. S. Richards (Oxford, 1973), 1–16, esp. 1–6.

75. Skylitzes, *Synopsis historiarum*, 143; *CMH*, 4:714–715.

76. The reading *Kourtōn*, if genuine, could refer to Kurdish mercenaries who were serving in Muslim armies in these years (Kennedy, *The Prophet*, 250–251). But the Kurds are called *Kourtoi* nowhere else in Greek literature.

77. Strabo, *Geographia*, 11.13.3 and 15.3.1. "*Kurtioi*," *P-W1*, 12:205. Polybius also mentions the *Kurtioi* (5.52.5), and they appear in Livy as *Cyrtii* (42.58.13) and *Cyrtaei* (37.40.9), all with reference to their service as mercenaries in Asia Minor in the third and second centuries B.C. The *Kurtioi* are almost certainly the ancestors of the modern Kurds: "Kurds, Kurdistan," *EI2*, 5:438–486, esp. 447–449; G. R. Driver, "The Name 'Kurd' and Its Philological Connexions," *JRAS* (1923): 393–403, esp. 397.

78. Gaza, *De origine Turcarum*, col. 1004.

79. On the reputation for wildness which all the peoples of this part of the world enjoyed in antiquity, see R. Syme's exhaustive survey, "The Cadusii in History and Fiction," *Journal of Hellenic Studies* 108 (1988): 137–150.

80. Gaza, *De origine Turcarum*, col. 1004.

81. Ibid., col. 1001. The source is Strabo, *Geographia,* 15.1.17 (F. Jacoby, *Die Fragmente der griechischen Historiker* [Berlin, 1929], IIb, fragment 139.35); Gaza may have added further details from ibid, 15.1.11 and 15.2.8–10.

82. Gaza, *De origine Turcarum,* col. 1004; Strabo, *Geographia,* 15.1.26.

83. Gaza, *De origine Turcarum,* col. 1004.

84. Strabo, *Geographia,* 11.7.1.

85. A. Diller, "Strabo," in *Catalogus translationum et commentariorum. Medieval and Renaissance Latin Translations and Commentaries,* 2 (Washington D.C., 1971), 225–230; E. Fryde, *Humanism and Renaissance Historiography* (London, 1983), 72–82.

86. Diller, *Textual Tradition of Strabo,* 114–124.

87. The edition, assigned to 1469, is Hain 15086. On Gaza's work for Bussi, see M. Miglio, "Bussi, Giovanni Andrea," *DBI,* 15:565–572, esp. 568; G. A. Bussi, *Prefazioni alle edizioni di Sweynheym e Pannartz, prototipografi romani,* ed. M. Miglio (Milan, 1978), 35; M. Manoussakas and N. Staikos, *L'attività editoriale dei Greci durante il Rinascimento italiano* (Athens, 1986), 24–28. Bussi thanked Gaza for his help in his preface to the Strabo; he also continued the polemic against Gaza's old enemy, George of Trebizond, which he began in his preface to the 1469 Apuleius (Bussi, *Prefazioni,* 11–19). Gaza also helped Bussi with the text of the 1468 *Epistles* of St. Jerome (ibid., 7–8), the 1469 Aulus Gellius (20), and the 1470 Pliny, *Historia naturalis* (44). In a letter dated 17 May 1470 to Bussi, Filelfo praises him and Gaza together for their editorial work: *Epistolae* (Venice, 1502), fol. 221r; see also fols. 225r and 229r.

88. A similar connection has been suggested between the editorial work Gaza did for Bussi in preparing the 1470 *Historia naturalis* of Pliny for the press and his frequent citation of Plinian information on dogs in his *Laudatio canis,* also composed around this time: Kindstrand, "Notes," 103–105.

89. E. Mioni, "I manoscritti di Strabone della Biblioteca Marciana," in *Bisanzio e l'Italia: raccolta di studi in memoria di Agostino Pertusi* (Milan, 1982), 260–273.

90. S. Lilla, "Gli excerpta di Strabone fatti da Demetrio Raul Cabakés nel codice Vat. gr. 2238," *Scriptorium* 33 (1979): 68–75.

91. Gaza, *De origine Turcarum,* col. 1004.

92. *BT,* 2, s.v.; also *CMH,* 4:566; text in Skylitzes, *Synopsis historiarum,* 176.

93. Gaza, *De origine Turcarum,* col. 1004.

94. Ibid., cols. 1004–1005.

95. Woodhouse, *Plethon,* 158, 226–227.

96. Cf. Pertusi, "Primi studi," 470, where Filelfo is said never to have mentioned Gaza's information.

97. Accounts of the controversy can be found in C. De Rosminis, *Vita di Francesco Filelfo Tolentino,* 3 vols. (Milan, 1808), 3:40–42; F. Gabotto and A. Badini Confalonieri, *Vita di Giorgio Merula* (Alessandria, 1894; reprint from *Rivista di storia, arte, archeologia di provincia di Alessandria* 2 [1893]), 115–118; L. A. Sheppard, "A Fifteenth-Century Humanist, Francesco Filelfo," *The Library,* 4th ser., 16 (1935): 16–20; Gualdo Rosa, "Filelfo e i Turchi," 114; Pertusi, "Primi

studi," 470; R. G. Adam, "Filelfo at the Court of Milan," Ph.D. dissertation, Oxford University, 1974, 105–106; and Hankins, "Renaissance Crusaders," 137–139.

98. Sheppard, "Filelfo," 16–17; Gabotto and Badini Confalonieri, *Merula,* 116.

99. Filelfo's letter is now lost, but we know of its contents because Merula quoted from it in the next letter in the exchange. Writing on 7 October 1480 to Bartolomeo Chalco, newly appointed secretary to the duke of Milan, Merula wrote, "Lest I perhaps seem . . . a frivolous imitator of *another* person's petulance . . . I shall reproduce below a sample of [Filelfo's] words to Giustiniani: 'The letter enclosed with these items contains an exhortation to launch a war against the *Turci,* whom certain ignorant compatriots of yours call *Turcae*'" (Giorgio Merula, *Duae epistolae contra Franciscum Filelfum* [Venice: Nicolaus Girardengus de Novis, after 13 Dec. 1480], *IGI* 6379, sig. a1v.) Diedo was Venetian ambassador to Milan from October 1479 to June 1480 ("Diedo, Francesco," *DBI,* 39:769–774, at 771), so Filelfo must have written to him after his return to Venice in June and before 7 October 1480, the date of Merula's letter defending himself against Filelfo's charge. Filelfo enclosed with his letter a crusade exhortation, which Adam identifies as a letter to Doge Giovanni Mocenigo, 13 Sept. 1480 (MS Bologna, Biblioteca Universitaria, 2948.36, fols. 190bisr–194v).

100. Merula, *Bellum Scodrense* ([Venice]: Gabriele di Pietro, [not before 10 Sept. 1474]), *IGI* 6376, fols. 2v, line 6; 10v, line 5; 11r, line 8. Cf. Gabotto and Badini Confalonieri, *Merula,* 116–117 and, following them, Adam, "Filelfo," 263n208, who assert that this work was the cause of the quarrel.

101. Merula, *Duae epistolae,* sig. a5v: "Scripsi saepius ad Bartholmaeum Chalcum . . . [et] gentem *Turcas* appellavi."

102. F. Babinger, *Mehmed the Conqueror and His Time,* ed. W. Hickman and trans. R. Mannheim (Princeton, 1978), 389–400.

103. Merula, *Duae epistolae,* sig. a1r–v.

104. Pomponius Mela, *Chorographia,* 1.116: "Regna Amazonum, fecundos pabulo, ad alia steriles nudosque campos tenent. Budini Gelonon urbem ligneam habitant. Iuxta Thyssagetae, Turcaeque vastas silvas occupant alunturque venando."

105. Merula, *Duae epistolae,* sig. a1r.

106. Francesco Filelfo, *Invectiva in Georgium Merulam* [Padua: Matthaeus Cerdonis, after 4 June 1481], *BMC* 7:924, sigs. a1r–a2r. Gabotto and Badini Confalonieri also found a copy of this letter in a Leipzig manuscript and reproduce its text in full (*Merula,* 117–119). Unfortunately, both their version and the incunable text are beset with errors.

107. Coined by Filelfo, apparently, from Greek *khezō* ("to defecate"); cf. his deliberate misspelling of Merula's name as *Merdula* throughout the letter.

108. Filelfo, *Invectiva,* sig. a1r.

109. Filelfo presumably means such names as *Geta, Scytha,* and *Dalmata,* which Merula had produced from Mela; on the other hand, he may be trying to ex-

plain the appearance of the particular spellings *Thyssagetae* and *Turcae* in some (but not, he implies, all) manuscripts of Mela.

110. Filelfo, *Invectiva*, sig. a1r–v.

111. E.g., Pomponius Mela, *Chorographia: Gynaecocratumenoe* (1.116); *Hamaxobioe* (2.2); *Hesperioe* (3.96). F. E. Romer, *Pomponius Mela's Description of the World* (Ann Arbor, 1998), viii–ix.

112. Incidentally, the spelling *Budinoe*, which Filelfo gives at the start of the passage he quotes, is not attested in any critical edition of Mela's text either: the manuscript tradition uniformly gives *Budini*.

113. The Greeks called the Italians *Italoi*, but no Latin form "Italoe" is found, in Mela or anywhere else. The Greek name for the Etruscans was *Tursēnoi* or *Turrēnoi*; no Greek form of the homegrown Italian names "Tusci," "Thusci" or "Etrusci" is recorded, nor do any of these names appear in Latin with the ending *-oe*.

114. Filelfo, *Invectiva*, sig. a1v.

115. L. Labowsky, *Bessarion's Library and the Biblioteca Marciana* (Rome, 1979), 27–28, 50, 57–59. Cf. V. Fera, "Itinerari filologici del Filelfo," in *Francesco Filelfo nel quinto centenario della morte (1981)* (Padua, 1986), 89–135, at 134–136, who cites this passage as proof that Filelfo did actually visit the library to consult manuscripts.

116. Adam, "Filelfo," 105.

117. Merula, *Duae epistolae*, sigs a1v–b4v. Gabotto and Badini Confalonieri (*Merula*, 117n3), relying on erroneous information from Mattaire, misdate the letter to 12 September 1480.

118. Merula, *Duae epistolae*, sig. a6r–v.

119. Ibid., sig. a6v: "Legat paulo diligentius Plinium apud quem *Tissagetae* et *Turcae* habentur." The passage of Pliny (*Historia naturalis*, 6.19) which Merula cites is a list of Scythian tribes, probably derived from the same source as Mela.

120. Ibid., sig. a6v.

121. Ibid., sigs. a6v–b1r.

122. Hankins, "Renaissance Crusaders," 137–139, relates their controversy to the larger fifteenth-century debate over the forms *Teucri* and *Turci*, thus endowing their comments with political implications which I do not think can really apply.

123. Merula, *Duae epistolae*, sig. a1r: "hic importunae inventionis magister."

124. Ibid., sigs. a1r–v and a6r. Merula ascribes the comment to a letter Filelfo sent to his friend Marco Aurelio, possibly concerning the 1474 siege. Merula himself commented on the names in his *Bellum Scodrense*, fol. 2r: "Urbem ipsam incolae suo et prisco vocabulo *Scodram*, Itali nunc *Scutarum* voce nova et barbara appellant."

125. Merula, *Duae epistolae*, sig. b1r–v. Pliny, *Historia naturalis*, 3.99–103.

126. Filelfo, *Invectiva*, sig. a1v: "Merdula noster Chezergius . . . grammaticulus imperitus."

127. Merula, *Duae epistolae*, sigs. a5v–a6r.

128. Ibid., sig. b2r.
129. Merula's *Bellum Scodrense* describes the siege of that city in meticulous detail, and Filelfo wrote something (although we do not know what) about the city in a letter to the Venetian Marco Aurelio (n. 125 above); Merula wrote letters to Bartolomeo Chalco about the Turkish sieges of both Rhodes and Otranto (n. 102), while Filelfo's letter to Doge Mocenigo (which I have not seen) probably discusses Turkish activity in the summer of 1480: see n. 100 above.
130. The question of whether Merula was right—whether Mela really did describe *Turcae* and, if so, whether these people were Turks—remains unresolved. All extant manuscripts reproduce the reading, and Pliny preserves the almost identical form *Tyrcae*. As early as the sixteenth century, however, it was recognized that the source for both these passages was either Herodotus or an earlier Greek authority used by him (Heath, "Renaissance Humanists," 457–459). Herodotus mentions among the peoples of Scythia both *Thussagetai* and *Iurkai*, with emphasis on their devotion to hunting (*Histories*, 4.22), suggesting that Mela's *Turcae* were in fact *Iurcae*. Recently, however, the Turkologist Denis Sinor has suggested that Herodotus himself may have got the name wrong and that Mela and Pliny were correct in calling these people *Turcae*. If Sinor is right, then a branch of the Altaic Turkic peoples, perhaps even proto-Türks, may well have been living in antiquity in the forest zone north of the Black Sea (Sinor, "Establishment and Dissolution," 285; but Sinor does not repeat his suggestion in a more recent essay, "The Türk Empire," in *History of the Civilizations of Central Asia*, 3, ed. B. A. Litvinsky [Paris, 1996], 327–335).
131. William of Tyre, *Chronicon*, ed. R.B.C. Huygens (Turnhout, 1986), 114–117.
132. On the lost *Historia Tartarorum* of Simon of St. Quentin, see G. G. Guzman, "Simon of Saint Quentin and the Dominican Mission to the Mongol Baiju," *Speculum* 46 (1971): 232–249; idem, "Simon of Saint Quentin as Historian of the Mongols and Seljuk Turks," *Medievalia et Humanistica* 3 (1972): 155–178. See P. Pelliot, *Notes on Marco Polo*, 3 vols. (Paris, 1963), 2:864–865, for "Turquie"; *Mandeville's Travels*, ed. Malcolm Letts, 2 vols. (London, 1950), 1:176–177 and 2:374 for "Turquestan." Mandeville's source was the *Flos historiarum terrae orientis* of Hetoum of Korikos, discussed below.
133. Aeneas Sylvius, for one, expressed serious doubts about the value of medieval or contemporary travelers' reports in his *Asia:* see Anastos, "Pletho's Calendar and Liturgy," 3–6; N. Casella, "Pio II tra geografia e storia: La 'Cosmografia,'" *Archivio della Società Romana di Storia patria* 95 (1972): 67–68, 77, 84; M. Meserve, "From Samarkand to Scythia: Reinventions of Asia in Renaissance Geography and Political Thought," in *Pius II: el piu expeditivo pontifice. Selected Studies on Aeneas Silvius Piccolomini (1405–1464)*, eds Z.R.W.M. von Martels and A. Vanderjagt (Leiden, 2003).
134. That is, the Khazars as seen by Syriac apocalyptic writers, especially ps.-Methodius, rather than those portrayed in Theophanes' more measured account.
135. On the negative image of barbarians in Christian thought, see the comments of

A. O. Lovejoy and G. Boas, *Primitivism and Related Ideas in Antiquity* (Baltimore, 1935), 339, 342–444; W. R. Jones, "The Image of the Barbarian in Medieval Europe," *Comparative Studies in Society and History* 13 (1971).

136. E.g., Hankins, "Renaissance Crusaders," 123–124, 142, 145–146; N. Bisaha, "New Barbarian or Worthy Adversary? Renaissance Humanist Constructs of the Ottoman Turks," in *Western Views of Islam in Medieval and Early Modern Europe: Perception of Other*, eds. D. R. Blanks and M. Frassetto (New York, 1999), 187–194.

137. R. Schwoebel, *The Shadow of the Crescent: The Renaissance Image of the Turk* (Nieuwkoop, 1967), 148; C. Göllner, "Legenden von der skythischen, trojanischen und kaukasischen Abstammung der Türken im 15. und 16. Jahrhundert," *Revue des études sud-est européens* 15 (1977): 50–51. Valla completed the translation in 1455: G. Mancini, *Vita di Lorenzo Valla* (Florence, 1891), 321–323; S. I. Camporeale, *Lorenzo Valla: umanesimo e teologia* (Florence, 1972), 202–203 and 447–448.

138. F. Cardini, "La crociata, mito politico," *Il Pensiero Politico* 8 (1975): 31–32; Hankins, "Renaissance Crusaders," 145–146; K. Fleet, "Italian Perceptions of the Turks in the Fourteenth and Fifteenth Centuries," *Journal of Mediterranean Studies* 5 (1995): 167, 169; Bisaha, "'New Barbarian,'" 189; J. Helmrath, "Pius II und die Türken," in *Europa und die Türken*, eds. B. Guthmüller and W. Kühlmann (Tübingen, 2000), 106.

139. Even though Filelfo owned a copy of the *Histories* in Greek, purchased during his stay in Constantinople, and at least a half-dozen other manuscript copies of the Greek text are recorded in Italy during the period considered, including one owned by Gaza's and Sagundino's patron and friend Bessarion. R. R. Bolgar, *The Classical Heritage and Its Beneficiaries* (Cambridge, 1954), 476–477.

140. The excurses on Turkish origins which he included in his oration at the Congress of Mantua and in *Europa* and *Asia* show little change from his writings of 1452–1454 except for the addition of Sagundino's information. It is, of course, impossible to prove that Aeneas did not know the text of Herodotus in translation. He actually quotes from the *Histories* on occasion: once before Valla's translation was done (in his 1452 oration for Frederick III's coronation, *Opera omnia* [Basel, 1551], 929, an aphoristic sentence which he could have found in a commonplace book) and twice afterward (geographical information, cited in the *Asia*: Casella, "Pio II," 76). Casella (99) notes two manuscript copies of Valla's translation in the Vatican Library which may be associated with Aeneas: one with the Piccolomini family arms but nothing to connect it to him personally; another dated Jan. 1463, by which time he had written all of his many accounts of the Scythian origins of the Turks.

141. A. Momigliano, "The Place of Herodotus in the History of Historiography," in *Studies in Historiography* (London, 1966), 127–142; cf. Schwoebel, *Shadow*, 148, who takes Momigliano's conclusions as evidence for Herodotus's popularity among and influence on the quattrocento humanists, particularly Sagundino, Gaza, Filelfo, and Aeneas Sylvius. See also Momigliano, "Polybius between the

English and the Turks," in *Sesto contributo alla storia degli studi classici*, 2 vols. (Rome, 1980), 1:125–141, at 131.

142. François Hartog argues that Herodotus actually describes the Scythians in such detail in Book IV in order to present them as a *positive* (i.e., brave, hardy, and virtuous) counterpart to the blustering and cowardly Persians: F. Hartog, *The Mirror of Herodotus: The Representation of the Other in the Writing of History*, trans. J. Lloyd (Berkeley, 1988), esp. 6–7, 32–33, 35–40.

143. Recent considerations of the issue include E. Hall, *Inventing the Barbarian: Greek Self-Definition through Tragedy* (Oxford, 1989); *The Birth of the European Identity: The Europe-Asia Contrast in Greek Thought, 490–322 B.C.*, ed. H. A. Khan (Nottingham, 1994).

4. Translations of Empire

1. N. Daniel, *Islam and the West: The Making of an Image* (Edinburgh, 1960), 79–108; idem, *The Arabs and Mediaeval Europe*, 2d ed. (London, 1979), 111–118, 232–237; R. W. Southern, *Western Views of Islam in the Middle Ages* (Cambridge, Mass., 1962), 27–32; M. Rodinson, "The Western Image and Western Studies of Islam," in *The Legacy of Islam*, 2d ed., eds. J. Schacht with C. E. Bosworth (Oxford, 1974), 9–62, esp. 9–23; B. Z. Kedar, *Crusade and Mission: European Approaches toward the muslims* (Princeton, 1984), 85–93; S. Luchitskaja, "The Image of Muhammad in Latin Chronography of the Twelfth and Thirteenth Centuries," *Journal of Medieval History* 26 (2000): 115–126; J. V. Tolan, *Saracens: Islam in the Medieval European Imagination* (New York, 2002), 135–169.

2. S. Runciman, "Byzantium and the Crusades," in *The Meeting of Two Worlds: Cultural Exchange between East and West during the Period of the Crusades*, ed. V. P. Gross (Kalamazoo, Mich., 1986), 15–22; idem, *HC*, 1:104–105. For Urban II's sermon at Clermont proclaiming the crusade as a universal campaign against all Muslims, see ibid., 237–249. The metrical *Gesta* of Robert Guiscard, written by William of Apulia after 1085 but before the launch of the First Crusade in 1095, offers an interesting contrast. Here the description of the Seljuk invasion of Anatolia recalls the perspective of the Byzantine historians: Guillaume de Pouille, *La Geste de Robert Guiscard*, ed. M. Mathieu (Palermo, 1961), 164:

> Horum temporibus Turcos orientis ab oris
> Ingressos fugit gens territa Christicolarum
> Qui Romaniae loca deliciosa colebant
> Maxima pars horum ruit interfecta nefandis
> Turcorum gladiis, et captis urbibus omnis
> Subditus his populus dans vectigalia fugit.

After 1095, Latin authors rarely expressed such interest in the ill effects of Seljuk incursions into Byzantine territory.

3. D. C. Munro, "The Western Attitude towards Islam during the Period of the Crusades," *Speculum* 6 (1931): 329–341; W. M. Watt, "Muhammad in the Eyes of the West," *Boston University Journal* 22 (1974): 61–69; collected studies in

M.-T. d'Alverny, *Connaissance de l'Islam dans l'Occident Medievale,* ed. C.S.F. Burnett (Aldershot, 1994), and *Medieval Christian Perceptions of Islam: A Book of Essays,* ed. J. V. Tolan (New York, 1996).

4. Guibert of Nogent (writing c. 1106–1109) was probably the earliest: his *Dei gesta per Francos* (ed. R.B.C. Huygens [Turnhout, 1996], 94–100) was a revised and enlarged version of the anonymous *Gesta Francorum.* He credited no written sources for his life of Muhammad but claimed to rely on oral reports. The second is Hugh of Fleury (writing 1108–1109), whose *Chronicon,* in two redactions (one composed before and one after his discovery of Anastasius's translation of Theophanes' *Chronographia*), is edited in part by Kedar, *Crusade and Mission,* 208–210, and discussed at 33 and 87. More extracts from the later redaction are in Hugh of Fleury, *Chronicon, PL,* 158:805–854. A. Wilmart, "L'histoire ecclésiastique composée par Hugh de Fleury et ses destinataires," *Revue Bénédictine* 50 (1938): 293–295; N. Lettinck, "Pour une édition critique de l'*Historia Ecclesiastica* de Hughes de Fleury," *Revue Bénédictine* 91 (1981): 386–397. Sigebert of Gembloux (writing c. 1112; *Chronica,* in *PL,* 160:118) was probably the most influential of the three, being a source for, among others, Vincent of Beauvais.

5. Guibert of Nogent, *Dei gesta,* 98–99.

6. Hugh of Fleury, second redaction, ed. Kedar, *Crusade and Mission,* 208; for his use of Theophanes in Anastasius's translation, ibid., 86–87. The account of the rise of the Arabs and their early conquests is in Anastasius, *Chronographia tripartita,* in Theophanes, *Chronographia,* ed. C. de Boor, 2 vols. (Leipzig, 1883), 208–214.

7. Hugh of Fleury, *Chronicon,* ed. Kedar, 210.

8. Sigebert, *Chronica,* col. 119: "[A.D. 632] Saraceni qui hactenus fuerant sub Persarum regno, eos bello victos versa vice sub suo redigunt dominio. Ab hinc pro regno Persarum titulandum est regnum Saracenorum."

9. E.g., Josephus, Eusebius, John of Damascus, and Isidore of Seville, cited by Southern, *Western Views,* 15–19; Rodinson, "The Western Image," 9–10; Daniel, *Islam,* 14; Kedar, *Crusade and Mission,* 91.

10. Daniel, *Arabs and Mediaeval Europe,* 118.

11. Hugh of Fleury, *Chronicon,* ed. Kedar, 208: "Saraceni, qui et Turci dicuntur."

12. Ibid., 209–210. For Khadiga as the *domina* of Khorasan, see Daniel, *Islam,* 324; idem, *Arabs and Mediaeval Europe,* 232–233.

13. Alan Murray explores biblical and contemporary literary traditions which may also have influenced the choice of Khorasan as the original home of the Saracens: "*Coroscane:* Homeland of the Saracens in the *Chansons de geste* and the Historiography of the Crusades," in *Aspects de l'épopée romane: mentalités, idéologies, intertextualités,* eds. H. van Dijk and W. Noomen (Groningen, 1995), 177–184. Byzantine authors, with their fondness for classicizing vocabulary, had also called the Seljuk Turks on their emergence from Khorasan "Persai."

14. And he adds an interesting detail—that their homeland of Khorasan was once known as the Caucasus. Guibert aspired to a refined style and elevated treat-

ment of his subject matter and found it necessary to explain why he used modern proper names instead of their classical equivalents: "The names of men, provinces and cities presented me with considerable difficulties . . . For example we inveigh every day against the Turks, and we call Khorasan by its new name; when the old word has been forgotten and has almost disappeared, no use of ancient sources, even if they were available, has been made: I have chosen to use no word unless it were in common use. Had I used Parthians instead of Turks, as some have suggested, Caucasus and not Khorasan, in the pursuit of authenticity, I might have been misunderstood." Guibert, *Deeds of God*, trans. Levine, 26, from *Dei gesta*, ed. Huygens, 82–83.

15. Ibid., 36, from *Dei gesta*, ed. Huygens, 100. See also 83.
16. Guibert probably refers to either the Seljuk overthrow of the Ghaznavids or their usurpation of the Buyids' role as protectors of the Abbasid caliphate.
17. *Dei gesta*, ed. Huygens, 100–101 and 158–159.
18. William of Tyre, *Chronicon*, 105: "doctrina pestilens."
19. Ibid., 106–107.
20. William of Tyre, *A History of Deeds Done beyond the Sea by William Archbishop of Tyre*, trans. E. A. Babcock and A. C. Krey, 2 vols. (New York, 1943), 70–71; text in *Chronicon*, 114.
21. Ibid., 114–115.
22. Ibid., 117.
23. The name "Türkmen" (in English, commonly "Turcoman") is first used in eleventh-century Arabic sources to describe members of the Oğuz Turk confederation—possibly only those who converted to Islam—around the Oxus and Aral Sea (i.e., modern-day Turkmenistan). The derivation and significance of the name remain uncertain: B. Kellner-Heinkele, "Türkmen," *EI2*, 10:682–685.
24. William of Tyre, *Chronicon*, 117.
25. The Mamluks, Kipchak Turks from the southern Russian steppes, served the Ayyubids in Egypt as a slave militia; after the Mongols defeated the Ayyubids in 1250, the Mamluks seized power in Egypt and Syria, where they remained until their overthrow by the Ottomans in the early sixteenth century.
26. William of Tripoli, *Notitia de Machometo. De statu Sarracenorum*, ed. P. Engels (Würzburg, 1992), 296.
27. Vincent of Beauvais, *Speculum historiale* 30.139–147, 150–151; 31.26–28 in *Speculum maius* (Douai, 1624), 4.1280–1284, 1294–1295. Vincent wrote in the 1250s and 1260s, only a few years after the first Mongol invasions: Guzman, "Simon of Saint Quentin and the Dominican Mission"; idem, "Simon of Saint Quentin as Historian," 162–167.
28. Roger Bacon, *Moralis philosophia*, ed. E. Massa (Zurich, 1953), 189–192, cited by Southern, *Western Views*, 58.
29. The text (in both French and Latin) is in *Flos historiarum terre orientis*, ed. C. Kohler, in *RHC Arm*, 2:255–363. See ibid., 1:469–470 and 769; D. D. Bundy, "Het'um's *La Flor des Estoires de la terre d'Orient:* A Study in Medieval Armenian

Historiography and Propaganda," *Revue des études armeniénnes* n.s. 20 (1986–1987): 223–235; Hetoum, *A Lytell Cronycle. Richard Pynson's Translation (c. 1520) of* La Fleur des histoires de la terre d'Orient *(c. 1307),* ed. G. Burger (Toronto, 1988), ix–xxix. Both Latin and French redactions of the text are found in dozens of manuscript collections of Oriental travel literature (*RHC Arm,* 2:lxxxv–cxxxi), many favored by such aristocratic book collectors as Philip the Bold of Burgundy, the dukes of Anjou and Berry, and Sigismund of Hungary. The Florentine chronicler Giovanni Villani recommended the work to readers interested in Eastern affairs (D. Webb, "The Decline and Fall of Eastern Christianity: A Fifteenth-Century View," *Bulletin of the Institute of Historical Research* 49 [1976]: 198–216, at 205). Extracts were copied into the *Travels* of Sir John Mandeville; the work was also used by the cosmographical poet Fazio degli Uberti.

30. Book I surveys the kingdoms and peoples of Asia; Book II rehearses Eastern history from the birth of Christ to the arrival of the Mongols in the 1240s; Book III reviews the Mongol conquests and their alliance with Armenia; Book IV sets out a plan for a joint Mongol-Christian crusade to free the Holy Land, including a history of the Mamluks and their territories in Egypt.
31. Hetoum, *Flos,* 274 and 275.
32. Ibid., 274.
33. Ibid., 276. In Hetoum, as in most medieval chronicles, "Persia" indicates all the lands once subject to the ancient Achaemenid and Sassanian dynasties—including the Iranian plateau, Mesopotamia, and northern Syria.
34. The correct sequence of events was not unknown to Latin historians: William of Tripoli, for instance, correctly dates the establishment of the Abbasid caliphate to the reign of the fifteenth caliph, the eponymous "Hebbas."
35. Ibid., 276.
36. The name gained currency only in the eleventh century (see above).
37. Tabari, *Chronique,* trans. H. Zotenberg, 4 vols. (Paris, 1958), 3:502–511.
38. The Eastern Türk confederation outlasted that of the Western Türks by more than a century: D. M. Dunlop, *A History of the Jewish Khazars* (Princeton, 1954), 54–55.
39. Hetoum's reliance on an Arabic tradition for this story may be confirmed by the fact that in his version the river the Turks cross is not the Oxus but the Phison, a reference quite inexplicable at first glance. The Phison was best known in the West as one of the four rivers of Paradise mentioned in Genesis (2:11); it was usually equated with the Ganges or Indus, or occasionally even the Danube (J. K. Wright, *Geographical Lore of the Time of the Crusades* [New York, 1925], 72). In medieval Armenian geography, too, the Ganges was called "Phison," but a second name, "Gehon," was also known. (In one seventh-century Armenian gazetteer, the Ganges is called both "Phison" and "Gehon": *The Geography of Ananias of Širak [Ašxarhac'oyc']: The Long and Short Recensions,* trans. and comm. R. H. Hewsen [Wiesbaden, 1992], 75 and *ad indicem s.v.* "Ganges.") If Hetoum, or an earlier Armenian author used by Hetoum, derived his infor-

mation on Yazdgerd's appeal to the Turks from an Arabic source, then it is quite likely that he misinterpreted the Arabic name for the Oxus— "Djihoun"—as indicating the river known in Armenian as the "Gehon," i.e., the Ganges. On this hypothesis, Hetoum, or his source, then substituted the more common Armenian name for the Ganges—"Phison"—for what he imagined to be the "Gehon."

40. Hetoum, *Flos*, 277: "Turquemanni autem, qui nullam legem penitus sequebantur, mandatis califfi faciliter consenserunt, et effecti perfidi Sarreceni."

41. Ibid., 277: "Sciverunt enim Turquemanni sub dominio Sarracenorum sagaciter pertransire, quousque rebellionis materiam invenirent."

42. Romanus IV Diogenes, who actually ruled a little later, 1068–1071.

43. Hetoum, *Flos*, 277.

44. Ibid., 279: "Solimanssa . . . fuit primus christiane fidei inimicus qui se belliger opposuit peregrinis."

45. Ibid., 279: "Obiit Alp Asalem, imperator Turquorum, et successit sibi . . . Melecssa. Et iste Melecssa mandavit precipiendo Artot, soldano Messapotamiae, et Solimanssa, soldano Turquie . . . ad obsidendam civitatem Antiochie"; 279–280: "Et tempore illo quo passagium Godoffridi de Boliono per Turquiam transivit, Belkiaroc erat imperator Persarum, et Solimanssa erat soldanus Turquie."

46. Ibid., 280: "Et ille soldanus Turquie tenuit pacifice regnum suum usque ad adventum Tatarorum, a quibus fuit postmodum debellatus."

47. This information was known to Italians as well. The Venetian Andrea Dandolo, writing in the mid-fourteenth century, reproduces a great deal of information from earlier chronicles on the rise of the Seljuks (whom he identifies as Persians) and their triumph at Manzikert: e.g., A. Dandolo, *Chronica per extensum descripta*, ed. E. Pastorello, in *RIS2*, 12.1 (Bologna, 1942): 214–215.

48. R. Arbesmann, "Andrea Biglia, Augustinian Friar and Humanist (†1435)," *Analecta Augustiniana* 28 (1965): 154–185; "Biglia, Andrea," *DBI*, 10:413–415; J. C. Schnaubelt, "Andrea Biglia (c. 1394–1435), Augustinian Friar and Renaissance Humanist," Ph.D. dissertation, Catholic University of America, 1976; idem, "Prolegomena to the Edition of the Extant Works of Andrea Biglia, O.S.A. (†1435)," *Analecta Augustiniana* 40 (1977): 141–184, esp. 143–145; idem, "Andrea Biglia (c. 1394–1435), His Life and Writings," *Augustiniana* 43 (1993): 103–159.

49. Biglia's *Commentaries* have not been published, although Schnaubelt produced a critical edition and translation of the dedicatory letter to Book I ("Life and Writings," 144–145, 156–158). The text survives in two late manuscripts (MSS Vatican City, Biblioteca Apostolica Vaticana, Vat. lat. 5298, fols. 83r–118v and Rome, Biblioteca Angelica, 1136 [S 4 5]). Webb, "Decline and Fall"; Schnaubelt, "Prolegomena," 161, and "Life and Writings," 145–146; G. Fioravanti, "*Commentarii Historici de defectu fidei et Orientis* di Andrea Biglia," *Rinascimento*, 2d ser. 19 (1979): 241–246.

50. D. Webb, "Andrea Biglia at Bologna, 1424–7: A Humanist Friar and the Troubles of the Church," *Bulletin of the Institute of Historical Research* 49 (1976): 41–59.

51. Aeneas was to recall, in his *De viris aetate sua claris:* "Hoc tempore etiam Andreas Mediolanensis ex ordine Augustinensium, quem Senis audivi, historiarum scriptor floruit." Cited by Schnaubelt, "Life and Writings," 140n185.

52. Fioravanti, *"Commentarii Historici,"* 246. Filelfo moved to Siena in Dec. 1434: L. De Feo Corso, "Il Filelfo in Siena," *Bulletino senese di storia patria,* n.s. 11 (1940): 181–209, at 186.

53. MS Vat. lat. 5298, fol. 83r: "Hortatusque est, si quid otii haberem, haec alio quodam scribendi genere facerem, nostris ut essent notiora."

54. Webb, "Decline and Fall," 201–205. The conciliarist cardinals to whom Biglia dedicated books were Jean de la Rochetaillée (Book I), Branda Castiglione (Book II), Domenico Capranica (Books III and IV) and Gerardo Landriani (Book V). Books VI and VII were dedicated to Antonio da Pisa, a commander of the Milanese army; Books VIII and IX to the imperial chancellor Kaspar Schlick; Book X to Eugenius IV; Book XI to the unofficial leader of the cardinals at Basel, Giuliano Cesarini; and Book XII to a "Batista," whom Webb identifies as a Genoese diplomat in Sigismund's service.

55. Ibid., 198–201. Filippo Maria was hoping for Sigismund's support in the war over Lucca, sparked by the Florentine capture of the city in 1429, in which Florence, Siena, Genoa, Venice, and Milan were all embroiled. The conciliarist cardinals at Basel also pinned their hopes on imperial support against Rome. Sigismund himself, while appreciative of these various appeals to his authority, wanted above all to secure his coronation by Eugenius IV, who opposed the claims of the cardinals at Basel and, as a Venetian, had little sympathy for those of Milan.

56. Ibid., 213–216. Schnaubelt ("Life and Writings," 145–146), unaware of the multiple dedications of the work, maintains less convincingly that Biglia wrote the *Commentarii* for Sigismund alone and that his choice of subject reflects Sigismund's longstanding interest in combating the Turkish advance.

57. Webb, "Decline and Fall," 210. Mignanelli attended the Council of Constance in 1416 to help with the interpretation of various Eastern languages; he wrote the biographies for the instruction of the council. W. J. Fischel, "A New Latin Source on Tamerlane's Conquest of Damascus, 1400/01 (B. de Mignanelli's *Vita Tamerlani,* 1416)," *Oriens* 9 (1956): 201–232; idem, *"Ascensus Barcoch:* A Latin Biography of the Mamluk Sultan Barquq of Egypt (d. 1399) written by B. de Mignanelli in 1416," *Arabica* 6 (1959): 57–74, 157–172.

58. Vat. lat. 5298, fol. 83v.

59. Ibid.: "Imperium tum habebat Heraclius . . . non tamen iusta apud barbaros autoritas imperii . . . Tanquam fastidio hominibus barbaris fuisset quod Romanum diceretur imperium."

60. Ibid.

61. Webb, "Decline and Fall," 207–209 and 211–213.
62. Vat. lat. 5298, fol. 108r–v: "Sic cecidimus mutata Romani imperii sede, quasi simul ac Romana cepit esse ecclesia, fides desierit esse catholica . . . Sic se res habet, postea quam Constantinopolim fasces abiere, claves deserte sunt . . . Coepit inde pessum ire Romanum imperium ac prorsus res Romana dissolvi ubi nec liberalitatis memoria nec ordinum tituli fuere."
63. Ibid., fol. 83v: "Hinc data late licentia *imperii simul ac fidei* hostibus, quicumque vellent, *iugum ac religionem* detrectare; quo factum est postea, ut *utriusque* vires plus in hoc orbe valerent, coniunctatis *fide ac potentia* principum." The italics are mine. Elsewhere, the Arabs attack Damascus, inspired "simul et ira et superstitione" (fol. 83v). During the siege of Antioch they are exhorted to fight for Muhammad, "beato prophete ac regi suo" and to show themselves "ut in templis pios ita in armis fortes" (fol. 84r). Later the inhabitants of Asia Minor submit to Arab rule, "partim novitate superstitionis seducti, partim potentia territi" (fol. 85v). Likewise, they capture Egypt both because the princes there fear the Arabs' military might and because the people have embraced Islam: "Nihil enim difficile, regibus aut metu ad vim inclinantibus aut per populos deditis, late enim priusquam vires accederent, superstitio gentes occupaverat" (ibid.).
64. Ibid., fol. 83v. The original source of the story is Theophanes (Anastasius, *Chronographia tripartita,* 210).
65. Ibid.: "Huius igitur quem diximus pseudoprophetae superstitionibus imbuti, primum ausi sunt discedere ab imperio et adversum finitimas arma capere . . . Stimulabat, ut diximus, et augebat iram ac perfidiam superstitio, qua nulla ad vim atque ad sanguinem res est acrior."
66. Ibid.: "Ita simul et ira et superstitione imbuti Saraceni nominis libertatem conclamant."
67. E.g., Heraclius is weak because of both "infirmitate virium" and "angustia nominis." Until his time, Christianity thrived in the East: "Nomen ad id tempus Christiane religionis in oriente preclarum et invidiosum manserat"; the lowly Arabs enjoyed "non . . . ullum usquam nomen, non pars ulla orientalis glorie" (all on fol. 83v). Elsewhere they are described as "Saraceni quorum nullum umquam fuerat nomen" (fol. 85v). The Persians, by contrast, have much to lose: "Conati tamen Persae invictum nomen regni adversus Arabum temulentiam defendere"; while the Turcomans are described as "gens ferox ac Saraceni nominis inimica" (both on fol. 85r). The Seljuks invade Persia because "nolle Saracenum nomen in Asya eminere" (fol. 86v); after the Mongols occupy Asia Minor, a Muslim counterattack is launched, "non difficile sperans posse ex omni Phrygia Tartarum nomen pelli" (fol. 91r–v).
68. Ibid., fol. 86r: "Puduit aliquando Sarracenos dici qui possent Dardani aut Phriges appellari; iam vero Teucri appellantur quos vulgo Turcos vocant."
69. Ibid., fol. 108v: "Per longas inde ac varias successiones, imperium vulgatum est cum, ut fit, purpura potentioris esset, ex qua orti nunc Henrici et Conradi, nunc Othones et Ludovici, ceterique iis nominibus illustres, Romanum imperium sine ullo romanae rei fastigio tenuere."

70. Ibid., fol. 83v: "Nec dubitaverunt cum Arabes clariori nomine dici possent, se pro veteribus Saracenis Saracenos [d]epresso et quasi toto orbe desueto atque abhominando nomine appellare."

71. Ibid., fols. 83v–84v: he scorns Muhammad's doctrine as a pastiche of Christian and Jewish theology, condemns the Prophet for encouraging worship of himself (a common medieval misperception), and repeatedly refers to the mosques established in conquered cities as temples dedicated to Muhammad. (Here he adds an interesting observation: that in encouraging his followers to pray to him, Muhammad may have been emulating the ancient Persian practice of king-worship.) He also decries Muslim atrocities—the destruction of churches and monasteries, slaughter of priests and hermits, and outright suppression of Christianity in so many of the Eastern cities where it first took root.

72. Ibid., fol. 85r: "Hec orantis cura potius quam res gestas scribentis esse debent."

73. Ibid., fol. 84r: "Nec deerant interim pseudoprophete et Machometi precones qui velut spem religionis ad sectandam ducis sui legem populos hortarentur, ex eo omnem Syriam Ciliciamque et usque ad Cappadociam atque hinc in Licaoniam vagati ad Pamphylium mare pervenerunt."

74. Ibid., fol. 84v: "Obsessa igitur Hyerusalem, tolleratis diu malis, altero anno in potestatem Saracenorum venit, letissimaque illis victoria velut quesita natali urbe, quod in lege Machometi non nunquam Judeorum patres, scripturarum nostrarum more, laudantur: Abraam, Jacob, Joseph atque alii eius generis."

75. Ibid., fol. 85v: "Post Sarraceni . . . ad Aegiptum quoque conversi Alexandriam obtinuerunt . . . Late enim priusquam vires accederent, superstitio gentes occupaverat. Sic inde Lybiam pervagati in Africam transiere, moxque omnis Africa, accepto perfide religionis signo, in ditionem concessit."

76. Ibid., fol. 84r–v: "Eo, collectis navibus, tanta erat hominum insania navigationem ad ipsam Constantinopolim quasi Christiani imperii caput parant, eosdem arbitrati futuros domi hostes, quos tuendis longinquis experti erant."

77. Ibid., fol. 85r: "Non multo igitur post simili audacia Saraceni Persarum regna lacessunt, quibus tamen et in ipsis nostra fides, ut olim, quasi peregrina versabatur . . . Frequentes vero in illis oris Christianorum populi, quos ab initio conditos Persarum reges ut qui regie liberalitati consueti essent, bonis legibus vivere sinebant."

78. Ibid., fol. 85v: "Nam Perse fidei iugum male retentis patrum suorum dogmatibus sepius abiecerant, neque Asia (tametsi nulla gens tam nobiles fidei primitias habuerat) Christianum nomen integrum servaverat, quasi mallent erraticos quosque quam veritatis documenta sectari."

79. Ibid., fol. 85r.

80. Ibid., fol. 87v: "Tam absurdos illa Machometi superstitio effecerat, ut penitus viderentur humanitatem repudiavisse. Omnis illa veterum *vel Grecorum vel Persarum* memoria exciderat, ut ne vestigium quidem cognite aliquando virtutis superesset." Italics mine.

81. Ibid., fols. 108v–109r: "Nec tamen eo tempore melius consultum hostibus nostris, quando nec illi iam aut Darios aut Ptolomeos aut eiusmodi nomina meminissent, quibus vix ipsarum Persarum aut Aegyptii nomen constaret."

82. Ibid., fol. 85v: "In occidente reges potentissimi Christianissimique erant, quam ob rem factus ex omni Gallia auxiliorum concursus, pugnatum adversus bestias." Biglia then describes (wishful thinking?) how the Arabs were not only driven from Spain but also pursued by locusts across the length of North Africa; these (nonhistorical) events are fixed in the eighth and ninth centuries.

83. Ibid., fol. 86r: "In Asia tam diu imperium mansit quod Sarracenorum appellaret dum, ut fit, superstitioni fides habita est . . . quod maiora erant hominum ingenia quam ut Arabum imperio regi se paterentur, paullatim subiit animos indignatio ac penitentia servitutis quam hactenus ignaviae genti exhibuissent."

84. Biglia remarks that the Byzantine emperors, like the ancient Greeks before them, had become more enamored of elegance than of power: ibid.: "Minus tamen in dies et fiducie et virium in Constantinopolitano imperio et iam frustra dicerentur Constantini reges, quos velut grecos facundia potius verborum quam rerum audacia iuvaret."

85. Hetoum, *Flos*, 277.

86. Vat. lat. 5298, fol. 86r: "Sed in Asia iam, ut diximus, et imperia et nomina mutabantur. Puduit aliquando Sarracenos dici qui possent Dardani aut Phriges appellari; iam vero Teucri appellantur quos vulgo Turcos vocant."

87. Hetoum, *Flos*, 277.

88. Vat. lat. 5298, fol. 86r: "[Teucri] ab Hellesponto intro ad orientem late patentes tum ubi Galatia, Bithynia maximeque ipsa Phrigia cum civitatibus quarum hodie celeberrima Nicomedia, Nicea, Nicopolis, cum ubi mons Olympus et omnino illa vetus Grecia quam et poete et hystorie predicant."

89. Ibid., fol. 86r–v: "[Teucri] regem eligunt vocatum ab illis Sabochum, nec prius ille institutus, quam de occupanda reliqua Asia cogitat . . . Defuncto Sabocho in regnum succedit filius Virogrissa, nec minus ille ad liberandam ampliandamque Asiam intentus." See Hetoum, *Flos*, 277–279.

90. Vat. lat. 5298, fol. 86v: "Non tamen excidit superstitio, qui adhuc venerandum Machometum decreverunt, quasi metu, ne a visendo illius sepulchro excluderentur, nec esset illo relicto quem colerent."

91. Ibid.: "Proinde illi Caliphae, quem velut summum sacerdotem barbari honorant, contestati sunt nihil se de veteri religione mutaturos, ceterum nolle Saracenum nomen in Asya eminere." Cf. Hetoum, who said simply that when the Turks overthrew the Saracens, they "caused no trouble" for the caliph: see *Flos*, 277.

92. Hetoum, *Flos*, 279.

93. Ibid.

94. Vat. lat. 5298, fol. 87r.

95. Hetoum, *Flos*, 280.

96. Vat. lat. 5298, fol. 87r: "Cum et Teucri in patriam rediissent . . . soldani Teucrorum potentia mire crevit, alienisque calamitatibus secura."

97. Hetoum, *Flos*, 280: "Et ille soldanus Turquie tenuit pacifice regnum suum usque ad adventum Tatarorum, a quibus fuit postmodum debellatus."

98. Ibid..
99. Vat. lat. 5298, fol. 87v: "[Tartari] nec Christiani nominis ignari paulo magis ad humanitatem sese inclinant." This echoes Hetoum's enthusiasm for Mongol rule. For the Western medieval tradition of identifying Christian elements among the Mongols, see Webb, "Decline and Fall," 209.
100. Vat. lat. 5298, fol. 87v.
101. Ibid., fol. 109r.
102. Ibid., fol. 114r: "Id crediderim fere in odium Sarraceni nominis divinitus permissum, veluti cuperet Machometi sordes Tartareis sordibus abolere."
103. Ibid., fols. 106r–107r.
104. Ibid., fol. 107r.
105. Biglia does not, however, deny that Bayezid had his flaws: he blinded and murdered members of his own family to ensure his succession to the throne and so deserved to pay a penalty for his evil deeds: ibid.
106. Ibid.: ". . .precipue vero Teucri omnium qui ad illud mare spectant, humanissimi habentur."
107. E.g., his description of the crusaders' difficult journey to Antioch: "Tandem vero, peragratis longis itineribus, cum multi fame defecissent, multi Turcorum insidiis interissent. . ." (fol. 109v); the state of the Holy Land after the fall of Jerusalem in 1187: "Brevi factum nusquam ut in omni provincia Christianum nomen audiretur, omnia in Turci potestate venere" (fol. 111r).
108. Arbesmann, "Andrea Biglia," 158, quotes letters from Sicco Polenton dated 1418 and 1419 congratulating Biglia on making Bruni's acquaintance.
109. D. J. Wilcox, The Development of Florentine Humanist Historiography (Cambridge, Mass., 1969), 3.
110. E. Cochrane, Historians and Historiography in the Italian Renaissance (Chicago, 1981), 111–112; Arbesmann, "Andrea Biglia," 180–182; Schnaubelt, "Life and Writings," 149–150; G. Ianziti, "From Biondo to Crivelli: The Beginnings of Humanistic Historiography in Sforza Milan," Rinascimento, 2d ser., 20 (1980): 3–39, at 10–13.
111. For Bruni's contributions to Renaissance historiography, see B. Ullmann, "Leonardo Bruni and Humanistic Historiography," Medievalia et Humanistica 4 (1946): 45–61; Wilcox, Florentine Humanist Historiography; R. Fubini, "Osservazioni sugli Historiarum Florentini populi libri XII di Leonardo Bruni," in Studi di storia medievale e moderna per Ernesto Sestan, 2 vols. (Florence, 1980), 1:403–448; Cochrane, Historians and Historiography, 1–9; H. Baron, In Search of Florentine Civic Humanism: Essays on the Transition from Medieval to Modern Thought, 2 vols. (Princeton, 1988), 1:43–93.
112. Leonardo Bruni, Historiarum Florentini populi libri XII, ed. E. Santini, in RIS2, 19.3 (Città di Castello, 1934), 5.
113. Ibid., 7–9.
114. Ibid., 9–13.
115. Ibid., 13: "Tunc igitur imperio ad Romanos traducto. . . . Etrusca virtus omnino consenuit, longe plus inerti otio quam hostili ferro depressa."

116. Baron, *In Search of Civic Humanism*, 53–60.
117. Bruni, *Historiarum Florentini populi*, 14.
118. Ibid., 14–15.
119. Ibid., 15.
120. Ibid., 15–22.
121. Ibid., 7 and 22–23.
122. Ibid., 23–24.
123. For Bruni's influence on Biondo, see W. K. Ferguson, "Humanist Views of the Renaissance," *AHR* 45 (1939): 1–28, at 11–16; Ianziti, "From Biondo to Crivelli," 5–10. See also D. Hay, "Flavio Biondo and the Middle Ages," *Proceedings of the British Academy*, 45 (1960); N. Rubinstein, "Il Medio Evo nella storiografia Italiana del Rinascimento," *Lettere italiane* 24 (1972): 431–447 at 433–434; A. Mazzocco, "Decline and Rebirth in Bruni and Biondo," in *Umanesimo a Roma nel Quattrocento*, eds. P. Brezzi and M. de Panizza Lorch (Rome, 1984), 249–266; Cochrane, *Historians and Historiography*, 35–36.
124. His account is in *Decades*, 122–125.
125. Ibid., 123: "Macometus quidam, ut aliqui Arabs, ut alii volunt Persa. . ."
126. Shiroe ("Syrochus") was the son of Chosroes II. After murdering his father in 628, he had himself crowned with the name Kavad II, but he died later in the same year. His infant son Ardashir III ("Adhaeser") succeeded him but died in 629. After him, a series of Sassanian princes and one princess were elevated and deposed in quick succession; among these was one who took the name Hormizd V, but he lasted no longer than any of the others (*CHI*, 3:170–171). The events Biondo describes all took place during the reign of the prince who ultimately won the succession struggle but lost the empire, Yazdgerd III.
127. Anastasius, *Chronographia tripartita*, 205; P. Buchholz, *Die Quellen der* Historiarum Decades *des Flavius Blondus* (Naumberg, 1881), 114. Contrary to Anastasius, the Persian king Hormizd V ("Hormisdas") was not killed by the Arabs but deposed, and the Persians went on to resist Arab attacks on their country for a good ten years after Yazdgerd III, whom Theophanes does not even mention, succeeded to the throne in 632. In fact, the Arabs did not launch a serious campaign against Persia, much less overthrow the dynasty as Anastasius describes, until after they had defeated the Byzantines at the River Yarmuk in 636. Their first major assault on Persia came in 636 or 637, at the battle of Qadisiyah, after which they took the capital, Ctesiphon. They finally destroyed the remnants of the Persian army at the battle of Nihavand in 642. Yazdgerd, the last Sassanian ruler of Persia, wandered as a fugitive through his eastern territories until his murder in 651: *CHI*, 4:8–17. Anastasius does include a second account of the fall of the Persian king (whom he still calls "Hormisdas") much closer to the correct date, possibly indicating his reliance on two different sources: Anastasius, *Chronographia tripartita*, 213–214.
128. Heraclius evacuated the True Cross from Jerusalem before the Battle of the Yarmuk in 636; Antioch fell to the Arabs shortly after (G. Ostrogorsky, *History of the Byzantine State*, 2d ed., trans. J. Hussey [Oxford, 1968], 111). The Arabs

took Jerusalem in 637 or 638, after a two-year siege (A. A. Vasiliev, *History of the Byzantine Empire*, 2d ed. [Oxford, 1952], 211).

129. *CHI*, 3:29–33.

130. Anastasius, *Chronographia tripartita*, 205: ". . . Hormisdas, quo a Saracenis pulso, factum est regnum Persarum sub Arabibus usque in hodiernum."

131. Biondo, *Decades*, 151.

132. Ibid., 207: "Paucos ante annos, gens e Perside Agarena (quam vos corrupte Saracenam dicitis) sanctam civitatem Hierosolymam, sanctae terrae loca invadens cepit . . . Omnes Romano quondam imperio, et post Romano pontifici, parentes a Turcis Saracenisque nostris (imo Christi domini et immortalis Dei) hostibus possideri, neminem esse vestrum qui ignoret certum habemus. . ."

133. Ibid., 208: "Fuit hactenus in extremis ad septentriones Europae partibus Constantinopolitanum imperium obex, et tanquam murus, qui maiores omnia prostraturas Turcorum Saracenorumque alluviones continuit prohibuitque, ne Hungaros, Polonos, Bohemos et ipsos Alemannos primo, deinde caeteros obruerent Christianos. Pulsus vero ante paucos annos Asia imperator, de retinendis Constantinopoli propinquis Europae regionibus laborat."

134. Ibid., 208: "Melius, filii, et maiori cum gloria nostri progenitores inchoatam, ut altiuscule repetamus, Romae, et in Italia et viribus Europae auctam dignitatem ad totius orbis monarchiam extulerunt, per cuius omnes provincias et regiones nomen floruit Christianum—quod nomen nostris temporibus ad parvum orbis angulum coangustari, et quotidie de excidio periclitari videmus." In his *Roma triumphans*, Biondo advised the pope that a revival of ancient Roman virtues and institutions was the only sure way of overcoming the contemporary Ottomans. See Mazzocco, "Decline and Rebirth;" D. Mertens, "*Claromontani passagii exemplum:* Papst Urban II. und der erste Kreuzzug in der Türkenkriegspropaganda des Renaissance-Humanismus," in *Europa und die Türken*, eds. Guthmüller and Kühlmann, 65–78.

135. It is not clear whether Biondo knew and used Biglia's work as a source. Biondo certainly drew on some of the same medieval texts, and he treats many of the same events of medieval Eastern history. In later books of the *Decades*, Biondo uses information from Biglia's *Milanese History:* Ianziti, "From Biondo to Crivelli," 10–13.

136. MS Vatican City, Archivio Secreto Vaticano, Indice 71, fols. 90r–102v. The MS is not in Filelfo's hand but is probably a fair copy of his original. L. Gualdo Rosa ("Filelfo e i Turchi: un inedito storico dell'Archivio Vaticano," *Università di Napoli. Annali della facoltà di lettere e filosofia* 2 [1964–1968]) published the text of the notebook and an analysis of its contents. Unaware of Biglia's work, she suggests that Filelfo extracted his information directly from the text of Hetoum and added details from other medieval sources. In fact, all the material in the early pages of the notebook derives from Biglia, and it was he who added material from the medieval Theophanes tradition to Hetoum's basic narrative. Gualdo Rosa's investigations into possible medieval sources for the early pages

are still useful, however, since they apply to Biglia's text just as well as to the notes Filelfo derived from it. Filelfo's reliance on Biglia was first suggested by Fioravanti, "*Commentarii Historici*," 246.

137. Text ed. Gualdo Rosa, "Filelfo e i Turchi," 131–155. The remaining three leaves contain notes on Western conflicts with Muslim powers from the time of Charlemagne on, extracted from Fazio degli Uberti's *Dittamondo* and from the universal chronicle of Martin of Troppau: ibid., 156–165.

138. Filelfo moved to Siena in December 1434, nine months before Biglia; he may have met the humanist friar and read his work at this time.

139. Filelfo to Charles VII, *Epistolae* (Venice, 1502), fol. 58r.

140. A few years later, Filelfo was openly lobbying for employment at Charles's court: D. Robin, *Filelfo in Milan: Writings, 1451–1477* (Princeton, 1991), 82–85, 88–90. The encomiastic nature of the 1451 letter is underscored by Filelfo's *Ode* 3.1, which is also addressed to Charles VII. Filelfo seems to have composed it at the same time as his letter (it repeats many of the same arguments), but the focus is almost entirely on praising the French king rather than promoting the crusade.

141. F. Babinger, *Mehmed the Conqueror and His Time*, ed. W. Hickman and trans. R. Mannheim (Princeton, 1978), 66–67.

142. Filelfo to Charles VII, *Epistolae*, fols. 55r, 56r–v.

143. Ibid., fols. 57r–58r.

144. Ibid., fol. 55v: "Duo sunt infidelium genera. . ."

145. Ibid., fol. 57r.

146. Ibid., fol. 57v. The story of the Arab revolt is also told by Theophanes (who is the original source: Anastasius, *Chronographia tripartita*, 210), Sigebert of Gembloux (*Chronica*, col. 119), and Biondo (*Decades*, 124–125).

147. Filelfo to Charles VII, *Epistolae*, fol. 57v.

148. Text in Gualdo Rosa, "Filelfo e i Turchi," 133.

149. The injury actually occurred during a skirmish between the Qurayshites of Mecca and Muhammad's Muslim forces at Uhud, outside Medina, in September 625: M. Rodinson, *Muhammad*, trans. A. Carter, 2d ed. (London, 1996), 177–183. For Western accounts, see Jacques de Vitry, *Historia orientalis*, ed. F. Moschus (Douai, 1597), 13 ("A quodam autem praelio dentibus suis a dextera parte excussis, labro superiori conciso et genis confractis, vultu lacerato et deturpato [Mahometus] vix evasit"), and Daniel, *Islam*, 91–95.

150. For instance, in the oration he delivered in the presence of Aeneas Sylvius at the Congress of Mantua in 1459, after describing Bokhan's capture of Cimmerian Bosporus in the sixth century, Filelfo claimed that the Turks continued to pursue a life of undistinguished brigandage until, by unspecified turns of good fortune, they were able to challenge first Alexius Comnenus in the eleventh century, then the Cantacuzenus pretender in the fourteenth, for control of Byzantium itself. F. Filelfo, *Orationes* [Milan: Leonardus Pachel and Uldericus Scinzenzeler, 1483–1484], *IGI* 3905, sig. H3r; also the text translated in the following note.

151. In 1444, Filelfo included a shorter version of this story in his letter to Wladyslaw of Poland. After describing Bokhan's raid on Cimmerian Bosporus and the Turks' subsequent invasion of Persia during the reign of Heraclius, he continues (*Epistolae*, fol. 37v): "These brigands . . . disgracefully expelled that bandit Mahomet, the most wicked and depraved of all depraved men, whose impious religion they had embraced most enthusiastically of all peoples, on account of the attractions of the wicked behaviour [Islam allows]. Thereafter . . . progressing gradually and little by little and meeting no one to oppose them, the Turks settled in the regions close to the Adriatic Sea, disturbing, despoiling and laying waste to everything in their path—so completely had the courage of Christian princes fallen asleep, languished and wasted away."

152. Biglia, too, uses the form "Saboch"—a corruption of "Salioch," Hetoum's name for Seljuk.

153. Filelfo to Charles VII, *Epistolae*, fols. 57v–58r.

154. Ibid., fol. 57v.

155. See n. 103 above.

156. Filelfo to Charles VII, *Epistolae*, fol. 58r.

157. Ibid., fol. 56v.

158. At the end of the excursus (ibid., fol. 58r), Filelfo rapidly brings his account of Turkish history up to recent times. Despite his attempt to make Saladin the key transitional figure, it seems he did not really understand how power had passed from the medieval Seljuks to their Ottoman successors. (Biglia does not treat this matter, since Osman's conquests fell between the periods covered by Hetoum, whose work ends with the fall of the Seljuks in the 1240s, and Mignanelli, who describes Tamerlane's career in the late 1300s.) Filelfo, after paraphrasing Biglia on the reigns of the early Seljuk sultans Toghril Beg and Artuq, skips ("Et ne videar omnem historiam recensere") to the middle of the fourteenth century, to the moment in 1354 when the Byzantine pretender Cantacuzenus ferried his Ottoman mercenaries into Europe. In his letter to Wladyslaw, Filelfo treats the problem of the Turks' activities between their first appearance in Asia and the rise of the Ottomans some seven centuries later even more vaguely: he simply states that they expanded into new territories—from Persia to the Adriatic!—so gradually and with such stealth that no one thought to oppose them: see n. 151 above.

159. Aeneas Sylvius, *Oratio habita in conventu Mantuano*, 26 Sept. 1459, in *Opera omnia*, 905–914, at 905: "Ostendamus quaenam sunt illa quae amisimus, quas nobis et Deo nostro iniurias intulerunt Turci."

160. Ibid., 906: "Nunc quo nos Turci et Saraceni redigerint [*ex* redigerunt] . . . docebimus."

161. Ibid., 906.

162. In the winter of 1431–1432, Aeneas was a student at the University of Siena, where Biglia was his teacher. He later described Biglia as a "historiarum scriptor" (see n. 51 above), but conclusive proof that he knew Biglia's *Commentaries* remains to be found.

163. The universal "heathen" threat against Christendom is a theme Aeneas first proposed in his 1452 oration for Frederick III, but the idea that the Turks led the movement is new to this oration.

164. Aeneas Sylvius, *Oratio habita in conventu Mantuano,* 906: "Hi sunt termini vestri, o Christiani, sic circundati estis, sic in angulum coartati potentissimi quondam domini et orbis possessores."

165. Ibid., 906–907: "En quantum imperium permisistis? Quot nobiles urbes, quot ditissimas provincias perdidistis? Inter quas etiam Iudaeam neglexistis, terram nobilem, terram sanctam, terram lacte et melle fluentem, terram in qua primi nostrae fidei flores apparuere."

166. Aeneas Sylvius, *Supra Decades Blondi ab inclinatione imperii . . . Epitome,* in *Opera omnia,* 144–281.

167. Ibid., 176: "Et hi ex Persis facti Saraceni."

168. Ibid., 187: "Convenit autem inter Saracenos et Turcos ut restituto Persarum regni nomine, quod Saraceni Focae et Eraclii temporibus in suum confuderant, Turci per se appellarentur."

169. Hay, "Flavio Biondo," 61.

170. Platina, *Vitae pontificum* ([Venice]: Johannes de Colonia and Johannes Manthen, 11 June 1479), *IGI* 7857, sig. k6r.

171. Francesco Sforza to Pius II, 25 October 1463, in Aeneas Sylvius, *Opera omnia,* 865–868, at 865–866.

172. Ibid., 866.

173. Ibid.

174. E.g., Filelfo to Ludovico Foscarini, 1 August 1463, in *Epistolae,* fols. 131v–136v, at 132r: "Nam qui genere Turci sunt, eos omnis Asiaticos esse constat. Quos autem milites et quanta robustitate aut audentia viros Asia gignere consueverit, et Graecae et Latinae docent historiae. Sunt inquam Turci natura omnes ignavi, molles, effoeminati, id quod fieri arbitror partim coeli non tam claementia quam laxitudine quadam enervata partim dissolutiore vivendi ac victitandi luxu."

5. Wise Men in the East

1. S. A. Quinn, "The Timurid Historiographical Legacy," in *Society and Culture in the Early Modern Middle East,* ed. A. J. Newman (Leiden, 2003), 19–31, at 26. For Timur, see B. Forbes Manz, *The Rise and Rule of Tamerlane* (Cambridge, 1989); *CHI,* 6:42–97.

2. *Prester John, the Mongols, and the Ten Lost Tribes,* eds. C. F. Beckingham and B. Hamilton (Aldershot, 1996); B. Wagner, *Die "Epistola presbiteri Johannis" lateinisch und deutsch. Überlieferung, Textgeschichte, Rezeption und Übertragungen im Mittelalter* (Tübingen, 2000); A. Knobler, "Pseudo-Conversions and Patchwork Pedigrees: The Christianization of Muslim Princes and the Diplomacy of Holy War," *Journal of World History* 7 (1996): 181–197.

3. J. Richard, "The Mongols and the Franks," *Journal of Asian History* 3 (1969):

45–57; J. A. Boyle, "The Il-Khans of Persia and the Princes of Europe," *Central Asiatic Journal* 20 (1976): 25–40; V. Minorsky, "The Middle East in Western Politics in the 13th, 14th, and 15th Centuries," *Journal of the Royal Central Asian Society* 27 (1940): 427–461.

4. Kings Charles VI of France, Henry IV of England, and Martin of Aragon all sent enthusiastic letters congratulating Timur on his defeat of Bayezid in 1402: A. Knobler, "The Rise of Timur and Western Diplomatic Response, 1390–1405," *JRAS*, 3d ser., 5 (1995): 341–349, at 343–344, 346.

5. W. J. Fischel, "A New Latin Source on Tamerlane's Conquest of Damascus, 1400/01 (B. de Mignanelli's *Vita Tamerlani*, 1416)," *Oriens* 9 (1956): 203–204. The account is summarized in *Chronographia regum Francorum*, ed. H. Moranvillé, 3 vols. (Paris, 1891–1897), 3:199–223; idem, "Mémoire sur Tamerlan et sa Coeur par un Dominicain en 1403," *Bibliothèque de l'Ecole des Chartes* 55 (1894): 433–464; A. Kern, "Der *Libellus de notitia orbis* Johannes' III. (De Gonfalonibus?) O. P., Erzbischofs von Sultanyeh," *Archivum Fratrum Praedicatorum* 8 (1938): 82–123.

6. Thomas Walshingham, quoted by Knobler, "Rise of Timur," 344. John Capgrave, *The Chronicle of England*, ed. F. C. Hingeston (London, 1858), 277, reports the victory of a "King of Lettow" over the great Turk in the year 1402. See also Knobler, "Pseudo-Conversions and Patchwork Pedigrees."

7. Knobler, "Rise of Timur," 349; idem, "Timur the (Terrible/Tartar) Trope: A Case of Repositioning in Popular Literature and History," *Medieval Encounters* 7 (2001): 101–112. See also R. W. Battenhouse, "Tamburlaine, the 'Scourge of God,'" *Proceedings of the Modern Language Association* 56 (1941): 337–348.

8. T. Nagel, "Tamerlan im Verständnis der Renaissance," *Oriente moderno*, n.s. 15 (1996): 203–212, discusses Mignanelli and Fregoso but concentrates on Marlowe. Other articles in this special issue treat other northern European observers of Timur. O. Intze, *Tamerlan und Bajazet in den Literaturen des Abendlands* (Erlangen, 1912), surveys several post-1500 sources; U. Ellis-Fermor, ed., *Tamburlaine the Great in Two Parts*, 2d ed. (London, 1951), 23–41, discusses some fifteenth-century texts, but the chronology is not reliable.

9. Adam of Usk, *The Chronicle of Adam of Usk*, ed. and trans. C. Given-Wilson (Oxford, 1997), 130. Adam was in Rome in 1402 but did not return to England, and to the writing of his chronicle, until about 1411: ibid., xlvii. His account is rather garbled (Timur did not sack Jerusalem at this time) and less appreciative of Timur than Knobler suggests.

10. Knobler, "Rise of Timur," 342.

11. Giorgio Stella, *Annales Genuenses*, in *RISI*, 17:1194.

12. Giovanni Cornaro, letter dated 4 September 1402, quoted in Sanudo, *Vite de' Dogi*, in *RISI*, 12:795.

13. "Chronacetta veneziana dal 1402–1415," ed. V. Joppi, *Archivio veneto* 17 (1879): 301–325, at 302–303.

14. Jacopo Delaito, *Annales Estenses*, in *RISI*, 18:975. Other Italians who see Timur as an agent of divine providence include Beltramo de' Mignanelli, *Vita*

Tamerlani (1416), ed. Fischel, "A New Latin Source," 225–226, 229; Andrea Redusio, *Chronicon Tarvisinum,* in *RIS1,* 19 (after 1428); Giorgio Stella, *Annales Genuenses* (after 1435), col. 1195; Francesco Filelfo, *Orationes* [Milan: Leonardus Pachel and Uldericus Scinzenzeler, 1483–1484], *IGI* 3905, sig. H3v (1459); Matteo Palmieri, *Liber de temporibus,* ed. Gino Scaramella, *RIS2,* 26.1 (Città di Castello, 1906–1915); Antoninus Florentinus, *Chronica* (Nuremberg: Anton Koberger, 31 July 1484), *IGI* 608, 3:148r.

15. Fischel, "A New Latin Source," 225.

16. Most of Mignanelli's *Vita Tamerlani* is translated by Fischel, "A New Latin Source," 208–230. The complete text is in É. Baluze, *Miscellanea novo ordine digesta et non paucis ineditis monumentis . . . aucta,* ed. J. D. Mansi, 4 vols. (Lucca, 1761–1764), 4:131–141. A. M. Piemontese, "Beltramo Mignanelli senese, biografo di Tamerlano," *Oriente moderno,* n.s. 15 (1996): 213–226, surveys the *fortuna* of Mignanelli's text.

17. Fischel, "A New Latin Source," 225.

18. Mignanelli, *Vita Tamerlani,* ed. Baluze, 140.

19. Stella, *Annales Genuenses,* col. 1194.

20. U. M. Ellis-Fermor notes similar ambivalence among Byzantine authors of the period: *Tamburlaine the Great* (London, 1930), 23–26.

21. Redusio, *Chronicon Tarvisinum,* cols. 800–804. The text, which starts at Creation, does not end with Timur's career (cf. E. Cochrane, *Historians and Historiography in the Italian Renaissance* [Chicago, 1981]) but continues to 1428.

22. Redusio, *Chronicon Tarvisinum,* col. 801: "'Canis ex genere canum, habuisti animum contra potentiam nostram arma sumere?'"

23. Ibid.

24. Ibid., col. 804: "Sic barbarus ille . . . fidem barbaram comprobavit."

25. Ibid., col. 805.

26. Ibid., col. 801.

27. Palmieri, *Liber de temporibus,* 120–121 (=*Eusebii Caesariensis episcopi chronicon . . . ad quem et Prosper et Mattheus Palmerius et Matthias Palmerius . . . complura quae ad haec usque tempora subsecuta sunt adiecere* [Paris, 1512], fol. 149v). See also Antoninus Florentinus, *Chronica,* 3:148r ("Et quocunque eius transcenderat nomen sola fama, quasi a deo missus fuisset scelerum ultor terribilis imminebat"). Antoninus notes, nevertheless, that Timur was reputed to have been friendly to Christians ("qui Tamburlanus dicitur fuisse benivolus christianis").

28. Poggio, *De varietate fortunae,* ed. O. Merisalo (Helsinki, 1993), 107.

29. Ibid., 109. Piemontese, "Beltramo Mignanelli," 222–226, suggests that Poggio may have drawn details for his life of Timur from Mignanelli.

30. "Magni Themurlani seu Themurlibei et progressus et mores et regnum," ed. B. Figliuolo, in *La cultura a Napoli nel secondo Quattrocento* (Udine, 1997), 226–243, with remarks at 181–182. Compiled between 1460 and his death in 1492–1493, Ranzano's *Annales* include several short studies composed earlier in his career. His life of Timur purports to have been written in late 1444 or

445, shortly after Ranzano met and interrogated an elderly Sicilian eyewitness, Nino da Noto, who was resident in Damascus at the time of Timur's conquests. Arguing against this date is the fact that Ranzano also derives information from Poggio Bracciolini's 1447 *De varietate fortunae*. Other details come from the 1403 account of his fellow Dominican Jean of Sultaniyya.

31. Ranzano, "Magni Themurlani . . . ," 231–232. Ranzano departs from Jean of Sultaniyya, who says Timur despised *Christians* for engaging in sodomy (*Chronographia regum Francorum*, 216).

32. Ranzano, "Magni Themurlani . . . ," 232. Jean of Sultaniyya also mentions Timur's regard for learning: *Chronographia regum Francorum*, 210.

33. B. Nogara, *Scritti inediti e rari di Biondi Flavio* (Rome, 1927), 33.

34. Filelfo, *Orationes,* sig. H3v.

35. Battenhouse, "Tamburlaine," explores this commonplace thoroughly.

36. Platina, *Liber de Vita Christi ac omnium Pontificum,* in *RIS2,* 3.1:293.

37. E.g., Cornaro, Delaito, Mignanelli, Redusio, Biglia, Stella, and Palmieri.

38. E. Hall, *Inventing the Barbarian: Greek Self-Definition through Tragedy* (Oxford, 1989); F. Hartog, *The Mirror of Herodotus: The Representation of the Other in the Writing of History,* trans. J. Lloyd (Berkeley, 1988).

39. Cicero wrote fondly of the copy of the *Cyropaedia* he kept to hand (*Epistolae familiares* 9.25). For manuscripts of the text in the Renaissance, see Bolgar, *The Classical Heritage and Its Beneficiaries* (Cambridge, 1954), 492–494. For translations, see David Marsh, *Xenophon,* in *Catalogus Translationum et Commentariorum: Mediaeval and Renaissance Latin Translation and Commentaries,* ed. P. O. Kristeller (Washington D.C., 1992), 7:75–196, at 81 and 116–123. In the middle decades of the fifteenth century, Valla made a translation of the first book, and Poggio and Filelfo produced complete translations. The 1470s saw further translations into Italian and French. In 1504, Petrus Crinitus noted the "mirificam sane ac memorandam disciplinam" of the kings of Persia (directly after an opening anecdote about Timur, discussed below) in his commonplace book, *Commentarii de honesta disciplina* (Florence, 1504), sig. a1r.

40. A. Momigliano, *Alien Wisdom: The Limits of Hellenization* (Cambridge, 1975).

41. Xenophon, *Cyropaediae libri VIII,* trans. Francesco Filelfo [Milan: Archangelus Ungardus, before 18 Feb. 1477], Hain 16227, *IGI* 10404, fols. 1r–4v.

42. Aeneas Sylvius to Nicholas of Cusa, *Briefwechsel* 3:209–210.

43. Biondo, *Scritti inediti,* 33.

44. Aeneas Sylvius, *Asia,* in *Opera omnia* (Basel, 1551), 312–313.

45. It is not clear where Aeneas found this story. Jean of Sultaniyya mentions that Timur raised a black standard when he wished his troops to sack and destroy the territory they were invading: *Chronographia regum Francorum,* 219.

46. Aeneas Sylvius, *Asia,* 313. Aeneas worked up a briefer account of Timur's career in his 1458 *Europa* (*Opera omnia,* 395); here the context is not the history of Persia but rather the origins of Ottoman power, and Aeneas argues that Bayezid I would have conquered Constantinople had not Timur suddenly ap-

peared on the scene to foil his plans in spectacular style. In *Europa*, Aeneas does not identify Timur as ethnically Parthian or Persian (instead, he borrows the moniker "ille Scytharum praepotens rex" from Sagundino's 1456 treatise, *De origine Turcarum*, 187), but he compares him favorably to Darius and Xerxes and presents his appearance in history as a clearly positive thing.

47. *Commentarii rerum memora bilium*, ed. A. van Heck, 2 vols. (Vatican City, 1984), 1: 322.

48. One example, among many that could be cited, is Antonio Cornazzano's vernacular *canzone* of 1470 (with the Latin title *Ad italicos principes pro Turci adventu*), on Mehmed's capture of Negroponte: "Un novo Xerse, un perfido Pillato/mentito al mundo el gran sangue di Troia/sui nostri litti el suo standardo ha fisso." Note both the comparison to Xerxes and Pilate and the charge of presumption, for falsely claiming Trojan blood: A. Comboni, "Alcune puntualizzazioni sulla tradizione delle rime del Cornazzano con una canzone inedita sulla minaccia turca," *Bolletino storico piacentino* 80 (1985), 206.

49. Jacopo Filippo Foresti, *Supplementum chronicorum* (Venice: Bernardinus Benalius, 23 August 1483), *IGI* 5075, 154–155; Hartmann Schedel, *Liber cronicarum* (Nuremberg: Anton Koberger, 12 July 1493), *IGI* 8828, fol. 237r.

50. Crinitus, *Commentarii de honesta disciplina*, 1.1 (sig. a1r). Nevertheless, Crinitus also discusses Timur's cruelty to Bayezid in a chapter on excessive harshness in princes: 13.4 (sig. h6v).

51. Battista Fregoso, *De dictis factisque memorabilibus a rerum humanarum primordio usque in praesens tempus, : . . .* (Paris, 1518), fol. 90v. Fregoso also discusses Timur's treatment of Bayezid in his chapter on "Pride" (fol. 292v), but the criticisms leveled there are balanced by several more examples of Timur's virtue in the chapter on "Abstinence and Continence" (fol. 118r).

52. Antoninus Florentinus, *Chronica*, 3:148r.

53. A. M. Piemontese, "La représentation de Uzun Hasan sur scène à Rome (2 mars 1473)," *Turcica* 21/23 (1991): 191–203; C. Falletti, "Le feste per Eleonora d'Aragon," in *Spettacoli conviviali dall'antichità alle corti italiane del Quattrocento* (Viterbo, 1983), 269–289 at 276–280.

54. Piemontese, "La représentation," 195–196, 202–203.

55. "Uzun Hasan," *EI2*, 10:963–967; J. Woods, *The Aqquyunlu: Clan, Confederation, Empire*, rev. ed. (Salt Lake City, 1999), 87–123.

56. L. Pastor, *The History of the Popes from the Close of the Middle Ages*, trans. F. I. Antrobus, 40 vols. (London, 1891–1953), 2:408.

57. Woods, *Aqquyunlu*, 88–89.

58. Antony Bryer, "Ludovico da Bologna and the Georgian and Anatolian Embassy of 1460–1461," *Bedi Kartlisi* 19–20 (1965): 178–198, at 180–181 and 187; Aeneas Sylvius, *Commentaries*, ed. van Heck 1:322.

59. "Uzun Hasan," *EI2*, 10:965; Callimachus Experiens (Filippo Buonaccorsi), *De his quae a Venetis tentata sunt Persis ac Tartaris contra Turcos movendis*, ed. A. Kempfi (Warsaw, 1962), 38–50; E. Cornet, *Le guerre dei Veneti nell'Asia 1470–1474* (Vienna, 1856); G. Berchet, *La Repubblica di Venezia e la Persia* (Turin, 1865); V. Minorsky, *La Perse au XVe siècle entre la Turquie et Venise* (Paris, 1933);

idem, "The Middle East," 438–448; B. Palombini, *Bündniswerben Abendländischer Mächte um Persien 1453–1600* (Wiesbaden, 1968), 8–37; G. Scarcia, "Venezia e la Persia tra Uzun Hasan e Tahmasp (1454–1572)," *Acta Iranica,* ser. 1, 3 (1974): 419–438; K. Setton, *The Papacy and the Levant (1204–1571),* 4 vols. (Philadelphia, 1976), 2:315–321; A. M. Piemontese, "The Nuncios of Sixtus IV in Iran," in *Iran and Iranian Studies. Essays in Honor of Iraj Afshar,* ed. K. Eslami (Princeton, 1998), 90–108; F. Babinger, *Mehmed the Conqueror and His Time,* ed. W. Hickman and trans. R. Mannheim (Princeton, 1978), 305–327.

60. M. Dabrowska, "Uzun Hasan's Project of Alliance with the Polish King (1474)," in *Mélanges d'histoire byzantine offerts à Oktawiusz Jurewicz* (Lodz, 1998), 171–185.

61. Woods, *Aqquyunlu,* 100–106.

62. Callimachus, *De his quae a Venetis tentata sunt,* 40: "rege a christiana professione alieno."

63. Aeneas Sylvius, *Commentaries,* ed. van Heck, 1:322; Sixtus IV in Setton, *Papacy and Levant,* 2.316: "insignis princeps Zuncassan Christianorum amicus."

64. V. Todesco, "S. Cassiano o uno Scia di Persia?" *Atti del Reale Istituto Veneto di Scienze, Lettere ed Arti* 86 (1926–1927): 1369–1378, esp. 1375, 1377–1378; A. Medin, "Per l'origine della voce 'sancassan': Le *gesta* di Husun Hasan in un cantare del sec. XV," *Atti del Reale Istituto Veneto di Scienze, Lettere ed Arti* 87 (1927–1928): 799–814. Thanks to Cristelle Baskins for the references.

65. Domenico Malipiero, *Annali Veneti dall'anno 1457–1500,* eds. T. Gar and A. Sagredo (*Archivio Storico Italiano,* ser. 1, 7.1 [1843]), 33–34. Uzun Hasan was not a direct descendant of Timur, but his aunt had married a grandson of the conqueror: Woods, *Aqquyunlu,* 47.

66. Malipiero, *Annali,* 25; see Todesco, "S. Cassiano," 1374–1375.

67. *EI2,* 965–966. Venice had pursued secret negotiations with Uzun Hasan since 1463, but the relationship did not become public until 1472. The ambassadorial reports of Zeno, Contarini, Barbaro, and others, so useful to modern scholars of relations between Uzun Hasan and the West, seem not to have had a wide circulation in Italy at the time, though Contarini's *relazione* was published in 1487: *Viaggio ad Usun Hassan re di Persia* (Venice: Hannibal Foxius, 16 Jan. 1487), *IGI* 3182.

68. Palombini, *Bundniswerben,* 120–122; Malipiero, *Annali Veneti,* 79: "Queste preparazion . . . dà gran speranza che l'impresa debbia riuscir." Callimachus, *De his quae a Venetis tentata sunt,* 44, also describes the Venetian response to the news. Callimachus was writing in Poland, where he was employed by the Jagiellonian king, with a view to encouraging Casimir to join Venice and Persia in their war against the Turks.

69. Filelfo to Ludovico Foscarini, 23 Feb. 1473, in *Epistolae* (Venice, 1502), fol. 256v.

70. Filelfo to Bernardo Giustiniani, 13 Sept. 1470, in *Epistolae,* fols. 226r–228v, at 228v.

71. Filelfo to Marco Aurelio, 10 November 1473, MS Milan, Biblioteca Trivulziana

873, fols. 452v–453r. Text in M. Meserve, "From Samarkand to Scythia: Reinventions of Asia in Renaissance Geography and Political Thought," in *Pius II: el piu expeditivo pontifice. Selected Studies on Aeneas Silvius Piccolomini (1405–1464)*, eds. Z.R.W.M. von Martels and A. Vanderjagt (Leiden, 2003), 37.

72. MS Milan, Biblioteca Trivulziana, 873, fol. 453r: "Adde quod de vobis hoc est Venetis bene meruerat rex Assam, nosseque debuerat ex illo vetere Persarum instituto nullum esse ingratitudine detestabilius vitium."

73. Xenophon, *Cyropaedia* 1.7.

74. Filelfo discussed an edition with Giovanni Andrea Bussi, using the Italian proto-typographers Sweynheym and Pannartz; the project was never realized, and the first edition appeared in Milan about 1477 (see above). The passage on ingratitude is at sig. [a]7r–v.

75. Piemontese, "La représentation," 195, 198.

76. C. Baskins, "The Bride of Trebizond: Turks and Turkmen on a Florentine Wedding Chest, circa 1460," in *The 'Turk' and Islam in the Western Eye (1453–1832)*, ed. James Harper (forthcoming).

77. *Esortazione ai Veneziani ("Al nome sia di Dio. . .")* [Florence: Nicolaus Laurentii, Alamanus, about 1477], *GW* 487; for the text see A. Medin, "Per l'origine," esp. stanzas 9–10. The alliance is also mentioned by Coriolanus Cepio, *Petri Mocenigi imperatoris gesta* (Venice: Bernhard Maler, Erhard Ratdolt, and Peter Löslein, 1477), *IGI* 2684, reprinted in Clauser, 348.

78. Angelus Cato Supinas, *De cometa anni 1472* [Naples: Sixtus Riessinger, after 1 March 1472], *GW* 6385, fol. 12v. Mattia Palmieri also associates Uzun Hasan's rise with the comet of 1472 (*Eusebii chronicon . . .*, fol. 161r–v). These comments emerge from a general conviction that the comet of 1472 presaged the outbreak of war in Asia: Thuricensis physicus [Eberhard Schleusinger?], *Tractatus de cometis* [Beromünster: Helias Heliae, after April 1472], *GW* 7252, fol. 8r; Jacobus Angelus de Ulma, *Tractatus de cometis* [Memmingen: Albrecht Kunne, 1490], *GW* 1891, sigs. b4v–c2r. See V. F. Brüning, *Bibliograhie der Kometenliteratur* (Stuttgart, 2000), 6–8. Octavius Vivianus, *Comete quot fuerint, quibusque annis apparuerint, quos effectus produxerint, ex scriptorum monumentis* [1525?], s.a. 1472, also makes the connection with Uzun Hasan explicit.

79. Giovanni Gioviano Pontano, *Centum Ptolemaei sententiae . . . e Graeco in Latinum translatae atque expositae* (Florence, 1520), fol. 142v. On 142r, Pontano explains that the comet of 1402 likewise presaged the triumphs of Timur in Asia.

80. Laudivius Zacchia, *Epistolae Magni Turci* (Rome: Philippus de Legnamine, 27 November 1473), *IGI* 5965, fols. 3r–4v. The first edition was printed in Naples in September of that year (*IGI* 5964); the text was reprinted twenty times in the fifteenth century: F. Babinger, "Laudivius Zacchia, der Erdichter der 'Epistolae Magni Turci,'" *Sitzungsberichte der bayerische Akademie der Wissenschaften*, philos.-hist. (Klasse, 1960); B. Wagner, "Sultansbriefe," *DLMV,* 11:1464–1465.

81. Woods, *Aqquyunlu,* 117–120.

82. Medin, "Per l'origine," 801–802.

83. Palmieri, *Eusebii . . . chronicon*, fol. 161r–v.

84. Schedel, *Liber cronicarum*, fol. 249v: "Sumcassianus appellatur, quod latine magnum virum significat." Uzun Hasan is literally "Tall Hasan" in Turkish.

85. Another positive notice on Timur is in Callimachus, *De his quae a Venetis tentata sunt*, 48–49, recording contemporary Venetian sentiments which very likely reflect his own opinion as well.

86. Fregoso, *De dictis factisqve memorabilibvs*, fol. 156v.

87. Sabellico, *Rapsodie historiarum enneades* (Paris, 1513), 2:320v–321r.

88. Raffaele Maffei, *Commentariorum urbanorum libri XXXVIII*, (Rome, 1506), fol. 104r.

89. R. Savory, *Iran under the Safavids* (Cambridge, 1980), 1–49; P. Brummett, "The Myth of Shah Ismail Safavi: Political Rhetoric and 'Divine' Kingship," in *Medieval Christian Perceptions of Islam: A Book of Essays*, ed. J. V. Tolan (New York, 1996), 331–359.

90. Marino Sanudo, *Sah Ismail I nei* Diarii, ed. B. Scarcia Amoretti (Rome, 1979), 3–4.

91. These are collected in ibid., 3–75. Other popular responses can be found in G. Ponte, "Attorno a Leonardo da Vinci: L'attesa popolare del Sofi di Persia in Venezia e Firenze all'inizio del Cinquecento," *Rassegna della Letteratura italiana* (1979): 5–19.

92. S. N. Fisher, *The Foreign Relations of Turkey, 1481–1512* (Urbana, Ill., 1948), 67–89.

93. Sanudo, ed. Scarcia Amoretti, 11: "quel signor, nominato Sophi, vien di Persia . . ."

94. Zuan Moresini, ibid., 140.

95. Ibid., 145, trans. Brummett, "Myth," 340.

96. "Nove de gran Sofi," in Giovanni Rota [*sic*], *La vita, costumi et statura de Sofi re di Persia et di Media et de molti altri Regni et paesi con le grandissime guerre quale ha fatto contra el gran Turcho et altri Re et Signori, et de la descriptione di paesi et vita et costumi de populi con molte altre cose piacevole* [Rome: Eucharius Silber, 1508], sig. c1r.

97. Costantino Lascari, in Sanudo, ed. Scarcia Amoretti, 38: "esser signor natural, et soi antecessori et parentato de imperio di Persia; e l'è vero, che questo Sophi se tien, intro la sua fede, molto catolico." Translation from Brummett, "Myth," 336.

98. Rotta, *La vita*, sig. a4v.

99. Ibid., fol. 3v: "Beve vino ma occultamente, e mangia carne porcina, ne havea per quanto me ha ditto un suo domestico ultimamente uno in casa nutrito grasso e grande, el qual per despregio del re turcho dal suo nome el dimandava el conducar Baisit." These are constant themes in the Italian literature on Ismail. Costantino Lascari noted that the Sophy ordered his pork from Christian Cyprus (Sanudo, ed. Scarcia Amoretti, 36). The "Nove de gran Sophi" in Rotta's tract mentions his consumption of both pork and wine (Rotta, *La vita*, sig. c1r).

100. *Le baptesme de Sophie roy de perse, contenant sa generation son estat sa condition et cor-*

pulence translate en françoys [Poitiers: 1508?]; G. Atkinson, *La Littérature géographique française de la Renaissance: Répertoire bibliographique* (Paris, 1927), 22.

101. Sabellico, *Rapsodie historiarum enneades*, 2:350r.
102. Ibid.
103. Maffei, *Commentariorum urbanorum libri XXXVIII*, fol. 104r. Moses veiled: Exodus 34: 32–35.
104. Egidio da Viterbo, "Fulfillment of the Christian Golden Age under Pope Julius II" (21 December 1507), trans. F. X. Martin, *Friar, Reformer, and Renaissance Scholar: Life and Works of Giles of Viterbo* (Villanova, Pa., 1992), 259.

Epilogue

1. Felix Fabri, *Evagatorium in Terrae Sanctae, Arabiae et Egyptii peregrinationem*, ed. C. D. Hassler, 3 vols. (Berlin, 1849), 1:2. For his wide reading, see H.F.M. Prescott, *Jerusalem Journey: Pilgrimage to the Holy Land in the Fifteenth Century* (London, 1954), 69–74.
2. Fabri, *Evagatorium*, 3:237–239.
3. Jacopo Filippo Foresti, *Supplementum chronicorum* (Venice: Bernardinus Benalius, 23 August 1483), *IGI* 5075, 83.
4. Janos Thuroczy, *Chronica Hungarorum*, eds. E. Galantai and J. Kristo (Budapest, 1985), 31–32.
5. Hartmann Schedel, *Liber cronicarum* (Nuremberg: Anton Koberger, 12 July 1493), *IGI* 8828, fol. 165r. Schedel thought highly of Aeneas's writings on the Turks: he also reproduced, at the end of the *Chronicle*, Aeneas's chapter on the Turks from *Asia* (272r–273v), his oration at the Diet of Frankfurt ("De expugnatione Constantinopolis," 274r–275r), and the entire text of *Europa* (278v–298v); E. Rücker, *Hartmann Schedels Weltchronik: Das grösste Buchunternehmen der Dürer Zeit* (Munich, 1988), 19, 82–83, 117.
6. Sebastian Brant, *De origine et conversatione bonorum regum et laude civitatis Hierosolymae cum exhortatione eiusdem recuperandae* (Basel: Johann Bergmann de Olpe, 1 March 1495), *GW* 5072, sig. IIr.
7. Marino Barlezio, *De obsidione Scodrensis* (Venice, 1504), sig. a3v: the Trojan theory is a *frivola argumentatio*. F. Pall, "Marino Barlezio, uno storico umanista," in *Mélanges d'histoire générale*, ed. C. Marinescu, 2 vols. (Cluj, 1938), 2:1–184, esp. 38–41 and 49.
8. Sabellico, *Rapsodie historiarum enneades*, 2 vols. (Paris, 1513), 2: 217r–v; A. Pertusi, "I primi studi in occidente sull'origine e potenza dei Turchi," *Studi Veneziani* 12 (1970): 492–497.
9. Chalcocondyles, a renowned Greek scholar and a pupil of George Gemisthos Plethon, fled Mistra for Venetian Crete after the Turkish conquest of the Peloponnese in 1460. It is uncertain whether he ever traveled to Italy. He lived into the late 1480s (the latest events described in his history date to 1487), and whether he died in Italy or Crete, a manuscript of his history appeared in Ven-

ice soon after its completion. Most of the twenty-nine surviving manuscripts stem from an early Venetian exemplar. N. Nicoloudis, *Laonikos Chalkokondyles: A Translation and Commentary of the 'Demonstrations of Histories,' Books I–III* (Athens, 1996); F. Grabler, "Aus dem Geschichtswerk des Laonikos Chalkokondyles," in *Europa im XV. Jahrhundert von Byzantinern Gesehen* (Graz, 1954), 13–97, esp. 13–15; A. Wifstrand, "Laonikos Chalkokondyles der letzte Athener: ein Vortrag," *Scripta Minora Regiae Societatis Humaniorum Litterarum Lundensis* 2 (1971–1972): 5–19; J. Harris, *Greek Emigrés in the West* (Camberley, 1995), 17.

10. Significantly, Sabellico inserted the excursus into his account of eleventh-century history, following a notice on the fall of Jerusalem to the Turks—thus stressing, as few previous historians had done, the importance of the Seljuk conquests as a link between the Turks' Scythian origins and recent Ottoman past.

11. Pertusi, "Primi studi," 480, 484–485, 497–513; idem, "Giovan Battista Egnazio e Ludovico Tuberone tra i primi storici occidentali del popolo turco," in *Venezia e Ungheria nel Rinascimento,* ed. V. Branca (Florence, 1973), 479–487. Pertusi traces some of their information to a crusade treatise written by Martino Segono for Sixtus IV in 1480, but this contains little information on Turkish history before the rise of Osman.

12. Sabellico, *Rapsodie historiarum enneades,* 2:345r.

13. Raffaele Maffei, *Commentariorum urbanorum libri XXXVIII,* (Rome, 1506), fols. 103v–104v.

14. Copies of these letters are in MS Venice, Biblioteca Marciana, lat. X.299 (3512), fols. 74v–77r and 80v–83r; for Caterino Zeno, see also N. Zen, *Dei commentarii del viaggio in Persia* (Venice, 1558).

15. For overviews of eyewitness literature from the fifteenth and sixteenth centuries, see Pertusi, "Primi studi," 466, 478–479, 482–489; R. Schwoebel, *The Shadow of the Crescent: The Renaissance Image of the Turk* (Nieuwkoop, 1967), 202–226; A. Wunder, "Western Travelers, Eastern Antiquities, and the Image of the Turk in Early Modern Europe," *Journal of Early Modern History* 7 (2003).

16. M. Rothstein, "Etymology, Genealogy, and the Immutability of Origins," *RQ* 43 (1990): 332.

Appendix: The Caspian Gates

1. The exact location and orientation of the Iranian Caspian Gates remains unclear, mostly because of the conflicting evidence in the ancient sources: Polybius, *Historiae,* 5.44.5; Strabo, *Geographia,* 2.1.27–34 *passim,* 11.8.9 (citing Eratosthenes), 11.9.1, 11.12.1, 11.13.7; Pliny the Elder, *Historia naturalis,* 6.43–45, 6.61–62, 6.76; Ptolemy, *Cosmographia,* 1.12; Diodorus Siculus, *Bibliotheca historiarum,* 2.2.3. See A. R. Anderson, "Alexander at the Caspian Gates," *Transactions of the American Philological Association* 59 (1928): 130–163, at 133–134; "Caspiae Pylae," *Dictionary of Greek and Roman Geography,* ed. W. Smith, 2

vols. (London, 1856–1857), 1:557–558; "Caspiae Portae," *P-W1*, 22:322–333; Appendix 8.9 in Arrian, *Anabasis*, trans. P. A. Brunt, 2 vols. (Cambridge, Mass., 1976–1983), 1:495–497; J. F. Standish, "The Caspian Gates," *Greece and Rome*, 2d ser., 17 (1970): 17–24.

2. Pliny, *Historia naturalis*, 6.44.

3. Arrian, *Anabasis*, 3.19–21; A. von Stahl, "Notes on the March of Alexander the Great from Ecbatana to Hyrcania," *Geographical Journal* 64 (1924): 312–329, esp. 318–320; G. Radet, "La dernière campagne d'Alexandre contre Darius," in *Mélanges Gustave Glotz* (Paris, 1932), 2:765–778; E. Badian, "Alexander in Iran," in *CHI*, 2:447–448; J. Hansman, "The Problems of Qumis," *JRAS* (1968): 111–139, esp. 116–119; A. B. Bosworth, "Errors in Arrian," *CQ* 26 (1976): 117–139, esp. 132–136; N.G.L. Hammond, "A Note on 'Pursuit' in Arrian," *CQ* 28 (1978): 136–140; A. B. Bosworth, *Conquest and Empire: The Reign of Alexander the Great* (Cambridge, 1988), 94–96; J. Seibert, *Die Eroberung des Perserreiches durch Alexander den Grossen auf kartographischer Grundlage* (Wiesbaden, 1985), 111–114.

4. Pliny, *Historia naturalis*, 6.45.

5. R. Lane Fox, *Alexander the Great* (London, 1973), 267–330.

6. U. Wilcken, *Alexander the Great* (London, 1932), 152–153; W. Tarn, *Alexander the Great* (Cambridge, 1948), 2:5–15; L. Pearson, "Notes on Two Passages of Strabo," *CQ* 1 (1951): 80–84; J. R. Hamilton, *Plutarch: Alexander* (Oxford, 1969), 116–119; idem, "Alexander and the Aral," *CQ* 21 (1971): 106–111; Appendix 12 in Arrian, *Anabasis*, trans. Brunt, 1:522–525; G. Huxley, "The Sogdian Tanais and Aristobulus," *Bulletin of the American Society of Papyrologists* 22 (1985): 117–121; Bosworth, *Conquest and Empire*, 109–110; idem, "Aristotle, India and Alexander," *Topoi* 3 (1993): 407–424, esp. 407–412 and 423; idem, *Alexander and the East: The Tragedy of Triumph* (Oxford, 1996), 80–82 and 120.

7. Oxus: Strabo, *Geographia*, 11.7.3 (citing Aristobulus), and Arrian, *Anabasis*, 3.29.2. Jaxartes: Arrian, *Anabasis*, 3.30.7–9.

8. Underground channel: Strabo, *Geographia*, 11.7.4 (citing Polycleitus). Caspian Sea an extension of the Maeotic Lake: Quintus Curtius, *Historia Alexandri Magni*, 6.4.18; Plutarch, *Vita Alexandri*, 44.1.

9. The error probably originated with Aristotle, *Meteorology*, 1.13 (350a, 22–25), who calls the Jaxartes "Araxes" and makes it the source of the European Tanais; reports of Alexander's campaign actually call the Jaxartes "Tanais." For this and the association of the river with European peoples and flora, see Strabo, *Geographia*, 11.7.4; Arrian, *Anabasis*, 3.30.7–9, 4.1.1, and 4.15.1; Quintus Curtius, *Historia Alexandri Magni*, 7.6.12 and 8.1.7; Plutarch, *Vita Alexandri*, 45.4; A. B. Bosworth, *A Historical Commentary on Arrian's History of Alexander*, 2 vols. (Oxford, 1980–1995), 1:377–379 and 2:15.

10. Arrian, *Anabasis*, 4.15.4; Lane Fox, *Alexander the Great*, 306–307; Bosworth, *Historical Commentary*, 2:105–106.

11. The meeting occurred at Zadracarta, capital of Hyrcania, just after Alexander passed through the Caspian Gates: Lane Fox, *Alexander the Great*, 276;

Bosworth, *Alexander and the East,* 81. For the transformation of this visit into an
encounter with Amazons of the Thermodon (originating with either
Polycleitus or Onesicritus and mentioned by Strabo, *Geographia,* 11.5.4 [citing
Cleitarchus]; Quintus Curtius, *Historia Alexandri Magni,* 6.5.24–32; Plutarch,
Vita Alexandri, 46.1; Diodorus Siculus, *Bibliotheca historiarum,* 17.77.1; Justin,
Epitome in Pompeium Trogum, 12.3.5 and 42.3.7), see Tarn, *Alexander the Great,*
2:326–329; W. Heckel, ed., Justin, *Epitome of the Philippic History of Pompeius
Trogus, Books 11–12* (Oxford, 1997), 200–203.

12. In the medieval *Alexander Romance,* Alexander's encounter with the Amazons
was transferred to their traditional realm near the eastern end of the Black Sea,
while his founding of a city on the "Tanais" (Alexandria Eschate, near modern
Khojend on the Jaxartes/Syr Darya: P. M. Fraser, *Cities of Alexander the Great*
[Oxford, 1996], 151–156) was symbolized by his dedication of a monumental
altar or pillar marking the farthest extent of his travels. On medieval maps, this
construction appears close to the European Don in southern Russia: Anderson,
"Alexander at the Caspian Gates," 139–141.

13. Strabo, *Geographia,* 2.1.1 (citing Eratosthenes; trans. H. L. Jones, 8 vols. [Cam-
bridge, Mass., 1949], 1:253), also 2.5.31; 11.8.1; 11.12.1–5; Pomponius Mela,
De situ orbis, 1.81; Pliny, *Historia naturalis,* 5.27; Diodorus Siculus, *Bibliotheca
historiarum,* 18.5.2–5; "Taurus Mountain Range," *OCD,* 1477.

14. Pliny, *Historia naturalis,* 5.99.

15. Quintus Curtius, *Historia Alexandri Magni,* 7.3.5–18 and 7.4.22–5; Arrian,
Anabasis, 3.28.9; Diodorus Siculus, *Bibliotheca historiarum,* 17.82.1–83.1; Strabo,
Geographia, 15.1.17, 15.1.26, and 15.2.8–10; "Paropamisidae" and
"Paropamisus" in *P-Wl,* 18:1778–1779 (including descriptions of the snow-
bound isolation of the area's inhabitants, the Paropamisidae). Modern accounts: T. B. Jones, "Alexander and the Winter of 330/29 B.C.," *Classical World*
28 (1935): 124–125; Lane Fox, *Alexander the Great,* 292–297; Bosworth, *Conquest and Empire,* 105–107.

16. Fraser, *Cities of Alexander the Great,* 73, 140–150; Arrian, *Anabasis,* 3.28.4;
Diodorus Siculus, *Bibliotheca historiarum,* 17.83.1; Quintus Curtius, *Historia
Alexandri Magni,* 7.3.23.

17. Strabo, *Geographia,* 11.5.5, 15.1.8–11; Arrian, *Anabasis,* 5.3.2–4 and 5.5.3, and
Appendix 12.3 in *Anabasis,* trans. Brunt, 1:523–524; Bosworth, *Historical Commentary,* 1: 333–334 and 2:213–217; D. Braund, *Georgia in Antiquity* (Oxford,
1994), 12–14. Local features confirmed the Macedonians in their error: they
were shown a cave in the Hindu Kush, supposed to be the site of Prometheus's
punishment (Diodorus Siculus, *Bibliotheca historiarum,* 17.83.1; Quintus
Curtius, *Historia Alexandri Magni,* 7.3.22); "Paropamisus," *P-Wl,* 18:1778–1779;
Bosworth, *Alexander and the East,* 118; Lane Fox, *Alexander the Great,* 296 and
533. Despite Strabo's demurral, the identification of the Hindu Kush with the
Caucasus was widely accepted: e.g., Cicero, *Tusculanae disputationes,* 2.22.53
and 5.27.77.

18. Pliny, *Historia naturalis,* 5.98: "Collisus . . . numeris nominibus et novis

quacumque incedit insignis: Imaus prima parte dictus, mox Emodus, Paropanisus . . . Taurus, atque ubi se quoque exuperat, Caucasus."

19. Quintus Curtius, *Historia Alexandri Magni,* 7.3.19–21.

20. *Etymologiae,* 14.8.2: "Mons Caucasus ab India usque ad Taurum porrectus, pro gentium ac linguarum varietate quoquo versum vadit, diversis nominibus nuncupatur. Ubi autem ad orientem in excelsiorem consurgit sublimitatem, pro nivium candore Caucasus nuncupatur." Also Solinus, *Collectanea rerum memorabilium,* 38.13; J. K. Wright, *Geographical Lore of the Time of the Crusades* (New York, 1925), 270.

21. Pliny, *Historia naturalis,* 6.30 (trans. H. Rackham, 10 vols. [Cambridge, Mass., 1947], 2:359).

22. Pliny, *Historia naturalis,* 6.40 (trans. Rackham, 2:367).

23. Dio Cassius, *Historia Romana,* 62.8; also Tacitus and Suetonius (cited below); J. Kolendo, "Le Projet d'expédition de Néron dans le Caucase," in *Neronia 1977,* ed. J.-M. Croisille and P.-M. Fauchère (Clermont-Ferrand, 1982), 23–30; A. Aiardi, "Interessi neroniani in Oriente e in Africa: l'idea di Alessandro Magno," *Atti del Istituto veneto di scienze, lettere ed arti* 138 (1979–1980): 563–572; B. Isaac, *The Limits of Empire: The Roman Army in the East* (Oxford, 1992), 403–405; Braund, *Georgia in Antiquity,* 216, 224–226.

24. Tacitus, *Historiae,* 1.6. Elsewhere Tacitus describes a "Caspia via" through Albania: *Annales,* 6.33.

25. Suetonius, *Vitae Caesarum,* Nero, 19.2.

26. Pliny's statement that veterans of Corbulo's campaign in Armenia (A.D. 58–67) also located the Caspian Gates in the Caucasus (see above) suggests that the idea was widespread; nonetheless, this campaign was undertaken in the reign of Nero, who may have encouraged their error.

27. There are in fact *two* passes through the Caucasus which have been known as the Caspian Gates: the pass of Dariel, running north–south through the middle of the Caucasus range, near Tblisi, also called *Portae Sarmaticae, Portae Iberiae,* or *Portae Caucasiae* (this is the one discussed by Pliny; see above), and the pass of Derbend, bypassing the eastern end of the Caucasus by the Caspian Sea and earlier known as *Portae Albaniae:* "Caucasus," *Dictionary of Greek and Roman Geography,* 1:570–573; "*Albaniai pulai,*" *P-W1,* 1:1305; "Sarmaticae Portae," *P-W2,* 2:13–14; Anderson, "Alexander at the Caspian Gates"; Braund, *Georgia in Antiquity,* 44–46, 226n117.

28. The fullest account of this legend and its *fortuna* remains A. R. Anderson, *Alexander's Gate, Gog and Magog and the Inclosed Nations* (Philadelphia, 1932), but Anderson's analysis is not without flaws. See the review by P. Barry, *Speculum* 8 (1933): 264–470 and further studies in nn. 42 and 43 below.

29. Josephus, *Bellum Judaicum,* 7.244–245 (*Josephus,* trans. H. St. J. Thackeray et al., 9 vols. [London, 1926–1965], 3:575).

30. A. B. Bosworth, "Arrian and the Alani," *Harvard Studies in Classical Philology* 81 (1977): 217–255, at 221–225.

31. Jerome, Epistola 77, *PL,* 22:695: "Ecce subito . . . ab ultima Maeotide inter

glacialem Tanain, et Massagetarum immanes populos, ubi Caucasi rupibus
feras gentes Alexandri claustra cohibent, erupisse Hunnorum examina quae
pernicibus equis huc illucque volitantia, caedis pariter ac terroris cuncta
complerent."

32. E.g., Hegesippus (*Historiae*, 3.5.2, 5.50.1), Procopius (*De bello Persico*, 1.10),
Jordanes (*Getica*, 7.5); Isidore of Seville (*Etymologiae*, 9.2.66), and Fredegar (*The
Fourth Book of the Chronicle of Fredegar with its Continuations*, ed. and trans. J. M.
Wallace-Hadrill [London, 1960], 54–55).

33. The development of the *Alexander Romance* tradition is extremely complex; no
copy of the original text—probably composed in Greek in the third century
A.D.—survives, only a great number of later recensions in Greek, Latin, Syriac,
Ethiopic, Armenian, etc. Chronologically, the Armenian recension is one of the
earliest witnesses, dating from the fifth century A.D. In it, Alexander travels
into a land of darkness at the end of the world (beyond Armenia), where he
encounters many marvels and monsters, including a talking bird who tells him
to leave the northern wastes and conquer India. Alexander recalls, "And turning back from that place, we set our guiding star by Arcturus and thus came
out in twenty-two days. And I put the gates together and carefully sealed up
the place" (*The Romance of Alexander the Great by Pseudo-Callisthenes. Translated
from the Armenian Version*, ed. and trans. A. M. Wolohojian [New York, 1969],
116).

34. Josephus, *Antiquitates Judaicae*, 1.123. The comment comes as Josephus attempts to amalgamate Jewish and Greek traditions regarding the origins and
early history of all the peoples of the world. However, although Josephus is
also one of the earliest sources for Alexander's construction of a gate against
barbarians, he did not establish any connection between these two ideas: he
never said that the tribes behind the gate (whom he identified in the *Bellum
Judaicum* as Alans) had anything to do with Gog and Magog or the apocalypse.

35. E.g., Ambrose, *De fide*, 2.16. O. Maenchen-Helfen, *The World of the Huns: Studies
in Their History and Culture* (Berkeley, 1973), 3–5. Some Christian theologians
resisted this sort of identification; Jerome reported it as a belief of others
(*Commentarii in Ezechielem*, in *PL*, 25:356: "Igitur Judaei et nostri Judaizantes
putant Gog gentes esse Scythicas, immanes et innumerabiles quae trans
Caucasum montem, et Maeotidem paludem, et prope Caspium mare ad
Indiam usque tendantur") and argued against it (*Hebraicae Quaestiones in
Genesim*, in *PL*, 23:999–1000); also Augustine, *De civitate Dei*, 20.11.

36. E. A. Wallis Budge, ed., "A Christian Legend Concerning Alexander," in *The
History of Alexander the Great* (Cambridge, 1889), 144–158. For the date, see F. J.
Martinez, "Eastern Christian Apocalyptic in the Early Muslim Period: Pseudo-
Methodius and Pseudo-Athanasius," Ph.D. dissertation, Catholic University of
America, Washington D.C., 1985, 48n74, and for the historical events that in-
spired it, 173–175; also *Die syrische Apokalypse des pseudo-Methodius*, trans. G. J.
Reinink, 2 vols. (Louvain, 1993), 2:xxxiv, n127.

37. Martinez, "Eastern Christian Apocalyptic," 25–33, suggests a date of A.D. 688–

689; S. Brock, "Syriac Sources for Seventh-Century History," *Byzantine and Modern Greek Studies* 2 (1976): 17–36, at 34–35, suggests 691–692. See also G. J. Reinink, "Ps.-Methodius' Concept of History," in *The Byzantine and Early Islamic Middle East: Problems in the Literary Source Material*, eds. A. Cameron and L. I. Conrad (Princeton, 1992), 149–187, at 167n73; Reinink, *Die syrische Apokalypse*, 2:vii–xxv.

38. On the transmission of the *Neshana* story to ps.-Methodius, see J. Trumpf, "Alexander, die Bersiler und die Brüste des Nordens," *Byzantinische Zeitschrift* 64 (1971): 326–328; Brock, "Syriac Sources," 34–35; Martinez, "Eastern Christian Apocalyptic," 2–57, esp. 5–8, 25–33 (with translation at 132–134); Reinink, "Ps.-Methodius' Concept of History," 167; idem, *Die syrische Apokalypse*, 2:vii–xxv. For the derivation of the Greek and Latin versions of ps.-Methodius from the Syriac original, see M. Kmosko, "Das Rätsel des Pseudomethodius," *Byzantion* 6 (1931): 273–296; K. Czeglédy, "The Syriac Alexander Legend," *Acta Orientalia* 7 (1957): 231–249; Martinez, "Eastern Christian Apocalyptic," 5–8, 25–32. The earliest MS of the Latin translation dates to about 720: Reinink, "Ps.-Methodius' Concept of History," 155.

39. Pfister (see below) thought the *Neshana* descended from an early version of ps.-Callisthenes and that the legend connecting Alexander to Gog and Magog was of Hellenistic Jewish origin and had already taken shape in the time of Josephus. But Czeglédy ("Syriac Alexander Legend," 235–238) points out that neither Josephus nor Jerome, the next important witness to the tradition, even hints at an apocalyptic dimension to the legend. See J. Trumpf, "Alexander, die Bersiler und die Brüste des Nordens," and his review of D.J.A. Ross, *Alexander Historiatus* (1st ed., London, 1963) in *Byzantinische Zeitschrift* 58 (1965): 149–151, taken into account by Ross in his second edition (Frankfurt-am-Main, 1988), 111.

40. The Syriac *Sermo de fine extremo*, once attributed to the fourth-century Ephraim Syrus and thus adduced as a source for the *Neshana*, actually used the *Neshana* as a source (Czeglédy, "Syriac Alexander Legend," 239–240; Brock, "Syriac Sources," 35; Martinez, "Eastern Christian Apocalyptic," 49n76). The so-called Metrical Discourse attributed to the sixth-century author Jacob of Sarug has likewise been redated to after the composition of the *Neshana*. The relationships between these texts and ps.-Methodius are, however, still unclear: Martinez, 18–20, 173n6.

41. This was recognized by Kmosko, reiterated by Czeglédy, and proven conclusively by the later studies cited in n. 38 above. The accounts of the Syriac works by Michael and Guzman (see below) are not reliable.

42. Anderson, *Alexander's Gate*; F. Pfister, "Ein kleiner lateinischer Text zur Episode von Gog und Magog," *Berliner Philologische Wochenschrift* (4 December 1915): 1549–1552; idem, "Gog und Magog," in *Handwörterbuch des deutschen Aberglaubens* (Berlin, 1931), 3:910–918; idem, *Alexander der Grosse in den Offenbarungen der Griechen, Juden, Mohammedaner und Christen* (Berlin, 1956), 30–32; G. Cary, *The Medieval Alexander* (Cambridge, 1956), 130–131; Ross, *Alex-*

ander Historiatus, 2d ed., 34–35; J. A. Boyle, "The Alexander Romance in the East and West," *Bulletin of the John Rylands Library* 60 (1977): 13–27; I. Michael, "Typological Problems in Medieval Alexander Literature: The Enclosure of Gog and Magog," in *The Medieval Alexander Legend and Romance Epic: Essays in Honor of David J. A. Ross,* eds. P. Noble et al. (Millwood, N.Y., 1982), 131–147; R. Manselli, "I popoli immaginari: Gog e Magog," in *Popoli e paesi nella cultura altomedievale,* 2 vols. (Spoleto, 1983), 2:487–522; A. C. Gow, *The Red Jews: Antisemitism in an Apocalyptic Age, 1200–1600* (Leiden, 1995), esp. 295–349; V. I. Scherb, "Assimilating Giants: The Appropriation of Gog and Magog in Medieval and Early Modern England," *Journal of Medieval and Early Modern Studies* 32 (2002): 59–84. Two recent studies which take into account the importance of the Syriac scholarship are S. Gerö, "The Legend of Alexander the Great in the Christian Orient," *Bulletin of the John Rylands University Library* 75 (1993): 3–9, and A. Samarrai, "Beyond Belief and Reverence: Medieval Mythological Ethnography in the Near East and Europe," *JMRS* 23 (1993): 19–42.

43. Jones, "Image of the Barbarian." For application of the legend to Khazars, see L. S. Chekin, "Christian of Stavelot and the Conversion of Gog and Magog: A Study of the Ninth-Century Reference to Judaism among the Khazars," *Russia Mediaevalis* 9 (1997). For Mongols, see C. W. Connell, "Western Views of the Origin of the 'Tartars': An Example of the Influence of Myth in the Second Half of the Thirteenth Century," *JMRS* 3 (1973); C.S.F. Burnett and P. Gautier Dalché, "Attitudes towards the Mongols in Medieval Literature: The XXII Kings of Gog and Magog from the Court of Frederick II to Jean de Mandeville," *Viator* 22 (1991): 153–167; G. G. Guzman, "Reports of Mongol Cannibalism in the Thirteenth-Century Latin Sources: Oriental Fact or Western Fiction?" in *Discovering New Worlds: Essays on Medieval Exploration and Imagination,* ed. S. D. Westrem (New York, 1991), 31–68. See also Westrem's own article, "Against Gog and Magog," in *Text and Territory: Geographical Imagination in the European Middle Ages,* eds. S. Tomasch and S. Giles (Philadelphia, 1988), 54–75, arguing that their presence in medieval maps is far rarer than often supposed. Also J. Tattersall, "Anthropophagi and Eaters of Raw Flesh in French Literature of the Crusade Period: Myth, Tradition and Reality," *Medium Aevum* 57 (1988): 240–251.

44. Roger Bacon, *Opus maius,* trans. R. Belle Burke, 2 vols. (Bristol, 2000), 2:644–645.

Acknowledgments

This book has been a long time in the making. I am grateful to Harvard University for a Frank Knox Memorial Fellowship, which first took me to the Warburg Institute in London, where the idea for the project took shape, I learned what I would need to pursue it, and the bulk of the work was done. For further research support and travel awards I thank the U.K. Committee of Vice Chancellors and Principals, the University of London's Central Research Fund, the Gladys Krieble Delmas Foundation, the Wolfenbütteler Arbeitskreis für Renaissanceforschung, the American Research Institute in Turkey, the Folger Institute, and the Institute for Scholarship in the Liberal Arts and the Department of History in the University of Notre Dame.

Material from Chapter 2 has been previously published in "Medieval Sources for Renaissance Theories on the Origins of the Ottoman Turks," in *Europa und die Türken in der Renaissance,* eds. B. Guthmüller and W. Kühlmann (Tübingen: Niemayer Verlag, 2000), 409–436. Material from Chapters 2 and 4 appeared in different form in "From Samarkand to Scythia: Reinventions of Asia in Renaissance Geography and Political Thought," in *Pius II: el piu expeditivo pontifice. Selected Studies on Aeneas Silvius Piccolomini (1405–1464),* eds. Z.R.W.M. von Martels and A. Vanderjagt (Leiden: Brill, 2003), 13–39, and in "Italian Humanists and the Problem of the Crusade," in *Crusading in the Fifteenth Century: Message and Impact,* ed. N. Housley (London: Palgrave, 2004), 13–38. I am grateful to the editors and publishers of all three volumes for permission to reproduce the material here.

In writing this book, I relied above all on the superb resources of the Warburg library, where the good and neighborly books opened up countless lines of inquiry. Thanks also to my former colleagues at the British Library, especially John Goldfinch, for coaxing early editions out of their hiding places, and to helpful and patient librarians and staff at the School of Oriental and African Studies, Institute of Historical Research, Institute of Classical Studies, Senate House, University College London, Bodleian Library, Cambridge University Library, Bibliothèque Nationale de France, Biblioteca Marciana, Biblioteca Trivulziana, Biblioteca Apostolica Vaticana, New York Public Library, Princeton University Library, Huntington Library, Newberry Library, University of Chicago Library, and the Library of the University of Notre Dame. Special thanks to Ian Jones for help with preparing the illustrations and to Philip Schwartzburg for preparing the map.

Over the years James Hankins has read many drafts and offered helpful comments, rewarding my many attempts to disagree with him with unwarranted kindness. Anthony Grafton challenged me to refine my thinking in ways both large and small, and I am grateful to him for good advice and many suggestions for improvement. I owe the greatest debt to Jill Kraye, who gave me the freedom to follow the humanists as far as I could down their bewildering trails, then drew me back to the present with her bracing marginal critiques. Her inspiration, guidance, and friendship have been invaluable.

I also want to thank the many colleagues, friends, and readers who have contributed something to this book, from years of tolerant companionship to a single vital moment of clarification: David Armitage, Wendy Arons, Eric Ash, Cristelle Baskins, Nancy Bisaha, Peter Burke, Charles Burnett, Dorigen Caldwell, David Chambers, Paul Cobb, Remie Constable, Martin Davies, Anthony D'Elia, Una Roman D'Elia, Filippo De Vivo, Cornell Fleischer, Peter Golden, Kenneth Gouwens, Brad Gregory, Mary Harper, Dag Nikolas Hasse, Kristine Haugen, Barbara Heck, Paul Heck, Colin Heywood, Norman Housley, Philippa Jackson, Ian, Jane, and Hattie Jones, Mary Laven, Sara Maurer, Alan Murray, Paul Needham, Emily O'Brien, Emily Osborn, Alessandra Petrina, Nick Popper, Eileen Reeves, Johannes Röll, Will Ryan, Alessandro Scafi, Jason Scott Warren, Zur Shalev, Marcello Simonetta, Tania String, Koenraad van Cleempoel, John Van Engen, Diana Webb, Andrew Wheatcroft, Jonathan Woolfson, and Amanda Wunder. Of course the faults remain my own.

Last, thanks to my family. I owe my parents, Hamilton and Helen Meserve, so much, for their support and enthusiasm, for their always provocative questions, and for a lifetime of experiences and ideas that each contributed something to the making of this book—from arranging an odd sort of babysitter for me in Riyadh to being babysitters themselves in Venice. I'm grateful to my brothers and sisters-in-law for precious glimpses of life beyond the library. Finally, without Robert Goulding's inspiration, advice, good humor, vast knowledge, and belief in me—alongside countless more mundane contributions—I would never, ever have managed to finish this project. In the meantime, Alice and Tommy gave me good reason to do so.

Index